AF328760

WORLDS OF UNFREEDOM

Worlds of Unfreedom

WEST CENTRAL AFRICA IN THE ERA OF GLOBAL ABOLITION

Roquinaldo Ferreira

PRINCETON UNIVERSITY PRESS

PRINCETON & OXFORD

Published by Princeton University Press
41 William Street, Princeton, New Jersey 08540
99 Banbury Road, Oxford OX2 6JX

press.princeton.edu

GPSR Authorized Representative: Easy Access System Europe - Mustamäe tee 50, 10621 Tallinn, Estonia, gpsr.requests@easproject.com

All Rights Reserved

ISBN 978-0-691-17758-8
ISBN (e-book) 978-0-691-18558-3

British Library Cataloging-in-Publication Data is available

Editorial: Priya Nelson and Emma Wagh
Production Editorial: Jenny Wolkowicki
Jacket design: Heather Hansen
Production: Danielle Amatucci
Publicity: William Pagdatoon
Copyeditor: Bhisham Bherwani

Jacket image: © National Maritime Museum, Greenwich, London

This book has been composed in Miller Text

Printed in the United States of America

10 9 8 7 6 5 4 3 2 1

CONTENTS

ACKNOWLEDGMENTS

THIS BOOK BENEFITED from the assistance and support of many scholars and colleagues. Tiago Caungo played a key role in a trip I took to Ambriz in 2022, and I owe him a great debt of gratitude for introducing me to local historians, particularly João Baptista Pedro (Twaka), and for the opportunity to learn from them. In the early stages of the project, Gareth Austin provided an intellectual home at Geneva's Graduate Institute, where I taught a seminar class that served as a space to conceive the basis for the book. I then tested several ideas in Luanda as a visiting professor at the Universidade Agostinho Neto, an opportunity I owe to my dear friend Virgilio Coelho.

The final product became better due to intellectual input from the late Joseph Miller, Alexandre Pelegrino, Sherri Cummings, Elena Schneider, Alejandro de la Fuente, David Gordon and Dale Graden. Tatiana Seijas read the book proposal and gave key input as the project was maturing in 2014. Marial Iglesias Utset and Reinaldo Funes supported me in Havana as I sought to track down Cuba's connections with Angola and Brazil. Flora Thomson-DeVeaux, Jackson Owen and Christina Poulin provided editorial assistance at different stages of the project. In Luanda, I have relied on support from and had intellectual exchanges with several people, including Herminia Barbosa, Conceição Neto and João Lourenço. I have also benefited greatly from intellectual exchanges with and the friendship of Aderivaldo Ramos de Santana, Andrea Marzano, Aline Helg, Ivana Stolze, Paulo de Jesus, João José Reis, Flávio Gomes, David Gordon, Carlos Francisco da Silva Júnior, Lisa Earl Castillo, Marcelo Bittencourt, Lucilene Reginaldo, Vincent Brown, Roberto Guedes Ferreira and Shobana Shankar.

The research that underpins the book was only possible with the support of several organizations. A research fellowship from the National Endowment for the Humanities (NEH) funded the early stages of the research in 2012. Brown University and the University of Pennsylvania provided multiple funding opportunities that made possible archival work in Angola, Cuba, Portugal, England, and France. Both universities provided research leaves that allowed me to focus on research and the writing of the manuscript. I owe a great deal to my colleagues at UPenn's History Department for providing an intellectually nurturing environment. Priya Nelson has been a wonderful editor at Princeton University Press, and I also thank Emma Wagh for her flexibility and help in steering the book as it came into production.

WORLDS OF UNFREEDOM

Introduction

[1]

IN SEPTEMBER 1856, an African man named Inbundo ran away from a caravan transporting forty enslaved Africans to the Congo River. There, a ship that had sailed from New York City was set to take him to Cuba, where a sugar boom based on enslaved labor had fueled significant economic growth. After a harrowing escape, Inbundo had a fateful encounter with a group of more than two thousand soldiers (an African ruler allied to the Portuguese colonial regime led about six hundred soldiers) making their way toward copper mines in the Bembe region, some two hundred kilometers from the coast and near the capital city of the Kingdom of Kongo. Dispatched by the city's Portuguese government, these soldiers had departed Luanda with a singular objective: to secure control over mines critical for a lucrative copper trade with British and American nationals along the coast.

Commanding the expedition was Francisco Salles Ferreira, a former slave trade sympathizer who viewed abolition as key to Portugal's geopolitical interests in the Congo region.* He interviewed Inbundo. With the help of a translator, the Kikongo-speaking man shared his ordeal and offered valuable intelligence on shipments of enslaved Africans near the Congo River. According to Inbundo, he and his fellow captives "had all been caught and would be taken to the Zaire River to be forced onto a ship then loading slaves." Antonio Jose da Costa Lima, a Portuguese man and local agent for a far-reaching slave-trading consortium based in New York City, was both the owner of the enslaved Africans and the leader of the slave caravan. Inbundo disclosed that "the remainder of Africans [those who did not manage to escape the caravan] had been escorted in shackles to the Zaire River with [. . .] Costa Lima," and other "shipments of slaves had already been organized several times by said person [Costa Lima]."[1]

---

* For background on Salles Ferreira, see Tracy Lopes, "Continuities between the Slave Trade, "Legitimate" Commerce, and the Serviçal Trade: a Look at Four Families in Angola in the Mid- to Late Nineteenth Century," *Canadian Journal of African Studies*, 58, 3, 2024, p. 567.

After Inbundo asked not to be returned to Costa Lima, the Portuguese took him inland to Bembe, where the African man was likely put to work in the recently occupied mines. For Portugal, the mines represented an opportunity to create a brand-new economy to replace the then-waning slave trade. Yet controversy soon emerged. African miners earned eight cowrie shells a day, with younger workers making half that, while those with monthly contracts received 30 cowrie shells a day, plus a piece of cloth.[2] The Portuguese authorities candidly admitted that these shells were essentially worthless.[3] Seizing upon such reports, British officials were quick to denounce conditions in the copper mines as a thinly disguised form of slavery.[4]

Inbundo's story provides an entry point into the broader themes and arguments in *Worlds of Unfreedom*. First, his capture highlights how the slave trade to Cuba fueled massive enslavement in West Central Africa, exacting a heavy toll on local populations. Second, the intelligence that the African man shared with the Portuguese expedition provides a rare example of enslaved Africans' participation in the suppression of the transatlantic slave trade— one of the most inscrutable themes in African history due to the scarcity of primary sources on subaltern groups' anti-slave trade politics. Third, the Portuguese military expedition to Bembe, ostensibly motivated to take over the mines but part of a broader effort to end the slave trade, reveals the strategic use of anti-slave trade efforts to promote territorial expansion in West Central Africa. Fourth, Inbundo's fate in the Bembe mines shows a direct link between efforts to end the slave trade and the emergence of new forms of labor exploitation in West Central Africa.

In theory, the campaign to end the transatlantic trade in human beings was a matter of laws and geopolitical calculations. In practice, however, it was also a gut-wrenching story of human lives lost, staggering in its scale and cruelty, or entrapped under ruthless exploitation under emerging colonialism. To grasp its human dimensions, *Worlds of Unfreedom* develops a minutely detailed approach invested in recovering the lives of individuals like Inbundo, who are usually left out of the usual historical narrative; "to retrieve from a recalcitrant archive that has until now either ignored them, drowned them in figure of trade or read them as socially dead."[5] In so doing, the book seeks to factor subaltern politics into the broader narrative of anti-slavery, thus furthering comprehension of its multiple and sometimes organically grounded forces.[6]

While emphasizing contingency, complexity, and humanity, *Worlds of Unfreedom* singles out particular situations, everyday interactions, and personal trajectories, which are then deployed as microcosms to explicate complex global phenomena. "A close analysis of a single case study may pave the way to a much larger (indeed, global) hypotheses."[7] By blending portraits of individuals' lives with large structural processes, the book seeks to break down "frontiers between social, cultural, economic and political histories."[8] A pointillistic approach teases out specific circumstances of individuals, providing greater levels of granularity and texture to webs of cultural, economic, and social networks.[9] The result is an Africa-centered global history that toggles between dense individual trajectories and the broader narrative of abolition, all while centering human agency.

By centering the narrative on the lived experiences and agency of enslaved Africans like Inbundo, *Worlds of Unfreedom* seeks to decenter Eurocentric perspectives that have tended to erase or marginalize African participation in the struggle against the slave trade. This approach aligns with historian Benedetta Rossi's emphasis on recovering the voices and actions of subaltern actors, particularly those who had directly experienced the horrors of enslavement, as vital forces in the fight for abolition. According to Rossi, "African enslaved persons and their descendants, acting within African or European institutions, were the most committed to abolition."[10] By foregrounding such acts, *Worlds of Unfreedom* contributes to a broader project of recasting enslaved Africans as central protagonists in the complex global story of slave trading and slavery's demise, thereby challenging triumphalist narratives that, as scholar Michelle Liebst notes, have tended to glorify European abolitionists while obscuring the multifaceted ways in which Africans shaped the course of abolition.[11]

The theme of African resistance to slavery and the slave trade has not been neglected by Africanist scholars in recent years. In West Africa, Sandra Greene notes that "dissenting voices" against slavery and the slave trade emerged "as a result of British antislavery efforts in the region."[12] In Senegal, Becca de Los Santos argues that "the authors of the many liberations that took place over the two decades after abolition were the enslaved and not the French colonial administration."[13] In Sierra Leone and Liberia, Bronwen Everill and Lisa Lindsay reveal that local authorities took significant military actions against shipments of captives and, in Liberia's case, prevented British attempts to ship "free" migrants to the Americas.[14] Paul Lovejoy argues that the Sokoto Caliphate withdrew from the slave trade of its own accord, not due to British pressure.[15] Philip Misevich has demonstrated how Africans rebelled against captivity in Sierra Leone following news of the end of the British slave trade.[16]

Nor have scholars of Angola failed to scrutinize the long history of resistance to slavery in the Portuguese colony. By the mid-nineteenth century, as noted by historian Aida Freudenthal, African resistance to slavery was so entrenched as to force colonial authorities to negotiate coexistence with runaway communities.[17] Mariana Candido points out that "enslaved individuals often escaped and moved inland by following the paths of long-distance trade routes, which may have led them back to their homeland or to inland markets to look for help or follow a trail."[18] As argued by José Curto, slave revolts formed the cornerstone of a veritable culture of resistance in the Portuguese colony.[19] Yet, while significantly advancing our understanding of African resistance to slavery and the slave trade, these studies leave out the specific role of enslaved Africans in the abolition of the transatlantic slave trade.

Worlds of Unfreedom seeks to address this gap by examining how enslaved Africans actively challenged the system that oppressed them, shedding light on the agency and resilience of these individuals in the face of unimaginable hardship. The book illuminates the ways in which their actions, often overlooked in traditional narratives, played a crucial role in undermining the foundations of the slave trade and hastening its demise. Drawing on the most comprehensive research ever conducted in Angolan archives, as well as extensive research in Brazil, Cuba, France, Portugal, and the United Kingdom, it centers the narrative on the lived experiences and resistance of the enslaved, contributing to a more balanced understanding of the complex forces that shaped the abolition of the transatlantic slave trade.

Worlds of Unfreedom pushes back on the notion that Africa played little, if any, meaningful role in the suppression of the trade in human beings. Robin Law states that "the suppression of the Atlantic slave trade was effected through the closing down of markets in the Americas, rather than the shutting off of supplies of slaves from Africa."[20] By contrast, this book situates West Central Africa's experience within wider circuits of ideas, people, and goods, highlighting the region's vital role in the story of slavery's global demise and living legacy. Following Adiele E. Afigbo's prescription, I view African contexts and peoples as essential to understanding how the transatlantic slave trade—one of the most painful chapters in the history of humankind—came to an end.[21]

From the outset, it is vital to stress that the campaign against the transatlantic slave trade, while successful in eliminating the transportation of enslaved Africans across the Atlantic, constituted a key tool for the creation of new forms of labor exploitation in the Atlantic and Indian Oceans. Several scholars have already highlighted the shortcomings of liberal abolition and its failure to deliver freedom to former slaves.[22] Yet a comprehensive understanding of how abolition enabled unfreedom is still lacking. Chapter 7 fills this gap by tracing connections between the legislation of abolition and the emergence of systems of forced labor and forced migration that plagued West Central Africa well into the colonial era of the twentieth century. While ostensibly aimed at ending the slave trade and slavery, Portugal's anti-slavery laws and decrees, such as those enacted in 1842, 1854, and 1858, were often crafted in ways that served the economic interests of colonial powers at the expense of freedom promised to Africans.

To understand this complex phenomenon and its far-reaching consequences, *Worlds of Unfreedom* offers a sprawling, densely plotted, people-focused global history that weaves together multiple historical threads spanning the Atlantic and Indian Oceans. Embedding West Central Africa within expansive networks of capital, people, and labor then spanning the globe, the book adheres to Antoinette Burton's recommendation to regard "marginal people as subjects rather than objects of global history."[23] It illuminates trans-imperial dialogues that shaped global labor regimes, demonstrating how ideas and practices tested across British, French, and Portuguese empires culminated in strategies that transformed abolitionist measures into tools for perpetuating labor exploitation. Moving beyond national and imperial boundaries as primary units of analysis, this approach reveals how the legal architecture of abolition, shaped by the exchange of ideas and strategies among colonial powers, perpetuated exploitative labor practices in the twilight of the slave trade era.

In conceptualizing a global history of abolition and its aftermath, *Worlds of Unfreedom* challenges the traditional divide between the Atlantic and Indian Ocean worlds. By tracing the circulation of ideas, practices, and peoples across these vast oceanic spaces, the book reveals the complex interplay of local and global forces that shaped the uneven and often contradictory processes of abolition and the rise of new forms of unfreedom. It examines how Britain's assertive anti-slave trade policies extended across the Southwest Indian Ocean, challenging Portugal's territorial claims in East Africa and beyond. Simultaneously, it situates West Central Africa within the broader context of Atlantic Africa, drawing connections between the impact of European interventions in regions such as Lagos, the Bight of Benin, and the Kingdom of Kongo. Recognizing interconnections across oceanic regions is essential for situating the transformations in Angola's labor systems within a global fabric of shifting imperial ambitions and evolving forms of unfree labor, where abolition—particularly its gradual iteration—redefined labor systems without fundamentally altering the underlying dynamics of exploitation.

Worlds of Unfreedom is anchored in West Central Africa, a pivotal battleground in the fight against the transatlantic slave trade. From Loango to Mossamedes, this region—culturally rich and geographically diverse—shouldered the heaviest burden of the slave trade from 1850 to 1867. A staggering 70% of the nearly 200,000 enslaved individuals deported from the continent during these years originated from West Central Africa.[24] The region's experience was shaped by complex dynamics, such as the fracturing of African sovereignty in the Kingdom of Kongo amidst intensifying European imperial competition and the rise of new forms of unfree labor under the guise of abolition. To unpack these developments, the book deploys a global history perspective that situates West Central Africa's abolition story (see Map 5) within a broader tapestry of interconnected processes spanning multiple continents and oceanic spaces.

We will never know how exactly Inbundo felt when he came across the Luanda military expedition, nor can we fully recover his feelings as the world he knew unraveled due to violence unleashed by the slave trade. Yet, by piecing together elements of his layered identity, we can restore his place in the narrative of African History. In his village, Inbundo would have abided by clearly defined cultural practices (how to cut one's hair, file one's teeth, and scarify one's body) that carried explicit social meanings: the number of sharpened teeth and their position in the mouth silently bespoke different levels of in-group status and belonging. As one observer noted, "in this custom (filing teeth) as well as tattooing, the various tribes [*sic*] are regulated by fixed principles, and the place of their nativity may be determined by it."[25]

Similarly, practices like scarification and body marking played a crucial role in defining ethnic identity, nurturing spiritual connections, and marking significant life milestones. These cultural expressions also provide insights into the devastating impact of the transatlantic slave trade on local communities. For instance, in Benguela, scarification was adopted by Africans to symbolize their altered status as enslaved individuals, with reports noting that "it is not uncommon to see negroes who have been robbed of their freedom sacrificing at their shrine of vanity [*sic*] by endeavoring to make some additional ornament to their bleeding wounds."[26] The practice of tooth filing also carried significant social meanings. As observed by Francisco Antonio Pinto, an extensive traveler and colonial official in Angola during the 1870s: "In Ginga, no one who appears without this distinction [having their incisor teeth filed] will be considered a free man."[27]

These markers of identity assumed additional layers of meaning in the diaspora. On the British-controlled island of St. Helena, individuals torn from West Central Africa would adopt the body marks of their peers, either as a gesture of solidarity, a source of comfort, or a mark of defiance. As a British doctor stationed on the British island explained, "they did [it] either as a compliment to their new associates, as a source of amusement or as an object of admiration."[28] Similar dynamics played out in West Africa, where Kru people would tattoo their foreheads to indicate their free status, "which the Portuguese respected even at the height of the slave trade."[29] For Inbundo and others like him, these cultural imprints were thus not just remnants of a past life; they were emblems of a shared heritage that could be deployed against the dehumanizing horrors of Atlantic slavery.

Inbundo and his fellow fugitives would also have relied on commonalities such as the Kikongo language, spoken across large swaths of West Central Africa. An early observer noted, "all these [people] speak a somewhat similar language."[30] William Bentley, a British missionary who traveled extensively in the lower and upper Congo, observed variations but noted that the Kikongo language was uniform enough to enable relatively easy communication in regions stretching from Loango to Angola. "From Loango to the border of Angola, and from the coast to within 15 miles west of Stanley Pool, I had little difficulty understanding and being understood when I spoke the pure Kongo of the capital."[31]

A direct consequence of the transatlantic slave trade, the extent of the violence inflicted on individuals like Inbundo is heartbreaking and difficult to process. Forced to journey from Africa's interior to the coast, they often did so "without any cloth, completely naked, tortured by hunger and thirst."[32] To reduce their perceived value in the eyes of slave dealers, mothers injured their own children.[33] Children born in barracoons (slave depots) were killed, adding a layer of tragedy to the already unimaginable suffering that Africans endured.[34] Upon reaching the coast, victims faced further acts of violence, such as having a hot iron applied to their ribs, hips, or chest. British physicians on the island of St. Helena, where thousands of Africans released from slave vessels were taken, referred to this dehumanizing act of violence as "aitchrimbo," a rendition of the Kimbundo language word kirimbu (meaning mark).[35]

In the same year Inbundo was enslaved, a man named Zau was given as *caução* (loan collateral) by his uncle, who had received goods from a coastal trading outpost in exchange for a loan. These loans or goods were used in various ways, including payment for dowries to consummate marriages and religious ceremonies (*entambes*) when someone passed away.[36] The creditor openly "boasted over the good deal that he had done, for he planned to sell the miserable black once the deadline for the loan to be paid was over." Overcome with fear, Zau took his own life to avoid life under slavery in the Americas.[37] For women, time on the coast was marked by sexual violence, often leading to despair as they were forced to bear the children of their assailants. "Some, after being forced to satisfy the bloodthirsty lust of their masters, were to be sold, and the anguish of an impending pregnancy further aggravated the agony of their fate."[38]

Life was no better for those taken by the British to St. Helena after being released from slave ships. Many were so devastated by their experiences in the slave trade that they would not have the strength to live. "They will reject all medicines, refuse even food, and their only wish seems to lie down undisturbed, and die." This decision often came after the painful realization of "the loss of relations and friends, and perhaps their own affliction by disease, far from their country and those who could speak and administer comfort to them."[39] In their grief, some would gather together at night, "with looks fixed on the far-moving waters, recall the memory of their distant lands, and raise a mournful and clamorous song in tribute of respect to their parents, and as an expression of their sorrows for the loss of their country and kindred, and all that was dear to them." In their songs, they would express their sorrow.[40] Yet very few expressed a desire to return to their home country, replying that "mammy was no more, and bapa (father) no more, and Portuguese catchy me again."[41]

To make sense of the devastation brought about by the slave trade, Inbundo would have relied on a cosmological belief system that divided the universe into the realm of the living (nza yayi) and the realm of the dead (nsi a bafwa).[42] Within this belief system, the capitalist motivations behind the slave trade became entwined with cosmological understanding. Africans believed slave dealers took their victims to an under-ocean world to produce goods for the consumption of white people. "People have been brought up in the belief that away under the sea, their relatives make cloth, etc., for us white folk."[43] Yet many were fully cognizant of underlying motivations behind the atrocities they suffered. "Every man I have conversed with indeed acknowledges [that] if white men did not come for slaves, the practice of kidnapping would no longer exist."[44] Most importantly, the notion that the trade must be stopped was not without support. "The [African] people at large most assuredly desire the cessation of the trade."[45]

In this context of extreme violence and desolation, the enslaved found ways to express resistance to their captors, some channeling their feelings into songs and chants that directly confronted their oppressors: "You have sent me to the sea coast, but my yoke is off in death. Back I will come to haunt and kill you."[46] Chapter 3 of this book details how escapes and revolts on slave vessels or onshore threatened a nascent post-slave trade economy in Benguela, pushing the Portuguese administration to take action against shipments of African people abroad. A decree that offered freedom to enslaved individuals who reported plans to transport captives across the Atlantic recasts the narrative of abolition, in a testament to enslaved people's crucial role in the fight against oppressive forces that sought to commodify their lives.

A crucial element of this story is Inbundo's status before being captured in the slave caravan. David Richardson states, "The vast majority of those entering the export slave trade were born free and were forced into it against their will."[47] In Inbundo's case, there are two possible scenarios. First, he may have been a free worker on one of the coastal trading outposts, known as feitorias, that facilitated the slave trade. He knew, after all, that his enslaver Costa Lima had already organized other shipments of enslaved people in Ambriz. This suggests that Inbundo may have been familiar with the workings of the slave trade before he was enslaved. His enslavement would then have mirrored that of Zau, the African man referred to above who made the dramatic decision of taking his own life instead of being taken across the Atlantic in the slave trade.[48]

It is also possible that Inbundo was born into slavery, as his name seems to suggest. As recorded by British missionary William Bentley: ondioyo Inbundo a Makitu (that man is a slave of Makitu).[49] Scholars have characterized African slavery as defined more by kinship and social dependence than labor extraction. Individuals like Inbundo would have come from a social milieu where "slavery" was primarily "a form of social dependence, not of forced or dependent labor."[50] This understanding is supported by the observations of British traveler John Monteiro, who spent almost two decades in Angola and Congo. According to Monteiro, the difference between an enslaver and an enslaved person was not always apparent, and someone who was not familiar with the institution of slavery might not even recognize it as such.[51]

Yet, while African slavery was characterized by complex dynamics of social dependence and kinship, the emergence of the transatlantic slave trade had a profound impact on these traditional practices. The trade ushered in a new, commerce-oriented form of slavery that significantly blurred the traditional distinctions between indigenous African slavery and emerging forms of commercial captivity.[52] Previously, Quisikos, or domestic slaves typically born into households, enjoyed certain protections and could even seek refuge with local authorities if wrongfully sold. In stark contrast, Mobikas, usually war captives, were viewed as absolute property without any rights. As the transatlantic slave trade intensified, however, established distinctions collapsed, subjecting individuals like Inbundo to an uncertain and often cruel fate.[53]

This transformation was intrinsically linked to shifts in the political landscape that empowered coastal lords at the expense of traditional monarchs.

In the interior, chiefs of the principal towns and villages profited from the transit of slaves through their territories by removing them to the sea coast. This practice led to a pronounced fragmentation of power. "Each locality has its separate government, and each village, however small, constitutes a sort of patriarchal monarchy, which is continually at variance and enmity with every petty state in its neighborhood."[54] In coastal kingdoms such as Ngoyo, increased trade activities led to the emergence of trading families as the traditional authority waned. According to anthropologist Wyatt MacGaffey, "the last invested king of Ngoyo died in 1830."[55]

While placing human agency at the center of anti-slave trade politics, *Worlds of Unfreedom* situates West Central Africa within larger trade circuits and imperial geopolitics then enveloping the world. Instead of being static, I argue, locality was embedded in, molded by, and interlocked with global dynamics.[56] As Inbundo remarked, his captor had been a slave dealer named Costa Lima, whose brother was then living in New York—the sanctuary city of the illegal slave trade in the 1850s—as a key member of an intercontinental network of traders with multiple centers in Rio de Janeiro, Lisbon, Cádiz, Havana, Luanda, and Benguela. In this deeply interconnected world, several cities, even those no longer directly receiving enslaved Africans, such as Rio de Janeiro, or where large-scale shipments of enslaved people no longer took place, such as Luanda, remained connected to the broader networks of the slave trade through a myriad of business, legal, social, and personal ties.

Inbundo's story thus only makes sense if set on an Atlantic canvas or, indeed, on a global playing field. By the time the runaway escaped the transatlantic slave trade, shipments of enslaved Africans from West Central Africa had undergone significant transformations due to the end of imports of enslaved people to Brazil, the largest market for African captives in the Americas until 1850. The widespread belief was that the transatlantic slave trade would end. Yet, with Cuban production of sugar escalating to global dominance, primarily driven by high demand in the United States and Europe as well as technological breakthroughs that transformed the means of transportation and integrated the island's economy, shipments of enslaved people in West Central Africa continued through the late 1860s.[57]

One of *Worlds of Unfreedom*'s key contributions is its in-depth exploration of the often-overlooked connections between West Central Africa and Cuba in the final decades of the transatlantic slave trade. Scholars such as María del Carmen Barcia, Jorge Felipe Gonzalez, Martín Rodrigo y Alharilla, and Lizbeth Chaviano Pérez have made key contributions to the study of Cuba's ties to the Upper Guinea coast.[58] Yet the same is not true about the Spanish island's key ties to West Central African regions such as the Congo River, Ambriz, and Cabinda, which supplied the vast majority of enslaved Africans to the Spanish island by the 1850s.[59] By delving into the partnerships between Cuban and Brazilian slave traders that facilitated Cuba's emergence as a major player in West Central Africa, the book reveals the intricate web of economic, social, and political connections that bound these regions together. Moreover, it demonstrates how these partnerships not only integrated West Central Africa into the global capitalist economy but also had far-reaching consequences for African societies, contributing to the intensification of internal enslavement.

Aspirations of Empire

The military expedition that "rescued" Inbundo from the slave trade in 1856 was just one of several interventions by the Portuguese government aimed at solidifying territorial claims in the lower Kongo during that period. In 1855, Portuguese soldiers were sent to seize Ambriz, a pivotal center of the slave trade and a focal point of contention with British, US, and French naval forces. The following year, the same expedition that liberated Inbundo proceeded to Bembe amidst a period of pronounced instability within the Kingdom of Kongo. This action secured Portugal a decisive role in the kingdom's political affairs during a succession crisis. Then, in 1860, in an act of support for a new ruler aligned with their interests, Portugal launched another expedition, this time to take control of Kongo's capital city.

These military actions highlight how abolition was deeply intertwined with Portugal's broader imperial goals in the South Atlantic. After losing Brazil in 1822, Lisbon policymakers saw Africa as essential to producing colonial goods for European markets, thereby boosting their domestic economy and reducing dependence on foreign powers.[60] In this context, Angola—primarily consisting of the coastal enclaves of Luanda and Benguela—soon emerged as a significant player in imperial geopolitics. "Of all Portuguese possessions that we still possess, the vast and richest territory of Angola is the one that offers us most advantages," an 1840 government report declared, "which is why the government has promoted its prosperity and development."[61]

Portugal's significant challenges in developing a cohesive empire-building strategy cannot be understated. After the end of a civil war in 1834, the country faced significant political instability, which was so high as to make "impossible the construction of long-lasting consensus about fundamental rules of social coexistence (there were three constitutions in a short time) and fueled political violence—with unrest, social revolts, military pronouncement and another civil war (1846–47)."[62] Further compounding Portuguese travails were its underperforming economy and precarious infrastructure.[63] By the 1850s, however, the country's restored political stability had paved the way for an "overhaul of administration, both domestic and ultramarine."[64]

Particularly significant here was the role played by Lisbon's *Associação Marítima e Colonial* in shaping imperial policies, including the recognition that abolishing the transatlantic slave trade would be key to transforming

Angola into a fully fledged colony. Historian Gabriel Paquette reminds us that the associação was part of a shift toward producing ideas about empires across Europe.[65] Tellingly, four of Associação's members would become governors of Angola between 1840 and 1848, pivotal years in eradicating shipments of enslaved Africans in Luanda and Benguela, Portugal's main hubs in West Central Africa. Among these was Pedro Alexandrino da Cunha, a seasoned naval commander who would take firm measures against the slave trade and strongly advocate for agricultural expansion in Angola based on slavery.[66]

Yet such goals could not be achieved without the crucial role played by colonial elites and local dynamics in Angola. A case in point is Luanda's businesswoman Ana Joaquina dos Santos Silva. As discussed in Chapter 5, her investments in sugar production, ownership of multiple ships, and extensive network of agents positioned her as a pivotal figure in shaping Angola's economic landscape. Ana Joaquina's strategic engagement with Nawej II, the ruler of the expansive Lunda Empire, established direct ties between Angola and this powerful African state, bolstering Portugal's broader ambitions to create a new economy in its African colony. Nawej II's decision to engage with the Portuguese was driven by complex political dynamics within the Lunda Empire, as the rise of independent trade routes by Chokwe and Ambakista traders destabilized traditional power structures. By accepting Ana Joaquina's invitation to send emissaries to Luanda, the African ruler sought to counteract these destabilizing forces and bolster his own power.

Ana Joaquina's bold trade diplomacy reveals how colonial settings like Angola served as incubators of colonial policies. Portuguese empire-making would not have been possible without individuals like her, whose actions aligned with and furthered the vision of Lisbon officials for a post-slave trade economy in Angola. Exemplifying the complex dynamics at play is the extraordinary journey of Ana Joaquina's enslaved emissary, Eufrazina, to the court of the Lunda ruler. The enslaved woman's experience complicates traditional notions of slavery and agency. While highlighting intricate intersections of gender, status, and power within both the Lunda kingdom and Portuguese Angola, it also reveals the multifaceted nature of empire-building in the colonial context.

While local actors like Ana Joaquina played a crucial role in shaping Angola's economic landscape, the impetus for change also came from the highest levels of Portuguese administration. As early as 1838, Lisbon officials had already issued instructions to newly appointed Governor Antonio Manoel de Noronha to combat the slave trade, declaring it "infamous and shameful to humanity," beyond being harmful to the country where it occurred. Lisbon officials then outlined a vision for economic development that positioned Angola as a competitor to their former colony in South America, Brazil. They argued that because labor costs were lower in Angola, crops grown there could be sold in Europe at a lower price than agricultural commodities from Brazil. The former colony of Brazil held such significance in the minds of Lisbon officials that they even proposed incentivizing Brazilian agricultural laborers to migrate to Angola. In their view, this migration should also involve Brazilian "capitalists" who could provide investment funds beyond the transatlantic slave trade.[67]

Yet Brazil also increasingly emerged as a rival in the eyes of the Portuguese, particularly due to Angola's attachment to the former Portuguese colony via the slave trade. Lisbon lamented the existing dynamics where Angola was seen merely as a source of enslaved labor for Brazil's booming sugar and coffee sectors. "We persuaded ourselves that we could profit from Angola without developing it, crudely uprooting its inhabitants to serve as slaves in foreign lands like Brazil."[68] With Brazil's independence, this resentment deepened. Officials noted the irony in importing sugar from Brazil, produced with labor taken from Portuguese colonies. They pointed out, "all the sugar we import comes from Brazil, but the labor used to cultivate that sugar originates from our colonies."[69]

Lisbon officials believed that abolishing the slave trade was crucial not only for Angola's agricultural and economic development but also for severing the deep-rooted ties that bound Angola to Brazil's slavery-based economy. Since the seventeenth century, these ties had transcended mere economic interests, forming a complex web of familial, religious, legal, and cultural bonds that spanned the Atlantic.[70] However, to Portugal's growing alarm, these connections had now acquired a political dimension following Brazil's independence in 1822. As Brazil's political landscape grew increasingly volatile in the wake of independence, the resulting shockwaves rippled across the Atlantic, stimulating identity formation among local elites in Luanda and Benguela and deeply unsettling Portuguese officials. As explored in Chapter 1, the specter of secessionist movements, inspired by events in Brazil and fueled by the dense network of transatlantic ties, cast a looming shadow over Portugal's efforts to end the slave trade and tighten its grip on Angola.

While Portugal faced the unique challenge of competing with its former colony, Brazil, for influence in Africa—a situation unparalleled by any other European power—it was not alone in leveraging the abolition of the slave trade as a tool for empire-building. This dynamic was also evident in the British Empire's parallel expansionist approaches leveraging anti-slave trade measures. This nexus has spurred debate among scholars; some, like Tom C. McCaskie, argue that British territorial expansion remained geographically restricted, while Martin Lynn casts doubts on Britain's capacity to foster imperialism in West Africa.[71] Rebecca Shumway describes British policy toward Africa as "ambivalent."[72] Seymour Drescher suggests that while anti-slave trade politics were imperialistic in methods, a definitive link between abolition and empire-building remains elusive.[73] John Darwin further complicates this debate, arguing that British imperial expansion was often driven less by a coherent strategic vision than by the interplay of private and official interests in regional hubs and in the metropole.[74]

In contrast, other scholars argue for a more direct link between abolition and European empire-building in Africa. Robin Law, for instance, states that efforts to end the slave trade led to European encroachment on African sovereignty and subsequent European rule.[75] Bronwen Everill echoes this perspective, stating that the British felt compelled to expand into Africa as a result of their stand against the slave trade.[76] Richard Huzzey states that the use of naval force against the slave trade in the 1840s "foreshadowed the following fifty years of colonial advance."[77] Lauren Benton and Lisa Ford see the anti-slave trade legal framework as a form of "legal imperialism," while Maeve Ryan contends that it justified "violence, legal destruction, and dispossession of property" by Britain, which accounted for the "accumulating power" on a global scale.[78]

Importantly, the strategic use of abolition for imperial ambitions occurred beyond the Atlantic. In the Indian Ocean, scholars such as Sujit Sivasundaram and Fahad Bishara illustrate how Britain skillfully used the struggle against the slave trade to craft relationships with local societies.[79] In Mauritius, Richard Allen adds, Britain's anti-slave trade stances allowed for political interventions, tweaking local dynamics.[80] Edward Alpers identifies analogous strategies in East Africa and the broader Indian Ocean from the 1840s, foundational to later British dominance.[81] Guillemette Crouzet and Behnaz Mirzai spotlight the Persian Gulf, where the campaign against the slave trade signified the ascendancy of British power.[82] Further, in the Western Indian Ocean, the British leveraged treaties and military victories to project their naval power and establish territorial control.[83]

Yet, while the strategic use of abolition for imperial ambitions was evident across various regions, it was in the Atlantic Ocean where Britain's empire-building impulse, often cloaked in anti-slave trade rhetoric, manifested most prominently. This imperial drive, which included but was not limited to military interventions, had far-reaching consequences, particularly in West Central Africa. Scholars have traced a turning point to the 1840s. Scholar Tamis Parron asserts that Britain's interactions with Brazil and Cuba primarily spurred this shift.[84] Yet Bronwen Everill associates this shift with the end of slavery in the British Empire in 1838, which enabled Britain to focus resources on curbing the slave trade.[85] Another inflection point was an anti-slave trade treaty that Britain imposed on the Portuguese in 1842, which followed a unilateral decision by the British government to seize Portuguese vessels suspected of engaging in the slave trade in 1839. These measures transformed West Central Africa into a key battleground for the abolition of the transatlantic slave trade.

To fully grasp this complex landscape, it is vital to recognize France's often-overlooked endeavors to gain a stronghold in West Central Africa from the 1840s onward. Historian Denise Bouche notes that while post-restoration France harbored territorial ambitions primarily in Algeria, there was a concurrent aspiration to extend its influence across the Pacific Ocean, Southeast

Asia, and West Africa.[86] According to David Todd, this effort predominantly employed a strategy of informal empire, favoring influence and economic dominance over the direct annexation of territory.[87] In Senegal, however, historian Joseph-Pierre Diouf highlights the early development of structures that would herald the onset of "total colonialism," marking a transition in French imperial tactics in Africa.[88]

By the 1840s, echoing sentiments of Lisbon's *Associação Marítima e Colonial,* France's Institute d'Afrique had emerged as a key proponent of abolishing the slave trade, promoting free trade, and advocating for European colonization across Africa.[89] These pursuits were initially marked by an inconsistent blend of state and private support, notably with Marseille's Régis house being a central player in the formulation of France's policy toward Africa. Yet as Britain's anti-slave trade activities along the African coast intensified, France stepped up its efforts, taking concrete actions such as establishing settlements for Africans liberated from slave ships and sending trade and missionary expeditions to regions like Gabon, seeking to replicate "the same power which they have in Senegal."[90]

It is against this dense fabric of geopolitical competition, further explored in Chapter 6 of *Worlds of Unfreedom,* that Portugal's reorientation of imperial focus toward Africa must be understood. As early as 1842, Portuguese officials declared that "Europeans' attention is no longer limited to its borders and has recently turned to Africa."[91] They recognized that the threats to their imperial aspirations stemmed not only from Britain and France but also from the United States, adding another layer of complexity to the already intricate geopolitical chessboard. This recognition, combined with the aspiration to harness Africa's economic potential and rekindle Portugal's former imperial glory by cultivating a "new Brazil" in West Central Africa, fueled Portugal's motivations to oppose the transatlantic slave trade.

However, as discussed in Chapter 1, Portugal's aspirations of empire unfolded in a deeply convulsed South Atlantic world, where Portugal found itself locked in a struggle for influence in Angola with Brazil, its erstwhile colony. This struggle transcended mere economic opportunities, territorial influence, and geopolitical goals, unfolding within a dense web of social, cultural, economic, and political connections tying Angola to Brazil across the South Atlantic. These networks fed into a political awakening among the elites of Luanda and Benguela, resentful of Portugal's increasingly intrusive presence in Angola's affairs—including its attempts to abolish the slave trade—and deeply attached to the newly independent Brazil, itself undergoing a deeply fractious nation-building process marked by political unrest with racial and anti-Portuguese undertones. The 1845 Benguela revolt, which will be explored in detail in Chapter 1, stands as a powerful manifestation of these complex dynamics.

In the context of Portugal's ambitions in Africa, the struggle was thus not merely against external powers but also against its history and imperial legacy, especially in relation to Brazil. The Atlantic world, particularly the South Atlantic sphere connecting Angola to Brazil, was not just a space for economic exchanges but also a nexus of political contestation and intellectual and cultural circulations. Ideological constructs concerning race, identity, and governance echoed back and forth across this oceanic conduit, creating a nuanced, dynamic backdrop against which Portugal's imperial aspirations in Africa unfolded. Far from being a one-dimensional quest for territorial expansion or economic exploitation, Portugal's imperial endeavor in Africa thus played out amid a broad array of local and global variables.

The Structure of the Book

Chapter 1 examines identity formation and political contestation in the nineteenth-century South Atlantic world through the life of José Ferreira Gomes, an influential African slave trader arrested in 1846 in Benguela for allegedly inciting racial war against Portuguese rule. The chapter frames the South Atlantic as a fluid space marked by the circulation of people, unstable racial constructs, and political ideologies derived from feedback loops across permeable imperial boundaries. It portrays Ferreira Gomes as emblematic of unstable circuits of power across the South Atlantic—born in Angola, educated in Brazil, with a lineage spanning slave trading ties on both sides. For anxious Portuguese officials, his political activism stemmed from reverberations of Brazilian political turmoil and anti-Lusitanism amid growing nativist consciousness among coastal elites in Luanda and Benguela. By emphasizing racialized perceptions and political loyalties as relationally forged and transient, the chapter underscores identity and race as globally constituted through intricate Atlantic entanglements.

Chapter 2 provides an immersive exploration of gender, culture, and politics in 1840s Luanda, Angola, a critical juncture in the city's history as the most important slave port in the transatlantic trade. By centering the narrative on Dona Francisca Joaquina do Amaral, a woman ensnared in a web of patriarchal violence due to accusations of infidelity, the chapter seeks to evince fracture points and power relations concealed under imperial modes of record-keeping. The narrative delves into the microcosm of her experience against the larger backdrop of Luanda's struggle to end the slave trade, offering a rich tapestry of ethnographic detail to reconstruct the social, cultural, and economic fabrics of the city. Focusing on details, such as the culturally loaded gift of kola nuts (makèzú) sent to her lover, the chapter challenges archival erasures by portraying Dona Amaral as a complex figure navigating and shaping her circumstances. The chapter interweaves personal stories, political machinations, cultural traditions, and the institution of slavery to create a vivid portrayal of life in multicultural Luanda, where African languages, beliefs, and customs prevailed over Portuguese influences. It not only reconstructs the layered life of Dona Amaral but also seeks to give voice to the city's enslaved residents and the influential role of African women, particularly the street vendors known as quitandeiras, in shaping the city's vibrant markets and cultural fabric.

Chapter 3 centers the narrative of abolition on the main victims of the slave trade: enslaved Africans themselves. Through original archival research, the chapter illuminates the overlooked but pivotal role of enslaved Africans as active agents in dismantling the transatlantic slave trade networks in Benguela, Angola's second slave port. It tells the story of Tabião, an enslaved man who escaped and alerted authorities about an impending shipment of 194 captives from a feitoria in Equimina in 1854. His bold actions led to a raid that liberated these enslaved people and resulted in new anti-slave trade measures, including a decree granting freedom to any enslaved person who assisted in reporting slave trading activities. The chapter shows how attempts to revive large-scale shipments of enslaved people posed a threat to Benguela's emerging post-slave trade economy, which relied on natural resource extraction through African slavery. In this context, enslaved people leveraged their value as workers to disrupt slave trading attempts and shape anti-slave trade laws. This revisionist narrative provides a more complex understanding of abolition by recasting enslaved people as agents of abolition and not merely as victims of the slave trade.

Chapter 4 offers a new transnational perspective on the complex dynamics of abolishing the transatlantic slave trade in the mid-nineteenth century, while also assessing its impact on African political fabrics. By tracing the intricate networks linking West Central Africa, Brazil, the United States, and Cuba, the chapter positions West Central Africa as a critical hub within the capitalist structures sustaining the illegal trade's twilight years. Focusing on the story of slave trader Augusto Garrido's acquisition of U.S. citizenship to bypass anti-slavery laws, the chapter illuminates how slave dealers adapted by exploiting tensions between intensifying global abolition efforts and national economic interests. Additionally, the chapter highlights the often-overlooked ties between Cuba and West Central Africa, underscoring the Spanish colony's significant influence as the transatlantic slave trade neared its end. Through a multi-sited analysis, the chapter develops a nuanced understanding of the concerted, transnational efforts to halt human trafficking across the Atlantic world, while also examining the trade's profound ramifications for African societies and politics during this period.

Chapter 5 probes the complex trade diplomacy between Luanda native Dona Ana Joaquina dos Santos Silva and Nawej II, the ruler of the expansive Lunda empire, set against the backdrop of the declining transatlantic slave trade. It examines the Lunda ruler's strategic initiatives to establish direct commercial links with Luanda to bolster political power and respond to a shifting economic landscape, while also highlighting how these initiatives aligned with the Luanda government's interests in expanding its influence and securing new economic opportunities. The chapter also illuminates the role of Eufrazina, an enslaved woman whose pivotal involvement as an emissary disrupts conventional narratives of servitude, revealing the intricate intersections of gender, status, and power within the Lunda kingdom and the broader context of West Central Africa. Furthermore, it explores the ongoing agricultural efforts near Luanda, where the continuation of slavery and the internal slave trade underpinned a nascent plantation economy, reflecting the enduring and adaptive nature of exploitative labor systems.

Chapter 6 shifts focus to the regions north of Luanda, from Ambriz to Cabinda—the epicenters of the illegal slave trade in the 1850s—to investigate how efforts to end the trade intersected with European empire-building in Africa. It argues that Portugal's actions to suppress the slave trade in the lower Congo were intrinsically linked to its territorial ambitions, as exemplified by the Ambriz takeover and the occupation of Mbanza Kongo. The chapter situates Portugal's endeavors within the broader context of European powers leveraging anti-slave trade campaigns to expand their influence, drawing parallels to British interventions in Lagos and French naval patrols in the Bight of Benin. Crucially, it highlights the French role in Kongo's succession crisis, with the Maison Régis firm backing one of the contenders for the throne as part of a forced migration scheme in the lower Congo. Moreover, the chapter demonstrates how Portuguese troops, initially deployed to combat the slave trade, were subsequently used to intervene in Kongo's succession crisis, underscoring the complex interplay between abolition efforts, imperial ambitions, and local political dynamics in the mid-nineteenth century.

Chapter 7 investigates the global dynamics of labor exploitation in the age of abolition, tracing the circulation of ideas and practices across the British, French, and Portuguese empires. The chapter reveals how legal efforts to end the slave trade and slavery gave rise to new forms of unfree labor through mechanisms like apprenticeship and the engagé system. These systems perpetuated coercion and exploitation, facilitating the forced migration of Africans to various colonies, including the British Caribbean and French-controlled Réunion Island in the Indian Ocean, and from Angola to São Tomé and Príncipe. By situating Angola's experience within a broader global context, the chapter highlights the interconnectedness of labor practices across vast geographies and demonstrates how abolition laws were manipulated to serve colonial economic interests, ultimately shaping the development of labor legislation in the post-slavery era.

CHAPTER ONE

Unraveling the South Atlantic

IN JANUARY 1846, José Ferreira Gomes, a black man, was arrested near Benguela, Angola's second-largest city, and charged with orchestrating a rebellion to overthrow the city's Portuguese administration and eradicate its white populace. A native of Benguela, Ferreira Gomes had held various roles in the civilian and military administrations, spending much of his life in close association with the political elite. Yet city officials accused him of "seeking to promote a revolt among the people of the Benguela *sertão* [backlands] to devastate that city [Benguela], murdering the governor of the district [of Benguela] and all *whites* who lived there."[1] His primary co-conspirator was identified as his younger brother, Johannes Ferreira Gomes. Benguela's authorities contended that "the Ferreira Gomes blacks are fierce enemies of white people and have constantly plotted against them."[2]

The revolt led by José Ferreira Gomes was not an isolated incident but rather a reflection of broader sociopolitical upheavals gripping the wider South Atlantic world at the time. With the decline of the transatlantic slave trade, Angola found itself at the epicenter of shifting imperial dynamics and economic imperatives orchestrated by its colonial ruler, Portugal. The abolition of the slave trade brought forth external pressures as Portugal's rivals, including not only Great Britain but also France and the United States, vied for influence along Africa's coast. Meanwhile, Brazil maintained enduring connections with the African colony. In this context, Portugal sought to consolidate its presence in Angola by moving against the slave trade and transitioning it into a fully fledged colony. Yet these moves disrupted long-standing power dynamics with urban elites who had long benefited from the slave trade—including the Ferreira Gomes family—and African rulers who saw their land expropriated to make room for a new post-slave trade economy.

The Benguela revolt had all the ingredients to produce a bloodbath of unimaginable consequences. According to the German traveler George Tams, who visited Benguela in the 1840s, there were only 300 whites in the city, and their number varied considerably every year due to the sailing seasons and dry-season travel in the interior.[3] Fifteen years later, another traveler estimated the number of whites at just 39.[4] In 1860, authorities estimated the population of Benguela proper at 5,442 residents, of whom 4,308 were slaves; nearby Catumbela's population stood at 5,860 people. More importantly, there were by then only 108 white individuals in these places—78 of whom lived in the city of Benguela.[5] These numbers strongly suggest that an African uprising could deal an irreversible blow to Portuguese control of Benguela.

Against this backdrop, the revolt was inseparably linked to deeply ingrained local grievances, particularly ongoing attempts to expropriate African land to build a post-slave trade economy. Yet it was also fueled by broader struggles over authority, sovereignty, and political agitation unfolding across a tumultuous South Atlantic world. Particularly relevant was Brazil's troubled nation-state-building process, marked by deep political instability until the 1840s, which Portuguese officials in Angola perceived as potentially destabilizing. By tracing the transatlantic movements and ties of the Ferreira Gomes family, this chapter uncovers how ideas concerning race, identity, and political contestation spanned the Atlantic Ocean, creating a complex web of relationships that defied Portugal's efforts to rebuild its South Atlantic empire after losing Brazil in 1822.

By the time José Ferreira Gomes was taken into custody, he had allegedly already committed "the greatest atrocities in the vicinity of Benguela, murdering, beating, burning orchella weed farms [feitorias], and inciting Africans against white residents of that city [Benguela]."[6] In Egito, a coastal region north of Benguela where the alleged rebel leader owned businesses, he had sought to "persuade the people of Catumbela to murder the [district] regent and travel to Benguela to kill white people who had taken over their lands."[7] After authorities arrested Ferreira Gomes, two Ndombe rulers, one of them his maternal uncle, took up the fight against the Portuguese, significantly escalating a crisis that shook the foundation of Portuguese rule in the region. Despite the deployment of considerable military forces, including warships and hundreds of troops, the Benguela government would spend nearly two years struggling to reclaim dominion over the strife-torn region.

The Benguela revolt's strategic locations in Catumbela and then Dombe Grande hold significant importance to this story. Both regions played a crucial role in Benguela's economy, supplying foodstuff, including beans, corn, and manioc, not only to the city but also Luanda. A short distance from Benguela (three léguas), Catumbela boasted fertile lands and an abundance of agricultural fields known as nakas. "After the periodic floods of the river subside, black people sow beans, corn, and cassava, and some sow throughout the year, irrigating with water drawn from the river."[8] As late as 1858, rebel leader José Ferreira Gomes was still the owner of six small farms (arimos) in the district.[9]

Ferreira Gomes's primary basis of support was initially formed in Catumbela, where he sought to persuade the local population to rise against the

Portuguese authorities. This support included close associates such as a black man named Manoel Dias de Oliveira, a former soldier in Benguela who had married the rebel leader's daughter. Dias de Oliveira died during the Benguela revolt, taking his own life as troops pursued him in Catumbela. Another supporter was a "mixed race man [*pardo*] named Antonio Nogueira da Rocha [who] had accompanied the Ferreira Gomes [brothers] in their terrible attacks on the whites."[10] Among the supporters were also Francisco Marques da Silva and António Joaquim Monteiro, "lately charged with complicity in plans to attack Europeans in Benguela, in addition to several crimes in collusion with José Ferreira Gomes."[11] These individuals were eventually arrested and taken to Luanda for "crimes [that] had undermined the government of the district of Benguela."[12]

From Catumbela, the revolt spread to the much larger Dombe Grande, eighty miles (12 léguas) south of Benguela, significantly escalating the crisis for the Benguela government. Known for its sulfur mines, which supplied approximately one hundred tons of the mineral to Brazil between 1808 and 1824, the region played a crucial role in Benguela's food supply.[13] Dombe Grande was then home to five chiefdoms (sobados), with men primarily engaging in pastoral activities while women and children cultivated agricultural fields. Emigrant groups from Kilengues (known as Muhumbes) stood out as the principal farmers, producing cassava and flour later sold in Benguela.[14]

To frighten Benguela's residents, Ferreira Gomes had apparently spread rumors that his African ally "Joannes Gaspar was preparing weapons to come to [Benguela] at night and attack the houses of some white people and that he might murder them and rob them."[15] A chief from Catumbela and until then a faithful ally of the Portuguese, Gaspar was the ruler [*soba*] of a *Ndombe* community that until then had largely coexisted peacefully with the colonial regime.[16] After the Benguela government arrested the Ferreira Gomes brothers, Gaspar became the revolt's leader, lending the movement a social dimension that significantly deepened a crisis that threatened the foundations of Portuguese rule.

Adding a key element to the unfolding drama, the African ruler was also José Ferreira Gomes's maternal cousin. His aunt, the Catumbela-born Florinda Josefa Gaspar, had married Ferreira Gomes's father in the 1820s. This marriage had been foundational for a commercial empire that the family had built on forcibly and violently transporting human beings across the Atlantic. In June 1824, one of their ships transported four hundred and fifty enslaved people to Brazil, about five percent of the overall number of Africans deported from West Central Africa by the Ferreira Gomes family.[17] Some of these people might have journeyed to the coast through territory belonging to Soba Gaspar. Now, rebel leader José Ferreira Gomes was bent on leveraging such ties to challenge Portuguese rule in Benguela.

Soba Gaspar, who would eventually be coldly murdered by the Portuguese, also directly disputed official views that the revolt led by his nephew was fueled by anti-white sentiments. When government forces sought to capture the younger Ferreira Gomes, the African chief refused to surrender him, asserting that "Africans considered him [Joanes Ferreira Gomes] as in the class of whites [and thus] it was up to white people to look for him."[18] This statement reveals a complex racial dynamic at play. The Portuguese colonial authorities, influenced by their own rigid racial hierarchies, saw the Ferreira Gomes brothers as Black insurgents driven by a desire to overthrow white rule. In contrast, Soba Gaspar and other Africans viewed the brothers as whites, likely due to their wealth, education, and Westernized mannerisms.

This chapter seizes on this dissonance to examine how ideas concerning identity, race, and political contestation developed in the broader canvas of a deeply integrated Atlantic world. Scholars have emphasized the formation of Angolan identity in relation to Portugal and the heightened efforts of the metropole to control the colony.[19] By contrast, this chapter braids together events unfolding in Angola and Brazil to demonstrate how ties between these two regions became a nexus for the circulation of ideologies concerning race, identity, and anti-colonial contestation. By following multiple threads of relationships, including legal battles, trade interactions, and family bonds, I argue that race formation and political contestation emerged relationally via webs of historical connectivity linking Luanda and Benguela to several Brazilian cities, including Rio de Janeiro, Salvador, and Recife.

The chapter argues that Portuguese colonial authorities, haunted by the loss of Brazil and the ongoing political instability there fueled by anti-Portuguese sentiment, viewed figures like Ferreira Gomes and the Benguela revolt through the lens of racial anxieties imported from Brazil. Yet the revolt was actually rooted in local grievances, particularly over land expropriation and the imposition of a new post-slave trade economic order. By uncovering this dissonance, the chapter illuminates how the South Atlantic space produced its own distinctive race-making dynamics, challenging the notion that racial ideologies originated solely from European thought. This finding suggests the need for a more expansive and relational approach to the study of race formation that attends to the specific histories and dynamics of interconnected regions such as the South Atlantic world.

To unravel the interconnected racial and political dynamics of the South Atlantic, this chapter will first delve into José Ferreira Gomes's background straddling Brazil and Angola, exemplifying persisting and complex bonds between the two regions. It will then analyze the rise of an Angolense identity opposing Portuguese control and more closely aligned with Brazil, fueled by enduring cultural, economic, and familial ties. By weaving together Angolan and Brazilian political histories, the chapter will uncover how Brazil's own political instability, fueled by racial tension and anti-Portuguese sentiment, heightened Portuguese anxieties and suspicions surrounding figures like Ferreira Gomes. In this context, Brazil served as a proxy for Portuguese fears of racial upheaval, and Benguela's close connection with Brazil made it a potential battleground for the political and racial instability percolating throughout the South Atlantic.

Straddling Two Worlds

This story cannot be told without considering rebel leader José Ferreira Gomes's wider world, particularly Benguela's complex connections with Brazil, Portugal's erstwhile colony. Historically, Benguela was intertwined with Brazil through brutal slave trading networks, much like Luanda, Angola's primary supplier of enslaved labor to the Atlantic.[20] The Ferreira Gomes family, notable for selling thousands of Africans across the Atlantic, was central to this relationship, fostering complex familial, cultural, and legal ties that spanned the ocean. José Ferreira Gomes, the son of a Brazilian slave trader with extensive South Atlantic dealings, emerged from this interconnected world, embodying the multifaceted bonds that bridged Angola and Brazil.

Nor can this narrative be fully comprehended without acknowledging how these ties increasingly stood in the way of Portugal's aspirations to firmly colonize Angola after losing Brazil in 1822. With the slave trade as a backdrop, the former South American colony remained deeply tied with what had by then become the jewel of the Portuguese crown, Angola. A novelty was the fact that these connections had acquired an unmistakable political dimension after Brazil's independence when part of the elites in Luanda and Benguela sought to sever ties to Portugal and join Brazil as overseas provinces of the independent nation.[21] Despite Brazil's independence, the ties between Angola and Brazil persisted, influencing political and economic relations. With Brazil's politics becoming increasingly volatile due to a troubled nation-state building that would last into the 1840s, political shockwaves rippled across the Atlantic, deeply unsettling Portuguese officials in Luanda and Benguela.

For all its complexities, Angola's ties with Brazil were not entirely sui generis. In West Africa, cities like Lagos, Whydah, and Porto Novo also shared intricate cultural, religious, and economic connections with Brazil, especially Salvador, Brazil's second-largest city.[22] A powerful slave dealer from Salvador played a vital role in the rise of King Guezo in Dahomey in 1818.[23] In another instance, a Lagos royal claimant garnered support from Brazilian slave traders in Whydah before setting off to Lagos to vie for power.[24] African ethnicity and religion played crucial roles in Salvador's labor organization and slave uprisings.[25] Faith-based connections facilitated constant transatlantic movements.[26] Yet nowhere were West African coastal elites ever accused of employing violent means to dismantle European ruling, nor were they ever charged with waging racial wars on white people.

As a living link between two worlds slowly drifting apart, Ferreira Gomes's life encapsulates how Angola and Brazil remained interlocked despite Brazil's

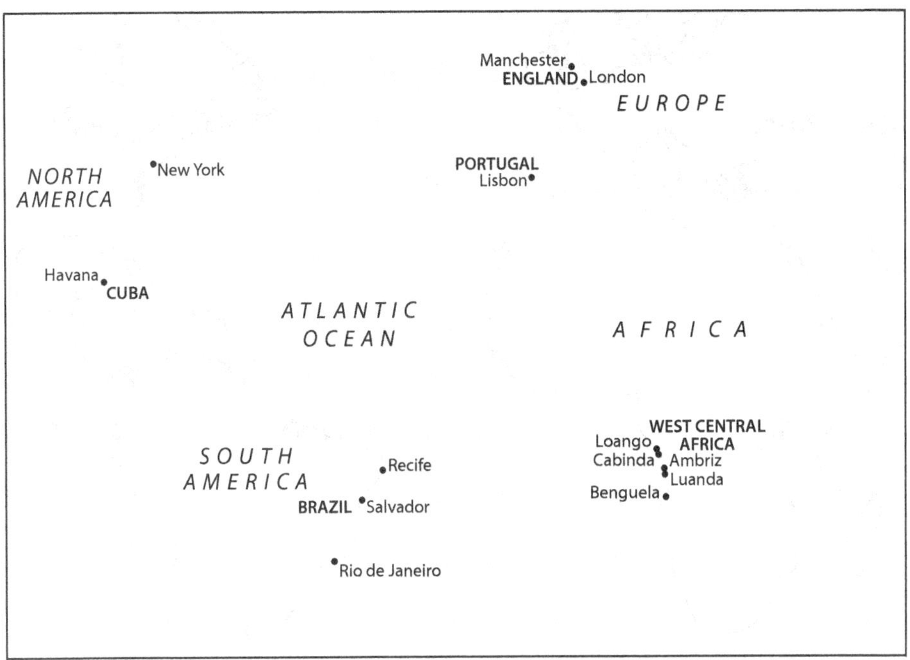

MAP 1. The Atlantic World

independence from Portugal in 1822. Born in Benguela in 1800, the alleged rebel leader was sent to Brazil at the age of 13 for education and managerial training. He stayed for about eight years in Brazil's capital, Rio de Janeiro. To some extent, his education in Brazil reflected the limited availability of Western education in Benguela. A European traveler who visited Benguela in the 1840s observed, "in the strictest sense of the word, there is no school instruction whatever in the town, although there is a population of 3,000 souls."[27]

Ferreira Gomes's stay in Rio de Janeiro is little known, yet it is likely that he was housed by one of his father's associates. Around the same time, Francisco Franque and Manoel Puna, members of Cabinda's trading family, were also sent to Rio for education with housing arrangements likely organized by the Portuguese colonial government, possibly staying with one of the city's slave dealers.[28] The patriarch of the Ferreira Gomes family, being a native of Rio de Janeiro with extensive business connections in the city, might have arranged similar accommodations for his son. Regardless of the specifics, José Ferreira Gomes would not have felt entirely out of place in Rio, a city with strong ties to Benguela.

Ferreira Gomes's trip to Rio de Janeiro fit into a broader trend of Luanda and Benguela elites shipping their offspring to be educated in Brazil. A father once mentioned sending his child to "one of the good primary education schools established in that city [Rio de Janeiro]."[29] Ernesto Gamboa, fluent in French, had studied the language in Rio de Janeiro, where his family sent him during his youth.[30] Arsenio Pompilio Pompeu de Carpo, one of Luanda's most active slave dealers, declared that he had lived in Rio "13 years for the education of his sons," with at least two of them born and raised in Brazil and one who studied briefly at the Colégio Pedro II in Rio de Janeiro.[31] Carpo would become a vocal leader of nativist politics in Luanda, leveraging his power to undermine anti-slave trade laws, as discussed in Chapter 2.

These trips were also relatively common among elites elsewhere in Africa. In the 1840s, Lagos ruler Kosoko had three children enrolled in schools in Salvador through his association with Brazilian slave dealers.[32] As historian Toby Green notes, "The hope was that by expanding their skill set, they would enable their children to achieve greater profits in business and political negotiations with the outside world."[33] Yet, in the unique context of the Angola-Brazil relationship, these educational voyages took on a different significance, shaping identities in ways that Portugal viewed as potentially threatening to its rule in Luanda and Benguela.

Once José Ferreira Gomes returned to Benguela, his trajectory gave no inkling that he would later take on the Portuguese regime. He experienced a steady ascent through the ranks of both civilian and military spheres. Esteemed as a "very diligent and highly regarded" officer in the Henriques battalion, previously led by his Brazil-born father, his reputation in administrative circles was steadily growing.[34] Serving as a justice of the peace, he was once said to have used this position to extract undue financial benefits from a local merchant's widow.[35] He also managed the royal stores and commanded the strategically crucial Fort São Domingos de Calundo, near Benguela.[36]

In subsequent years, Ferreira Gomes continued climbing the ranks of colonial society. After being promoted to major by Angola's governor Bressane in 1842, he reportedly persuaded the governor of Benguela, Chateauneff, to declare a war of retribution against Africans [Ndombe] who had attacked caravans he had dispatched upcountry to purchase enslaved people and commodities.[37] As late as 1844, just one year before the alleged revolt that led to his downfall, he schemed with the governor of Benguela, João Casimiro de Vasconcellos, to invalidate the testament of a Catumbela ruler so that he could become the ruler's heir, thus further enlarging his already considerable fortune.[38]

Notably, Ferreira Gomes's career unfolded against the backdrop of a continuing transatlantic slave trade, which thrived despite the official prohibition in 1836. In 1839, a slave dealer said in Rio that captives were embarked "during daylight in Benguela, in front of authorities of the country."[39] In 1840, the British reported that "at Benguela, slaves are said to be openly shipped in the port, and a capitation tax paid to the governor."[40] Thirty thousand people were shipped to Brazil between 1836 and 1840, many on ships that belonged to the Ferreira Gomes family, paving the way for the family's wealth on both sides of the Atlantic.

Evidence of Ferreira Gomes's participation in the slave trading operations abound. As early as 1824, having recently returned to Benguela from Rio de Janeiro, he requested a license to dispatch one barrel of gunpowder to Benguela's backlands, likely to supply inland trading expeditions.[41] The following year, he sought licenses to send carriers inland, highlighting his involvement in overland trade.[42] Alongside his father, he also applied to purchase enslaved people for their brig Maria in 1827.[43] His commercial ventures grew as he sent agents inland and requisitioned additional porters, dispatching as many as thirty, then one hundred at a time, over the following two years.[44]

While no evidence has surfaced about Ferreira Gomes's actively undercutting Portugal's efforts to end the transatlantic slave trade, his close associate and sometimes rival, Justiniano José dos Reis, did engage in such actions. Dos Reis, a Brazilian-born slave dealer, had become a major political player in Benguela in the early 1820s alongside the Ferreira Gomes patriarch, with whom he had co-owned at least one slave ship. In 1835, Dos Reis was named interim governor of Benguela after promising to fund the city's transfer to Catumbela.[45] In this capacity, he was responsible for enforcing Portugal's anti-slave trade law, which was passed the following year. While Dos Reis once ordered an investigation into slave ships, likely belonging to his competitors, entering the city's port, he also owned the brig Nova Sorte, which disembarked 444 enslaved Africans in Rio de Janeiro in 1836, revealing his own involvement in the illegal trade.[46]

By the 1840s, José Ferreira Gomes had long since become the primary administrator of the family's commercial empire, following his father's retirement to Rio de Janeiro in 1834, after thirty years of life in Benguela.[47] As discussed later in this chapter, the patriarch's relocation was clouded by accusations that, together with his oldest son, he was one of the leaders of a plot that would have overthrown the Benguela government. After a thirty-five-day Atlantic crossing, he arrived in Rio de Janeiro on December 6, 1834, taking with him two daughters, but without his wife Florinda Josefa Gaspar, who stayed behind in Benguela.[48]

Recounting his departure from Benguela, the patriarch would later state that "he had left his trading house and properties to the care of his wife [Florinda Josefa Gaspar], given the absence of his sons, José Ferreira Gomes and Johannes Ferreira Gomes."[49] This account sheds light on Florinda Josefa Gaspar's pivotal role in the family's business affairs. As pointed out earlier, her marriage to the Brazilian-born Francisco Ferreira Gomes was a turning point for the family's commercial ventures. Their union solidified his connections with a powerful family in the food-producing region of Dombe Grande, helping him benefit from his position in the Benguela administration and later likely helping his slave trade activities in Benguela. Notably, one of the ships owned by the family—Delfina da África—was named after her.[50]

A key point to note is the Ferreira Gomes patriarch's commercial activities after his relocating to Rio de Janeiro in 1834. Before leaving Benguela, he had been responsible for shipping approximately eight thousand enslaved Africans to Brazil. In Rio, in close association with his Benguela-based son, he adapted his business in response to a ban on importing enslaved Africans enacted three years earlier. This adaptability is evident by examining the voyages of two of his ships, the Maria and the Delfina of Africa. At the time, Montevideo had emerged as a key entry point for smuggling African slaves into Brazil. Slave ships departed from Angola would declare Montevideo as a destination, and around twenty percent of Africans brought into Brazil came through that city.[51] In November 1837, for example, the Delfina da Africa arrived from Montevideo, likely having disembarked enslaved Africans either near Rio or in Uruguay.[52]

From Rio de Janeiro, the Ferreira Gomes elders maintained robust connections with Benguela, retaining ownership of land, houses, and enslaved individuals even two decades after leaving the city. "The black woman Dionísia, also known as Juamutango, has always been a slave of the *justificante* [Francisco Ferreira Gomes] ever since he was a resident of this city [Benguela], having been bought from the late Francisco Joaquim Coelho Santiago, from the sertão of Galangue."[53] The patriarch once claimed that all the properties that a Benguela judge sequestered from his son belonged to him.[54] The ties stretched beyond materiality; through his oldest son, they contributed funding for restoring a church in Benguela on his father's behalf.[55]

From Benguela, the oldest son would take several business and family trips across the Atlantic, effectively connecting the two branches of the family. In 1825, he was described as "legally associated in a commercial partnership [with his father Francisco Ferreira Gomes]," wherein one of the partners had to travel to Rio de Janeiro.[56] In this capacity, he would travel to Rio alone in 1826 and 1827.[57] But these voyages were not only for business. In 1830, he took his whole family to Rio, where he met his father, who had traveled there the year before.[58] In 1849, he crossed the Atlantic again to take his niece Florinda Ferreira Gomes and his son Francisco Ferreira Gomes Neto to stay with their grandparents in Rio.[59] His last trip to Rio seems to have occurred in 1851 to retrieve his stepdaughter's dowry.[60]

A lawsuit from Benguela sheds light on Ferreira Gomes's activities during his time in Rio de Janeiro, despite the limited availability of specific details. In the suit, his stepdaughter Feliciana Ferreira Gomes Vianna and her husband accused him of misappropriating a dowry left by her mother, Gertrudes Ferreira Gomes. According to Ferreira Gomes, "the mother of his [step]-daughter, Gertrudes Ferreira Gomes, when she arranged the marriage of her daughter with [a man named] Manoel [Dias de Oliveira], gave the couple as a dowry four contos de réis in Brazilian currency."[61] Ferreira Gomes had promised to retrieve this money from Rio de Janeiro and obtained a power of attorney from the couple for this purpose. However, upon his return to Benguela, he failed to fulfill his promise, further straining the already tense family dynamics.[62]

The family legal battle illustrates what historian Mariana Dias Paes has termed a "shared legal culture" across the South Atlantic, pivotal in Ferreira Gomes's business ventures and others' alike.[63] This legal interconnectivity was facilitated by the mutual recognition of rogatory letters between courts in Benguela and Brazil. Yet it also often still necessitated transatlantic movement, as highlighted by a lawsuit that pitted Mariana Emilia de Mello Santos Palhares against Maria do Carmo Mantaury dos Reis in Rio de Janeiro. Following a verdict in Palhares's favor, she took steps to protect her interests in Luanda, initially appointing Joaquim Ribeiro de Brito, a known slave dealer, as her representative. Yet she later dispatched her son across the Atlantic to prevent Reis from liquidating her late husband's estate in Luanda.[64]

The trajectories of other slave traders, such as José Joaquim Teixeira, may shed some light on Ferreira Gomes's activities in Rio de Janeiro. Born in Porto but operating in Benguela during the 1840s, Teixeira was described as a 42-year-old white man.[65] He supported the formation of an agricultural company in the colony and was appointed commander of a Benguela fort. After sending one of his daughters for education in Rio de Janeiro, he traveled to the city for medical treatment in the 1840s.[66] Teixeira's involvement in the illegal slave trade is evident from the condemnation of three of his vessels by the Anglo-Brazilian Mixed Commission Court in Rio de Janeiro in the 1830s.[67]

Another illustrative example is Manoel Joaquim Teixeira, once described as Benguela's largest slave dealer alongside Ferreira Gomes and one of his frequent commercial partners.[68] In 1835, Teixeira sailed to Rio de Janeiro on a ship owned by Ferreira Gomes.[69] After being appointed interim governor of Benguela in 1844, Teixeira sought permission to travel to Rio just three days into his tenure.[70] While based in Rio, he maintained links to Benguela, even funding the city's hospital, while engaging in the slave trade through associates such as Bento Pacheco dos Santos, a Brazilian national still operating in the city. Teixeira's actions demonstrate how slave traders leveraged their transatlantic connections to maintain their business interests and influence in both Benguela and Rio de Janeiro.[71]

Manoel Joaquim Teixeira's involvement in the illegal slave trade is further highlighted by his co-ownership of the *Paquete de Benguela* with the above-mentioned José Joaquim Teixeira, possibly his relative. The ship was seized in 1840 off the coast of Rio de Janeiro with 280 enslaved Africans on board.[72] Following his eventual expulsion from Brazil, Teixeira resumed slaving operations from Benguela, focusing on shipping captives to Cuba in the 1850s. In 1853, authorities described him as "an old merchant in Benguela who had relocated to Rio de Janeiro in 1846, where he amassed a considerable fortune through illicit slave trading until being forced to leave Brazil by the imperial government."[73]

While the transatlantic journeys of these slave traders were primarily driven by their commercial interests, it is worth pointing out that they were part of a larger pattern of mobility between Angola and Brazil that encompassed individuals from diverse backgrounds and with varying motivations. From small-scale traders to skilled laborers, and from men to women, individuals of different social strata participated in these crossings, creating a complex web of personal, familial, and economic connections that spanned the Atlantic. A case in point was a Cabinda man named Antonio José Marinha, who departed from Rio de Janeiro to Angola with his wife and child on July 7, 1835.[74] In another example, Estevão Taviano Muri and his wife, both free individuals, had initially traveled to Rio de Janeiro for educational reasons, before later spending two years in Luanda and then deciding to return to Rio.[75]

Economic pursuits, ranging from small-scale trade activities to training opportunities, also underpinned crossings. Between June 11 and December 22, 1831, sixty-two free blacks, including eight women, were issued licenses to travel to Brazilian cities like Rio de Janeiro and Recife. While twenty of these individuals headed to Rio de Janeiro, thirty-three set out for Recife. Among them were Rafael Banzando, Bonifacio Mampeme, and Andre Zalumbe, three free Africans who paid 30,000 réis for a one-year authorization to stay in Rio de Janeiro, likely in pursuit of business opportunities.[76]

Others traveled in pursuit of professional training, which might have been the case for Sebastião de Souza, described as a "free black resident in Luanda," who applied for a license to stay in Rio de Janeiro for an entire year after paying thirty thousand réis.[77] Similarly, Antonio Francisco invested 30,000 réis in a license to travel to Rio, aiming to undergo welding training with the likely intention of applying this skill in a professional capacity upon his return to Luanda.[78] It is significant that, as late as 1867, Luanda authorities still had to specify the "free" status on passports for "persons of color" traveling to Brazil, underscoring the enduring nature of these transatlantic journeys.[79]

Highlighting that mobility was not exclusively a male domain, women also featured in these crossings. Likely sisters, free black women Josefa Maria and Ana Maria applied for a license to travel from Benguela to Rio de Janeiro in 1825.[80] Inácia Maria arrived in Rio from Luanda on a ship carrying 330 captives in 1830.[81] Ana Casanje, "a free black woman living in Luanda," paid thirty thousand réis for a license to travel to Rio de Janeiro, joining Ana Conga and Tereza Matamba, two other free black women from Luanda.[82] Catarina sailed to Rio on the *Paquete da Saudade*, accompanied by Rita and a man named José Batista Gomes.[83] Thirteen years later, four free black women (Maria Joaquina, Maria Luiza, A. J. Victorina, and M. Thereza) entered Luanda on the Andorinha after first traveling from Rio de Janeiro to Benguela on the General Rego.[84]

As a result of transatlantic crossings, Benguela hosted a community of individuals whose identities were fundamentally shaped by the Atlantic. A traveler once described the city as "frequented chiefly by Brazilians," with the number of Brazilian nationals permanently living there being calculated at twenty out of twenty-five foreign residents in 1853.[85] Among them was André Corrêa Homem de Cadillos, whom Ferreira Gomes appointed to manage his business after being arrested on charges of sedition in 1846.[86] Ten years later, Ferreira Gomes accused his former partner—then the legal representative of his parents, living in Brazil—of illegally owning land his parents had inherited from his African ruler uncle.[87]

Notably, Brazilian transplants' influence was not confined to the slave trade, with their reach extending into the very power structures of Benguela. A striking example was Justiniano José dos Reis, a native of Brazil who became an interim governor of Benguela, demonstrating the significant roles Brazilian transplants played in the city's administration. Another case in point was Veríssimo Lopes de Moura, who declared that "he had been born in the city of Salvador, a province of the empire of Brazil, and was baptized in the parish of Nossa Senhora de Santana."[88] Moura was at least once elected member of the city chamber and appointed an interim judge.[89] In another example, Bento Pacheco dos Santos, a known slave dealer in town, was at least once elected to the city chamber.[90] According to a registry of enslaved people in 1854, he was the owner of 124 enslaved people at the time.[91]

The employment of Brazilians came under scrutiny, however, as the movement to dismantle the networks of the slave trade gained momentum in the 1840s. In 1843, authorities in Luanda instructed the local government to dismiss José Campos Ribeiro Porto, who had moved to the city in 1841 after spending ten years as a bookkeeper (caixeiro) and trader with ties to the backlands (sertões) in Luanda. After arriving in Benguela, Porto worked as a clerk at the city's hospital before eventually moving on to the customs service and the government office that managed the estates of deceased residents. The Luanda government called for Porto's dismissal due to his nationality and involvement in the transatlantic slave trade.[92] They later commented that another Brazilian, José Pereira da Fonseca Guimarães, had no "cause or justification" for being in Benguela.[93]

The intensified surveillance of these individuals stemmed from their participation in the slave trade, now intertwined with the burgeoning trade of a lichen (orchilla), then in high demand in Europe. In 1845, the governor of Benguela declared that "[José] Ferreira Gomes had established a commercial house in [Benguela] and operated trading posts (feitorias) along the northern coast of the city."[94] By investing in the orchilla trade, Ferreira Gomes joined numerous other Benguela merchants, such as Jácomo Felipe Torres, who owned several trading posts along Benguela's northern coast, and Raimundo Lapinberg, a Brazilian trader likely involved in the slave trade, who also owned an orchilla trading post.[95] Another Benguela resident who owned orchilla trading posts was Veríssimo Lopes de Moura, already mentioned earlier, whose property was located south of Benguela in Lucira.[96]

Yet these investments drew scrutiny from officials then seeking to curb the transatlantic slave trade, since the orchilla trade often served as a facade for shipments of captives abroad. In 1844, authorities observed that these feitorias "caused great damage to the national treasure because they were points where contraband [of orchilla] takes place."[97] Despite these warnings, merchants like Ferreira Gomes persisted in requesting permission to visit their feitorias. Officials granted him a renewed license to travel to one in Equimina but cautioned that he would be held responsible if enslaved Africans were transported from the establishment.[98] To sidestep any allegations of involvement in the slave trade, Ferreira Gomes even asked to be accompanied by an inspector from the Benguela customs house when applying for a license to visit his feitoria in Egito.[99]

Identity Formation

The revolt led by José Ferreira Gomes must be understood within the context of growing discord between the Portuguese colonial administration and an increasingly assertive Angolense local elite in Luanda and Benguela. Comprising educated and influential individuals, emerging Angolense groups would draw sharp comparisons between the increasingly constricting reality of life under Portuguese rule in Angola and perceived possibilities for advancement in Brazil's "hospitable" society, where many of them had been educated and believed they could attain "the highest positions," including diplomatic posts.[100] Given José Ferreira Gomes's background, his having studied in Brazil and maintaining strong family ties there, it is plausible that the Portuguese would have associated him with such Angolense groups.

To express their discontent, Angolenses leveraged political clubs and freemasonry lodges as platforms for political agitation—a strategy that had been successfully employed in Brazil.[101] In 1840, officials noted that "almost all sons of the country harbored visceral hatred towards individuals from the kingdom [of Portugal]" and that these organizations aimed to "break away from the metropole and achieve the annexation of Angola to Brazil."[102] Jovem Luanda, a Luanda freemasonry lodge predominantly founded by slave dealers from Brazil, came under particular scrutiny, as its members were described as "sworn enemies of European Portuguese."[103] As tensions heightened, colonial authorities eventually sought a more cooperative approach with Angolense groups, going so far as to hold meetings with an organization charged with defending native interests.[104]

In Benguela, however, local authorities once reported confrontational behavior toward Portuguese nationals, remarking that "mulattoes from this district had demonstrated since last July with loud insults, rancorously treating the Portuguese as *Galegos* and saying publicly that the situation in Benguela would only return to normal when the Galegos had been excluded from public positions and these were filled with natives from the country."[105] Protesters included Pedro Ferreira de Andrade, a mixed-race judge partial to slave dealers, and José da Silva Maia Ferreira, the Rio de Janeiro educated scion of a powerful slave trade family from Luanda.[106] A Benguela governor lamented his lack of force to counter this rising tide of local discontent, stating, "I do not have sufficient force to block an insult against the whites who reside here, as the soldiers in Benguela are all naturals of the country."[107]

The widening chasm revealed how preferences for Portuguese-born individuals in administrative roles inflamed nativist sentiments among local elites, which surfaced during a selection process for the Luanda tribunal: "I considered myself uncomfortable given that I am European."[108] Heightening Portuguese concerns was the fact that non-white individuals were often elected as representatives of Angola in the Portuguese parliament and the Luanda city council. "Every time that elections have taken place, either to select voters for the national assembly or to the municipal chamber, those elected have always been either blacks or mixed-race individuals [*pardos*], and whites have been excluded."[109]

Yet what made tensions boil over was Portugal's implementation of an anti-slave trade decree passed in 1836, which elicited a fierce backlash from Luanda and Benguela elites who relied on the sale of African lives across the Atlantic to maintain their wealth and affluent lifestyles. A letter from Luanda captures how local opposition to the enactment of anti-slave trade laws intertwined with nativist attachment to Brazil, which was the destination of most of the enslaved Africans transported across the Atlantic from Luanda and Benguela. In the letter, a Luanda resident spoke about a "tendency to proclaim a union with Brazil, which disgracefully nothing will prevent given the inferiority of Portugal's navy."[110]

Notably, Portugal's reluctance to sign an anti-slave trade treaty with Britain stemmed from fears that fighting the slave trade could lead to secessionism in Luanda. During negotiations in 1838, Portuguese foreign minister Sá da Bandeira demanded that Britain guarantee substantial land and sea support to quell any disturbances or separatist movements resulting from the treaty. Britain's refusal to provide a comprehensive guarantee for Portugal's African colonies, along with Portugal's concerns over the treaty's potential to destabilize its colonial territories, ultimately sank it.[111]

Significantly complicating matters was Brazil's ongoing social and political upheaval, driven by pervasive anti-Portuguese sentiments and bouts of radical politics from below, which directly influenced Portuguese perspectives about Angola's nascent nativism. As early as 1835, while analyzing proposals to allow mixed race and black individuals to become commanders in the colonial army in Luanda, city officials expressed concern that "from the moment that blacks and mulattoes gain authority over whites, it will follow that Angola will be reduced to the state of anarchy currently afflicting parts of Brazil."[112] White members of the military opposed the proposal, and officials agreed that such a change could potentially lead to violent upheavals similar to the "bloody scenes of São Domingo [a reference to the Haitian revolution that had wiped out slavery and European power in a former French colony] that today are repeated in [the Brazilian province of] Pará" and the same would happen in Luanda.[113]

Luanda authorities' reference to Pará highlights the far-reaching shockwaves of the Cabanagem, a social uprising in northern Brazil from 1835 to 1840. This deeply organic movement was supported by commoners, including enslaved people, and managed to capture and control Belém, Pará's capital, for nearly a year. A civil war resulted in the loss of approximately thirty thousand lives and necessitated intervention from Brazilian troops and several foreign nations, including France, Britain, and Portugal. At its core, the movement was fueled by deeply embedded anti-Portuguese sentiments, with rebels strategically targeting Portuguese individuals while mounting a serious challenge to the province's social order.[114]

Brazil's anti-Portuguese sentiment extended far beyond the Cabanagem revolt and animated social movements throughout a country going through a troubled nation-building process. The anti-Portuguese sentiment was fueled by several factors, including resentment toward a Portuguese monarch and his advisors who held sway in independent Brazil.[115] Economic grievances also played a role, as Portuguese merchants were often accused of manipulating food supplies for speculative gains in Brazilian cities. Crucially, these anti-Portuguese sentiments found a particularly receptive audience among Brazil's non-white populations, stoking fears of a more expansive social revolution similar to the one that had ended French colonialism in Saint Domingue.[116]

Just as the specter of the Haitian Revolution haunted slaveholders in Brazil, evoking fears of a similar slave uprising that could upend the social order, Brazil's turbulent political landscape became a source of anxiety for the Portuguese colonial administration in Luanda and Benguela. In Brazil, the Haitian Revolution sparked intense debates and fears among slaveholders, who saw it as a cautionary tale of the dangers posed by enslaved Africans. As historian Flávio Gomes notes, news and rumors about the Haitian Revolution circulated widely in Brazil, fueling anxieties about the potential for slave rebellions and reshaping discussions about slavery and abolition.[117] In a similar vein, Brazil's own political instability and anti-Portuguese sentiment became a constant reminder to the Portuguese colonial administration in Angola of the fragility of their power and the potential for radical change emanating from across the Atlantic. Just as Brazil looked to Haiti with a mixture of fear and fascination, Portugal saw in Brazil a reflection of its own vulnerabilities and the risks of losing control over its African colony.

The circulation of news about Brazil's political instability and anti-Portuguese sentiment was facilitated by various means, including ships crossing the Atlantic. These vessels carried not only crewmembers with direct accounts but also private letters originating from Brazil, which often contained information about the political climate and social unrest. Despite delays in standard postal services, individuals with financial means could expedite their mail through well-connected ports like Pernambuco and Rio de Janeiro, ensuring a steady flow of information across the ocean.[118] These letters not only kept the Portuguese colonial administration informed about the turbulent events in Brazil but also heightened their anxieties about the potential spread of seditious ideas to Angola.

Brazilian newspapers, albeit few in number, also made their way across the Atlantic and were read in Luanda and Benguela, complementing personal reports and private letters. A striking example occurred in 1835 when the Luanda government declared three days of mourning upon receiving Brazilian newspapers reporting the death of Pedro IV in Lisbon.[119] Notably, news from Brazil was occasionally featured in Luanda's weekly gazette, the *Boletim Oficial da Província de Angola* (BOPA), further facilitating the circulation of information across the Atlantic.[120] This exchange of newspapers and the inclusion of Brazilian news in local publications underscore the deep interconnectedness between the two regions and the importance placed on staying informed about developments on both sides of the ocean.

The Portuguese colonial administration's awareness of this interconnectedness and its potential implications is evident in their actions and concerns. Tellingly, officials in Luanda once urged Lisbon to send more political exiles from Portugal to Angola, emphasizing that "whites, especially Portuguese, constitute the support to authorities here, and the primary source of stability for the province."[121] By making this request, they aimed to bolster Portuguese rule, which had become closely intertwined with notions of whiteness. However, transatlantic ties persisted, perpetuating lingering fears of unrest originating from Brazil. Antonio Manoel de Noronha, the first governor to oppose the slave trade and who would soon be forced to resign due to a backlash from local slave dealers, voiced apprehensions about the arrival of "proud settlers perhaps imbued with Brazilian ideas" in Luanda.[122] Noronha believed that a "Brazilian party" had emerged in Angola, comprised of mixed-race individuals advocating for independence from Portugal.[123]

Luanda officials would have paid particular attention to any instability affecting Rio de Janeiro, Brazil's capital, where many Angolenses had family and business connections or had been educated—including José Ferreira Gomes. At that time, Rio de Janeiro was a hotbed of popular politics characterized by racial tension and strong anti-Portuguese sentiments.[124] Street protests pitted radical liberals known as Exaltados against forces aligned with the Portuguese. The former advocated policies that included extending citizenship rights, gradual emancipation of slaves, and the establishment of a republic. Waves of popular politics enabled marginalized groups like blacks and poor people to voice economic and racial grievances, underscoring the development of a national identity from below. A strong anti-Portuguese sentiment marked these conflicts, exposing Portuguese nationals to bouts of violence that would have made the news in Angola.[125]

Similarly, in Salvador, Brazil's second city with strong ties to Luanda and Benguela, anti-Lusitanism was a dominant feature of political conflicts. Here, street clashes often pitted Portuguese supporters of Emperor Pedro I against his opponents. The latter were described as "barefoot men, blacks, and mulattos dressed in jackets and armed with sticks, as well as some whites who waved hats adorned with the national ribbon."[126] These confrontations, transcending race and class boundaries, hinted at the potential for a widespread social revolution grounded in anti-Lusitanism.[127] This social volatility came to a head in the Sabinada of 1837–1838, where non-white people—including free blacks, freedmen, and slaves—comprised the majority of the rebel forces.[128]

For Portuguese officials in Angola, news of Brazil's upheavals would have set off alarm bells, making them sensitive to any perceived or actual local dissent that could potentially unravel their fragile control over Luanda and Benguela. They would have certainly known about the movement known as Balaiada, in which around eleven thousand people waged what amounted to a civil war in Maranhão between 1838 and 1841. Non-white Brazilian-born rebels saw themselves in opposition to oppressors, prominently featuring Portuguese natives, with an alliance between free rebels and maroons emerging in the revolt's final phase and rebel leaders actively recruiting and arming slaves. In a call that echoed other movements in Brazil, they insisted on equal treatment for all citizens, irrespective of their color or "quality" and called for the expulsion of all Portuguese nationals from the province.[129]

While the Balaiada revolt highlighted the potential for large-scale, racially charged uprisings against Portuguese interests, events in Pernambuco a few years later would further underscore the precarious position of Portuguese nationals in Brazil. During the Praieira Revolt, Portugal had to deploy a naval force to Recife to protect its citizens from widespread violence. According to an official account, "the safety of Portuguese nationals has been guaranteed due to the presence of warships . . . but there is still great hostility against them."[130] Pernambuco's political violence would eventually prompt the creation of a colony south of Angola to accommodate Portuguese nationals seeking to escape anti-Portuguese protests in Brazil.[131] Once in Mossamedes, settlers reminisced about their lives in Brazil, stating that "even though Portuguese nationals were extremely useful for the [Brazilian] empire, they feared for their lives and properties, as demonstrated by events in Pernambuco on July 26th and 27th of 1848" during the Praieira revolution.[132]

Against this backdrop, the Portuguese colonial administration in Luanda found itself walking a tightrope, striving to suppress a growing Angolense political consciousness deeply rooted in feelings of kinship with the former

Portuguese colony while also grappling with the potential importation of seditious ideologies from Brazil. This concern was not merely hypothetical but founded on historical precedents. In the wake of Brazil's independence in 1822, secessionist movements had rocked Benguela and Luanda, as previously discussed. In the ensuing decades, the specter of these events would cast a long shadow over politics in the two cities, serving as a haunting reminder of the fragility of Portuguese rule and the enduring appeal of a union with Brazil. A Luanda judge astutely observed, "The highest ambition of the Angolense is a union with that empire [of Brazil]," noting that this sentiment was "a repetition of what they had done in another time."[133]

Political Activism

As Brazil's political instability reverberated across the Atlantic, the Ferreira Gomes brothers found themselves under the shadow of these broader political dynamics. The wider Atlantic context shaped perceptions about the family and its history of challenging Portuguese authority, particularly given their involvement in two previous acts of contestation of Portuguese rule in Benguela. In the first case, the Ferreira Gomes's patriarch found himself under arrest in 1824, accused of dispatching envoys to Rio de Janeiro in a bid for military aid. His audacious plan? Overthrow Benguela's Portuguese government and turn it into an overseas province of an independent Brazil. Although Portuguese authorities managed to quell this insurrection, its legacy was clear: not only had Angola's ties to Brazil become political in nature, but now they also posed a genuine threat to the fragile fabric of Portuguese rule in Luanda and Benguela.

The second episode of political contestation involving the Ferreira Gomes family occurred in 1835. Following the family patriarch's retirement in Brazil after thirty-four years in Benguela, the Ferreira Gomes brothers were arrested on charges of leading a "revolution that, if not suppressed, might have victimized the entire white race" in Benguela.[134] According to Benguela officials, the oldest brother's "revolution" involved "attacks on the nights of February 3rd, 6th, and 9th of [1835]," forcing the government to take a series of measures to restore order in the city.[135] In addition to prohibiting the firing of guns, the government determined that "no free or enslaved blacks, as well as other individuals, regardless of their legal status, could carry weapons [including knives, arrows, and swords] at night or during the day."[136]

Although away in Rio de Janeiro, the Ferreira Gomes patriarch was viewed as a crucial figure in the sedition. Benguela governor Justiniano José dos Reis, a Brazilian-born individual once accused of plotting against the Portuguese, claimed that the patriarch "had diabolically traveled to Rio de Janeiro to wait for the end of the undertaking" but was expected back in the city.[137] Upon his return to Benguela, according to official reports, the Ferreira Gomes patriarch would travel to Lisbon to seek support to reconstruct the city's economy without the transatlantic trade of enslaved Africans. In exchange for his efforts, the patriarch would receive a monopoly on exporting ivory from the city.[138]

While the notion of an Angolan rebellion orchestrated partially from Brazil might initially appear far-fetched, a revolt against physical punishment in Luanda lends credence to this scenario. In 1835, rebels murdered their commander, leading officials to note that "the people of color (who comprise almost all population and troop) are not in open anarchy, but they were convinced that they can do whatever they want without the risk of being punished, particularly politically."[139] One of the rebels was a soldier named João da Paixão Nogueira, condemned to death by hanging: "this condemned [man] is a black man without any culture, 37 years old, born in the Dembos."[140] Two of the insurrection's ringleaders, however, successfully evaded justice in Luanda, finding sanctuary in Rio de Janeiro.[141]

The dramatic escape provides glimpses into interconnected political dynamics in the South Atlantic. Yet what made the 1835 insurrection unique was the Ferreira Gomes brothers' attempt to incite "powerful sobas from the interior" to challenge the Benguela government. According to authorities, the brothers' plan to overturn Portuguese rule had two layers: the first involved provoking "blacks of the backlands into staging attacks on the outskirts of the city, and when people escaped to the city, take over the fort [of Benguela] by surprise, murdering white residents, and achieving their goals." The second plan was to incite "a war outside the city so that it would be left to the mercy of the plotters [*conjurados*]."[142] Yet the plot never came to fruition "due to the objections of some sobas who did not want to rebel against the white Portuguese."[143] When approached by the brothers, the African rulers dismissed them, stating that "they [African rulers] did not have weapons to battle the whites, and they lived and traded with them."[144]

A decade later, however, José Ferreira's efforts bore fruit as he gained support against the Portuguese from his maternal uncle, Joanes José Gaspar, a soba (ruler) in Catumbela—a pivotal region for Benguela's food supply and security. Control of Catumbela would have given rebels potential leverage over Benguela itself. As discussed earlier, the two men shared a bloodline through José Ferreira Gomes's mother, Florinda Josefa Gaspar, binding the rebellious nephew and powerful uncle together against the Portuguese. About four decades earlier, Florinda had married a black Brazilian man named Francisco Ferreira Gomes, who would go on to become one of Benguela's main slave dealers. The couple had several children, including José Ferreira Gomes, the future leader of the 1845 revolt against the Portuguese.

Through Delfina, the Ferreira Gomes family patriarch, a black man named Francisco Ferreira Gomes, forged crucial ties with her father, Joanes Gaspar, a Cabo in the colonial administration stationed in Dombe Grande. Described in 1798 as a 35-year-old man, Gaspar was an influential figure, owning thirteen enslaved Africans and married to Dona Leonor Pereira da Costa, a mixed-race woman with significant landholdings in the region.[145] His role as a Cabo entrusted him with various duties, including tax collection and managing the food supply from the local African population.[146] In 1811, now described as owning more enslaved people and dependents, Gaspar was appointed to command "auxiliary troops" in a campaign against Dombe Grande's rulers, one of the area's "main potentates."[147] Notably, his military responsibilities also entailed apprehending defectors, which became personal when his son fled to evade military service as an artilleryman in Benguela.[148]

To the Ferreira Gomes patriarch, the connection with a powerful father-in-law was invaluable. A case in point is Ferreira Gomes's role as the royal treasury's storekeeper between 1814 and 1819. This position mandated frequent liaisons with Dombe Grande's farmers to procure food for Benguela's military. In 1814, his purchases included sixty sacks of manioc flour from Dombe Grande; two years later, he procured another hundred sacks from Brazil and the district.[149] To fulfill his duties, the Brazilian son-in-law likely collaborated closely with Gaspar, his African father-in-law. As a Cabo, Gaspar would have been motivated to leverage his influential position in order to facilitate these vital acquisitions for his daughter's husband.

A turning point in the elder Gaspar's career came when the Benguela government appointed him soba in Dombe Grande. Traditionally, sobas were selected by following matrilineal customs. The heirs to sobas were not their sons but rather their sister's sons—their nephews. In 1829, Governor Nicolau Castelo Branco noted: "I have always heard that traditionally nephews who are sons of soba's sister, and not the soba's sons, are the ones who hold power [in the sobados]."[150] Nonetheless, it was not unusual for matrilineal customs to adapt over time, "since it is not always that eligible nephews are available, it would be unfair to leave sons" out of the process.[151]

In Gaspar's case, however, his appointment as soba was likely a recognition of his long record of loyal service and support from the population of one of the nine sobados in Dombe Grande. His case would have then paralleled the appointment of Braz Antonio in 1854. Originally serving as a "soldier from the artillery company of this city," Antonio was sent to Dombe Pequeno to mediate a succession dispute after the death of the previous soba. The Benguela administration noted, "The leaders of that community have not been able to come to an agreement in choosing one among them to succeed in the chieftainship."[152] Antonio's performance convinced makotas (local leaders) to petition the Benguela government to appoint him as their new soba.

By the 1840s, another member of the Gaspar lineage, Joanes Gaspar—son of the elder Gaspar—found himself ascending to the role of soba. Yet the appointment was not in Dombe Grande, where his father had gained prominence, but in Catumbela, just north of Benguela, a region that played a key role in the provision of food and water to the city. As early as 1826, well before being named soba, the younger Gaspar had been jailed and taken to Kakonda on the request of his brother-in-law, the Ferreira Gomes's patriarch.[153] No reason was stated, but Ferreira Gomes argued that Gaspar was "unruly."[154] Several years later, however, Gaspar re-emerged as one of Catumbela's sobas and the primary supporter of the revolt led by his nephew José Ferreira Gomes.

The alliance between members of the Benguela urban elites and the ruler of a chiefdom so close to Benguela was soon identified as potentially catastrophic. The prospect of attacks on Benguela itself sparked urgent concern, given the city's fragile hold on the surrounding periphery. Hundreds of troops were mobilized to apprehend the rebel brothers, with the youngest seeking refuge in territory under the control of his African ruler uncle. Yet, when authorities demanded Gaspar surrender his cousin, he refused, stating, "Even if he were at my house, I would not surrender him because he [Ferreira Gomes] is his relative."[155]

In taking such a defiant stance, Gaspar channeled escalating discontent among African rulers about land expropriation then taking place near Benguela. Historian Mariana Candido points out that since the 1820s, local rulers had resisted Portuguese encroachment on their lands, once even claiming that "the Portuguese had enough land and did not need to conquer more."[156] Two years before Ferreira Gomes's revolt, such tensions had already led to attacks on a delegation of high officials, including a Benguela governor, then traveling through Lobito. In response, the Benguela government retaliated by deploying a naval vessel, ninety-four soldiers, and two artillery pieces.[157] According to Benguela officials, Africans "considered themselves the owners of the land near Benguela."[158]

As the government grappled with the growing threat, they sought ways to neutralize the Ferreira Gomes brothers, with the initial phase of the revolt unfolding between mid-1845 and January 1846. Yet the limits of Portuguese rule soon became evident. Despite the deployment of troops, the government eventually had to rely on an African ally named Gury to capture José Ferreira Gomes.[159] After Ferreira Gomes's arrest, he was swiftly taken to Luanda to prevent any attempts by his allies to rescue him.[160] By August 1847, over a year after his arrest and two years after the beginning of the revolt, Ferreira Gomes remained detained in Luanda.[161] His younger brother died while attempting to escape the government's forces on the way to Luanda.

Yet the arrest of the revolt's ringleader failed to restore order, with Soba Gaspar emerging as the movement's new leader and forcing the Benguela government to deploy a large military force to crush it. Hundreds of soldiers, artillery pieces, and warships mobilized under the governor's command, requiring approval from Luanda.[162] Government forces burned villages, seized livestock, and reinstated a deposed ruler.[163] A commander recounted "incalculable losses" suffered by the Ndombe, including imprisoned sobas.[164] Gaspar's arrest saw the return of the government's African ally, Gury, who had been instrumental in detaining José Ferreira Gomes.[165] The African ruler was swiftly executed on his own land, without any legal proceedings.[166]

By then, however, the revolt had spread to Dombe Grande, a much larger region that presented significantly more challenges to the government's forces. As discussed earlier, the region was crucial for the supply of foodstuff to Benguela and the location of sulfur mines. It was also a territory not entirely under the control of the Portuguese, where many runaways found refuge. In 1825, the region's strategic importance was underscored by the Benguela government's decision to swiftly take measures when robberies on roads disrupted the supply of food to Benguela.[167] Portuguese officials believed that, if provoked, these chiefdoms could unite, mustering a force of 400 to 500 well-armed and disciplined men, making external control difficult.[168]

By then, the primary leader of the revolt was a soba named Handa, recognized as the most influential among the five sobas of Dombe Grande. He became the main target of a ten-day military campaign organized by the Portuguese government of Benguela, when "dwellings were reduced to ashes and farm fields destroyed." During one operation, prompted by suspicions of a planned rebel invasion of Benguela, colonial forces claimed the lives of forty individuals.[169] Some of these casualties were seemingly not even associated with the insurgents. Africans apprehended by the colonial forces were transported to Luanda and enslaved, an action justified by the assertion that they had revolted against Portuguese dominance.[170]

Gaspar and Handa's defiance reflected simmering tension due to attempts to build a new economy in Angola at the expense of African land. According to an eyewitness, policies aimed at the dispossession of African lands served as the "single reason why Africans had decided to expel whites from their lands."[171] Yet Portuguese officials, haunted by racial anxieties imported from across the Atlantic but also facing a local backlash against policies to end the slave trade, could only perceive African resistance through a racial lens. The 1845 revolt was thus local in origin but Atlantic in cause.

To rationalize scorched-earth tactics, the Portuguese fell back on the familiar narrative of African hostility toward whites—a narrative they previously used to justify military action against the Ferreira Gomes brothers. However, this narrative was challenged by contemporaries. Luso-African scholar Joaquim de Carvalho e Menezes contended that Soba Handa harbored "no animosity against whites, among whom he hoped to find exile and protection."[172] Menezes further posited that Gaspar's most grievous transgression "was attempting to escape the tyranny of this government's crushing crusade."[173] Handa, the third leader of the revolt, was executed along with sixty supporters after going to Benguela for peace talks with the Benguela government.[174]

Following the military campaigns' conclusion, official statements made the Benguela government's underlying motives evident. As they proclaimed,

"Everyone knows these lands belong to the king [of Portugal]."[175] Historian Mariana Candido observed that this coincided with a pivot toward formal land documentation and a change in how land ownership was conceptualized. As Candido shows, the shift was not just procedural but also a key incentive for commercial agriculture in a post-slave trade world.[176] Supported by Benguela merchants, a fort was built in Catumbela. These merchants were assigned the duty of "reorganizing the peoples of Dombe de Benguela, who had previously been hostile and rebellious, but had recently been subdued and pacified by Her Majesty's forces." Alongside the loss of their land, Africans faced increased taxes under the emerging colonial regime.[177]

The land confiscated from African people would soon become the backbone of an emerging post-slave trade economy, as several examples demonstrate. In 1854, Egito was noted as "one of the most important points of this province, which supplies food to Benguela and Mossamedes, exporting more than thirty thousand arrobas of goma copal and five thousand arrobas of urzela."[178] In 1856, Dombe Grande was identified as the most profitable district of Benguela and a significant provider of food to Benguela.[179] Subsequently, the number of farms in Dombe Grande, Egito, Catumbela, and neighboring regions was estimated at forty, including three belonging to a single Benguela farm owner where hundreds of African workers toiled with little or no pay.[180]

While African leaders like Gaspar and Handa were executed for their defiance, José Ferreira Gomes experienced a fall from grace that led him to lose most of the wealth he once enjoyed. In April 1847, Benguela officials informed him that a verdict had been issued in his case in Luanda.[181] Shortly thereafter, he requested permission to access the estate of his younger brother, who had died in Portuguese custody en route to Luanda.[182] Although Ferreira Gomes still maintained some of his former wealth, as evident when he challenged the requirement to pay taxes on the one hundred captives transported from Benguela to Luanda, his influence and resources were already declining.[183]

The former rebel leader's diminishing status became increasingly apparent in the following years. After gaining authorization to harvest orchella weed along the Benguela coast, he soon faced setbacks, petitioning to close down his Egito enterprise shortly afterward.[184] An official petition identified him merely as a resident of Benguela rather than a merchant in the city, a downgrade from his previous social status.[185] Further evidence of his reduced circumstances came from a Brazilian power of attorney document that labeled him a "small farmer"—a stark contrast to his family's former slave trade empire.[186] An old Brazilian associate summed up Ferreira Gomes's then reduced status by saying, "I knew the defendant [José Ferreira Gomes] at another time when he was a wealthy person, but now he had decayed [financially]."[187]

Conclusion

To tell Ferreira Gomes's story is to tell a story of an intensely integrated South Atlantic world where events taking place in Brazil had ripple effects on coastal Angolan cities such as Luanda and Benguela. An ocean stood between Angola and Brazil, yet instead of separating them, it was, in fact, a conduit for social, economic, cultural, and political exchanges. By reading Angola through the eyes of Brazil, then convulsed by political instability fueled by anti-Portuguese sentiment, the Portuguese involuntarily revealed how the South Atlantic remained tightly integrated even while Portugal strived to sever multi-century-long ties that connected Angola to Brazil.

All too aware of Angola's profound ties to Brazil and still reeling from the loss of its most valued colony in South America, Portuguese officials in Angola responded with suspicion and anxiety to the prospect that the political instability that plagued Brazil during its nation-building process might somehow inspire Angolense groups to break away from Portugal. These fears were encapsulated by the Ferreira Gomes family's complex web of connections across the Atlantic and record of political activism in Angola. For the Portuguese, they signaled that ties between Angola and Brazil had morphed into a political nexus across the Atlantic that stood at odds with Portugal's efforts to strengthen ties with the African colony.

By situating the Benguela revolt within the broader context of Luso-Brazilian relations and the circulation of ideas across the Atlantic, the chapter offers a nuanced understanding of how local conflicts intersected with broader transatlantic dynamics. It highlights the need to look beyond simplistic racial narratives and consider the complex interplay of economic, political, and social factors in shaping acts of resistance and colonial perceptions. In doing so, the chapter contributes to a more expansive and relational approach to the study of identity and race formation in the nineteenth-century South Atlantic world.

Against this backdrop, Ferreira Gomes's ties with Brazil cast a long shadow over him. Because black men like him were revolting against the Portuguese in Brazil, there was just one way to understand Ferreira Gomes's politics in Angola: through the prism of race. Yet instead of racial war, the Benguela revolt was rooted in African discontent over land expropriation aimed at developing a post-slave trade economy at the expense of African land ownership near Benguela. A deep rift developed between the Portuguese and African rulers as the Benguela government engaged in projects to appropriate lands for agricultural projects. Portugal's efforts to modernize Angola's economy thus set it at odds not only with coastal groups who derived wealth from selling enslaved people across the Atlantic but also with African populations who had long coexisted relatively peacefully with Portuguese rule.

Ultimately, the chapter underscores the importance of situating Angolan history within a broader South Atlantic framework, attentive to the circulation of people, ideas, and anxieties across this interconnected space. It highlights how local conflicts, like the Benguela revolt, were shaped by transatlantic influences and colonial perceptions, even as they were rooted in specific grievances and power dynamics. By uncovering the dissonance between Portuguese racial anxieties and the actual motivations behind the revolt, the chapter challenges simplistic racial narratives and points to the need for a more nuanced understanding of identity, race, and political contestation in the nineteenth-century South Atlantic world.

CHAPTER TWO

Makèzú

ON DECEMBER 12, 1846, a woman named Francisca Joaquina do Amaral found herself alone with two doctors who took her into a private room in her father's house in Luanda. The doctors performed a physical examination of her intimate areas to establish the truth about "the pregnancy of three or four months that she had been accused" of having by her estranged husband Joaquim Olavo Gamboa, a lieutenant in the Angolan army. They found that she exhibited physical signs consistent with a recent abortion. Her cervix was very red, swollen, dilated, and also releasing blood, while "the size of her belly was somewhat expanded and the uterus was enlarged." She was also lactating. After establishing that Dona Amaral was feverish and had a pulse, the doctors concluded that an abortion had occurred, although they could not determine the stage of the pregnancy or the means by which the abortion was induced.[1]

This invasive medical examination was the cornerstone of the drama that upended Dona Amaral's life after her estranged husband filed a lawsuit against her on the accusation of adultery. In what can perhaps be termed a vengeful suit by a deeply resentful husband, Gamboa claimed his motivations for filing the case were not "hatred, malice, or ill-will" but instead to "safeguard his rights." These statements barely scratch the surface of the lawsuit's underlying psychological motives. As a public figure in Luanda and an amateur actor in one of the city's theater companies, Gamboa was likely driven by anger and humiliation due to Dona Amaral's alleged involvement with Braklami, a direct aide to anti-slave trade governor Pedro Alexandrino da Cunha. He even publicly admitted his great "scandal and offense" at her alleged actions. In a profoundly patriarchal society, the lawsuit was fueled by a wounded sense of male honor. Gamboa's actions were deeply rooted in the prevailing gender norms of the time.

Dona Amaral's personal drama unfolds against the backdrop of Luanda's sociopolitical climate, marked by intense battles over the transatlantic slave trade and the interplay of patriarchal, colonial, and cultural dynamics. Efforts to curtail the slave trade were met with fierce resistance from entrenched local interests, complicating the colonial administration's governance. Within this volatile environment, gender and power dynamics played out in intimate and often brutal ways, reflecting broader societal tensions. Women like Dona Francisca Joaquina do Amaral found their personal lives deeply entangled with these larger forces, their bodies and choices scrutinized and controlled by both personal vendettas and the colonial state's legal apparatus. This chapter explores how the intersections of personal, political, and cultural spheres shaped Luanda's individual experiences and broader historical trajectories.

Inspired by the work of Angolan anthropologist Óscar Ribas, the chapter employs a granular approach, focusing on intimate details and everyday practices to shed light on larger issues of gender, power, and cultural influence in Luanda. By centering on a gift of kola nuts (makèzú) sent by Dona Amaral to her alleged lover, the narrative illuminates the complex web of African cultural traditions that shaped social interactions and personal relationships across several social strata, including the privileged class to which Dona Amaral belonged. Makèzú, a traditional African gift symbolizing respect, friendship, and social bonds, serves as a powerful cultural artifact that underscores the deep-rooted and enduring customs in African societies. This focus on intimate exchanges and personal artifacts reveals the subtle ways in which African cultural norms persisted and adapted even within the context of colonial oppression.

By weaving together the experiences of various groups, from the enslaved workers in Dona Amaral's household to the street vendors (quitandeiras), the chapter creates a vivid and multifaceted portrayal of life in Luanda. Despite the oppressive institution of slavery and the increasingly stringent colonial power structure, it emphasizes the agency and cultural influence wielded by African people in shaping the city's rich social and cultural fabric. Through detailed accounts of legal proceedings, personal testimonies, and everyday interactions, this chapter demonstrates the endurance of African customs and practices, offering a nuanced understanding of the complexities of life in a slavery city.

Before their marriage broke down in May 1846, Dona Amaral and Gamboa had been a couple for eight years, during which they had three children. In a lawsuit filed seven months after their separation, the husband justified leaving her by citing Dona Amaral's alleged "bad temper," revealing an embittered man who used past marital incidents to justify his current actions. His anger was likely exacerbated by Dona Amaral's actions after their separation. Instead of moving in with her father as promised, she went on to rent a house "on her own account," an act the estranged husband likely viewed as an act of defiance, leading him to level several accusations against her, including that she received "visits by men late at night" in the house and was "three or four months pregnant."[2]

In Portugal, Angola's increasingly assertive colonial ruler, adultery laws were grounded in patriarchal notions of marital fidelity and the preservation of "family honor." Under the prevailing Roman law tradition, adultery charges were typically directed only at wives and their alleged lovers, while husbands often escaped such accusations. To substantiate adultery allegations, authorities often required concrete proof, such as evidence of sexual activity or pregnancy.[3] It is within this legal framework that the actions of the doctors sent to examine Dona Amaral must be understood. While they did conclude that she had recently had an abortion, they could not definitively establish whether she had engaged in an adulterous relationship while still living with her husband. Yet, based on witness testimonies, they decided to issue an arrest warrant against her and her alleged lover.

Dona Amaral's drama provides insight not only into a tangled web of alleged infidelity, sex, and patriarchal revenge but also illuminates Luanda's cutthroat anti-slave trade politics. Despite a sharp downturn in direct shipping, the city was still a vital node in the web of transatlantic trade. As an urban center, it provided slave dealers with a supportive legal system for their business across the Atlantic and maintained deep connections with African polities in the interior. It also had enduring connections to business and financial centers in the Americas and Europe, giving it a crucial role as a logistical and economic hub. Most importantly for this story, Luanda was home to a lobby of slave dealers fiercely opposed to the implementation of Portugal's anti-slave trade laws.

The lawsuit against Dona Amaral, orchestrated by her husband and fueled by the city's pro-slave trade faction, exemplifies how personal disputes could be weaponized to undermine the anti-slave trade efforts of the colonial administration. Only six years prior, slave trade supporters had ousted a governor for attempting to enforce anti-slave trade laws in the colony. Now, this same lobby viewed the lawsuit against Dona Amaral as an opportunity to undermine the administration of another governor—Pedro Alexandrino da Cunha—committed to the anti-slave trade cause. Dona Amaral was thus a victim not only of patriarchal violence but also of Luanda's toxic political machinations.

The lawsuit serves as a microcosm for understanding how accusations of female infidelity could be leveraged as instruments to assert male dominance in a society coming under the tightening grip of colonialism. "Nowhere are such [colonial] designs more spectacularly apparent than in discourses and practices aimed at controlling [women's] sexuality and the body."[4] Targeting women's sexuality and bodily autonomy, these colonial designs were starkly evident in both legal discourse and practice. Significantly, Dona Amaral's case was not isolated. A notable case was a young woman who had to prove her virginity to divorce her husband, highlighting the intrusive nature of patriarchal mandates.[5]

Portugal was, of course, not the only colonial power to seek to regulate and surveil women's intimate lives. Under Dutch colonialism, the policing of non-marital sex was also a tool of social control, albeit with distinct strategies shaped by their colonial milieu. While European men's extramarital relations with non-European women could be categorized as "improprieties" and managed with relative leniency, analogous to European men's relationships with locals in colonies like Angola, women were treated with harshness if they engaged in such relationships. While pointing to a broader pattern of controlling sexuality to uphold and reinforce gender hierarchies, such policies paved the way for the intimate lives of native-born individuals like Dona Amaral to become entangled with overarching objectives of governance under an increasingly strict colonial order.[6]

In Luanda's colonial archive, the record of gendered violence is obviously stacked against Dona Amaral—the central character in this narrative. She never had a chance to defend herself before officials, and her voice is conspicuously absent from the historical record. It is possible that her testimony was deliberately excised from archival files, reflecting the machinations against her. In the extant documentation, Dona Amaral is obliquely conceived solely as the recipient of patriarchal violence, devoid of human agency, reflecting what historian Marisa Fuentes would perhaps call "mutilated historicity."[7] We are left to wonder about Dona Amaral's perspective on Gamboa's accusations and her own understanding of the tumultuous events that upended her life.

Recognizing the need for a more inclusive historical narrative and pushing back on archival erasures, this chapter sketches out a portrayal of Dona Amaral defined not only by actions imposed on her by men but also by her own motivations and subjectivity. It seeks to present a picture of her life as textured and nuanced as possible, acknowledging the limitations of the available sources while still striving to illuminate her experiences and perspective. As Natalie Zemon Davis points out, "rightly done, such history is always relational: the history of women involves men, the history of peasants involves proprietors; the history of workers involves employers."[8] What emerges is a contested sociocultural environment where a plurality of historical agents—not only men empowered by the status apparatus but also free elite women and enslaved people—vied over economic, cultural, and social capital.[9]

Beyond seeking to illuminate the obscured agency and voice of Dona Amaral, this chapter recognizes the experience of the enslaved girl who played a key role in this story as the messenger between her and her lover. Though only briefly mentioned in the documentation, her coerced role enabling the relationship provides insight into the severe imbalances of power, violence, and vulnerability endured by enslaved women and girls in Luanda households and society at large. One testimony noted that the girl would cry when she could not find Braklami, fearing that Dona Amaral would beat her.[10] While Dona Amaral navigated patriarchal oppression as a privileged woman, the intersectionality of race, class, and gender amplified the vulnerability of enslaved women and individuals like this unnamed enslaved girl.

Even if unable to fully recover all hidden voices from slavery's margins, this chapter aims to counterbalance omissions in the archives of colonialism by developing a layered perspective of enslaved people's presence in Luanda. The objective is not merely to assess slavery's economic significance but to explore Luanda's cultural and social tapestry from the viewpoint of the majority of people living in the city: enslaved people. Here, African subjectivities take center stage, and Luanda residents are seen not as data points in economic analyses but as active participants in a landscape marked by contested beliefs, practices, and expressions. What this perspective seeks to develop is a nuanced understanding of Luanda's society around the humanity of those who lived and struggled within the constraints of a slave society, a humanity often overshadowed in historical records and sometimes not sufficiently explored in historical narratives.

To restore Dona Amaral to the narrative of Angolan history, the chapter seizes upon a minute but significant gesture by her—a gift of makèzú (kola nuts) that she sent to her alleged lover. This gift was delivered by the unnamed enslaved girl. As witnesses deposed by Luanda officials testified, the domestic servant made multiple visits to the headquarters bringing a "handkerchief wrapped in the shape of a heart that contained kola nut and ginger." Through the makèzú gift, Dona Amaral displayed affection and extended a coded invitation for Braklami to visit her under the cover of night. Notably, Braklami "took half of the kola nut and ginger, rewrapped the handkerchief, and handed it back to the girl."[11] In so doing, he demonstrated command of elaborate codes of courtship that not only natives but also foreigners like himself followed to engage in romantic courtship in Luanda.

The cultural significance of makèzú in Angolan society and its enduring legacy are captured in the poem "Makèzú" by Viriato da Cruz, a prominent figure in Angola's struggle for independence from Portugal in the 1960s. The poem tells the story of Grandma Ximinha, an elderly street vendor (quitandeira) who continues to sell makèzú despite the changing times and the younger generation's embrace of Westernized practices. Through Grandma Ximinha's steadfast adherence to tradition and her belief in the strength derived from consuming makèzú, the poem serves as a poignant reminder that even in the face of colonial oppression and societal changes Angola's cultural roots were resilient and unbreakable. It was not only a powerful symbol of their connection to their ancestral heritage but a cultural weapon that could be leveraged against Portugal's colonial domination.

For Dona Amaral, makèzú provided a brief escape from the confines of a deeply patriarchal society, allowing her to exert some agency in the most intimate aspects of her life. Yet, even with the ability to exert some autonomy, Dona Amaral's life was not free from the confines of a male-dominated society. This became evident when Gamboa posted a note in a local Luandan paper years after the dispute with his wife. Now at the height of his military career, he thanked those who had attended his father-in-law's funeral—the same man who once sided with Dona Amaral against him. Gamboa "apologized to those who had not been invited [to the funeral]," attributing this oversight to the "state of consternation" that had overwhelmed him upon learning of his father-in-law's death.[12] This family dynamic was further tested by the tragic loss of their son, Ernesto Gamboa. Having traveled and studied in places like America, Lisbon, and Rio de Janeiro, Ernesto was remembered "for the honest, serious, and well-mannered man" he had become.[13]

Although neither note sheds light on the specific circumstances that prompted Dona Amaral's decision to return to her marriage with the man who had previously tormented her, societal pressures might have played a role. A suggestive example is a case that played out around the time of Dona Amaral's drama, in which a Luanda judge ruled a lawsuit filed by a woman named Dona Maria Joaquina do Amaral against her husband, Antonio Balbino Rosa. In the suit, the woman accused the man of abusing her. In his ruling, the judge required the couple to live apart for two years. Yet the sentence also conveyed "a well-founded hope that they would soon reconcile" and reunite as a couple.[14]

Anti-Slave Trade Politics

The lawsuit against Dona Amaral must be considered within the context of political battles resulting from efforts to end shipments of enslaved Africans in Luanda during the administration of Governor Pedro Alexandrino da Cunha. Cunha believed the slave trade hindered Angola's potential for commercial agriculture. In a speech to Lisbon's *Associação Marítima e Colonial*, he once expressed that enslaved people should provide labor to Angolan plantations rather than those in Brazil. Cunha's firm actions against the slave trade earned him praise and the trust of British officials. The latter once remarked, "The measures pursued by the present Governor General of this province appear to have succeeded in suppressing all direct attempts at the slave trade in Portuguese vessels."[15] Yet his efforts sparked an intense backlash among slave trade supporters in Luanda.

The reaction reflected the central role that the slave trade played in the city's economy and society. As early as 1825, when Brazil signed a treaty with England and Portugal that included the elimination of imports of enslaved people by 1830, Luanda authorities voiced concerns about possible unrest in Luanda and Benguela. The year before, as discussed in Chapter 1, the city had been shaken by secessionist movements aiming to seek annexation to Brazil, largely due to trade exchanges related to the slave trade. In 1828, with the end of shipments of captives looming increasingly large, Governor of Angola Nicolau de Abreu Castelo Branco explained, "The idea of a blockage or the simple prohibition of the dispatch [of ships] from Brazil to this port makes this city's inhabitants tremble since it could destroy their fortunes with a stroke."[16]

FIGURE 2.1. View of Luanda

Cunha's anti-slave trade position tied in with Portugal's geopolitical interests at the time, as demonstrated by a petition in which Porto merchants argued that Angola should be treated as a colony, trading mostly, if not exclusively, with Portugal. They contended that low import duties on foreign goods, particularly from Brazil, were detrimental to Portugal's competitive edge in Angolan markets.[17] The situation was exacerbated by the inconsistent enforcement of metropolitan laws in Luanda, which allowed Brazilian ships—mostly geared toward the slave trade—unfettered access well into the 1840s. To a large extent, it underscored slave traders' power in the city's political establishment, enabling them to effectively circumvent Portuguese laws in favor of sustaining the slave trade, the backbone of the city's economy.

The entrenched position of slave dealers in Luanda's power structures played a pivotal role in resisting Governor Cunha's anti-slave trade efforts. Their influence was so extensive that they managed to have most city officials on their payroll, openly engaging in bribery to maintain their operations. "Each ship had to give 1,500,000 réis to trade in slaves, of which 800,000 réis [were given] to the governor of Angola."[18] The British take on the situation, essentially tying the situation to Luanda's structural dependence on the slave trade, is relevant here: "They were entirely dependent upon revenues derived either directly or indirectly from such traffic to support their colonial establishment."[19] This dependency was evident in Angola's financial records a year after Portugal's first anti-slave trade law in 1836, which showed revenues totaling 351,156,528 réis, exceeding expenses by 226,500,865 réis. The surplus was notably deposited into the royal treasury in Rio de Janeiro.[20]

By the time Cunha was appointed Governor of Angola, he had accumulated significant experience as a naval officer conducting operations against the slave trade on the Angolan coast. Yet he was likely still taken aback by the fierce backlash when two well-known Luanda slave dealers, Augusto Garrido and José Matozo da Câmara, were arrested on the accusation of shipping enslaved Africans near Luanda. A direct challenge to Cunha's anti-slave trade policies, the incident made the British fear for the governor's life. "We are sorry to hear that His Excellency appears to be very harassed and uneasy and that his manner to those who have seen him betrays considerable anxiety."[21] The crisis forced Cunha to order "crews of the Portuguese warships, now in port, to be landed and to occupy the fortress of Sao Miguel."[22] Ultimately, Garrido and Câmara "succeeded in escaping the immediate penalty [imprisonment] by obtaining bail in the sum of three contos, or about six hundred pounds, each."[23]

Of paramount importance to this story is the fact that one of Cunha's local opponents was precisely the judge who presided over the lawsuit against Dona Amaral, José Maria Gonçalves. The governor was acutely aware of Gonçalves's loyalties and saw his maneuvering as an attempt to politicize the lawsuit against Dona Amaral. According to him, the judge was a "protector of slave dealers" and had disregarded a report that would have cleared her of adultery allegations, replacing it with a report by someone who would condemn the defendants "as ordered by the judge."[24] While Cunha's motivation to contest the lawsuit was to protect his aide, not solidarity with or empathy toward Dona Amaral, his efforts eventually saved her from being sentenced for engaging in an adulterous relationship that could theoretically be punished with the death penalty.

A far more powerful foe was a slave dealer named Arcenio Pompilio Pompeu do Carpo, who had gone to Luanda as a political exile in the 1820s. He was among the approximately one thousand white men living in Luanda at the time, most of whom were of Portuguese and Brazilian origin, along with some who were born locally.[25] In the 1830s, Carpo spent time in Pernambuco and Rio de Janeiro and even traveled to the United States. By the late 1830s, having amassed a large fortune after returning to Luanda, he had become a powerful voice against anti-slave trade policies. He once declared, "If British warships sank ships carrying textiles used to purchase slaves, on the pretext that they were meant for the slave trade, what commodities (gêneros do país) would be purchased in the sertões, where there is no other currency?"[26]

Carpo's opposition to anti-slave trade policies was not merely rhetorical. He had once played a vital role in the resignation of Antonio Noronha, one of Cunha's predecessors, who had to escape from Luanda after a fierce backlash against attempts to end shipments of enslaved people in the city.[27] Having voiced opposition to the slave trade when he was still an official in Lisbon in 1827, Noronha sought to moderate his position once in Luanda, stating that actions against the slave trade "would still have to begin and that they would be as slow as not to harm merchants."[28] Yet he soon took measures that shook the status quo, establishing that ships could not have more than five enslaved people onboard, nor could they leave Luanda after 5 p.m. or be approached by small boats upon departing from the city.[29] The governor also ordered an investigation into the actions of Benguela administrators accused of involvement in the slave trade.[30] Crucially, he signed an agreement with a commander of the British naval forces that significantly expanded British power to seize slave ships off the coast of Angola.[31]

While Noronha's actions against the slave trade earned him accolades from the British, just as Cunha's would seven years later, they were sabotaged by members of the Luanda administration. One illustrative episode occurred when Noronha ordered authorities to inspect ships docking in Luanda from April to September 1839; they suspiciously reported all forty-four visiting vessels free of slave trading.[32] Another dispute pitted him against a city judge sympathetic to local opponents. Noronha suspended and dismissed the magistrate to Portugal. To bolster his anti-slave trade efforts by circumventing obstructionists within the colonial ranks, Noronha created an all-black volunteer troop, feeding into accusations that he tried to pit whites against blacks in Luanda.[33]

By the mid-1840s, Carpo was likely at the heyday of his power, leveraging formidable influence in Luanda's establishment to undermine anti-slave trade policies. In 1843, alongside other merchants in the city, he attempted to obstruct the provisioning of supplies to Portuguese warships.[34] These same merchants would also propose reducing the number of ships in the Portuguese naval station.[35] When Governor Pedro Alexandrino da Cunha came to power in 1846, one of his first measures was to jail and deport Carpo from Angola.[36] Yet, after the governor's tenure ended, the slave dealer returned to Luanda and went on to occupy several positions in the colonial administration.

Whether Gamboa's path ever crossed with Carpo's is unclear. According to scholar Tracy Lopes, the former was a military man "born in Lisbon and enlisted in the colonial army in 1833."[37] When he tormented his wife, Gamboa was still a lieutenant in the early stages of what would turn out to be a highly successful military career. By 1852, however, he had become a captain, later completing an interim term as commander of the Luanda battalion.[38] He would also serve as the second-ranking member of the expedition sent to seize copper mines in Bembe, near the capital city of the kingdom of Kongo.[39] Following the Bembe expedition, Gamboa held several critical positions in the military, including serving in a military tribunal in Luanda and commanding inland.[40] In the 1860s, as Lopes points out, he would become the chief police officer of Luanda.

What is certain is that accusations of involvement in the trade of enslaved Africans were at the basis of deep animosity between Gamboa and Governor Cunha. These accusations had led Cunha to once block Gamboa's promotion to chief government officer in Ambaca, a strategic outpost in the Luanda hinterland due to its role as a crossroad for the trade between Luanda and its commercial backcountry [sertões]. In Cunha's words, Gamboa was "suspected of having protected contraband of slaves while stationed in Libongo," near the Dande River. Although the governor did not have concrete evidence to prosecute him criminally, he launched a scathing attack against Gamboa. "I judge it improper to have someone like Gamboa as the officer in charge of that place [Ambaca] because he lacks the necessary prudence and indispensable honesty to govern people like those from Ambaca."[41]

Unraveling Adultery Allegations

Gamboa's prominent public presence in Luanda is relevant to this story. The military man was an active member of one of Luanda's two theater groups, which organized events attended by the city's wealthy residents, Angola's governors, and naval commanders. "The company consists of the principal people of the town, as they perform only three or four times a year; they go to Brazil for the necessary materials for every play."[42] It is worth noting that women were not permitted to participate in these plays, and male actors performed female roles, which was likely consistent with Portuguese customs at the time. British traveler John Monteiro suggests that attendance reflected Luanda's wider society. "The boxes on a gala night may be seen filled with the swells of the place, accompanied by the many black, mulatto, and white ladies, examples of the very elastic states of morals in fashion in Angola."[43]

Gamboa was satisfied when state forces promptly responded to his lawsuit against Dona Amaral, conducting a physical examination on her just two days after he filed his complaint. The swift action suggests that the examination was a deliberate effort to discredit and punish her rather than a legitimate medical procedure. Noticeably, there was no shortage of midwives in Luanda who could perform abortions and physical examinations on women. "Pregnant women delivered in the yards of their houses, not indoors, under tents where they remained overnight, if necessary, with the help of *milongueiras* [traditional doctors] and midwives."[44] Unlike colonial authorities elsewhere, however, Luanda authorities denied Dona Amaral the respect and privacy due to a woman of her considerable social standing.[45]

Yet, to Gamboa's great disappointment, critical elements of his claims failed to hold up. Although the doctors came away convinced that Dona Amaral had recently terminated a pregnancy, they could not establish whether she had carried out a sexual relationship with another man while still living with him. According to them, there was no evidence that Dona Amaral had "demeaned her matrimonial fidelity" [*fé conjugal*] by having "carnal commerce with a man other than her spouse [Gamboa]." In fact, the judges appeared to side with Dona Amaral, which certainly upset Gamboa. By moving out of his house, they argued, he had denied his wife her rights of *marital duty*, the notion that couples have a reciprocal sexual obligation.[46]

In response to the inconclusive findings, Gamboa, likely jealous that Dona Amaral had started another relationship so soon after their separation, filed another petition. He requested authorities to investigate when Dona Amaral's pregnancy had been terminated. Since the couple had split in May 1846, Dona Amaral would have been at an advanced stage of pregnancy if she had become pregnant while living with Gamboa. More likely, she had begun her relationship with Braklami after Gamboa left their house and then become pregnant. In his petition, however, Gamboa asked authorities to probe whether the recently terminated pregnancy "could have proceeded more than six months, in light of her physical state when they undertook a bodily exam on her."[47]

To support his claims, Gamboa requested that judicial authorities conduct a new round of interviews with witnesses who had already been deposed and gather new testimonies. Several of the new individuals interviewed by authorities were military men like him. Likely out of male solidarity, they all provided testimony against Dona Amaral. One soldier, Sebastião Rodrigues de Moura, said he had mounted a surveillance operation to confirm rumors among her neighbors about her relationship with Braklami. Moura testified that on several nights in mid-1846, "around eleven o'clock or midnight," he saw "Lieutenant Braklami entering the defendant's house and later being at the window with her," and even noted one night when "they left together through the garden gate, arm in arm."[48] Moura also mentioned that he occupied himself with watching the house to verify the truth of what he had been told by neighbors, confirming that "what he saw was true."[49]

A previous witness was Joaquim Jose Cardozo da Silva, a widowed Captain of the Infantry Battalion in Luanda, who relayed an incident that confirmed Gamboa's sense of wounded masculinity. At the request of Gamboa, a man named Sebastião was asked to declare what he knew about the behavior of his wife in front of several people. According to Sebastião, he had gone to the trouble of spying on Dona Amaral to verify whether neighbors' gossip about her was true or not. He then stated that "one night around two o'clock in the morning, while he was at the window of his house, he saw a wrapped figure coming from the direction of the college straight to the house of the defendant." When the figure noticed that Sebastião's window was open and people were awake, it turned to leave. However, "the same figure arrived again at the defendant's house and looked upstairs to see if it could enter, and by the voice, it was recognized as Ensign Braklami."[50]

Manoel Martins Cardozo, a 20-year-old unmarried corporal from the city of Porto, stated that he had often seen Braklami, wrapped in a cloak, entering Dona Amaral's house between 9 and 10 p.m. Cardozo also shed light on the role of an enslaved girl in facilitating the relationship. He testified that when Braklami failed to appear at Dona Amaral's house by 10 p.m., the girl would be sent to search for him at the battalion headquarters, sometimes making up to three trips in a single night. If the girl was unable to find Braklami by the third attempt, she would begin to cry, explaining to the sentinels that she feared Dona Amaral would beat her, as was customary when she failed to locate the ensign. This detail underscores the vulnerability and coercion the young enslaved girl faced in her role as a messenger between the two alleged lovers.[51]

José Ferreira, an unmarried 23-year-old soldier from Abrantes, recounted that he had once sought to deliver a letter to Braklami but could not locate him at his home. Upon being informed that Braklami was at the defendant's house, Ferreira "went to the tall house and climbed the stairs," where he witnessed "Braklami and the Defendant hugging and kissing each other in the living room." Embarrassed, Ferreira "stomped his feet," prompting Braklami to come to the door to receive the letter.[52]

All these witnesses shared a military background with Gamboa and might have acted in cahoots with him. Others, however, were not connected to him but still provided information supporting the notion that Dona Amaral had indeed engaged in a relationship with Braklami. Significantly, they all lived in her household. A black woman from Benguela named Roza José, who worked as a street vendor and could not speak Portuguese, testified through a translator that she had seen Braklami at Dona Amaral's house at night. According to her, "one night, they [Braklami and Dona Amaral] had asked her to cook fish, which he and the defendant ate and then went to her room alone, leaving behind her, her female companions, and the children."[53] Roza José's testimony, coming from someone within Dona Amaral's household but not directly connected to Gamboa, added weight to the allegations of an intimate relationship between Dona Amaral and Braklami.

Several of these testimonies established that meetings between Dona Amaral and Braklami would take place late in the evening, sometimes lasting as late as 1 a.m. Given Luanda's social norms and the rhythms of daily life, this timing would have provided an opportune moment for them to meet privately, as the streets would have been almost deserted. Typically, the city's residents would rise around 5 a.m., have breakfast by 8 a.m., and mostly stay home. According to Italian traveler Tito Omboni, who spent ten months in Luanda in the 1830s, "no European, except for some urgent need, leaves the house after sunrise, and only a few blacks are seen lying on the sands or running through the streets shouting drunk [*sic*] with brandy."[54]

Until 2 p.m., businesspeople, including influential businesswomen known as donas, attended to various affairs, such as "receiving trade caravans from the interior and engaging in the trade of slaves, selling them to ship captains from Havana or Brazil." Well-to-do people would then indulge in lavish meals and "would not receive even the governor himself if he came for any purpose other than feasting."[55] Nightfall brought with it distinctive cultural scenes: "While young people date and enjoy the pleasures of kizomba, old people congregate around fireplaces to grill cacusso, bagre, and other dry fish that they eat with manioc flour [fungi] and roasted ginguba. At the same time, they entertained themselves with legends of their oral literature. They call this Ku xinguilé."[56] More importantly, by 1 a.m., the majority would have retreated to their homes, making the timing of Braklami's visits to Dona Amaral particularly convenient.

Yet, despite all the details gathered about Dona Amaral's relationship with Braklami, the new testimonies still failed to substantiate Gamboa's accusation that she had engaged in a criminally adulterous relationship while still living with him. Still, despite the lack of concrete evidence backing up Gamboa's contention, judge Gonçalves issued an arrest warrant against her and Braklami for adultery, drawing a sharp rebuke from Angola governor Pedro Alexandrino da Cunha. According to Governor Cunha, the judicial procedure against Dona Amaral was invalid because Gamboa had bribed witnesses to testify against his ex-wife. Cunha even accused Gamboa of bragging in Luanda taverns about his success in bribing witnesses to provide false testimony. As a result, the governor used the power of his office to shut down the lawsuit.[57]

Makèzú: "Symbolical Language" of Love

Dona Amaral's gesture of sending makèzú (kola nuts) to her secret lover, Braklami, not only sheds light on her personal life but also reveals the deep cultural significance of this fruit in Luanda and beyond. As discussed earlier, Manoel Martins Cardozo testified that Dona Amaral's enslaved servant made multiple visits to the Luanda battalion headquarters, carrying a heart-shaped handkerchief containing a kola nut and ginger. Braklami's response of taking half of the offering and returning the rest to the servant signified his agreement to visit Dona Amaral's house at night, demonstrating his understanding of the elaborate codes of courtship that both locals and foreigners followed in Luanda.

Dona Amaral's use of the kola nut to convey secret love was just one way this fruit significantly influenced social and cultural fabrics across Africa. In many parts of the continent, the fruit played a vital role in various ceremonies, from weddings and baptisms to trials and traditional medicine practices. In Sierra Leone, they featured in trials for grave crimes and had roles in birth and wedding ceremonies, predicting outcomes based on how they landed when dropped.[58] Across many cultures, including Luanda's, kola nuts also served as a powerful symbol in courtship rituals, enabling women to navigate and assert some control over their romantic relationships.[59]

In West Central Africa, kola nuts' significance can be traced back to earlier historical encounters and ceremonial practices. As early as the sixteenth century, the kola nut had been presented to Portuguese visitors at the court of the Ngola as a sign of trust from the rulers. The fruit was also widely used in ceremonial functions, including the production of ritual paintings applied to the body of the Ngola to represent his lineage affiliation.[60] In the Congo, where the kola nut was used to make peace in intra-lineage disputes, it was also carried to the funerals of individuals who were fond of the fruit in life. In this case, the belief was that it could foster communication with the departed.[61]

Significantly, kola nuts spread through the transatlantic slave trade to the Americas. As early as the seventeenth century, they were spotted in Cartagena, where newly arrived enslaved Africans received the nuts to cope with health ailments.[62] From the Bight of Benin, they were exported across the Atlantic to Brazil, where they were known as obi and widely used in Candomblé.[63] As shown by historian João Reis, they were key to the small-scale transatlantic trade conducted by free Africans who crisscrossed the Atlantic.[64] In Jamaica, enslaved Africans from the Gold Coast created a demand for kola nuts, leading to imports from Africa.[65] From Angola, slave ships would take kola nuts to Brazil, "where these products are always in high demand among slaves brought from Africa."[66]

In Luanda, kola nuts, known locally as "makèzú" or simply "kezu," were primarily imported from the "kingdom of Congo, and the blacks bring it to sell in the city of St. Paul of Assumption [Luanda], and the inhabitants use it almost every day."[67] Although the bulk came from afar, they were also sourced from nearby regions like Mbaka. Street vendors, called coleiras or mukwa makezu nijinjibidi, were ubiquitous, displaying the nuts on stands or peddling them in the streets.[68] Roaming vendors traversed different neighborhoods, while others stationed themselves at lively open-air markets, where the nuts joined a vast array of commodities. The nuts' price hinged on their flavor profile, with less bitter, smoother varieties fetching a premium.[69] For convenience, they were sold in small bags named "rifunda."[70]

Luanda's demand for the nut stemmed from its multiple uses in the city. According to scholar Óscar Ribas, older Luanda women would often eat kola and ginger with quitoto, a beer made of corn.[71] Others relied on the fruit as a source of energy for their daily work, as kola nuts were so nutritious that "if they eat a slice of it in the morning, they will not remember to have to eat lunch."[72] Enslaved Africans, who were often deprived of the means to provide for themselves, were particularly keen on consuming the fruit. They would "chew one of two [kola nuts] early in the morning with a portion of ginger or *mundongo* root to, as they say, strengthen the stomach."[73] Yet the nut was also used for more prosaic reasons, including to disguise the bad quality of water in Luanda. According to Italian traveler Tito Omboni, "it is commonly used in the country, and a piece is offered to anyone asking for water to drink."[74]

Beyond their practical uses in daily life, kola nuts held a significant place in Luanda's social and cultural fabrics, playing a role in various ceremonies and traditions. During funerary ceremonies known as entambes, mourners would offer kola nuts "to convey condolences to those mourning a loved one."[75] They were also used in cooking and presented as sacred offerings by healers known as quimbandas, and even gifted during traditional wedding ceremonies called alembamento.[76] The nuts were "highly esteemed by women, who send some to each other as a sign of friendship, and almost all of them use it, as the Indians with tea, in the stated manner."[77] Significantly, makèzú remained a symbol of cultural authenticity well into the twentieth century, invoked by musicians seeking to question Portuguese colonialism in the 1970s.

This cultural role was also exemplified in romantic courtship rituals, closely matching Dona Amaral's case. As eighteenth-century historian Elias Alexandre da Silva Corrêa observed, "the general custom is to offer it as a gift in formal and casual moments to signify friendship or love."[78] Not just locals but foreigners who made Luanda their home adopted this practice when forming relationships with the native population. Souza Corrêa highlighted this, observing that "no European, American [Brazilian], or Asian refused to eat kola if they wanted to be a lover."[79] Detailing the symbolic gestures of love involving kola nuts, naturalist Frederico Welwitsch, who visited Angola in the 1850s, provides valuable insight. "When a boyfriend wants to confirm mutual feelings with a lover, he will send her a half-dozen kola nuts as a present. A pact is consummated if the lover accepts the present, and she will become his bride."[80]

The intricacies of these courtship rituals, as documented by various travelers, reveal a complex "symbolical language" deeply embedded in the city's diverse social and cultural fabrics.[81] Portuguese traveler Ladislau Batalha's account provides a nuanced understanding of these rituals. The act of offering a piece of kola nut and ginger, he notes, served as a declaration of love, with the woman's response holding profound symbolic meanings. Accepting and chewing the kola nut signified not only the reciprocation of love but also an affirmation of the woman's virginity, reflecting the high value placed on female chastity in Luanda's society. In contrast, accepting the offering without chewing implied prior romantic experiences, while refusing it altogether indicated a lack of interest in the courtship. These intricate rules governing the exchange of kola nuts highlight the central role of this ritual in negotiating romantic relationships and social status in Luanda. As Batalha emphasizes, "kola nut and ginger have an important symbolism in youth love [amores da mocidade] in the province of Angola. A black man declares love to a young woman by offering her a bit of kola nut and ginger".[82]

In the case of Dona Amaral and Braklami, there is no doubt that they were well-versed in kola nut courtship. Chronicler Elias Alexandre da Silva Corrêa, describing practices he observed in the eighteenth century, noted that Luanda lovers would send a "triangularly folded handkerchief at the center of which they put the kola or any other gift of small volume." The intricate details of this courtship tradition were of paramount importance. According to Silva Corrêa, handling the kola nut the right way ensured the recipient understood her intentions. By sending a kola nut with a piece of the fruit still attached, she conveyed deep affection. Sprinkling small pieces of kola around the fruit signaled to her lover how much she missed him. Returning the kola gift back without a piece of fruit indicated that Braklami planned to visit her that night.[83] Through her firm grasp of Luanda's "symbolical language" of love,

Dona Amaral thus displayed a profound understanding of one of the most deeply embedded cultural practices in her city.

Women and Urban Slavery

Offering kola nuts to her secret lover was just one example of how Dona Amaral seamlessly fit into Luanda's social and cultural landscape. After her husband left her, she rented a house and became the head of a household including herself and her three children. Although this may seem bold, it did not entirely upend societal norms. From 1823 to 1832, the Luanda administration conducted yearly assessments of a section of the Nossa Senhora do Rosário parish. These assessments revealed that out of 228 people living in 62 households, several women were heads of their households, living alone or with free and unfree individuals. For example, in 1824, 37-year-old Ignez Antonio and 30-year-old Engrácia Matheus, both free black women, lived together before being joined the following year by a 40-year-old black man named Felipe. Additionally, 38-year-old free black woman Maria Luiza lived unmarried with two enslaved black women, 48-year-old Barbara Matheus and 44-year-old Maria José. In the same neighborhood, four single women, three of whom were white seamstresses, lived alone that year.[84]

While these women did not possess the title of Dona, several women in the same neighborhood did. Dona Rita da Conceição, a white woman aged sixty-eight, was the head of a household that included 43-year-old Dona Francisca Xavier, another white woman, a free white man named Boaventura Lemos, and an enslaved man of mixed background named João, along with another enslaved African. Similarly, Dona Luiza Matoso, aged seventy, lived with her six enslaved women, mostly sewists, whom she likely hired out or took in for tailoring work. Another example is Dona Maria Bonini Tavares, a white woman identified as forty-one years old in 1826. She was the head of a household that included five infants and 44 enslaved Africans, of whom half were sewists.[85]

Within this context, Dona Amaral's social standing determined her racial identity as "white." In 1849, approximately 5,500 women resided in Luanda; the majority (4,464) were classified as black, 699 as mixed-race, and only 313 as white. About half (147) of these white women were verifiably born in Europe, while the remaining 166 were born in Angola. Despite this, they maintained a socially constructed white identity, even though they were likely the offspring of relationships between white European men and mixed-race or black women. Intriguingly, the number of white women born in Angola surpassed that of white men born in the colony, potentially due to the "whitening" effect associated with the donas category.[86]

Interestingly, not all white women were identified as donas, even though all but one dona was classified as white. From 1826 to 1831, several white women, including 31-year-old Francisca Rosa and 18-year-old Izabel Joaquim, were not granted the title, suggesting that the distinction of "dona" was not exclusively about race. Furthermore, this title appears to have been inherited or passed down from mothers to daughters in certain cases. Dona Maria Roza, a white woman who lived with her husband, Bento José da Silva, a captain and commander in the Angolan army, provides an illustrative example. The couple had eleven enslaved Africans in their household, most of whom were seamstresses. They also had two daughters, Eugênia and Maria Eugênia, aged five and six, respectively. Both girls were designated as donas by Luanda authorities.[87]

Dona Amaral's household was fundamentally shaped by larger forces operating within Luanda society, especially the institution of slavery. In 1844, just at the onset of efforts to curb shipments of enslaved Africans from the city, Luanda was home to approximately 5,600 people. By 1848, this figure had swelled to around 9,300 people, with enslaved Africans accounting for half of the populace.[88] The mid-1850s witnessed a further rise in the number of enslaved individuals, wherein women made up over half of the enslaved segment.[89] Two-thirds of these enslaved individuals fell within the age bracket of 10 to 29 years, and the majority hailed from regions near Luanda, like the city itself or regions such as Ambaca, Matamba, and Casanje.[90]

Enslaved people engaged in various activities in Luanda, from domestic services to specialized tasks. They learned domestic tasks like washing, ironing, and cooking; some even managed taverns and shops.[91] Some enslaved individuals had relative autonomy, such as those reported by Brazilian diplomat Souza e Oliveira as roaming "the street with *lancetas* bleeding others in exchange for twenty-five or fifty réis."[92] Specialized activities were mostly male-dominated, with carpentry, masonry, and metalwork being common occupations among enslaved men.[93] By contrast, many enslaved people in semi-specialized roles, particularly in domestic services and street vending, were female. The training of an enslaved person in a specialized trade was considered an investment by the owner, as historian Vanessa de Oliveira demonstrates, with skilled enslaved people having higher market value and earning wages, a portion of which would go to their owner.[94]

The increasing population of enslaved Africans in Luanda was met with a diverse demographic of enslavers. An 1856 assessment revealed that each Luanda slaveholder owned, on average, nearly seven enslaved Africans.[95] Women comprised 26.6 percent of Luanda slaveholders, and men owned, on average, more enslaved people than women. The largest male slaveholder in Luanda owned almost twice as many enslaved people as the largest female slaveholder. Donas, for instance, were the owners of eleven percent of the captives in Luanda.[96] The high value placed on skilled enslaved individuals, such as Maria, a seamstress who was sold for 100,000 réis, underscores the economic incentives that drove slave ownership among various demographic groups in the city.[97]

Yet slave ownership was not exclusive to the city's white and mixed-race population. In 1826, Pedro Lourenço, a free black tailor who lived with his free black wife Elena S. Thiago in the *Nossa Senhora do Rosário* neighborhood, owned ten enslaved Africans, five of whom were also tailors. Brazilian diplomat Saturnino de Souza Oliveira once reported on "a free black [man], bricklayer, who owned about 14 slaves."[98] The pervasiveness of slave ownership across various strata of Luanda society, from the elite donas to free black artisans, highlights the deeply entrenched nature of slavery in the city's economic and social fabric.

In Dona Amaral's household, two individuals—Celestina and Jesuína—reflected broader trends shaping the fabric of Luanda's slavery. Celestina, an enslaved woman from the Dembos region north of Luanda, underscores Kikongo-speaking individuals' significant presence and influence in the city's sociocultural landscape. She also played a special role in Dona Amaral's relationship with Braklami, guiding him to a specific room on one of his visits so he could wait for her mistress' arrival. This role suggests that Celestina was a mucama, one of the many domestic servants working in Luanda's households. Both in Luanda and Benguela, as historian Vanessa de Oliveira points out, such enslaved servants performed multiple roles, helping manage households while participating in social and religious events with their masters and mistresses.[99]

While scholars have associated mucamas with household work and slaveholders' prosperity, they also illustrate the sort of violence that slavery inflicted on women, including sexual violence. According to nineteenth-century linguist J. D. Cordeiro da Matta, the word "mucama" derives from a blend of the Portuguese "cama" (bed) and the Kimbundo prefix "mu-," indicating a place, thus connoting "in bed" and alluding to the enforced concubinage of these women.[100] In Brazil, as historian Lorena Telles argues, the term carried similar connotations, encompassing both domestic labor and sexual violence.[101] Many, as scholar Marcus de Carvalho documents, were further punished with sale to other provinces after becoming pregnant by owners or after bearing their children.[102]

As for Jesuína, her presence in Dona Amaral's household encapsulated the murky aftermath of liberation from slave ships, as she navigated an unstable status somewhere between bondage and freedom. As a liberta African from Benguela, she embodied many released from vessels intercepted by British and Portuguese forces, whose escape from the Middle Passage did not guarantee true emancipation, as further discussed in Chapter 7. While individuals like Jesuína were freed from slave vessels and the Middle Passage to the Americas, they faced conditions very similar to slavery in Luanda and elsewhere under an apprenticeship system. As Jesuína's guardian, it is doubtful that Dona Amaral saw her any differently from any other enslaved person in her household.

Celestina and Jesuína did not merely symbolize Luanda's labor dynamics; they played pivotal roles in Dona Amaral's household and personal life.

Therefore, when authorities investigated the accusations of infidelity against her, it was natural for them to take testimonies from the two women, who staunchly defended their mistress. Celestina, who had lived with Dona Amaral for a long time and remembered her separation from Gamboa, testified that "she had never seen any man visiting the house late at night."[103] Jesuína largely echoed this testimony. Although she could not confirm Dona Amaral's daytime activities, since she spent most of the day away from the household as a street vendor in Luanda's streets, she also sought to rebuke accusations against her mistress. In her words, she had "never heard that men had visited the house of the defendant late at night."[104]

While these testimonies suggest closeness between the two unfree women and Dona Amaral, it is worth pointing out that their relationship was based on power imbalances that could easily veer into violence. Take, for example, the testimony of the enslaved female teenager tasked with taking gifts of kola nut to Dona Amaral's lover, Braklami. As observed by a soldier named Manoel Martins Cardozo, she lived in fear. When questioned about why she cried, she would answer "that it was because she was afraid that her mistress would beat her as always because she could not find the said Braklami."[105] Another soldier, Antonio Pinto, recounted that the girl approached him while he was stationed as a sentinel at the Palace, asking if he had seen Braklami enter the house. Later that night, she returned, revealing that her mistress had sent her and had already punished her for not finding him.[106] These testimonies paint a picture of the girl's constant fear and the looming threat of violence that hung over her as she navigated her role as a messenger in the clandestine affair.

Dona Amaral's physical punishment of the enslaved girl contravened recently established regulations governing slave punishment, which dictated that enslaved individuals would be publicly punished at their owners' behest at the public pelourinho (whipping post). In 1846, for example, Mateus Guellette requested that authorities punish one of his captives for being "brazen, thieving, and drunk."[107] Later, two men were publicly flogged for drunkenness and brawling, demonstrating that the pelourinho also served to discipline enslaved individuals engaging in disorderly conduct in town.[108] Generally, enslaved Africans would be returned to their owners after receiving punishment. In 1847, authorities declared that a man who "had been caught stealing sugar cane in a tavern should be punished in the *pelourinho* and then released to his owner."[109]

Despite these new regulations, a mere twenty enslaved Africans were punished in the Luanda Pelourinho between February and October 1847, averaging less than one per week and suggesting that owners continued to administer punishment in the privacy of their homes and workshops.[110] From 1853 onwards, the administration introduced a regulation prohibiting owners from conducting punishments altogether. While stipulating that all punishments be carried out publicly, officials also decided that owners could no longer shackle their slaves' hands or feet or place iron collars around their necks. To enact punishment, they would have to prove that enslaved people had committed a crime or demonstrated disobedience.[111] Owners failing to comply with these regulations would face fines imposed by the State.[112]

These guidelines were used to punish eight men on January 28, 1854. Three men—José, Arcenio, and Joaquim—received 200 lashes each due to the fact they had refused to perform work duties. Another—Ndala—was punished for being prone to running away.[113] A few slaveholders seem to have been admonished for still punishing enslaved people in private.[114] Still, as historian Vanessa de Oliveira demonstrates, slave punishment remained pervasive and out of compliance with the law.[115] To justify these actions, which seem to have targeted enslaved women more than enslaved men, some owners would sometimes even invoke the Brazilian penal code, thus violating Portugal's own laws.[116] Historian Tracy Lopes shows that 7,420 enslaved people were sent to Luanda's chief of police for "correction" between 1857 and 1869. Owners exercised arbitrary discretion in so doing, and enslaved women sent into "correction" made up the majority of women imprisoned at the time.[117]

Quitandeiras' Economic and Cultural Roles

While Celestina and Jesuína's experiences shed light on the complex dynamics within Dona Amaral's household, they also reflect the broader realities of slavery and the roles of enslaved women in Luanda's society. Jesuína's work as a street vendor, or quitandeira, exemplifies a critical aspect of the city's economic and cultural landscape, one in which enslaved and free women played a significant role. Predominantly women, these vendors were a familiar sight in the city's streets and markets, offering a diverse array of goods, from food items like fish and manioc flour to various groceries and alcoholic beverages. Some specialized in specific products, including selling kola nuts (makèzú), while others provided a broader range of goods. Their presence and activities were integral to the local economy, serving both the resident population and transient visitors. In 1845, there were at least 127 registered quitandeiras, not counting those unregistered, roaming Luanda's streets.[118]

According to Ladislau Batalha, the term "quintandeira" and the cognate term "quitanda" revealed "Brazilian influence [on Angola], which derived from the many ties that Angola held with Brazil in the old times of the slave trade."[119] However, its exact etymology remains a topic of debate. Angolan anthropologist Óscar Ribas posits that the word originates from the Kimbundo term "kutanda," meaning "walking far."[120] In contrast, scholar Ana de Sousa Santos believes "quitanda" is derived from "kutandela," which translates to "display."[121] Yet another definition is provided by essayist Domingos Van-Dúnem, who argues for the centrality of the Kimbundo word "itânda," which means a woven stick platform that served as a bench, display stand, and even as a measure.[122]

FIGURE 2.2. Street vendor in Benguela

While Jesuína held the status of a liberta, most quitandeiras were enslaved women. For enslavers, owning them was a strategic investment, as they provided a reliable income stream generated by these workers.[123] The economic incentive for slave owners to exploit the labor of these women was significant, as quitandeiras played a crucial role in Luanda's vibrant informal economy. For instance, Jerônima de Carvalho Menezes owned five enslaved women engaged in street vending in Luanda. Augusto Teixeira de Figueiredo owned sixteen captives, all quitandeiras.[124] These enslaved women were tasked with selling a wide variety of goods, from fresh produce to textiles and beads, and their profits were funneled back to their owners.

The relationship between quitandeiras and their enslavers was not always one of complete subjugation, with some managing to negotiate a degree of autonomy and even accumulate personal wealth through their trade activities. For some quitandeiras, as historian Vanessa de Oliveira shows, their jobs provided a pathway to accumulate enough capital to purchase their own freedom.[125] This highlights the complex dynamics at play within Luanda's slave society, where the line between slavery and freedom was not always clear-cut, and where some enslaved individuals could sometimes leverage their economic activities to improve their social standing and ultimately secure their manumission. Yet the overarching reality remained one of exploitation and oppression, with the vast majority of quitandeiras toiling under the yoke of slavery to enrich their owners.

Further insight into these street vendors comes from Portuguese traveler Ladislau Batalha, who visited Angola in the 1860s. According to Batalha, "a quitandeira is a businesswoman" who deals in a wide range of items through bartering, with "no specialized item to trade. Sometimes they trade in flour, salt, fish, etc. Other times they only sell textiles [*chita* and cotton]. There are days when they sell only beads [*missangas*]."[126] They either moved around the city selling their goods or congregated in Luanda's four street markets.[127] They could hail from multiple places, as historian Vanessa de Oliveira shows, some as far away as territories under the control of the kingdom of Kongo and the Lunda empire.[128]

An incident involving two quitandeiras—Luiza Francisco and Luiza Antonio—sheds further light on the world of quitandeiras. While Francisco was enslaved, Antonio was a free individual. The women were accused of assaulting male African traders who had arrived in Luanda from the interior to sell their goods.[129] The altercation likely centered around a failed transaction, potentially related to credit that the African traders had from Francisco and Antonio that they had failed to repay. Such an incident implies that quitandeiras did not just engage in direct selling but also financed trade, extending their influence to Luanda's hinterland. As Ladislau Batalha notes, quitandeiras "easily realize large transactions," and "some stores sell to them on credit as they consider them great clients."[130] A portion of their profits likely resulted from lending trade goods to African traders venturing into the Luanda hinterland, "enabling them to have products available for sale during harvest time."[131]

In another case, a transaction by a free black woman named Engrácia Antonia Fernandes suggests that at least a few quitandeiras attained significant social mobility, even to the point of owning enslaved individuals. Fernandes lived in the Luanda neighborhood of Cafaco, known for its concentration of free black traders, and her status was uniquely high.[132] In 1855, she signed a contract to repay, within one year, goods (fazendas) that she had borrowed from Antonio Pereira de Lemos, an owner of one of at least fifteen establishments that sold fazendas to quitandeiras in Luanda. Fernandes had managed to establish a thriving business, selling goods throughout the city's streets. The terms of her mortgage contract further underscore her business acumen. To secure her debt, she offered as collateral "all her current and future assets as well as a two-bedroom cubata in the Cafaco neighborhood," along with six enslaved Africans whom she likely employed as street vendors.[133]

Some quitandeiras invested in land on Luanda's outskirts to accumulate generational wealth. In 1864, Maria André da Paixão and Felippa Pedro das Dores engaged in a complex transaction—including transferring money to Portugal—to purchase a plot of land (muceque) from Luis Gomes Ribeiro and Dona Maria Gomes Ribeiro, who were then living in Coimbra, Portugal.[134] According to anthropologist Óscar Ribas, Luanda muceques were used to grow crops such as cashew trees, cassava roots, and peanuts.[135] In 1847, there were more than one hundred such properties near Luanda.[136] The plot bought by the two women was about three square kilometers in size, including a water dam and a house, as well as twenty enslaved Africans who worked and lived on the land. According to them, they had purchased the muceque "for their children, who were named Margarida, José, Theodoro, and Francisco (also known as Pacífico) for the first buyer, and Francisca and Sebastião for the second buyer."[137]

Yet it is also crucial to recognize that quitandeiras played a role that extended beyond economy and business transactions. They contributed in vital ways to Luanda's vibrant cultural and social spheres. In one of the city's bustling markets—quitanda grande—over a hundred quitandeiras hawked their wares daily until dusk. Afterward, "only quitandeiras who sold fried fish stayed, and a large group of male and female blacks came to their market stands to play drums, talk, and party."[138] A vivid depiction of Luanda's largest market comes from American physician Charles Thomas's otherwise prejudiced account: "There were at least five hundred women there, having goods for sale, and all talking at once, seemingly at the highest pitch."[139]

In the bustling markets of Luanda, quitandeiras, seated amidst the vibrant hustle and bustle on the ground, were a sight to behold. Each woman, wrapped in vividly colored cloths known as meléle commanded attention. "They are very sharp traders, and all squat or lie down at full length on the hot sand, enjoying the loud gossip and chatter so dear to the African women with their friends and customers."[140] Their unique attire, unfamiliar to the unacquainted eye, included immense ad hoc hats with brims so wide they could rival the size of "a wheel of a cart." They would arrange goods in quindas (baskets) in front of them, sitting with their knees drawn up close to their chests, while their hats covered their backs and bodies entirely. Such interactions were not just transactions but also offered glimpses into how *quitandeiras* engaged outsiders on their own cultural terms and claimed markets as African spaces.

Beyond economic exchange, their stalls provided a gastronomic journey through Luanda's diverse and rich culinary landscape, featuring everything from kola nuts and ginger to dishes such as roasted rats skewered and presented in a manner that was deeply rooted in local customs. "Every kind of delicacy to captivate the negro palate and fancy is to be had there."[141] By effortlessly switching from Kimbundo and Kikongo to Portuguese, they added a layer of linguistic richness to the marketplace.[142] The crowds and noise created a dizzying cacophony—a discordant mixture of voices and movement that overwhelmed the senses. As one traveler described the scene, "the streets, when we left, were still swarming with negroes, and the hum of the market throng fell on our ears like the sounds of a distant cataract."[143]

In this context, quitandeiras performed a role akin to cultural curators of Luanda's tapestry of cultural traditions and tastes. Adept at distinguishing foreigners in the crowd, they would call them out using Kimbundo, Kikongo or Portuguese—"Ai u eh! N'gana iame!" ("Ah! Ah! Ah! My lord!"), or "Tambula fubá!" ("Take fubá!"), and "Iza'no, jungo!" ("Come here, my dear white [person]!"). According to Italian traveler Tito Omboni, they would dye their feet and legs red with clay collected around the city, and some painted stripes on their forehead, nose, and cheeks as well. In the evening, some would visit husbands and partners at Luanda taverns, joining in traditional dancing and music that further nourished the city's sense of community.[144]

The multifaceted roles of quitandeiras in Luanda's economy and society underscore their importance as cultural intermediaries and agents of change. Through their economic activities, social interactions, and cultural practices, these women navigated the complex dynamics of a slave society while asserting their agency and shaping the city's vibrant cultural landscape. Their experiences, ranging from the exploitation and oppression faced by enslaved quitandeiras to the social mobility and economic success achieved by some free women, reflect the broader tensions and possibilities within Luanda's social fabric. As the city underwent profound changes driven by the waning transatlantic slave trade and the influx of diverse African populations, quitandeiras stood at the forefront of cultural exchange and transformation.

Cultural Fusion in Dona Amaral's Luanda

Dona Amaral's Luanda was characterized by a degree of cultural fusion deeply shaped not only by the experiences of women like quitandeiras but also by the constant influx of enslaved individuals from interior regions like Ambaca, Matamba, and Casanje. These newcomers catalyzed a dynamic cultural convergence, a "babel of the black race," where their languages, customs, and beliefs mingled and reshaped the urban tapestry.[145] Despite the constraints of slavery, these individuals were far from passive; their vibrant cultural heritage injected new life into the city's social fabric, affecting everyone, including households like Dona Amaral's. Thus, Luanda emerged as a complex mosaic, where economic, social, and cultural influences were deeply entwined, impacting every resident's life, regardless of their legal status or race.

Dona Amaral certainly spoke Portuguese as her first language, yet she was also familiar with, if not fluent in, Kimbundo and Kikongo, two languages widely spoken in the city. Her linguistic capabilities were a necessity, as the inflow of Africans to Luanda endowed the city with a polyglot milieu, where multiple languages coexisted and intermingled. According to an anonymous observer of Luanda's social and cultural scenes in the 1850s, some slaveholders spoke "more Kimbundo than Portuguese, which these [enslaved servants] understand but cannot speak."[146]

Among the African languages spoken in Luanda, Kimbundo was the most dominant, and Dona Amaral would certainly have been conversant in it. The Portuguese traveler Ladislau Batalha once described Kimbundo as a "perfect language," suggesting that it had remained relatively resistant to change despite the "influx of European languages and neighboring languages."[147] However, even Kimbundo was not entirely insulated within Luanda's cauldron of cultural exchange. According to Brazilian physician Saturnino de Souza Oliveira, the language was in constant flux due to borrowings from Portuguese. As Souza Oliveira noted, "it is not rare to hear Kimbundo and notice many Portuguese language adverbs and prepositions."[148]

These language dynamics were intrinsically linked to social hierarchies, as anthropologist Óscar Ribas noted. According to Ribas, Kimbundo was a language in tension with an increasingly assertive Portuguese language seeking dominance. Luanda residents from the popular class would shift from Kimbundo to Portuguese when interacting with someone of a "superior condition," such as those of higher social status or authority, illustrating social hierarchies embedded in language use.[149] Still, their speech retained traces of their native syntax and phonetics, as the prevalent vowel endings in their Portuguese—a vestige of Kimbundo influence—revealed an inherent resistance to the complete linguistic assimilation that Portuguese dominance sought.[150] As Brazilian physician Saturnino de Souza e Oliveira pointed out, "the dominance of the Angolense language among natives of the country has modified the pronunciation of the Portuguese [language]."[151]

Beyond the realm of language, Dona Amaral's household served as a miniature reflection of Luanda's African culture in various other ways. She frequently enjoyed Angolan cuisine and notably served it to her lover Braklami. In the city's culinary tradition, fish was a staple that "provides the basis for the diet of the majority of the people, who make it the principal (and sometimes only) meal, adding flour and sometimes beans, with salt, palm oil, and peppers."[152] A particular favorite was moamba, a savory stew traditionally made with chicken or fish and enriched with tomatoes, onions, and a generous amount of palm oil, giving it a unique flavor and reddish hue. Alongside this, funge, a thick, smooth paste made from manioc, was typically served with richly flavored meat, fish, or vegetable stews. These dishes often featured a small but intensely fiery chili pepper known as jindungo, adding a distinctive heat that embodied Luanda's vibrant and diverse tastes.[153]

Likewise, although she had certainly married her husband Gamboa in a Catholic church, Dona Amaral was familiar with an elaborate African traditional wedding ceremony known as alambamento, a rite deeply rooted in the customs and identity of Luanda residents. As Angolan anthropologist Óscar Ribas noted, the ceremony served as an introduction to marital life and was considered indispensable for a successful pregnancy, childbirth, and the well-being of the couple's offspring.[154] During the eight days leading up to the ceremony, the bride was secluded and confined to a darkened room where she received instruction "in various things pertaining to the state of matrimony" from someone known as quibolo ou vilembo.[155] After this initiation period, a public parade known as cu bandulula took place, during which the bride worshiped an idol known as iteque.[156] The celebration culminated in three days of festivities, with Africans dancing and enjoying local delicacies such as the abovementioned funge and pirão, the latter being "a dish made from cassava flour mixed with sauces and highly regarded by soldiers, sailors, and convicts."[157]

The alambamento ceremony's widespread appeal, bridging divides of legal status, race, and nationality, not only underscores Dona Amaral's deep connection with this tradition but also highlights the complex cultural exchanges between native Africans and the wider colonial society. Its participants ranged from locally born whites to foreigners from Brazil and Portugal, illustrating its broad integration into Luanda's social fabric. Yet the ceremony's acceptance was not universal. It faced scrutiny and criticism from various quarters, particularly from those within the colonial establishment. Observers, often adopting a colonialist perspective, decried the participation of white Christians in what they referred to as a "heathenish custom."[158] Figures like Brazilian doctor Saturnino de Souza e Oliveira and Angolan intellectual Joaquim de Carvalho e Menezes captured such views, criticizing this embrace as an unwelcome validation of African cultural practices. According to Souza e Oliveira, "the majority of Europeans have adopted, and still adopt, [alambamento], adhering to and supporting thus an African custom against which they should instead protest."[159]

Just as Dona Amaral was well-versed in the rites of marriage through alambamento, she was equally familiar with Luanda's deeply entrenched funeral practices, such as the entambe ceremony. This ritual, described by Batalha as a ceremony "in which the profane mixed with the sacred," was another cultural cornerstone reflective of the community's approach to life's pivotal moments. When someone passed away, the air would fill with the sound of weapons firing to announce the departure, and "a large number of people of both sexes would gather around the corpse, publicly displaying their grief and crying loudly." The entambe, usually held eight days after the passing, was a communal event "in the deceased's backyard," featuring singing, instrumental music, and batuque dances, all aimed at ensuring that "the soul (zumbi) of the deceased would depart in peace and joy." In instances where resources for the ceremony were scarce, families sometimes provided a member as collateral, known as the gunge, to secure the necessary funds.[160]

Entambes underscore the fact that Western religion was not the only sacred space for Luanda's residents, including Dona Amaral. Luanda residents believed in entities like the benign N'gana Zambi and an array of spirits, often displaying protective amulets and rituals to placate them. Connection to these forces was mediated by venerated authorities called ngangas and quimbandas, revered in communities for their ceremonial mastery, medicinal plant knowledge, and other secret wisdom.[161] This multifaceted religious landscape, fusing African and Portuguese elements, created a rich cultural environment that Dona Amaral navigated adeptly in ways that could confer advantages over outsiders unaware of its complexities, like her lover Braklami.

Though identifying as Christian, the Luanda native most likely engaged daily with her city's rich spiritual practices, reflecting a blend of Western and African religions. As noted by anthropologist Óscar Ribas, residents often invoked both for different needs and blessings. "What God does not give us, [African] spirits will concede."[162] This blending extended beyond Luanda, influencing practices across urban and rural areas alike. For instance, Ladislau Batalha, a Portuguese traveler, recounted a religious ceremony near Calumbo in which a group of African peasants chanted the mucungi, "a Christian gospel in Quimbundo to ask [God] for rain for their harvest and sowing."[163]

In this environment, Dona Amaral likely did not rely on Western medicine to terminate her pregnancy. With only two hospitals and a minimal number of doctors in town, westernized medical care was not readily available, and the city's population largely resorted to traditional medicine. Healers ngangas and quimbandas dealt in divination and rituals for afflictions. They also provided remedies to "fend off bad luck, bring back harmony to marital lives, and stir enmity."[164] According to Brazilian physician Saturnino de Souza e Oliveira, "among the lowest class of the people of Luanda, there was greater confidence in curandeiros (traditional healers)" than in Western physicians.[165]

Several scenarios shed light on how she might have proceeded. In 1848, the Luanda administration listed three *casas de maternidades*, or maternity facilities where midwives helped local women deliver babies. It is possible that Dona Amaral sought the help of their health specialists.[166] Most likely, however, she obtained herbs to provoke a miscarriage. In Luanda, the use of biomedical herbs was widespread among the populace, sometimes without input from traditional healers. African traders would bring medicinal herbs to Luanda markets, "where they are in high demand by the black population, who use them to prepare several medicines."[167] As pointed out by Welwitsch, an herb named *Canbundo* was highly sought after in "drug markets, particularly by pregnant women, who rub it [*cingir*] on the head or arm with *bambundo* so that through this sorcery [*sic*] their newborn children could be spared from illnesses."[168]

Dona Amaral likely consulted one of Luanda's many quimbandas and ngangas. "I have seen many ngangas or healers who have achieved amazing cures by simply treating [people] with herbs," notes an account.[169] One example might have been a woman named May Ngumlu, a free black woman living alone in Luanda's Nossa Senhora do Rosário neighborhood between 1823 and 1826. The only person in the entire parish who used an African name, she likely offered services as a healer to her Luso-African and European neighbors.[170] If May Ngumlu was indeed a healer, she would have learned her skills from her parents and inherited her status. Patients who visited quimbandas contracted a moral tie with them, according to Ribas, who suggests that these healers held more immediate and personal power than government authorities in Luanda.[171] In a society where colonial oppression and patriarchal control sought to suppress and erase African identity, the enduring presence and power of traditional healers like May Ngumlu and the quimbandas Dona Amaral likely turned to in her time of need stand as a testament to the unbreakable spirit and resilience of African culture and religion, which continued to shape the lives and experiences of Luanda's inhabitants despite the forces arrayed against them.

Conclusion

This chapter provides a deeply layered portrayal of power dynamics, gender relations, and slavery at the apex of the campaign to end the transatlantic slave trade. At its core, the narrative intertwines the lived experience of Dona Amaral, a woman trapped within the confines of patriarchal norms, and larger sociopolitical developments in Luanda, a major city in the throes of the Atlantic slave trade. Dona Amaral's personal ordeal, stemming from allegations of infidelity, serves as a microcosm of the broader systems of power in place. By seizing on the intimate act of her secret communication with Braklami through a gift of kola nuts (makèzú), the narrative adds complexity and gives voice to women's experience within the larger context of gender, power, slavery, and anti-slave trade politics. In so doing, it seeks to depict Dona Amaral as a fully dimensional character whose story challenges male-dominated historical narratives focused narrowly on economic and political transitions orchestrated by men.

By drawing attention to Luanda's courtship rituals and the everyday lives of its residents, the chapter underscores the value of small, often overlooked details, leveraging them to excavate nuanced, hidden stories of gender and power within a patriarchal colonial order. This strategy generates insights into women's subjectivity—their desires, strategies, and agency—in a society that often sought to erase them. By focusing on cultural practices surrounding kola nuts, the chapter centers the intimate and the everyday as sites of historical inquiry, utilizing seemingly small gestures, intimate exchanges, and personal relationships as pathways to explore broad societal features, elucidating how macro-historical forces manifest in individual lives.

The narrative weaves together various threads—personal stories, political machinations, cultural traditions, and the institution of slavery—to create a rich and intricate portrayal of life in Luanda at a critical juncture. Dona Amaral's personal story is interwoven with the larger political battle over the slave trade, showing how individual lives were deeply affected by broader historical currents. The chapter highlights the multicultural nature of Luanda, with African languages, beliefs, and customs blending with Portuguese influences to create a unique social and cultural fabric. Despite lacking formal political power, Africans in Luanda wielded significant cultural influence, shaping the city's social norms, religious practices, and everyday life in ways that even the privileged, like Dona Amaral, could not escape.

The experiences of different groups—the privileged Dona Amaral, the enslaved workers in her household, the quitandeiras in the markets—are all part of this complex tapestry, each thread contributing to Luanda's vibrant cultural fabric. Despite the city's colonial structure and the institution of slavery, Luanda emerges as an utterly African city when viewed through a cultural lens. African languages, such as Kimbundo and Kikongo, were spoken by all strata of society, including the Portuguese elite. Traditional African religious practices, such as the veneration of spirits and the reliance on ngangas and quimbandas for healing and spiritual guidance, coexisted alongside Christianity. The city's vibrant markets, dominated by African women known as quitandeiras, served not only as centers of economic exchange but also as hubs of cultural interaction and expression. The foods consumed, the rituals observed, and the social norms followed all bore the indelible mark of African cultural influence. Thus, while the institution of slavery shaped the economic and social realities of Luanda, it was the African cultural foundation that truly defined the character of the city and its inhabitants.

Power imbalance and violence were endemic in Luanda. Yet this chapter seeks to depict the city's unfree residents as more than mere economic units devoid of volition and flattened by the oppression of slavery. In this narrative, African individuals emerge as complex human beings who actively shaped Luanda's social and cultural fabrics despite the constraints they faced. From the blended languages spoken on the streets to the syncretic religious practices embraced by all strata of society, the imprint of African cultures is evident across myriad facets of urban life. Even Dona Amaral, despite her relative privilege, lived a life profoundly shaped by African influences. From the cuisine she ate to the courtship rituals she engaged in, her experiences were imbued with cultural practices and beliefs rooted in African traditions. Foodways, healing traditions, music, and ceremonies all bore the profound but often overlooked influence of African beliefs and customs shaping colonial fabrics.

CHAPTER THREE

Agents of Abolition

ON NOVEMBER 16, 1854, a runaway slave named Tabião went to the interim governor of Benguela, Vicente Barruncho, to alert him that "a large number of slaves were shackled and readied to be shipped abroad" from an orchella weed [*urzela*] station [*feitoria*] in Equimina, south of Benguela.[1] At the time, Benguela's economy relied heavily on exporting orchella weed, a highly sought-after dyeing lichen in Europe. Tabião had "freed himself from the *libambo* [coffle]" and had come to alert authorities about the planned shipment.[2] As a ladino enslaved person who spoke Portuguese, he could "designate the place where [the feitoria] was located and even [divulge] the names of the owners."[3] Tabião's information was urgent as he "had heard from another slave [. . .] that the ship on which they would be sent was already off the coast of Mossamedes."[4] Four days later, he guided Portuguese forces to the *feitoria*, where 194 enslaved people were "found in irons and ready to be shipped" to Cuba.[5]

Tabião's significant role in the successful operation was openly acknowledged by João Maximo da Silva Rodovalho, a seasoned Portuguese naval commander who was reputed to be the "terror of the slave dealers on this coast, having captured and burned some slavers and destroyed some barracoons (slave depots)."[6] Rodovalho led the troops into the feitoria and stated that Tabião had been their guide. In his words, "Through the black man [Tabião] that served as a guide on this expedition, I learned that this was [. . .] where the enslaved Africans we were searching for were held."[7] At three o'clock, forty soldiers quietly waited to overrun the orchella farm. "When they realized they would be released from the shackles and the captivity that tormented them," the African captives "began to clap out of happiness."[8]

In the conventional wisdom, the abolition of the transatlantic slave trade is still often framed—at least when it comes to Africa—as mostly a matter of white people pulling the levers of powers in Europe. The enslaved come across as mostly nameless; their side of the story is rarely if ever told. Recent scholarship has begun to challenge this narrative by highlighting instances of Africans pushing back on the trade in human beings. As early as 1836, historian Michael Odijie notes, Gold Coast rulers expressed support for Britain's abolition of the trade.[9] Yet, while such examples point to hostility toward shipments of enslaved Africans to the Americas, the agency and resistance of enslaved Africans themselves still remain largely overlooked in dominant narratives.

By contrast, this chapter recasts the story of abolition by highlighting the active roles that enslaved Africans played in opposing the transatlantic slave trade, specifically in the Benguela region in the 1850s. The actions of individuals and groups ranged from singular acts, such as the one performed by Tabião, to more organized escapes and revolts. By bringing these instances of agency to the forefront, I showcase how enslaved Africans actively contributed to the dynamics of abolition, revealing a complex interplay between their actions, the economic motives of a Portuguese administration then seeking to remake Benguela's economy, and the evolving political structures of colonial rule. This perspective challenges the notion that abolition was solely the result of external actors, instead presenting the resistance of the enslaved as a critical and influential force in the fight against the sale of African lives across the Atlantic.

The notion of the enslaved playing a role in the abolition of the slave trade is not a novel concept. As scholars Flávio Gomes and Dale Graden have detailed, fear of slave revolts contributed to the Brazilian government's passing legislation to halt the flow of captives into the country.[10] In Brazil's Amazonia, as recognized by British sources, the existence of fugitive slave communities was "the principal cause of the early cessation of the Slave Trade," with marron communities causing "insecurity of slave property" that dissuaded slave owners from engaging in the slave trade well before Brazil seriously cracked down on imports of African captives in the early 1850s.[11] Similarly, as discussed in Chapter 4 of this book, fear of slave revolts also influenced the decision to end the slave trade in Cuba.

Recent scholarship further illuminates enslaved people's agency in Brazil's abolition process. As historian Isadora Mota argues, "the contested phasing out of human trafficking expanded the political field in which enslaved, freedpeoples, and quilombolas (maroons) in Brazil claimed the authority of abolitionism for themselves in the nineteenth century."[12] Mota reveals how enslaved people crafted their own abolitionist visions, often ascribing radical meanings to antislavery efforts that exceeded British intentions. This phenomenon resonates with dynamics in Benguela, where enslaved individuals similarly interpreted Portuguese antislavery efforts as potential support for their struggles, highlighting how enslaved agency shaped abolition processes across the South Atlantic world.

When it comes to Africa, however, the narrative of abolition has largely overlooked the role of enslaved Africans. As historian Robin Law points out, "The story of the ending of the Atlantic slave trade is usually told from a European perspective, with the role of Africans remaining that of passive spectators or, at best, active opponents of the abolitionist project."[13] In few if any other instances, however, has enslaved agency played as crucial a role in abolition as in Benguela, where individuals like Tabião actively assisted government-led operations to shut down the networks of the transatlantic slave trade. As Rebecca Shumway points out, abolition cannot "be fully understood without taking into account the vital contribution of a variety of actors located around the Atlantic basin, including those on the African continent."[14]

The Equimina raid was significant enough to be reported in the *Periódico dos Pobres*. This Rio de Janeiro newspaper stated that the Africans apprehended during the attack were taken to Luanda "to be presented to an appropriate tribunal."[15] In fact, the reality was more complicated. After the raid, both Inácio Xavier, one of the owners of the feitoria, and the enslaved Africans were held in one of Benguela's forts.[16] Three months later, twenty Africans had either died in custody or escaped, with one of the latter being caught while attempting to make his way to Caconda in the backlands of Benguela.[17] The remaining 174 enslaved Africans were taken to Luanda, where dozens were placed in the city's hospital for medical care. The rest were handed over to a state board responsible for Africans who had been liberated from slave vessels.[18]

Tabião's actions stand in sharp contrast to the usually pervasive complicity with the slave trade in Benguela. In 1851, a governor mentioned, "Your excellency will certainly not doubt the difficulty faced in Luanda to find someone willing to testify in court about any exportation of Africans."[19] In 1854, a judge from Luanda conducted interviews with 20 individuals across several trading posts along the Benguela coast. Implausibly, only a single witness admitted that shipment of enslaved people had ever taken place from these establishments.[20] Later, Portuguese commander Rodovalho, who had led the 1854 raid on the Equimina feitoria, stated: "All witnesses [in Benguela] would give testimonies in favor of slave dealers," making it impossible to press charges against them.[21] Notably, complicity extended to some of the workers on feitorias, who "would rather die than confess that they had any part in such operations."[22]

Tabião's actions took place at a critical moment in the efforts to end the trade of enslaved Africans. By the mid-1850s, with Brazilian importation of captives ended, officials described the state of the Angolan slave trade "as one of stagnation rather than of extinction."[23] According to Governor of Benguela Francisco Tavares de Almeida, no enslaved person had come through the city's customs house since the beginning of his term.[24] French navigator Kerhallet and naval commander Bouët-Willaumez also observed decreased shipments and a transition to a licit trade economy. While Kerhallet stated that shipments of enslaved people had been "almost entirely halted by military cruisers," Bouët-Willaumez remarked that a transition to a licit trade economy was already taking place, suggesting that the slave trade was being phased out.[25]

Since 1853, however, signs of a possible resumption of large-scale shipments of captives had begun to emerge, driven primarily by the arrival of ships seeking to take enslaved Africans to the Spanish island of Cuba, then the sole market to newly arrived enslaved Africans in the Americas, which was going through a sugar production boom. According to authorities, "news has circulated that a ship from Cuba had brought the proceeds of the first sale of slaves in that Island in December of the last year."[26] Some accounts suggest that each captive purchased in West Central Africa could be sold at a price up to twenty times larger in Havana. "A negro that might be worth in the Havana from four to five hundred dollars can now be bought on this coast for fifteen or twenty" dollars.[27]

Tabião's decision to stand up against the slave trade not only changed his life—he was granted freedom as a reward for his actions—but also led to new measures to prevent shipments of enslaved people to the Americas. These included the construction of a military fort in Equimina to "see that traffic is not carried on in his district," as well as a heightened commitment to action against those "who remain responsible for every negligence or connivance in that traffic." Moreover, captives working in feitorias, likely numbering in the thousands by then, could no longer be held in chains or restrained with iron collars and fetters, and setting up a new feitoria required prior approval from the Benguela government.[28] Most significantly, and as will be detailed later in this chapter, Tabião's act of defiance inspired the colonial state to issue an edict that emancipated any enslaved person who contributed to anti-slave trade initiatives.

The decision by the Portuguese to leverage African resistance against the slave trade raises intriguing questions about the motives underlying Portugal's move toward abolition at that time. What was then central for the Benguela government was establishing a post-slave trade economy, focusing on commercial agriculture and extractive products such as orchella. The emerging belief was that a resurgence in large-scale enslavement would undermine this goal by stripping a burgeoning economy of its labor force. It is within this context that Tabião's actions must be viewed. When he delivered a crucial tip-off about an impending shipment of captives in Equimina, not only did authorities act on his information, but they also came to realize the efficacy of incentivizing similar conduct among others. As will be discussed later, this approach proved to be effective, with instances of enslaved Africans reporting on planned shipments and assisting authorities in tracking down slave traders in Benguela.

While Tabião's actions represented a specific form of resistance against the slave trade, it is crucial to recognize that African resistance against the slave trade had its own autonomous legacy, intricately woven into the region's historical fabric, independent of its strategic utility to the Benguela government. This resistance was not a singular phenomenon but a complex tapestry of rebellion, survival, and community building. It was a force with its own momentum, often running counter to colonial plans and, at times, directly shaping policy due to its unignorable impact. An independent force with significant historical roots, multifaceted resistance—in the form of ship revolts, and maroon communities, and strategic escapes—collectively exerted pressure that directly challenged colonialism, impacting and sometimes even steering colonial policies that led to the eventual decline of the slave trade.

One illustration was a revolt that occurred on a ship that left Benguela in 1827. According to officials, "only one Spanish sailor remained [. . .] alive so that he could pilot the vessel to Hanha," north of Benguela. The revolt was led by an enslaved African named Domingos Caetano, who "disembarked all slaves, murdered the last sailor so he would not come to the city [of Benguela] to inform" authorities, and took refuge in the district of Dombe Grande. Caetano then "established a large *quilombo* of runaways," many of whom had evaded the slave trade in Benguela. Even local sobas of Dombe Grande could not capture him, with Caetano becoming a counterpoint to the colonial government in Benguela. He was only captured nineteen years later, with the Portuguese eventually resorting to a substantial military operation. His end was tragic and brutal: after being savagely whipped at the Benguela pelourinho (whipping post), Caetano was paraded through the city streets before being murdered.[29]

Benguela's status as a slave trade hub mattered in this story. Like Luanda, the city was the departure point of voyages into Brazilian and Cuban slavery for hundreds of thousands of victims of the slave trade. Yet its close connections to the Atlantic also provided a path for escape and return for some enslaved Africans. Some would cross the Atlantic to escape enslavement in Angola or Brazil. Others returned to Africa after obtaining freedom through manumission. Bartolomeu and Vicente, two highly skilled enslaved individuals who may have been sold to Luanda by José Cerqueira de Lima, one of Salvador's largest slave dealers, fled from Luanda with two young children. Their owner then placed an advertisement in a Rio de Janeiro newspaper to request their return, suggesting the group may have crossed to return to their home country.[30] Serafim, his wife, and two children attempted to escape enslavement in Brazil by crossing the Atlantic with the aid of a white man connected to Angola.[31] Another example is Luiza Teixeira, referred to as "Angola, preta forra," who appears to have returned to Angola after gaining manumission in Brazil. Teixeira was one of four passengers aboard a ship departing from Rio de Janeiro for Luanda on March 25, 1838.[32]

Those who most often took advantage of Benguela's ties to the Atlantic world were enslaved sailors, who comprised a large number of crewmembers on slave vessels. In 1828, fourteen out of twenty-seven crew members on the *Cometa*, a ship entering Rio de Janeiro from Cabinda, were enslaved sailors.[33] An American traveler observed that "the crews [of vessels in the harbor] are generally composed of slaves, in charge of the owner or a driver, who is captain of the boat."[34] According to a Luanda merchant who once applied for licenses for seven enslaved sailors on one of his ships, the practice of employing enslaved sailors stemmed from the "lack of sufficient white sailors for the said ship."[35]

Maritime life undoubtedly provided opportunities for enslaved Africans to escape bondage and the slave trade. A prime example was the revolt on the Eclipse, a slave vessel bound for Rio with human cargo in 1827. The unnamed rebel leader, originally from Rio de Janeiro, had almost certainly gone to Benguela with his owner's approval, mirroring the case of Caetano José, who worked as a sailor in Benguela while his owner resided in Rio.[36] The future rebel, however, seized the chance to drift away from slavery entirely. Similarly, two enslaved men belonging to Inácio Jose Silva, a ship owner in Benguela, escaped after being "seduced" by a third sailor on Silva's vessel.[37] In another case, a free cook on a slave vessel decided to break his contract with the master of the ship after arriving in Benguela from Salvador, even petitioning to receive payments for his labor.[38]

Yet the future rebel leader's life of disguised freedom—he had been living in Benguela incognito—came to an end after his Rio de Janeiro-based owner caught news of his whereabouts. The owner then asked Benguela authorities to either apprehend and return him to Rio or allow him to purchase himself out of slavery. After finding himself en route to slavery in Rio de Janeiro, the sailor led a revolt that resulted in the Eclipse returning to Catumbela. By the time Benguela troops found the vessel, all rebels were gone, except for thirty-five captives, a female passenger, and a crewmember. While acknowledging that slave ship revolts were far from atypical, authorities expressed hope that at least part of the escapees would turn up for sale again in Benguela after being apprehended by African traders and sold to the city's *sertanejos*.[39]

Against this backdrop, Tabião's actions in 1854 stand out as undoubtedly unique. Instead of fleeing or revolting, Tabião utilized his knowledge and command of Portuguese to become an effective informant, collaborating with authorities against the slave trade. While his actions aligned with the state's emerging economic interests—which made officials receptive to his assistance—they also underscored his awareness and shrewd understanding of anti-slavery efforts. Many outsiders, clouded by prejudice, held misconstrued views of the enslaved Africans. An American sailor who once visited Luanda even claimed that enslaved people's "intellects are too much enfeebled from their degraded state to comprehend the meaning of the word freedom, or liberty."[40] Yet, in Tabião, we see a stark contrast: a deep awareness that challenges prejudiced views while adding depth and complexity to a narrative frequently dominated by colonial and international diplomatic perspectives.

The chapter proceeds as follows: I first unpack the symbiosis between the slave trade and Benguela's emerging orchella factory-based economy, starting with the Equimina feitoria as a microcosm of this complex relationship. This analysis reveals the intricate connections between Benguela, Cuba, and New York City, highlighting the global nature of the slave trade even as it was being phased out. I then delve into how Benguela's orchella boom not only strengthened Portuguese maritime trade but also catalyzed the growth of slavery. As the enslaved population grew, so did the frequency and complexity of resistance, from individual escapes to organized rebellions. These acts of defiance forced officials to act against the slave trade and shaped colonial policies.

Throughout the chapter, I examine the power dynamics between slave dealers, colonial officials, and enslaved Africans, revealing how the latter's agency played a crucial role in undermining the slave trade networks. I track the ground-level reverberations of Portugal's groundbreaking decision to grant freedom to enslaved people who reported attempts to ship captives abroad, a policy directly inspired by Tabião's actions. The experiences of figures like Tabião, Egídio Sebastião, and Antonio Joaquim exemplify the risks and potential rewards faced by enslaved individuals who actively resisted the trade. By emphasizing enslaved people's precarious yet impactful agency, I seek to craft an alternative narrative of abolition that foregrounds African resistance against the violent structures of the transatlantic slave trade, challenging conventional wisdom that frames abolition primarily as a top-down process driven by European powers.

Equimina: A Trade Nexus

The Equimina feitoria was a microcosm of the broader transformation occurring in coastal Angola as the transatlantic slave trade was phased out. These coastal hubs were precursors to Benguela's emerging post-slave trade economy. As the British noted, "the establishment at Equimina cannot strictly, perhaps, be called a barracoon, consisting, as it does, of one or more substantial residences and exhibiting some indication of agriculture and works of a licit character."[41] Tellingly, not all enslaved Africans found on the property were seized; those engaged in agricultural and fishing activities were left undisturbed.[42] However, the British also highlighted that the site had been a significant depot for enslaved people, fostering and supporting the slave trade in the south of Angola.[43]

The Equimina incident not only highlighted the local infrastructure of the slave trade but also exposed the extent of the connection between Benguela slave dealers and Cuba. One of the owners of the Equimina feitoria, Ignacio Teixeira Xavier, had recently traveled to the Spanish island on a vessel full of captives shipped from his property.[44] Xavier was arrested on the spot, an event sufficiently remarkable to be mentioned in letters exchanged by slave dealers from New York City at the time.[45] While he did spend time in a Benguela jail, his stay there was most likely short, and he was soon reported as traveling to Cuba to escape further punishment in Benguela. "It seems that from there he will travel to Cuba," wrote Portuguese commander João Maximo da Silva Rodovalho, "where both he and his partner are owed the proceeds of five shipments of slaves lately carried out from the south of Benguela."[46]

Although Xavier's attempt to flee to Cuba did not ultimately come to fruition, several of his peers regularly traveled to the Spanish island as part of efforts to reestablish shipments of enslaved Africans from Benguela. Among these individuals was José Lucas Henriques da Costa, a well-known slave dealer in Benguela. Described as having one lame foot and "more or less forty years old, standard height, [with a] long nose and face," he developed a close business relationship with some of the island's most important slave dealers, including Julian Zulueta, J. Mazorra, Martin Rivera, and Nicolau Valdevez.[47] Costa's connections in Cuba had a direct impact on his ability to engage in the slave trade in Benguela, as he was known to offer "as much as fifty and sixty mil réis per head, ready money" to feitoria owners who were willing to ship their enslaved workers abroad.[48]

Costa, like other Benguela slave dealers, was also connected with investors in New York City who played a role in the slave trade to Cuba. He once sent a letter from New York to his Benguela associate, a Brazilian man named Bento Pacheco dos Santos, announcing the purchase of a four-year-old ship in the United States. According to the letter, the vessel had cost 7,200 pesos, of which 2,000 pesos came from his Benguela-based Brazilian partner. Lucas planned to send the ship to Benguela and then travel to Cuba to oversee the arrival of the vessel and the sale of its cargo of captives.[49] However, Lucas's plans were eventually thwarted by an investigation underway in Benguela, with the slave dealer being ultimately arrested in New York in 1856.[50]

Individuals like Xavier and Costa could not have operated without the support of Benguela's economic and political elite. A case in point is José Luiz da Silva Vianna, Xavier's leading partner in the Equimina factory. According to Governor of Benguela Francisco Tavares, Vianna was "the most important merchant and owner in this city."[51] A Portuguese man residing in Benguela since at least 1839, when he obtained a passport to travel to Rio de Janeiro, the slave dealer was once described as a tall, blue-eyed 32-year-old man.[52] He held several positions in the city's administration, including head of the Benguela city council and interim governor of Benguela.[53] He regularly hosted high-ranking officials, including governors of Angola Adrião Acácio da Silveira Pinto and José Rodrigo Coelho do Amaral, taking them on official trips to explore economic opportunities in recently conquered territories near Benguela.[54]

Vianna had been involved in the slave trade since the early 1840s. In 1842, for example, he requested a license from the Benguela government to send 50 barrels of gunpowder—a product usually traded for enslaved people—to the Benguela highlands.[55] He soon became one of the wealthiest merchants in town, regularly providing financial backing to others and endorsing bills of exchange to trade abroad. He also advanced goods on credit to African authorities as far away as Mossamedes.[56] Like Ana Joaquina dos Santos Silva, the famed Luanda slave dealer whose career will be analyzed in Chapter 5, he supported projects to develop commercial agriculture in Benguela.[57]

Before the Equimina raid, Vianna had apparently refused to sell enslaved people to the captain of a slave ship, reportedly due to outstanding payments from Cuba. As the British explained, "no payment having been made for them, the application on the present occasion for a fresh supply was hurt by a demand for payment of the previous cargo and an intimation that, until that demand was complied with, no more enslaved people would be furnished."[58] However, his slave trading activities were soon resumed. In 1854, Vianna was accused of owning 10 out of 107 enslaved people who were intercepted en route to Dombe Grande, where they would have been shipped to Cuba.[59] He was also allegedly involved in the kidnapping of six free Cabinda sailors by a Spanish vessel.[60]

It should be noted that Vianna was not the sole merchant who participated in both the slave trade and other legitimate business activities. For instance, in 1848, Miguel Lino Ferreira, a resident of Luanda, received a large shipment of orchella weed from a feitoria he owned in Cabo de São Brás, located just south of Luanda.[61] Lino Ferreira had been traveling to Benguela since at least 1841 and was described as a 25-year-old white man from Braga, Portugal.[62] However, he was also one of the Luanda correspondents for the firm of João Alberto Machado, a Portuguese slave trader based in New York City with connections to associates in Ambriz and Benguela.[63] In 1849, one of Lino Ferreira's ships was sold to Brazilian nationals in Rio de Janeiro to avoid anti-slave trade measures by obtaining Portuguese passports.[64] In 1855, he shipped between 60 and 100 enslaved people from Lucira to Cuba, eventually being arrested for such an act.[65]

The economic benefits and power men like Vianna derived from their involvement in the transatlantic slave trade could not be overstated. As a German traveler noted during a visit to Benguela in the 1840s, the slave dealer owned the finest garden in the city and was eager to hire a European gardener, "whom he was willing to pay between 600 and 800 dollars per year."[66] Additionally, he was the owner of a tile and brick factory located near Benguela.[67] This wealth was channeled toward projects that benefited Benguela while further bolstering Vianna's place in the local society. As the city's most prominent benefactor, he once offered to fund the construction of a road between Benguela and Catumbela while also contributing to restoring the town's main church.[68] These projects not only enhanced Vianna's status within the community but also served to promote Portuguese interests in the region.

At the time of his death in 1855, Vianna's business interests extended across several parts of southern Angola, including Equimina, Cuio, Hanha, Dombe Grande, Mossamedes, and the interior regions of Caconda, Quilengues, and Bié. He had business interests abroad in Brazil, Cuba, and Portugal. In Rio de Janeiro, for instance, a man named Antonio Ferreira Alves owed him five thousand réis. He was also a partner of the Hungarian traveler Ladislau Magyar in the fishery business in Lucira to the city's south. In addition, the famed

Angolan poet and slave trader José da Silva Maia Ferreira, who lived in the United States, owed him money. Vianna owned 200 captives who worked in several feitorias and farms (arimos) in regions near Benguela. Even though this human property constituted just 2.5 percent of his overall assets, it was still an important part of his wealth and power.[69]

Two episodes highlight how Vianna's political power and connections hindered Portugal's ability to suppress shipments of enslaved people in Benguela. In 1847, despite solid evidence of slave trading, Vianna successfully pressured a governor of Benguela to release a boat apprehended for engaging in the transatlantic trade of human beings.[70] Vianna's ability to manipulate local authorities illustrates the corruption and complicity that allowed the transatlantic slave trade to thrive in Angola. In 1851, British forces in Lobito seized four of Vianna's slaves, who had already been branded for shipment abroad, when they ran away from Benguela. However, British troops had no legal authority to confiscate enslaved Africans found onshore. As a result, they handed the African runaways over to Benguela authorities, who promptly returned them to Vianna.[71] This episode highlights how Vianna's influence over local authorities undermined efforts to combat the transatlantic slave trade.

Against this backdrop, it is not surprising that Vianna felt sufficiently confident to file a lawsuit seeking financial compensation from the colonial government for the apprehension of the enslaved Africans in Equimina in 1854. In the lawsuit, he sought to persuade a judge named Luiz José Mendes Afonso that the enslaved people found during the raid worked in agricultural activities and were only shackled because they might flee their duties. But his main target was Tabião, the enslaved African who boldly took on the transatlantic trade in human beings: "All this procedure, it is said, resulted from the false tip given to the governor of this district [. . .] by the runaway named Tabião, who had recently been bought in this city by the manager Xavier and had been sold because he was irremediably lazy."[72]

Six years before the Equimina raid, Judge Luiz José Mendes Afonso had been sent from Luanda to Benguela to investigate official collusion with the transatlantic trade in human beings. In his report, he wrote, "It is widely said and confirmed even by slave dealers that the governor of Benguela allowed the continuation of the slave trade."[73] After presiding over the Equimina trial, the judge gained a reputation as an enemy of slave dealers. In 1856, for example, he not only suggested the creation of military outposts along the Angolan coast to end shipments of captives but also advocated a "law to deprive contrabandists of slaves from some legal protections that individuals under judicial investigation enjoyed." In his view, individuals implicated in slave trading should receive the severest punishment short of capital punishment.[74]

During the hearings on the 1854 lawsuit, however, the judge's bias was palpable. He fiercely defended Vianna's interests, arguing that Commander Rodovalho had transgressed Portuguese law by not gathering testimonies from witnesses during the raid. Objects confiscated at the scene, which could have been conclusive evidence of illicit slave trading, were dismissed by him. Moreover, he not only disparaged Tabião's testimony, deeming it unreliable, but also derogated all enslaved Africans. He branded them as "vile and despicable beings" who were inconsistent in their statements and lacked comprehension of the Portuguese language. The blatant prejudice not only reveals how deeply embedded the slave trade was in Benguela society but also stands in stark contrast to the actions of enslaved Africans like Tabião, who risked everything to challenge and expose the very system that sought to diminish and dehumanize them.[75]

Orchella Boom and Slavery

Although we do not have concrete information on how Tabião ended up in the Equimina feitoria, he was a product of a world dramatically shaped by the growth of slavery in Angola. In 1849, an estimated 30,000 Africans were enslaved in the Portuguese colony, which had doubled to approximately 60,000 by 1854, reflecting the increasing restrictions on shipments of enslaved people to the Americas.[76] The number of enslaved people in Luanda and its environs was estimated at around 15,000, while Benguela and its surrounding regions had about 8,000 captives.[77] A sample of about 2,500 Africans shows that captives were drawn from over two hundred localities, both near and far from Benguela city, with seven regions emerging as the largest suppliers of enslaved labor: Bié (9.73%), Bailundo (7.7%), Hambo (5.6%), Galangues (4.3%), Ganguelas (5.8%), and Caconda (3.3%).[78]

The expansion of slavery was the result of two interrelated factors. The first factor was the decreasing number of enslaved individuals being shipped abroad, which led to a significant decrease in the prices of captives. In 1847, the British representative to the Luanda anti-slavery mixed commission observed that "the low price at which an able-bodied negro may now be purchased in this province [is] about one-half what would have been given to him two or three years ago."[79] In the 1850s, Hungarian traveler Ladislau Magyar wrote about the Benguela hinterland, noting that "prices of enslaved people are presently very low. Since shipments have been prevented, prices have fallen by a third."[80] At that time, the prices of enslaved individuals ranged from 25,000 to 45,000 réis, depending on their age and agricultural skills.[81]

Secondly, the decreasing prices of enslaved people facilitated the development of a post-slave trade economy based on commercial agriculture and the extraction of natural resources. This is exemplified by the orchella trade, which experienced significant growth beginning in the 1830s. In 1838, a governor of Angola reported that "a prodigious amount of orchella has been discovered everywhere in this province, which some investors have begun to collect."[82] Unlike the variety of orchella commonly consumed in Europe, Angola urzela was collected from trees "because it contains a stronger and plentiful dying substance."[83] One of these investors was a Portuguese man named José Ribeiro dos Santos, who "had the ambition of proving that fazenda trade could replace the slave trade." Having previously served as a diplomat in Denmark and Germany, Santos invested heavily in this new economy by establishing feitorias along the coast.[84]

In Angola's post-slave trade economy, while ivory, wax, and other products played significant roles, the importance of orchella cannot be overstated. By 1848, this lichen had become the second most valuable export in Luanda, surpassed only by ivory.[85] The scale of the orchella trade was substantial: from 1854 to 1856, more than two thousand tons were exported from Luanda alone, with exports reaching one thousand arrobas (approximately 14,688 kg) in 1859.[86] Benguela's trade was equally impressive, with more than 170 small boats transporting about 11,000 arrobas of orchella weed from Egito in 1858.[87] The economic impact was significant; Luanda's weekly gazette reported that duties on orchella exports accounted for half of the city's export revenues between 1855 and 1861.[88] This burgeoning demand for orchella in Europe led to the proliferation of feitorias (trading posts) along the Angolan coast, even in areas beyond Portuguese control, as noted in a government report.[89]

While it is impossible to provide a comprehensive account of the lives of enslaved workers on feitorias, two key points are evident. Firstly, their lives were characterized by unrelenting hard work, and secondly, they faced a constant threat of violence and death. In 1856, for instance, three enslaved women, Luiza, Luzia, and Joaquina, "who were slaves of Dona Tereza de Jesus Ferreira Torres Viana," fled from Equimina, located south of Benguela, after one of their friends was beaten to death on the orders of Manoel Ferreira Torres.[90] In 1858, the manager of another feitoria was required to pay a ransom to retrieve an enslaved woman who had fled from his property. The cruelty of her experience is evident from the runaway's threat to commit suicide if she were forced to return to her owner, causing the manager—who intended to sell both the woman and her children—to keep her on his ranch.[91]

In terms of Portugal's strategic objectives in Angola, the orchella trade played a vital role in enhancing Angola's maritime trade with Portugal, thereby reversing multi-century trends in the South Atlantic that had made Brazil Angola's primary commercial partner and relegated Portugal to a secondary role. As early as 1830, the governor of Angola noted that "trade relations with the motherland [Portugal] are much reduced."[92] Between 1830 and 1832, only eleven ships arriving in Luanda were from Portugal, whereas over ninety ships were bound from Brazil.[93] These figures resulted not only from economic fluctuations across the Atlantic but also from favorable conditions for commerce with the former Portuguese colony created by the Luanda authority's refusal to comply with metropolitan rules to increase duties on goods imported from Brazil.[94]

This trend remained unchanged in the subsequent decade, frustrating Portugal's efforts to strengthen trade relations with the African colony. In 1836, Portuguese officials noted that "today this kingdom [Angola] has trade relations more active with Brazil, a foreign country," and receives from Brazil "all goods produced in Europe."[95] In 1840, a group of merchants from Porto expressed dissatisfaction with the state of trade exchanges with Angola. They pointed out that, due to a decree passed three years earlier, overseas territories were now considered "national colonies." However, they saw their expectations frustrated after sending six ships to Luanda between 1838 and 1840, as goods from "foreign countries" were freely allowed entry, despite the decree stating that "only those directly shipped from Portugal were to be admitted" there.[96]

By then, however, a discernible shift in Portugal's trade relations with Angola had begun to emerge, partly due to the orchella trade and other products. In 1840, 16 ships sailed to Lisbon and Porto from Angola, with many carrying cargos of orchella. That year, the orchella trade accounted for half of the colonial products re-exported from Lisbon to trading partners elsewhere in Europe.[97] By the early 1850s, according to Portuguese traveler Carlos José Caldeira, direct trade between Angola and Portugal involved some 20–25 ships annually, transporting not only orchella but other products such as wax and ivory, which were similarly in high demand in Europe.[98] By the late 1850s, Portugal's share of Angola's trade relations had grown to about 75%, significantly surpassing other commercial partners.[99]

These figures stemmed partly from Portugal's monopoly over the orchella trade, which required all orchella exports from Angola to be shipped to Lisbon and transported on Portuguese vessels. While this policy contributed to the reorientation of Angola's economy away from Brazil, it hurt the business of local investors in Angola. In response to local pressure, Luanda authorities initially authorized exports of orchella on foreign vessels. However, this decision faced a backlash in Portugal, forcing them to abandon the policy.[100] As a compromise, in 1848, local investors were allowed to export up to 30,000 arrobas on foreign vessels, almost half of the official exports of orchella at the time.[101] Despite this concession, the monopoly largely remained in place. Nearly a decade later, British officials bemoaned how this policy continued to stifle the industry's growth. According to them, this "valuable article, which might otherwise have become a source of considerable industry and trade in this province, cannot be shipped in foreign vessels."[102]

More importantly, the growth of the orchella trade led to a substantial increase in the size of the enslaved population. In 1854, Benguela slaveholders stated that "residents of this district have perhaps more than two thousand slaves" employed in several activities, including the extraction of orchella weed.[103] Around the same time, British national John Monteiro, who spent several years in Angola, reported that he "knew men who had their two or three hundred slaves thus engaged, collecting as much as two to three tons [of orchella] a day."[104] One such man, Muango, "an enslaved African born in Libolo, aged about twenty-five years and unmarried," belonged to a merchant named Miguel Antonio Lino, later implicated in an investigation into illegal slave trading triggered by the actions of enslaved people.[105] As the number of enslaved people in Benguela and its environs grew, so did the frequency of escape attempts, which will be explored in the following section.

Slave Flights

The surge of slavery in Benguela paralleled a marked rise in escape attempts by enslaved individuals, even within the city's heart, where colonial authority was believed to be most formidable. This pattern echoed broader trends across Angola, particularly as endeavors to establish a post-slave trade economy gained momentum. Historian Tracy Lopes, centering her analysis on Luanda, highlights that escaping was the second most frequent reason for the incarceration of enslaved Africans, citing at least 1,622 documented escapees between August 1857 and April 1860.[106] This uptick occurred despite the institution of protocols like curfews to deter escapes.[107] Challenging the prevalent notion that enslaved women, due to their familial connections and roles as caregivers, were less inclined to escape, Lopes demonstrates that a notable number of women also made such attempts.[108]

The trend of enslaved individuals fleeing bondage took place against the backdrop of increased measures to deter escapes. An American sailor visiting Benguela in 1845 noted that enslaved people were "kept chained to deter them from fleeing into the backcountry. With no barriers like St. Paul's, this method was deemed necessary to stop them from escaping."[109] A whipping post initially positioned on the outskirts of Benguela was moved to the city's central square, allowing for public lashings aimed at exerting greater control over the enslaved population.[110] In an attempt to stem the tide of "ongoing losses from slave flight," a local merchant once requested the Luanda government to deploy empacasseiros (African warriors from the Angolan army) to Benguela.[111] Mostly, however, slaveholders took measures to stop flights individually. "All houses with large numbers of enslaved Africans" had shackles installed.[112] As the city still lacked a permanent police force, however, these fell way short of effectiveness.[113]

Flight attempts were said to be particularly acute among enslaved Africans recently brought to the coast. "Blacks who have recently come from the backlands know the way back home, and they will escape as soon as the opportunity presents itself to join runaway communities or lands that belong to rulers opposed to the colonial regime."[114] However, the issue was clearly not confined only to new arrivals. As Governor of Angola Adrião Acácio da Silveira Pinto once pointed out, all "blacks had a natural and to some degree excusable" inclination to escape slavery.[115]

FIGURE 3.1. Whipping post in Benguela

To be sure, slave resistance often took varied and covert forms, reflecting enslaved people's attempts to reclaim their humanity within a system of oppression. A case in point was an enslaved woman named Cristina, who used spiritual practices as an act of defiance against her owner. According to the master, "the enslaved woman Cristina not only practiced but also learned black magic." Believing that another enslaved woman had influenced the enslaved, the master searched Cristina's belongings, finding some of his clothes, which the woman allegedly used in her spiritual practices against him. As a punishment, he imprisoned her in shackles, constraining her agency and movement. In response to this oppression and perhaps as a final assertion of her autonomy, Cristina chose to take her own life.[116]

Fleeing was, however, commonly the preferred method of escaping bondage in Benguela and its neighboring areas. Enslaved individuals often ran away to their nearby native communities, taking advantage of their proximity. In 1854, a judge recognized the challenge this presented, remarking, "It is more difficult to hold and subject to heavy work slaves from these possessions as they are close to their homeland, where they were born and to where they escape continually."[117] Historian Raquel Gomes's research reveals that approximately 60% of escapees from Luanda and nearby regions originated from areas close to the coast.[118] This connection between geography and slave flight led to a proposal to import enslaved labor from Mozambique, on the assumption that a lack of familiarity with Angola's terrain would deter escape attempts.[119] Although this plan was not executed, the underlying logic might have influenced a Benguela merchant to transport 110 captives to Luanda in exchange for enslaved workers from more distant regions.[120]

Yet several other factors shaped slave flights, not least of which were Benguela's trading relationships with its hinterland. Every day, many African traders streamed into the city to sell from surrounding or distant places, forming ties with enslaved Africans that could facilitate escapes. For instance, in 1848, a Benguela merchant promised retaliation after free traders from Kilengues helped sixteen of his slaves flee.[121] In 1855, two enslaved men were apprehended just outside Benguela while trying to reach the colony's interior. Their owner was Bento Pacheco dos Santos, a prominent slave trader from Brazil who had a significant presence in Benguela, owning 124 enslaved people at that time.[122] More importantly, the runaways had received aid in their escape attempt from Saquipindi, an African trader who had traveled to Benguela to trade wax.[123]

Cases of this nature became so prevalent that authorities came to conclude that African traders played a role in abetting slave flights. In their assessment, the situation was an unintended consequence of increasingly successful efforts to curb shipments of enslaved Africans abroad. By assisting enslaved Africans in their escapes, African traders would have forced Benguela merchants to procure new captives as replacements for the escapees. This tactic was perceived as a means for these traders to offset debts accrued with Benguela's merchants by furnishing them with fresh captives.[124] This dynamic was not unique to Benguela; a similar situation transpired in Luanda. In 1852, Ambaquista traders also faced accusations of aiding runaways, ostensibly to diminish Luanda's enslaved population, thus boosting their leverage in selling captives to the city's inhabitants.[125]

However, the roots of slave flights were evidently more complex and multifaceted than officials could grasp. Personal and romantic relationships could play into the decision to run away. In one instance, it appears that Marcelina and Antonio had just become a couple when they made a failed attempt to run away together.[126] In another example, Rosa was arrested with two female enslaved friends on the accusation of plotting to run away after paying an extended visit to her Cabinda lover, José Mocambo, in Benguela. Mocambo stated that "Rosa had been his lover for a long time and [had visited his house] with the consent of her mistress," who had received money to allow them to have a relationship. However, according to the accusation, Rosa and her friends had planned to escape to Celes sertões with Mocambo and his friends.[127]

Enslaved Africans seeking to escape bondage on the coast faced numerous challenges, one of which was the presence of slave catchers, some of whom were themselves enslaved people. An overseer of a trading post once reported that three runaways were returned to him in just two days, all by enslaved or free Africans.[128] In 1826, two Africans petitioned Francisco Pedro to pay them for their work in capturing enslaved people who had fled from him.[129] In another instance, a group of captives belonging to Ana Joaquina arrested an enslaved African who was owned by a black man from Ambaca, likely due to suspicions that the man was a runaway.[130] There were, however, instances when the catching was undertaken by members of the colonial army, habitually in exchange for bounties.[131]

In their efforts to escape bondage, the enslaved were also influenced by their cultural background. Among the cultural practices that played a role was a system known as chimbika or tombika, which existed in their original communities. This elaborate social convention allowed enslaved individuals to seek a change of masters. It involved the enslaved person going to the residence of a headman—usually, someone wealthy and influential, whom they had previously selected—and there, in the presence of witnesses, performing a ritual that typically involved the sacrifice of a dog, goat, sheep, or another domestic animal. Others would rip a cloth belonging to their desired owners and then offer themselves as enslaved people to compensate for the damage.[132] The Portuguese traveler Silva Porto, who traveled extensively across the Benguela highlands, noted that *tumbicamento* was a widespread social practice. To change masters, enslaved Africans and individuals held under pawnship (*penhor*) would "affront" their new master by ripping his cloth and thus becoming his "slave."[133]

The death of slave owners was yet another factor that contributed to flights, as enslaved people feared the loss of customary rights secured under current masters. Governor of Angola José Rodrigues do Amaral recognized this issue, observing that "when slaveholders die, slaves become anxious about their future, fearing that their new owners will mistreat them and curtail their customary 'rights.'"[134] This pattern is evident in several incidents across Angola. In 1856, officials reported that the slaves of Manoel Jose da Costa, a military captain who had recently died in Pungo Andongo, caused significant damage to his estate, and many escaped due to fear of being sold.[135] In 1859, twenty-five of Victoriano de Faria's slaves, a merchant who had recently died, "came from the bush armed and demanded their letters of freedom, which their owner had promised them when he was alive."[136] In 1866, over four hundred enslaved individuals fled from a coffee farm owned by the largest coffee producer in Cazengo, and an observer noted that cases of captives who escaped after the death of their owners had "already happened hundreds of times."[137]

Against this backdrop, officials would implement a series of measures to curb enslaved people's unrest when their owners died. When the number of enslaved people was small, police forces would hold them until they accepted their new owners.[138] New slaveholders would keep newly acquired captives under close supervision until they became "accustomed" to their new circumstances.[139] However, as officials were quick to admit, such measures were not as effective when the number of enslaved people was large or government forces were unavailable to subdue them. According to Governor of Angola José Rodrigues do Amaral, "they know this [the balance of force that favored them against owners] because, no matter how much someone wants it, it is not possible to lower them entirely to the level of brutes."[140]

What is also important to highlight is that the impact of slave flights extended beyond the loss of workforce. As runaways formed or joined quilombos (runaway communities), they disrupted the commercial networks between Benguela, Luanda, and their hinterlands.[141] Governor of Angola Adrião Acácio Pinto once declared that "the incessant attacks that they conducted on the roads near their Quilombos were a serious matter and should no longer be tolerated."[142] In response, the government launched attacks that resulted in the capture of numerous escapees.[143] To prevent the constant escape of captives, authorities considered establishing fortifications around the city and made it mandatory for enslaved Africans to carry a pass if out after 10 p.m.[144] Nevertheless, some runaways returned to Luanda to persuade others to join quilombos.[145]

Near Benguela, Dombe Grande emerged as a particularly welcoming region for enslaved people seeking escape from bondage. Its relative remoteness from colonial authority enabled the formation of quilombos that provided refuge for runaways. As these communities grew, they increasingly disrupted trade flows between Dombe Grande and Benguela.[146] Trade caravans were subject to frequent attacks along roads near quilombos, seriously obstructing commerce between the two regions. Thus, through both their acts of flight and subsequent raids, enslaved individuals in Dombe Grande undermined Benguela's economic networks tied to the coast and hinterland.

Given these circumstances, slave flights posed a formidable obstacle to the viability of Angola's nascent post-slave trade economy. Governors José Rodrigues do Amaral and Sebastião Lopes de Calheiros e Menezes expressed their concerns about the impact of these escapes. Do Amaral went on record to claim that African laborers were unreliable because "they run away," further noting that "it is well-known that farmers and other investors cannot rely on local black labor."[147] Others stated that it was surprising that commercial agriculture had developed at all.[148] Similarly, Governor Calheiros e Menezes voiced pessimism about Angola's commercial agriculture ever reaching the productivity levels of other regions. In his view, it would "never be as productive as in São Tomé, Havana, Brazil or the United States because blacks can easily escape," implying that the ease with which enslaved people could flee made the establishment of a reliable workforce nearly impossible.[149]

Nowhere, however, was the situation direr than in orchella stations, which were particularly vulnerable to slave flights due to their remote coastal locations. In one such instance, a factory agent wrote a letter stating that "eleven of the best [enslaved Africans] escaped" during just the second trip to collect orchella.[150] He further reported that "of the newly bought slaves whom I had brought [here], nine are missing," not to mention the "old" enslaved people, 42 of whom had run away.[151] The overseer noted that the impact of slave flight was twofold. Firstly, the loss of labor lowered the extraction of the lichen. Secondly, runaways often took food supplies and equipment with them. "Young enslaved Africans [moleques] steal all they can when they run away."[152]

The lack of supervision of enslaved workers in orchella stations was a significant factor contributing to slave flights. Many enslaved workers, given the nature of their duties, often operated with minimal supervision or were entirely unsupervised. Some would return to their bases bi-daily, while others might be away for as long as six days, journeying considerable distances from the feitorias to gather orchella weed. Multiple examples underscore this reality. In 1850, a government commission identified over two hundred enslaved individuals gathering orchella south of Benguela, largely unsupervised, though they belonged to the city's residents.[153] Similarly, in 1860, four enslaved people, after facing an assault by Ndombe warriors, revealed they had been on their own, collecting urzela.[154] A property manager once mentioned his inability to track enslaved workers tied to a recently deceased owner, as they were out "collecting orchella."[155]

Without question, the pivotal role of orchella factories within the slave trade ecosystem was the most significant factor influencing enslaved individuals' decisions to flee. The factory owners relied heavily on enslaved labor for orchella production, which gave the enslaved workers a degree of leverage. However, this precarious balance of power was constantly threatened by the owners' temptation to sell enslaved Africans to American-bound ships sailing along the Benguela coast. Eager to profit, owners were frequently swayed by the lucrative deals and immediate cash payments offered by agents from these vessels who would sometimes come ashore. When enslaved laborers disappeared, they were reported as having escaped by the owners to reconcile their accounts.[156] This participation in the slave trade not only depleted the orchella industry's labor force but also created a climate of fear and instability among enslaved workers.

The slave trade's disruption of the orchella industry had far-reaching consequences for Angola's emerging post-slave trade economy, a fact that did not go unnoticed by proponents of economic change. By 1854, officials had noted that shipments of enslaved Africans from orchella factories were stalling economic activities, with "Portuguese ships being docked in Benguela for months without completing their cargoes."[157] According to Governor of Angola José Rodrigues Coelho do Amaral, "the factories that they had along the coast for harvesting lichen—the cornerstone of Benguela's economy at the time—and other lawful purposes were depopulated."[158] This depopulation resulted in a shortage of orchella, a product used to pay a large part of the business costs to the Lisbon ships. Consequently, factory owners failed to fulfill their commitments to these ships and lost credit, preventing them from obtaining goods on credit to barter with the interior regions.[159] The decline in orchella export volumes from 1,022 tons in 1854 to 743 tons three years later—a thirty percent drop—quantifiably illustrated the economic toll for the Portuguese.[160]

For the enslaved, however, the consequences were of an entirely different magnitude. The slave trade endangered their very lives, severing family and community ties. The fear clearly extended beyond those directly affected; free Africans, including fishers, often forsook their trades, fearing capture by slavers. One account captures this terror: "The Moroca blacks are more active and generally the healthiest on the coast south of Benguela. Many practice hunting, and some practice fishing. However, they are very fearful of the latter after a Spanish ship lured them onboard with gifts and then set sail (once they had enough) to sell in Havana or another port."[161] Yet it was no doubt the enslaved people laboring on feitorias, situated at the volatile nexus of the illicit slave trade, who were most at risk of being shipped abroad.

To be sure, the link between the slave trade and slave flights was not exclusive to orchella factories. As early as 1839, Portuguese officials remarked that "slave ownership was precarious because many slaves believed they were destined for Brazil, prompting them to flee and causing significant losses for their owners repeatedly."[162] In 1853, "50 slaves who belonged to Manoel da Costa Souza had been sent to the environs of Dombe Grande to be shipped [but] . . . they became suspicious about their fate and fled."[163] Nor was this connection unique to Angola. In Whydah, one of West Africa's most significant slave ports, British officials observed a marked increase in enslaved person escapes linked to a revival of the slave trade. They especially noted this trend among domestic slaves who spoke Portuguese: "They all state as the cause of their desertion the dread of being sold to Spanish slave dealers and carried away from the country."[164]

Portuguese officials were acutely aware of the high stakes in the Benguela region, the heart of the orchella trade, prompting a series of measures to protect the developing economy. As early as 1850, they mandated that orchella factory owners register their enslaved workers, in a bid to maintain control over the labor force.[165] Officials also took action when a shipment occurred near Dombe Grande, with a local official facing sanctions for negligence.[166] To prevent escapes, forces even escorted captives to coastal establishments and enhanced naval patrols after 1855.[167] Still, these measures did little to stem the tide of slave flights and growing unrest among the enslaved, with officials reporting that "after a shipment, slaves had fled feitorias."[168]

The depth of enslaved people's opposition to the slave trade is vividly illustrated by a rebellion near Mossamedes in 1860, which underscores that they could by then not only engage in individual escapes but also mobilize through more extensive unrest. Thirty-three enslaved workers escaped from a sugar and orchella farm to join an existing runaway community called Munda Evambo. Upon returning to the farm, rebels tried to murder owner Manoel de Paula Barboza. Although Barboza managed to escape, the farm's overseer was not as fortunate, falling victim to brutal torture, decapitation, and subsequent burning. The rebels went on to liberate over 60 fellow captives and set the farm on fire before returning to Munda Evambo. Rumors soon spread that they planned to attack other feitorias and farms.[169]

The catalyst for the revolt was enslaved people either witnessing or being told about the recent sale of two hundred captives by a Brazilian named Manoel José Correa. Having previously invested in the trade in enslaved Africans in Benguela, Correa had shifted his focus to commercial agriculture. His cotton, tobacco, and sugar investments earned him praise from the Angolan government. However, he was eventually drawn back into the Atlantic trade, even visiting a slave vessel that had recently arrived from Cuba and then inviting slave dealers to his property. His actions soon became known to enslaved workers. "The slaves of the neighboring feitorias saw shipments of captives that Manoel José Correia organized with a Spanish ship," leading to "large-scale escapes of captives from several nearby coastal factories."[170]

What distinguished this revolt was not merely its size but also the surprising stance of some orchella and fishing factory owners who denounced the efforts to reintroduce large-scale shipments of captives as the cause of the movement. In a petition to the Benguela government, they affirmed that "the slave trade has ceased completely" and had been replaced with several types of commercial activities, including orchella extraction, which "has produced great wealth." Intermittent efforts to transport captives overseas remained a source of concern, however, as they instilled fear among the enslaved workers, making them believe that "the slave trade had resumed and that they would soon be victimized by it."[171] According to the owners, many enslaved individuals were determined to "escape because they thought and even said that they did not doubt that after many and long years of work, they would be shipped abroad."[172]

O Processo da Escravatura

Undoubtedly, the most significant outcome of Tabião's actions was Portugal's groundbreaking decision to award freedom to enslaved people who, like him, reported impending shipments of enslaved Africans. This measure was formalized through an executive order issued by the Portuguese government to the Governor of Angola on June 14, 1855. According to the order, "that slave who shall denounce anyone as possessing slaves in irons, or any ready for embarkation (such being a true statement) shall be immediately redeemed at the cost of the state, in conformity with the decree of the 14th of December of 1854."[173] Though it did not specifically mention Tabião, the order referenced his action, endorsing the decision already taken in Angola to liberate him. The British pointed out that the order catered "especially for the case of the slave [Tabião] who gave information of the intended embarkation at Equimina."[174]

This landmark decree was pioneering in acknowledging and institutionalizing enslaved Africans' role in anti-slave trade initiatives. Enslaved people who reported slave trade activities were to become libertos, attaining freedom after a specified period of apprenticeship, following stipulations laid out in a decree issued on December 14, 1854. While reflecting Portugal's intentions to phase out slavery in Angola, this decree would later be manipulated, laying the groundwork for the rise of forced labor in Angola, as will be further discussed in Chapter 7. However, many former enslaved people leveraged their "liberto" status to claim rights that were not accessible to those still enslaved.

By transforming potential victims into active agents of abolition, the measure indicated evolving perceptions of the slave trade in Benguela. At that time, the government aimed to develop a post-slavery economy centered around extractive activities and commercial agriculture. This vision heavily depended on the labor of enslaved Africans who were at risk of deportation. Thus, a resurgence in large-scale deportations posed a considerable threat to this emerging economy. In this context, the Portuguese recognized Tabião's actions as a potential deterrent against the slave trade and aimed to incentivize similar actions by creating a legal framework that rewarded enslaved individuals who opposed the trade.

The decision must also be seen from the viewpoint of Portugal's complex ties with Britain, which was then pushing for the end of the slave trade in West Central Africa. While lauding the Portuguese initiative, the British framed it through an economic lens. "The partial revival of the slave traffic, which we now witness, by again depriving the province of manual labor, still more retards their development."[175] They also contextualized the law within the larger framework of the anti-slave trade campaign in West Central Africa. Although they anticipated "complaints" from slaveholders fearful that the policy might "foster a vindictive spirit among the slaves," they firmly believed it would "prove, no doubt, very instrumental in attaining the object it has in view."[176]

A case that unfolded in Luanda casts doubt on how consistently and broadly the Portuguese government was willing to enforce the policy. In 1860, two enslaved Africans went to officials after escaping from a vessel about to depart Luanda with enslaved people on board. According to the Africans, "they had crept in the night from the brigantine's [*Equimina's*], got into the boat lying astern, let go the rope, and allowed her to drift with the tide, hoping it might carry them on shore."[177] Their escape and subsequent report implicated the ship in the slave trade. The two Africans "informed [officials] that there were more blacks" on the slave ship, leading to a search of the *Equimina* that found "twelve blacks, of whom several were minors, who were taken to the Portuguese warship." The latter then told sailors from a Portuguese warship that they "were slaves and that the *Equimina* had already transported slaves to the north" of Angola.[178]

This intelligence was met with suspicion by Luanda officials, likely because the city had long lost its status as a major site of shipments of captives. Portuguese officials said they "did not believe immediately in the declarations provided by the Africans and were still skeptical about their veracity." The case was eventually turned to a Luanda tribunal set up to judge slave ships apprehended by the Portuguese navy [*tribunal de presas*].[179] Following their testimonies, a trial eventually ensued. The Africans denied the ship owners' allegations that they were simply crewmembers of the vessel, noting instead that they had been "embarked from several points along a beach in [Luanda] at different hours, some at night and other[s] after eating [dinner], some on the same day they had been bought and others a few days later." Due to these testimonies, Luanda judges deemed the vessel a *boa presa, a* ship seized legally for its involvement in illegal slaving.[180] Yet, unlike Tabião, the enslaved Africans were not "liberated" as a result of their actions.

In Benguela, however, evidence suggests that the new policy of granting freedom to enslaved individuals who reported impending shipments may have indeed encouraged such reporting. A case in point was an enslaved man named Joaquim Inocêncio, who, like Tabião, escaped from a feitoria in Equimina. His owner was a known slave dealer from Benguela named Manoel de Paula Barboza. The runaway informed officials that the feitoria contained "a great number of enslaved people who belonged to several individuals [of this city]" and that "he was convinced that his fate was to be shipped abroad along with his fellow Africans."[181] Inocêncio added, "The people designated for such purposes are hidden in the interior, not far from Equimina, and he could indicate the location where they were and even the names of their owners."[182] His actions exemplified the policy's potential to disrupt slave trade operations.

Inocêncio's case occurred as the legal framework continued to evolve, expanding its scope. The initial executive order had stipulated that any enslaved person who identified individuals in chains or prepared for shipment would be "redeemed at the cost of the state." However, subsequent adjustments sought to strengthen the policy's impact. First, owners of slaves found in chains were no longer financially compensated by the state. More importantly, the policy now redeemed any enslaved individual offering information about "any other slaves being placed in irons on any point of the coast . . . on such information being verified."[183] This broadened approach meant that the policy addressed any scenario where enslaved Africans were restrained, not solely during captive shipments.[184] These changes potentially amplified the policy's effectiveness in encouraging reporting and disrupting slave trade activities.

This policy might well have inspired actions taken by two enslaved Africans—Egídio Sebastião and Antonio Joaquim—who helped officials track down Luiz Antonio de Souza Monteiro, a slave dealer accused of participating in the voyage of the *Pierre Soulé*, a ship that took 479 slaves to Cuba in 1855.[185] A well-known slave dealer, Souza Monteiro had once traveled to Cuba on the first slave voyage seeking to reopen the Benguela slave trade in 1853.[186] Although officials initially overlooked his early engagements in the trade, they pursued him diligently two years later, when his participation in the *Pierre*

Soulé incident came to light. Monteiro was not only responsible for managing the feitoria in Lucira, where the captives were dispatched from, but he also owned or had a stake in the ownership of 84 of those enslaved on that ship. The remaining 47 were the property of various other individuals on board.[187]

To fully appreciate the significance of Sebastião and Joaquim's actions, it is crucial to examine the broader context of the *Pierre Soulé* voyage and its place within the patterns of slave trade in Benguela. This voyage, like other attempts to rekindle the slave trade in the region, relied extensively on the involvement of Cuban slave traders. Upon arriving in Cuba, the captives were handed over to Mazorra, Martin Riera, and Nicolau Veldevez.[188] Prior to this, however, they were disembarked in sugar mills equipped to receive newly arrived enslaved Africans from abroad.[189] Another similarity was the reliance on New York City to route funds to Angola. A ship named *Flying Eagle* set sail from this city laden with the proceeds from the sale of the enslaved people in Cuba: 432 British gold coins, or sovereigns, which was widely used by slave dealers in Benguela and ports of north Luanda. According to British traveler John Monteiro, sovereigns "can be readily obtained at moderate rates from the [slave] traders."[190]

By the time the *Flying Eagle* arrived in Benguela, local officials, forewarned by their Luanda counterparts, were already on high alert, swiftly launching a raid that led to the capture of the vessel and the arrest of 41 individuals. Among those detained was Ignacio Teixeira Xavier, a resident of Benguela and owner of the aforementioned Equimina feitoria. At least five of those detained were not from Angola.[191] Despite the fact that many eventually managed to slip through the authorities' grasp, British officials lauded the operation as a significant setback for the slave trade, expressing hope that "the blow now struck will, it may be hoped, prove effective in deterring any further attempt of the same kind."[192]

Yet Monteiro, a pivotal player in the *Pierre Soulé's* voyage, managed to dodge arrest, seeking refuge in an associate's home in Benguela. The prospect of his capture was uncertain, more so given that several of his associates had successfully evaded justice in the past. It was at this critical juncture that Egídio Sebastião and Antonio Joaquim played a crucial role. Their actions not only led to Monteiro's capture but also had broader implications for the struggle against the slave trade in Benguela. Specifically, they provided officials with vital information about Monteiro's whereabouts. Relying on this intelligence from "one of his own slaves," authorities located Monteiro, finding him "hidden in his residence."[193] The involvement of Sebastião and Joaquim in this high-profile case underscored the potential impact of enslaved individuals in disrupting slave trade operations, a factor that Portuguese authorities had begun to recognize and leverage in their anti-slave trade efforts.

By revealing their owner's whereabouts, Sebastião and Joaquim's actions had far-reaching consequences, becoming central to the so-called "*processo da escravatura*"—an extensive investigation of the Lucira shipment that dealt a significant blow to Benguela's slave networks. This probe, facilitated by the information Sebastião and Joaquim provided, exposed the intricate and often problematic relationships between slave dealers and government officials. For instance, Governor José Rodrigues Coelho do Amaral argued that Ignacio Teixeira Xavier seemed to have renounced the slave trade and had even alerted British cruisers of shipments of captives.[194] This stance laid bare how some officials were still willing to overlook transgressions in the interest of economic development in Benguela. According to Vicente Barruncho, who had just been appointed interim governor of Benguela, Xavier "deserved protection and indulgence despite past mistakes."[195]

The official tolerance of the slave trade persisted even as legal proceedings unfolded. Governor of Angola José Rodrigues Coelho do Amaral, while urging exoneration for those who had been indicted on the basis of "merely flimsy or compromised evidence," noted that three defendants faced "public opprobrium and constraints."[196] This stance revealed the ongoing official support for individuals brought to trial, which became even more apparent when Governor Amaral unabashedly called for an end to the so-called Benguela slave trade trial [*processo da escravatura*], stating: "I do not see how to end the decay of Benguela but by closing down the infamous lawsuit, which had implicated almost all the wealthy residents" of Benguela.[197]

Despite local officials' efforts to protect slave traders, the investigation aided by Sebastião and Joaquim's actions eventually succeeded in undermining the slave trade in Benguela, largely due to pressures from Portuguese authorities in Lisbon. For these authorities, the judicial procedure provided a unique opportunity to demonstrate commitment to eradicating shipments of captives from Angola. They even went so far as to overturn a judge's ruling in favor of the slave traders, overriding local attempts at leniency.[198] These efforts bore fruit, transforming the landscape that figures like Monteiro had once dominated. In 1858, a US naval commander received news in Benguela that the "trade in slaves had not been carried on from that vicinity for several years past."[199] By 1860, while reporting on shipments of captives in the south of Angola, a British diplomat observed that "the traffic [of enslaved Africans] in that direction has for the present fallen into decay and is rapidly being supplanted by legitimate commerce."[200]

Yet, instead of being rewarded with freedom for their courage, as mandated by law, Sebastião and Joaquim paid the harsh price that many Africans paid for their actions against the slave trade. Their owner, convinced of their role in his arrest, ensured they were punished for their involvement. Despite orders from Luanda authorities to place them under the custody of the Board for the Protection of Slaves and Freedmen, a newly established government agency, a Benguela judge disregarded these instructions, instead assigning them to Joaquim Luiz Bastos, who had direct ties to the *Flying Eagle* trip.[201] This decision underscored the persistent local resistance to anti-slave trade efforts. Tragically, before their transfer to Luanda, Sebastião and Joaquim endured torture by Bastos as retribution for their actions.[202] Their case underscores both the potential impact of enslaved resistance and the formidable challenges faced by those who dared to challenge the slave trade system from within.

Conclusion

In 1889, a Portuguese narrative of abolition, self-laudatory in nature, listed the Equimina raid as a testament to Portugal's commitment to eradicating the transatlantic slave trade and slavery.[203] This narrative was strategically crafted to bolster Portugal's international standing in the face of mounting criticism over the continued prevalence of slavery in its African colonies. Portugal sought to equate its abolitionist efforts with those of the British, despite the latter's complicated relationship with the cause. Notably absent from this account was Tabião's pivotal role in the Equimina raid, as well as the contributions of other enslaved Africans who helped dismantle the networks of Benguela's slave trade. In contrast, a counternarrative centered on bottom-up forces, as presented in this chapter, underscores the necessity of incorporating marginalized voices and experiences to construct a more complex (and ethical) narrative of abolition. Without such perspectives, we risk perpetuating views rooted in colonial erasures.

In Benguela, efforts to end the slave trade, as narrated through the lives of enslaved Africans like Tabião, Egídio Sebastião, and Antonio Joaquim, reveal a side of abolition often left in the shadows of dominant narratives. Tabião's act of defiance, by his escaping from his captors and alerting authorities of an impending shipment of enslaved people, prevented the sale of almost two hundred people across the Atlantic while also inspiring a groundbreaking decree that granted freedom to enslaved people who reported cases of impending shipments of slaves. This legislation formally recognized and rewarded enslaved Africans' pivotal contributions to the anti-slavery cause by granting them freedom for reporting future illicit slave shipments. This significant shift effectively transformed potential victims into instrumental agents of abolition, highlighting their active roles against the very system that sought to destroy their humanity.

The experiences of enslaved Africans like Tabião reveal the complex calculus behind acts of resistance against the slave trade. Their motivations ranged from the deeply personal, such as preserving familial bonds, to the political, such as undermining the slave trade's operations. Acts of resistance involved careful assessment of risks, costs, and potential rewards. For some, like Tabião, reporting slave trading activities to colonial authorities resulted in freedom — a precedent that would later be formalized into law. For others, escape and open rebellion enabled autonomy, even if temporarily. Their decisions reflected not just boldness but also sophistication in leveraging circumstances toward liberation.

Yet the intertwined complexities of politics, economics, and individual courage presented a landscape riddled with contradictions and challenges. As Egídio Sebastião's and Antonio Joaquim's tales unfold, they shed light on the inherent dangers and sacrifices these individuals faced. Their information led to significant disruptions in the slave trade networks, yet they endured torture and betrayal as a price for their actions. Still, their example shows that resistance was not solely led by foreign pressures or government mandates but was also propelled by enslaved Africans themselves, directly challenging and undermining the brutal machinery of the transatlantic slave trade.

This story, set against the backdrop of the burgeoning post-slave trade economy, underscores the inherent entanglement of economic transformation with the oppressive structures of the slave trade. As Portugal began to perceive the shipments of captives as a threat to the nascent licit economy, focused on natural extraction products, including orchella weed, enslaved Africans like Tabião seized the opportunity to disrupt the slave trade networks. For the Portuguese, what was at stake was the viability of a new economy that hinged on the enslavement of Africans. For people like Tabião, however, the struggle transcended economics—it was a fight for Africans' very existence, for the preservation of their families, communities, and the fundamental right to be human in a world that sought to commodify them.

CHAPTER FOUR

Interlocking Networks

IN 1854, Augusto Garrido, a high-profile slave dealer in Luanda, returned from a trip to New York City proudly claiming newfound protection against anti-slavery laws in Africa: American citizenship. Although Luanda was no longer a hub for the transatlantic slave trade, it maintained a significant role in illegal commerce due to its connections with various slave-loading points along the northern coast, as well as its strategic alliances with cities across the Atlantic. Despite spending just over a year in the United States and still needing permanent documentation, Garrido boldly leveraged his new status to bypass anti-slave trade laws in Angola. According to Governor of Angola José Rodrigues Coelho do Amaral, "Garrido has returned from New York calling himself an American citizen and furnished with some document from the authorities of that state prior to his becoming so."[1]

This chapter uses Garrido's trip as a springboard to delve into the intricate interplay between anti-slave trade efforts and the operation of the transatlantic slave trade in its twilight years. The chapter seeks to gain new purchase into the history of abolition by examining Brazil, Cuba, the United States, and West Central Africa within the same analytical framework. When it comes to the transatlantic slave trade or abolition, any single national history—whether Brazilian, Angolan, Portuguese, Spanish, or any other—will only tell part of the story. By exploring interconnections between these regions and their roles in the abolition of the transatlantic slave trade, the chapter sheds light on the complex dynamics of abolition in different settings, revealing how efforts to end the slave trade unfolded across multiple geographies and societies.

Garrido's newly acquired citizenship proved advantageous during a trip to Ambriz, a hub of the illegal slave trade just eight miles north of Luanda, in 1858.[2] However, once his involvement in the illegal trade came to an end, he promptly disavowed it. As a member of Luanda's Associação Comercial, he tried to distance himself from his previous life. He admitted to traveling to the US once but claimed that "he had never been naturalized as an American citizen" as "this would have required many years of residence in the country." Instead, he asserted that he had "always considered himself a Portuguese subject because I was born in Lisbon and am a son of Portuguese parents." He then vaguely referred to "special circumstances at the time that were well known by authorities in this city [Luanda]" when asked about the reason for his trip to the United States.[3]

While Garrido downplayed the significance of his U.S. citizenship in his slave trading activities, the examples of other slave dealers show that this strategy was not uncommon. A case in point was Joaquim Pamplona, who reportedly traveled to "the United States for the purpose, it is said, of residing there a sufficient period to enable him to claim naturalization papers, and then return here."[4] The strategy had a noticeable impact on the implementation of anti-slave trade policies in Angola. As Governor Amaral noted, "Being those merchants' citizens of the United States by adoption, there is little or nothing that the government of her [British] majesty can do to derail the speculations in which they are, with reason, presumed to be involved."[5]

Exploiting the US government's deep-seated animosity toward Great Britain's global anti-slavery campaign, Garrido's strategy must be understood within the wider context of the unprecedented global repression of the transatlantic slave trade in the mid-nineteenth century. As abolition efforts intensified and anti-slave trade laws were enforced more stringently, slave traders like Garrido were forced to adapt, finding new ways to evade detection and continue their illicit activities. Within this framework, the strategic acquisition of US citizenship served the purpose of sidestepping anti-slave trade enforcement, effectively granting slave dealers a shield of immunity from international anti-slavery statutes.

Yet Garrido's acquisition of U.S. citizenship was not merely a tactic to evade anti-slave trade laws in Angola; it was also a reflection of his deep involvement in the global networks that sustained the illegal trade. His first destination was New York City, then a booming hub of global capitalism. From there, he also went to England, stopping in London and Manchester, where he toured textile factories and financial institutions, engaging in business transactions that tied back to the slave trade. He then returned to New York. For officials then seeking to track Garrido's movements, the question was whether he would travel to Cuba, the destination of most vessels crossing from Africa into the Americas at the time. "Senhor Garrido seems to have been very actively employed, passing to and from the United States to England, if not to Havana."[6] Garrido's travels, in other words, were emblematic of the intricate financial, industrial, and logistical ties that linked the slave trade to the burgeoning networks of global capitalism.

Garrido's extensive travels challenge prevailing perceptions of West Central Africa's role in the nineteenth-century global economic order. Scholars have recently built upon Eric Williams's pioneering research to demonstrate how deeply connected slavery and capitalism were.[7] Yet the dominant narrative still tends to overlook the African ramifications of the happy marriage between capitalist and slave trading networks.[8] By contrast, Garrido's story offers an illustrative counterpoint that shows an African continent closely tethered to economic and logistical chains powering the trade in enslaved Africans. By tracing his trajectory, the chapter thus provides a deeper, more intricate understanding of the relationships between West Central Africa and circuits of trade and anti-slavery then enveloping the globe.

Garrido's travels also raise questions about the connections between West Central Africa and Cuba, which had become the primary destination for ships carrying enslaved Africans across the Atlantic by the mid-nineteenth century. Historians Nicolau Pares and Manuel Barcia have highlighted the dense ties between Cuba and West Africa's regions like the Bight of Benin, often facilitated through alliances with Brazilian and Portuguese counterparts.[9] Jorge Gonzalez highlights that Cuba's close ties with the Upper Guinea coast were so influential that they catalyzed the rise of the Galinas kingdom.[10] The Spanish island, as Lizbeth Pérez points out, played the role of a shadow colonial power for Spain, manipulating regional dynamics to establish the Galinas area as a strategic point for metropolitan imperial endeavors in Africa.[11] Martín Rodrigo y Alharilla further underscores the presence and activities of Spanish slave trading factories along the African coast, particularly in the Gallinas region, which functioned as an informal Cuban protectorate.[12]

Despite the well-studied connections between Cuba and other regions of Africa, the robust links between the Spanish colony and West Central Africa remain largely neglected in the existing scholarship. This stands in sharp contrast to the importance of regions such as Ambriz, Cabinda, and Molembo to the slave trade to Cuba from the 1840s onward, which cannot be overstated. By the early 1860s, according to British accounts, "nearly the whole of the slaves now landed in Cuba are shipped between the Equator and Ambriz, an extent of about 500 miles of the coast."[13] This development was the result of a combination of factors, including not only successful anti-slave trade efforts curtailing shipments from regions like the Bight of Benin but also the evolution of trade networks toward West Central Africa, which was historically the largest provider of enslaved people to the Americas.

This dynamic was intricately connected to a broader wave of globalization that integrated the slave trade into the fabric of global financial and industrial capitalism. Traders from the United States, France, and Britain became increasingly active in West Central Africa during this period. In the traditional narrative, these networks—particularly those formed by Portuguese and Brazilian traders—were subordinate to the so-called Portuguese firm, a syndicate of slave dealers from Brazil and West Central Africa who assembled in New York City as the slave trade came under attack in the 1850s.[14] Scholars like John Harris describe this as the final triangle of the transatlantic slave trade, linking Africa, the US, and Cuba. Meanwhile, historian Sean Kelley perceives New York as a mere "satellite" of Cuba, suggesting the Portuguese Company had only a marginal impact on Cuba's slave market.[15]

This chapter moves beyond this paradigm by tracing Cuba's direct links with West Central Africa, which were largely facilitated by the Spanish island's long-standing connections with Brazil since the early nineteenth century. It examines how Brazil served as a crucial intermediary in establishing and maintaining Cuba's slave trade networks in regions such as Ambriz, Cabinda, and Molembo, which became increasingly important to the slave trade to Cuba from the 1840s onward. The chapter explores the dynamics between Cuban and Brazilian slave traders, such as their collaboration in navigating the complex political and economic landscape of West Central Africa, and how these relationships evolved over time.

The chapter also sheds light on often-overlooked ground-level political and social ramifications of foreign connections on West Central African societies. By examining how the influx of traders from the United States, France, and Britain and their alliances with local rulers transformed power dynamics and economic structures in African coastal communities, it underscores how these relationships increased dependence on the slave trade for imported goods. This analysis illuminates how global capital reshaped local economies, shifting them toward producing captives for exchange. This approach contributes to a more nuanced understanding of the transatlantic slave trade in its final decades, highlighting the importance of African contexts and perspectives. It reveals how African polities and traders became indispensable agents within networks that operated simultaneously at local, regional, and global levels.

New Partnerships with Cuba

Before the end of the transatlantic trade in enslaved Africans, Garrido had a very successful trading operation in Luanda, acting as the agent of Francisco Ruviroza y Urzellas, a Cuban slave dealer based in Rio de Janeiro. Garrido was considered "one of the merchants and agents of the slave trade who operated on the largest scale and was most well-known in Rio [de Janeiro]."[16] When Brazil halted enslaved African imports in 1850, however, his fortunes took a downturn, leading to his bankruptcy amid a general crisis in Luanda's economy. He came back after being recruited by Brazilian slave dealer Francisco Antonio Flores, with whom he would form a close business relationship lasting nearly a decade. Significantly, it was on Flores's behalf that Garrido traveled to the United States, England, and perhaps Cuba.

Flores's early career in Angola established a remarkably consistent pattern of business operation, as he not only invested in the slave trade but also legitimate activities.[17] While based in Luanda, he soon began investing in Ambriz and Cabinda, establishing ties with African rulers that would later help him play an important role as an architect, diplomat, and financier of Portuguese colonial expansion to Ambriz and Congo, as discussed in Chapter 5. In 1846, he received a passport to travel to Cabinda, being then described as a 29-year-old Brazilian who had been born in Rio Grande [do Sul].[18] In the same year, he was already listed as one of the only twenty-one merchants entitled to "sign and endorse bills" to ship goods through the Luanda customhouse.[19] In 1849, he traveled (with a mixed-race servant) to Ambriz, soon to become a focal point for his business activities.[20]

Garrido's partnership with Flores exemplifies how slave dealers adapted to the end of the Brazilian slave trade by reorienting shipments of enslaved Africans to Cuba. In early 1851, British diplomats reported that Flores had departed from Luanda, "entrusting one of his clerks with the task of winding up the business operations there."[21] Flores then traveled to Rio de Janeiro to meet with the city's slave dealers and plan the use of Ambriz as a base for shipping enslaved Africans to the Spanish island.[22] The already mentioned Spanish merchant Francisco Ruviroza y Urzellas, then living in Rio de Janeiro, tasked Flores with relocating to the African territory to lead this new operation. As discussed later in this chapter, Ruviroza y Urzellas had relocated from Havana to Rio de Janeiro about ten years earlier.

Flores's meeting in Rio de Janeiro did not go unnoticed. In 1852, British diplomats reported that "wealthy and enterprising residents at Rio de Janeiro are forming a company with ramifications at Lisbon to carry on the slave trade to Havana on a large scale."[23] The intelligence was soon relayed to officials in Luanda, who promised to prevent the new organization from becoming operational.[24] Yet they later conceded that "measures are now in progress, directed by Flores and other known parties in this city [Luanda], for the shipment of slaves from this part of the coast, connected, probably, with the Cuban and Brazilian association denounced originally by her majesty minister at Rio de Janeiro, and the existence of which has been since confirmed from various sources."[25]

The new company should be contextualized within long-standing collaborative frameworks between Portuguese and Brazilian slave dealers tracing back several decades. As early as the 1790s, as historian Jorge Felipe González notes, Havana commercial houses were already strategically recruiting experienced Portuguese captains familiar with slave voyages to purchase captives in Africa and were forging ties with slave dealers based in Brazil.[26] By the 1820s, as historian Manuel Barcia shows, Cuba-based commercial houses were "sending their own men to the coast to learn the trade and often to act as their exclusive agents."[27]

Some of these individuals would have relied on partnerships with Portuguese and Brazilian slave dealers to establish themselves on the African coast. According to historians María del Carmen Barcia and Luis Nicolau Parés, Havana's commercial firm of Cuesta y Manzanal maintained business relationships with Domingos José Almeida Lima and Antonio Ferreira Coelho, merchants from Salvador, Brazil, who owned a coastal station in Onin, West Africa.[28] This association offers a glimpse into a somewhat overlooked trade of enslaved Africans from Brazil to Cuba between 1809 and 1815, when, as scholars María de los Ángeles Meriño Fuentes and Aisnara Perera Díaz point out, over two thousand enslaved individuals would have been shipped from Bahia, Brazil, to Cuba.[29]

As the slave trade faced increasing legal bans, the intricate ties between Cuba and Brazil's slave dealers deepened, seemingly undeterred by Spanish anti-slave treaties signed in 1817 and 1835.[30] By the 1830s, as scholars Dale Graden, Michel Zeuske, Adriam Camacho Dominguez, and Luis Nicolau Parés note, Havana slave traders had already forged robust connections with counterparts in Brazil.[31] A glimpse of these ties comes from British diplomatic reports from Cuba. "I have reason to believe that the Portuguese are mostly deeply engaged in the traffic [of slaves to Cuba], which is principally carried on the most remote parts of the Island."[32]

The journey of the ship named Eagle, which was apprehended off the Lagos coast in 1838, illustrates the intricate nature of these trade networks. Setting sail from Havana, its intended destination was Whydah, but it eventually made port in Salvador. From there, it journeyed back to Cuba, its hold filled with enslaved Africans. Departing Havana, the Eagle headed to Lagos to acquire another group of captives, readying for its transatlantic voyage. Instead of making a beeline back to Havana, it returned to Salvador, where it loaded up on tobacco before crossing the ocean again to Lagos. Tellingly, these trips were orchestrated by Joaquim Jose Duarte da Costa, one of Salvador's leading slave dealers and a former resident of Havana, and Don Joaquim Andreo, a Havana merchant operating in Lagos.[33]

Another example of these intricate networks is the career of Spanish trader Juan José Zangroniz Junior. The Whydah representative for his family, a prominent slave-dealing family with ties in Cuba and Spain, Zangroniz Junior was second only to his Brazilian collaborator Francisco Felix de Souza in the Whydah slave trade. Tellingly, he once journeyed to Salvador to engage with local business associates.[34] In another case, André Pinto da Silveira, previously an administrator of a short-lived factory in Onin established by Havana's Cuesta y Manzanal in 1816, would also become a partner of Cuban-based slave dealers.[35] Another significant individual in this network was Joaquim d'Almeida. Originally enslaved and brought to Salvador in the 1810s, Almeida obtained his freedom and subsequently returned to West Africa multiple times to participate in the slave trade. On several occasions, he conducted business there on behalf of Cuban slave dealers, further illustrating the complexity of these networks.[36]

Given this background, the reliance of Cuban-based slave dealers on partnerships with Brazilian and Portuguese counterparts to expand into West Central Africa by the 1840s becomes more comprehensible. Historian

Gustau Nerín's insights shed light on how Spanish factors, following an anti-slave trade treaty Spain signed with Britain in 1835, gradually entrenched themselves in the region, particularly around the mouth of the Congo River and Cabinda. This expansion extended further south as well. Here, the strategic significance of Luanda as the bustling commercial hub of Angola provided fertile ground for the establishment of Spanish trading networks, which, despite ostensibly legal fronts, often facilitated illicit slave trading activities.[37]

Illustrating wider Atlantic networks that fueled this trend is the collaboration between Havana's Pedro Toreado and the Rio de Janeiro-based influential Brazilian slave dealer José Bernardino de Sá.[38] Bernardino de Sá, known for his extensive slave trading infrastructure centered around Rio, extended his operations across the ocean to Ambriz in the 1840s, where he employed agents like Antonio Severino Avellar.[39] At this stage of his career, Avellar was likely serving as a ship captain, marking the beginning of his involvement in the slave trade network. His role would expand significantly in later years, as will be further discussed in this chapter. According to historian Mary Karasch, Toreado and Bernardino de Sá shared the ownership of a vessel at the time, underscoring the depth of these partnerships and their pivotal role in sustaining the transatlantic slave trade.[40]

Of course, Toreado was not the only Cuban-based trader who built connections with Rio de Janeiro slave dealers. Several others did as well. Spanish-born Pedro Martínez owned a ship with Rio's Manoel Pinto da Fonseca, another slave dealer from Rio with extensive African connections, centering mainly on Cabinda.[41] According to British accounts, Pinto da Fonseca owned feitorias in Cabinda, where he kept "goods of the invoice amount of seven hundred contos réis or about 140,000 pounds sterling."[42] Through Fonseca, Martínez once dispatched an agent to Luanda, the capital of Angola. According to British reports, "a Spanish, an agent of the concern, has lately made a hurried and secret visit to this capital [Luanda], the object of which is believed to have been to arrange for the shipment of more than one cargo of slaves to be landed on Spanish ground."[43]

In the case of Garrido, while he appears to have never made it to Cuba, evidence found on the *Newport*, a ship seized by the British in 1854 en route from London to Ambriz, shows his continued involvement in facilitating the slave trade to the Spanish island. According to authorities, the *Newport* would not have sailed from London without Garrido's involvement as "the traveling agent or a partner of Mr. Flores." Garrido had been responsible for purchasing goods loaded on the *Newport*, including "Manchester piece goods" (likely textiles) and "25 cases of muskets." These were sent to Ambriz "via Lisboa, and others by way of New York." Notably, Garrido "acknowledged the receipt of letters from Havana, which he intended to bring to Ambriz when he returned" to Angola.[44]

New York via Ambriz

When Garrido left Luanda for the United States, he was already a cosmopolitan man who spoke French, English, Italian, and German.[45] On the way to New York, he predictably stopped in Ambriz, where his Brazilian boss Francisco Antonio Flores had relocated from Luanda after his rendezvous in Rio de Janeiro. This stopover had immediate consequences; one British observer noted that it led to "various shipments of slaves which were either effected or attempted for the Cuban market."[46] About one year later, Garrido's return to Ambriz from New York City was eagerly awaited by slave dealers. He had become a crucial conduit for news and documents related to the slave trade, including payment of bills, proceeds from selling captives in Brazil and Cuba, and acquiring vessels to transport enslaved Africans.[47]

Situated just eight miles north of Luanda, Ambriz served as a sanctuary for slave dealers seeking to evade tightening anti-slave trade laws in the Angolan capital. As per British reports, "Ambriz, being immediately beyond the Portuguese territory and in close proximity to Luanda, afforded such ample facilities to the slave dealer that it might be considered the slave port of Luanda."[48] The African territory's strong ties with Luanda greatly facilitated slave trade operations due to the availability of resources from the capital of Angola. The British referred to Ambriz as "the place where most of the operations of the slave dealers at Luanda, the capital of Angola, are carried out."[49] Tellingly, the Luanda administration once reported that it was common for individuals to travel to this African port without prior governmental authorization.[50]

Ambriz's trading infrastructure hinged on coastal establishments known as feitorias, which served multifaceted purposes. Beyond being storage centers for imported goods, feitorias doubled as residential quarters and negotiation hubs. Historian Susan Herlin contends that the rise of these coastal outposts was a strategic response to intensifying anti-slave trade patrols along the coast, affording traders a nimbler setup.[51] Yet, as scholar Ana Lucia Araújo underscores, feitorias predated the rise of the anti-slave trade campaign in the nineteenth century. According to Araujo, they symbolized African dominion over the slave trade, distinguishing areas like Malembo, Cabinda, and Ambriz from locales such as Luanda and Benguela, where maritime commerce was predominantly under the sway of Portuguese and Brazilian individuals.[52]

The goods traded with Africans in Ambriz initially came primarily from Rio de Janeiro, but as the slave trade evolved, they increasingly originated from other points of the Atlantic. In 1845, José Bernardino de Sá, one of Rio's most prominent slave traders, had "goods to a considerable amount belonging to that firm that are now deposited in their factories at Ambriz, being generally brought over from the Brazils and landed without any risk from American vessels freighted for that purpose."[53] A year later, the British reported that "that three or four cargos of merchandise had recently been landed at that place from the Brazils and deposited in the slave factories."[54] As the trade network expanded, it began to incorporate sources beyond Brazil. This diversification is vividly illustrated by Hungarian traveler Magyar, who once remarked that goods of "almost incalculable value" were brought to Ambriz from "Brazil and the Antilles (Cuba)."[55]

The provenance of imported goods widened further as traders from various countries flocked to the coast from the 1840s onward. German naturalist Georg Tams visited Ambriz in the 1840s, reporting that American nationals owned three feitorias and Portuguese nationals owned four.[56] This trend had begun even earlier; a notable precursor was the appointment in 1839 of a U.S. national by the Salem-based firm of Farham and Fry as the manager of their factory in Ambriz. This former shipmaster of an American vessel was tasked with facilitating trade exchanges with the local population, procuring ivory and wax in return for imported goods such as "cloths, handkerchiefs, beads, and other trinkets, suited to their wants or tastes."[57] Such developments illustrate the increasingly global nature of commerce in Ambriz, intertwining legitimate trade with the ongoing slave trade operations.

This trend of internationalization continued to accelerate. By 1857, the diversification of foreign control had furthered: of nineteen coastal trading posts (feitorias), only three sourced goods from outside Britain and the United States.[58] As a British naval commander observed: "The exporters [of enslaved people] were Portuguese, but the importers of goods were British, Dutch, and French. They sold goods to the Portuguese, and the Portuguese purchased enslaved people with the goods."[59] Notably, Augusto Garrido, then Flores's representative in Luanda, at one point accepted goods shipped from London on his employer's behalf, which were later disseminated across various parts of the African coast.[60]

This evolving landscape reflected Ambriz's deepening entanglement with global capitalist networks, illustrating how the slave trade became increasingly intertwined with legitimate commerce. An account by British engineer John Monteiro reveals the economic incentives driving this integration: "Traders in Ambriz and further north often received hard cash in Spanish gold, at a profit of two to three hundred percent for the goods of pious Manchester and Liverpool, with which almost every one of the thousands of slaves were bought."[61] This staggering profit margin underscores how the slave trade fueled and was fueled by the expansion of global capitalism.

The presence of American and Liverpool-based trading houses further exemplifies this integration. As Monteiro noted, these firms would sell "for hard cash, Manchester [textiles] and other goods . . . to slave dealers from Cuba and Brazils, with which goods the slaves from the interior were all bought by barter from natives."[62] This complex chain of transactions demonstrates how ostensibly legitimate businesses became complicit in the slave trade, blurring the lines between legal and illegal commerce. It also highlights

FIGURE 4.1. British factories in the Congo River

the global nature of the trade, with goods from industrial centers like Manchester being exchanged for enslaved individuals destined for plantations in Cuba and Brazil.

The social and political ramifications of the growth of foreign trade cannot be overlooked. This transformation of coastal regions into nexuses of global trade networks had profound implications for local power dynamics and economic structures. Searching for efficiency, foreign traders sought to establish direct ties with African rulers who controlled coastal trade networks, which often resulted in complex, interdependent relationships. According to historian Norm Schrag, some local rulers leveraged their position by requiring "annual rent for the ground that the factories stood on" and forcing "foreign traders to hire a large number of local hangers-on."[63] This practice demonstrates how African leaders actively shaped their engagement with the global trade system, often to their economic advantage.

The depth of these relationships is illuminated by an episode from 1840: a Cabinda-based slave dealer instructed a peer in Rio de Janeiro, then planning a trip to Molembo, to go to the house of an African chief named Mambuco Manivaba to ask about his whereabouts.[64] This situation was far from unique. As described by a British commander in the 1850s, slave dealers were "closely connected with the native chiefs, and so entirely at their mercy," paying an amount of goods to trade in African land.[65] These accounts reveal how the slave trade became deeply embedded in local power structures, with African rulers playing crucial roles in facilitating and benefiting from the trade.

These connections between foreign traders and African rulers extended beyond immediate coastal interactions, reaching into the nearby hinterland and reshaping local power structures. The experience of a North American slave ship captain in Cabinda in 1846 exemplifies this trend. After arriving in this major hub of the 1840s slave trade, the captain not only became an employee of José Bernardino de Sá's prominent Rio-based firm but also "visited the interior and saw one of the kings of the Africans in the state."[66] Such direct engagement blurred the lines between maritime commerce and inland politics, with profound implications for African politics, as will be discussed in Chapter 6.

The intermingling between foreigners and local rulers had a profound impact on various aspects of African society, including religious and cultural practices. One striking example is the Khimba initiation cult, which played a crucial role in the power dynamics and trade networks of Mboma society. Mboma chiefs relied on this exclusive cult to assert their authority and control trade routes extending deep into the interior. During lengthy periods of isolation in the forest, young initiates learned sacred knowledge, rituals, and a secret language, all while adhering to complex rules and taboos. Interestingly, Mboma brokers who joined this trading brotherhood would often adopt Khimba names of Portuguese origin, reflecting the growing influence of Luso-Brazilian trade on local customs and identities.[67] This fusion of African and European elements in the Khimba cult underscores the far-reaching social and cultural repercussions of foreign trade in the region, as local practices and beliefs became increasingly intertwined with the dynamics of global commerce.

In this evolving landscape, agents from Havana-based commercial houses carved out a significant, yet often overlooked, role. By building upon existing infrastructure Portuguese and Brazilian slavers established over the preceding decades, Cuban traders entrenched themselves in local settings. A case in point was a Spanish man named Antonio Huerta, who once invested $8,000 worth of goods in a slave voyage together with "the house of Ximenes, Martinez, and Lafitte, a wealthy Havana firm connected both with Paris and London."[68] Yet another example was a man named Antonio Jose Fernandez, who was apparently mostly based in Luanda.[69] Tellingly, both men often stayed at the Luanda house of the Brazilian trader Francisco Antonio Flores, another piece of evidence about close collaborations between "Spaniards" and Brazilians on the African coast.

By the 1840s, Cuban firms' footprint on the African coast had expanded considerably. In Gabon, as historian Samba Mampuya argues, "Spaniards" agents operating on behalf of Havana's commercial houses were active.[70] But their primary focus would have been southward, with at least nineteen Havana trading posts—notably referred to as "Spanish factories"—in key slaving centers like Mboma, Porto da Lenha, and Porto Rico.[71] According to historian Norm Schrag, "a single Havana agent once procured four hundred slaves in the space of one month."[72]

The influence of Cuban firms in West Central Africa extended beyond mere trade to encompass sociopolitical dimensions, particularly in their interactions with African rulers. An incident is revealing. In 1857, Mangobo Fernando, a coastal chief in Congo, sent his son, Singa, on a slave ship to Cuba. One of the ship's sailors described the event, recounting, "A young negro came, the son of the king of some country, who entrusted his son to the captain and gave the captain some slaves to sell in Havana." Taking the offspring for education in Brazil had long been part of Portuguese and Brazilian traders' playbook, as it helped to strengthen ties between foreign traders and local leaders. As high-lighted by scholar Martín Rodrigo y Alharilla, this gesture not only immersed Singa directly into the intricate web of the Cuban slave trade's dynamics but also strengthened the ties between Cuban traders and African leaders like Mangobo Fernando.[73] By fostering such connections, Cuban firms could secure their access to captives and maintain their influence in the region, even as international pressure against the slave trade intensified.

The strong relationships between Cuban traders and African rulers had far-reaching consequences, not only facilitating the continuation of the slave trade but also undermining efforts by other powers to suppress it. A case in point was a British attempt to sign an anti-slave trade treaty in Loango in 1853. According to British accounts, "if ships do not arrive to take away slaves, and the Portuguese, in consequence, will not purchase them, the question will be settled in a few months." Yet the prospect of signing the treaty faded as "Span-iard" agents "collected their forces for another push at the trade." They had come on a recently arrived ship that brought three agents of Cuban houses, who established themselves in a feitoria that had recently been managed by a Portuguese slave dealer. As a result, "the king of this country will not accept the treaty at present, although pressed to do so upon several occasions."[74]

A Haven for Slave Traders

After Ambriz, Garrido sailed to New York City on one of the several ships that connected West Central Africa to the United States. In New York City, Garrido met several individuals connected with the so-called Portuguese firm, several of whom had previously lived in Luanda and already knew him. Among them was José da Silva Maia Ferreira, an Angolan-born poet and son of a prominent slave trader. Maia Ferreira had grown up in a family deeply involved in the Angola-Brazil slave trade, and had himself worked in the customs houses of Benguela and Luanda in the late 1840s and early 1850s before abruptly leaving for the United States in 1851. In New York City, he became a key member of the infamous "Portuguese Company" that financed and organized slave voyages to Cuba, working alongside several individuals, including Portuguese consul César Figanière, Manoel Basílio da Cunha Reis, and João Machado.[75]

Several factors attracted these individuals to the city. For one, New York provided slave dealers with a rapidly expanding international financial center with connections with several parts of the world, including Cuba and West Central Africa. With Cuba, American support had been central to the expansion of Cuba's very well-developed railroad system, which played a key role in the island's sugar industry. American trading houses also played a key role in Cuba's sugar trade, with the US accounting for more than one-third of Cuba's external trade by 1850.[76]

While the US economy would prove ideal to move capital across boundaries, it also mattered that the country's economic ties with West Africa were growing and that Portugal had just signed a commercial treaty with the United States in 1840. Under this treaty, American ships paid import taxes as low as Portuguese ships entering African ports, including Luanda and Benguela.[77] An 1841 agreement further facilitated trade by allowing entry of US and Portuguese citizens, enabling slave dealers to use commercial ties with Cuba to mask illegal slaving activities.[78]

One consequence of these economic ties and trade agreements was the relocation of US nationals to hubs under Portuguese control in West Central Africa. A case in point was John Willis, who had previously served as the captain of a ship from Salem entering Rio de Janeiro in 1838.[79] Willis later moved to Luanda, where he became close with Francisco Barboza Rodriguez, a notorious local slave dealer working for Francisco Antonio Flores at the time.[80] Willis went on to become the representative for Salem's Robert Brookhouse commercial house, which he likely had ties with from his previous voyages to Rio de Janeiro. The Salem firm was then one of only two U.S. firms with stationed agents in Luanda.[81]

During the 1850s, according to historian George Brooks, the Robert Brookhouse firm would outfit "six to eight voyages [to Angola] annually."[82] For Willis, this represented opportunities as a trader and beyond in Angola. By 1854, largely due to his association with the firm, Willis was appointed U.S. commercial agent in Luanda.[83] In this capacity, he once partnered with Simon Stodder, a US trader then based in Luanda, to pressure local authorities to reduce duties on an American vessel.[84] As late as 1857, when he took a trip to Salem on behalf of the firm, Willis remained connected with the Robert Brookhouse firm.[85]

The Brookhouse firm played a key role in merging the illegal slave trade into the structures of global capitalism.[86] Not only did the firm sell goods to slave dealers, but it also accepted bills of exchange from them, enabling traders to integrate their illicit business into the global financial fabric and facilitating the flow of slave trade proceeds back to Africa. The ship *Mary Smith*, captured in 1856 with over 300 enslaved Africans aboard, exemplifies these intricate Atlantic connections. Its journey involved transactions and meetings spanning Luanda, Ambriz, and New York City before it was seized off the Brazilian coast. Had the *Mary Smith* not been apprehended, the proceeds from the slave sales would have been routed back to Africa through Salem, likely via the Brookhouse firm's networks.[87]

The Brookhouse firm's involvement in the illegal slave trade underscores the critical role that U.S. commercial houses played in sustaining this illicit commerce. However, the firm's decision to end its Luanda operation in 1864, just two years after measures to suppress the transatlantic trade in human beings gained traction in the United States, suggests that the changing political and legal landscape was beginning to impact the networks that had long facilitated the slave trade.[88] As anti-slave trade efforts intensified on both sides of the Atlantic, firms like Brookhouse found it increasingly difficult to maintain their involvement in this illegal commerce, leading to a gradual unraveling of the complex web of relationships that had sustained the trade for decades.

Yet slave dealers were drawn to the US not only because of the country's financial might and trade links but also due to the lax implementation of anti-slave trade laws, particularly in New York City. Indeed, by 1861, a mere twenty individuals had been sentenced to jail for involvement in the slave trade, half of whom received presidential pardons, with corruption among city officials hampering efforts to dismantle slave trade networks.[89] In this context, New York City emerged as a citadel of the slave trade, with individuals like Garrido arguably operating with greater freedom there than in cities like Rio de Janeiro and Luanda, where anti-slave trade laws were by then more rigorously enforced. This leniency toward the slave trade is further evident in an 1860 report by officials, stating that "about twelve vessels are fitted out every year at New York for the African slave Trade."[90]

By moving part of the logistics of the business to US soil, slave dealers became eligible to apply for US citizenship, which proved to be a useful strategy not only to evade anti-slave trade laws but also to facilitate the trade itself. The example of a French man named François Désirée Kraft is revealing. Having once served as a slave factory agent on the African coast, Kraft moved to Rio de Janeiro in 1843 to represent Toreado, a merchant based in Cuba then allied with José Bernardino de Sá. Interestingly, despite seemingly lacking enough time to apply for legal residency in the United States, the slave dealer was still able to become a naturalized US citizen. While in Rio, Kraft then used his citizenship to obtain sea letters from the US consulate, enabling him to sail to the African coast without fear of arrest by British vessels.[91]

The strategic advantage of U.S. citizenship was further harnessed by João Machado, a native of the Azores islands who had previously operated out of Ambriz and was one of the first slave dealers to relocate to New York City in the 1840s.[92] Even in 1856, long after his departure from Angola, Machado was still widely known as a slave dealer in Luanda, where his brother still lived.[93] During the 1850s, when one of Machado's slave ships fell into British hands, he boldly leaned on his American citizenship, appealing to the pro-slavery sentiments of U.S. President James Buchanan for assistance. Machado portrayed himself as a victim, stating that his "lawful business was broken up, and my ruin produced." Despite Machado's well-documented involvement in slave trading, the U.S. government rallied behind his request for compensation from the British government.[94]

Most importantly, using New York City as a logistical basis meant that slave dealers could also rely on the US flag to send their ships to Africa, thus shielding them from anti-slave trade patrolling by the British. In 1840, the British made a deal with the commander of American vessels off Liberia to retain American vessels until the arrival of an American cruiser to inspect them. However, the American government disavowed the deal.[95] Two years later, they participated in the negotiation that led to the Webster-Ashburton treaty guaranteeing reciprocal rights of search with France, Prussia, and Austria. Yet the United States government ultimately refused to allow the right of search and visit and instead dispatched naval forces to Africa to prevent the participation of the US flag and ships in the trade in enslaved Africans.[96] As late as 1854, American naval commander Andrew Foote stated, "the deck of an American vessel under its flag is the territory of the United States, and no other authority but of the United States must ever be allowed to exercise jurisdiction over it."[97]

Broadly speaking, the US stance on the slave trade was fueled by a strong distrust of the motivations of Britain's campaign against the slave trade. Adding to the suspicion was a free-soil policy in which the British government freed any enslaved person who entered its Caribbean territories, including those who had revolted on board slave ships.[98] The US hostility also reflected the government's support for the institution of slavery domestically and abroad. As an American consul in Rio de Janeiro pointed out, "in immediate connection with this subject of the slave trade is that of interference by Great Britain with the domestic slavery of the United States."[99] Regardless, the US position seriously undermined efforts to end the slave trade abroad. Tellingly, Portuguese diplomats in London once drew a direct connection between the election of slavery-friendly James Buchanan as the President of the United States in 1856 and the transatlantic slave trade. In their view, the newly elected president would not only "defend the continuation of slavery [in the United States] but also issue a decree reopening the slave trade."[100]

Brazil's Shift from the Slave Trade

While the US built up a committed record of support for slavers, Brazil had by the mid-1850s largely withdrawn from the transatlantic slave trade, surprisingly emerging as a staunch advocate for anti-slave trade measures both within its borders and in West Central Africa. By 1851, the British reported the rise "powerful, active, and skillful anti-slave trade movement that is welcomed by the government, supported by the press, and has many supporters in the [Brazilian] lower chamber."[101] Four years later, they noted that "public opinion is declared to be decidedly against the slave trade," with funds previously invested in the human traffic now "taking a new direction."[102] They praised Brazil as an exemplar for Cuba to follow, asserting that "Brazil has set a noble example of perseverance in the suppression of the slave trade . . . which may be equally accomplished elsewhere."[103]

Yet Brazil's transformation from a slave-trading nation to an anti-slave trade role model was not linear. In 1829, the Brazilian government declared its intention to send two warships to West and East Africa to notify slave vessels of an upcoming deadline for bringing captives into Brazil.[104] After enacting an anti-slave trade law in 1831, the government started intercepting ships attempting to enter Brazil with captives and expelling Portuguese slave traders.[105] This policy also encompassed efforts to forge agreements with European powers to repatriate Africans seized from slave ships to their territories in Africa.[106] However, by the end of the 1830s, the momentum behind anti-slave trade repression waned due to a conservative political realignment that favored the slave trade as the best way to supply labor for Brazil's booming coffee plantations.[107]

Support for the trade of enslaved Africans was deeply embedded in Brazilian society. Portuguese consul João Batista Moreira observed that most of the Brazilian population "judged indispensable the introduction of Africans for agricultural and even domestic labor in the cities."[108] Slave dealers wielded substantial influence over Brazil's policymakers, "either by corruption or intimidation," which "has overridden all sense of right and wrong, and all regard for legal and international obligations."[109] As historian Marcus de Carvalho demonstrates, the illegal slave trade supported a domestic service economy that employed hundreds of individuals, which partly accounts for its widespread appeal.[110]

In such a context, the slave trade shaped not only domestic politics but, much as with the US government, also influenced international relations. The Brazilian government even went so far as to challenge the Portuguese government over the capture of slave ships that flew the Brazilian flag off the coast of Angola, prompting Portugal to direct its navy to refrain from seizing such ships.[111] In a particularly telling incident, a commander of a Brazilian warship once attempted to intervene on behalf of Brazilian slave dealers awaiting trial in the British vice-admiralty tribunal in St. Helena. While British judges "refused to admit any interference with the proceedings, as the prisoners had already pleaded," the incident underscores the Brazilian state's commitment to the trade in African lives.[112]

By then, however, several factors were already beginning to slowly shift Brazil away from the slave trade. Chief among these was the British naval operations along the Brazilian coast, directly threatening Brazil's sovereignty.[113]

Yet other elements also played a role, including fear of slave insurrection. "Public men of every shade of political opinion" agreed that "an imported slave may prove an enemy and never can be a friend."[114] Following a planned revolt by Mina enslaved people in Pelotas, a Rio de Janeiro-based British diplomat remarked that he had "no doubt that this is the people charged by Providence with the dreadful and inevitable retribution of Africa."[115]

Another relevant factor was the emerging belief that the slave trade contributed to spreading diseases from Africa to Brazil. A Rio de Janeiro newspaper even attributed a recent outbreak of yellow fever to this cause, stating, "The yellow fever that this year has been so lethal was a gift from Africa."[116] Moreover, with the rise of scientific racism, some Brazilians felt that the influx of enslaved Africans threatened the nation's moral fabric. "We act as tyrants towards them and reduce them to brutal animals. They give us their immorality and all their vice."[117] A report by British consul Hudson echoed these sentiments, depicting Brazil "gradually and visibly retrograding and becoming more deeply tinged with the blood of the most worthless offcasts of the most worthless family of the human race."[118]

Also relevant was a dominant anti-Portuguese sentiment that played a substantial role in the country's internal politics, as highlighted in Chapter 1. Historian Aline De Biase provides evidence of this sentiment by pointing to Recife's slave trader Ângelo Francisco Carneiro, who felt compelled to return to Portugal due to the growing anti-Portuguese feelings in Pernambuco.[119] A belief in sectors of society was that Portuguese nationals had manipulated the slave trade for their gain, detrimentally affecting Brazil's broader interests.[120] At a ceremony celebrating the establishment of an anti-slave trade association, one member remarked, "the independence of Brazil was illusory as long as Portuguese were allowed to remain in the land, turning its population into a vicious mass of slaves and slave masters."[121]

Brazil's shift away from the slave trade might also have been in part a function of the strategic thinking that preserving slavery necessitated the end of the slave trade. This perspective found resonance with the US consul in Rio de Janeiro, Henry Wise. Although a staunch slavery advocate, Wise opposed the slave trade, primarily due to geopolitical concerns. He argued that the trade in enslaved Africans presented Britain with an avenue to intervene in the internal matters of nations like Brazil and the US.** As we will discuss later, this rationale would also shape Spain's eventual stance against importing enslaved Africans to Cuba.

Whatever the case, Brazil robustly enacted its second anti-slave trade law, which was passed in 1850. In a bid to demonstrate its commitment to end

---

** Karp, *This Vast Southern Empire*, p. 80. Roberto Saba, *American Mirror: The United States and Brazil in the Age of Emancipation* (Princeton: Princeton University Press, 2021), pp. 19–27. For Wise, see also Horne, *The Deepest South*, Chapter 4.

the slave trade once and for all, the Brazilian government deployed a fleet of sixteen warships to patrol the nation's coastlines, while also conducting operations on estates near Rio de Janeiro.[122] This newly found anti-slave trade mood would prompt hundreds of Portuguese nationals, many of whom were involved in the slave trade, to return to Portugal in the early 1850s.[123] The exodus mirrored a political atmosphere where aggressive actions targeted those suspected of slave trading. While Portuguese diplomats voiced their disapproval of these measures, British officials lauded them as an "effective means for repressing the traffic when the action of penal law cannot reach the parties" and even suggested that Portugal should enforce similar policies in Angola.[124]

Remarkably, Brazil's newfound commitment to ending the slave trade reached as far as Angola. A recently appointed consul in Luanda was instructed to monitor the slave trade, including any official involvement in the shipment of captives, signaling a significant shift in Brazil's foreign policy.[125] In 1857, interim consul Ignacio Jose de Moraes reported to the British that "a cargo of Africans is being prepared in the river Zaire Cabinda for exportation to Havana" and that the same might be attempted toward Brazil.[126] Moraes suggested that the Brazilian government deploy a warship to stop the shipment of captives from Angola.[127]

Another consul assured the British commissioners that he was "from a strong conviction of its evil, a decided enemy to the slave trade, and that he holds instructions from his government to keep a strict watch over the proceedings of any parties suspected of being concerned in that traffic."[128] The statement revealed not only a personal conviction against the trade in enslaved Africans but also Brazil's official position, now in alignment with international pressures against the trade of enslaved Africans. The diplomat later shared with the British the schemes "entertained by parties in Angola for introducing slaves into the Brazils, by landing them in Guyana, and afterward removing them overland to Pará and the other northern provinces of that empire."[129]

From Brazil to Cuba

Despite its active anti-slave trade policies, Brazil's entanglements with the slave trade were far from over. According to scholar John Harris, "major slaving ports such as Luanda and Rio de Janeiro, long the key hubs in Africa and the Americas, finally closed, and the pivotal axis between West Central Africa and Brazil disintegrated."[130] Yet a mere two years following the passage of Brazil's second anti-slave trade law in 1850, Portuguese officials reported a meeting of slave dealers in Rio de Janeiro. Their objective? To establish a new company dedicated to the illicit trafficking of slaves to Cuba.

The creation of the new company was detailed in a memo sent to Angola by Portuguese officials, revealing Rio de Janeiro as a key hub of what amounted to a sprawling transnational network. Primary investors included Joaquim da

Fonseca Guimarães & Company, which owned trading posts (known as "factories") in Ambriz, and Oliveira Brandão. Both had long-standing ties to the transatlantic slave trade. A key player was Francisco Antonio Flores, a prominent Brazilian slave trader who managed operations in Ambriz for Fonseca Guimarães & Company. At the time of the meeting, Flores was visiting Rio de Janeiro but was soon to return to Ambriz to supervise the shipment of captives to Cuba. The firm would dispatch agents to strategic locations across the Atlantic, including Ambriz, Luanda, Lisbon, and Havana. José Gonçalves Moreira, for example, was sent to Havana alongside Rodrigo José de Abreu, while José de Sá Miranda initially headed to Lisbon.[131]

These agents quickly engaged in the familiar pattern of crisscrossing the Atlantic that characterized slave dealers' operations. From Lisbon, Sá Miranda moved to Luanda, a city where he had previously spent time as a slave dealer. In 1853, British consuls in the city reported his return by pointing out that he had "so long figured as the head of the slave trade interests at this place [Luanda] and eventually established himself at Rio de Janeiro."[132] In Luanda, Sá Miranda took residence in Flores's house, a known point of passage for slave dealers. According to the British, the slave dealer carried with him "a large sum of gold and is now living at Flores's house."[133]

The complex transactions within the syndicate are further illustrated by a letter from Salvador de Castro Jr., a prominent Cuban slave dealer. Castro revealed he had received a shipment of enslaved Africans from Ambriz, sent by agent Antonio Jose da Costa Lima. However, the rightful recipient of the sale's proceeds was unclear. Rodrigo Jose de Abreu, recently arrived in Havana from Rio de Janeiro, speculated that the profits might belong to L. Vianna, based in New York City. Yet, according to Castro, only Francisco Antonio Flores—the supervisor stationed in Ambriz and likely knowledgeable about the transaction's details and intended beneficiaries—could clarify this murky situation.[134]

Castro Jr.'s involvement in the syndicate underscores the sprawling nature of these networks. His family dominated the slave trade in Trinidad, a region that accounted for 18 percent of Cuba's slave trade.[135] Uncorroborated reports suggest that he might have once spent time in Rio de Janeiro, which would provide further evidence of a direct link between Brazil and Cuba through the slave trade.[136] During his alleged stay in Rio, he would have offered "himself to the contrabandists to receive the remittances of Africans, assigning the sum of 500 mil réis for each one."[137] Castro Jr.'s purported presence in Rio de Janeiro, combined with his prominent role in the Cuban slave trade, highlights the interconnectedness of these networks and the persistent role of Rio de Janeiro in facilitating the illegal trade, despite Brazil's efforts to suppress it.

Tellingly, Castro Jr.'s letter was addressed to a former Havana resident who had made a fortune as a slave dealer after relocating to Rio de Janeiro in the 1840s: Francisco Ruviroza y Urzellas. Back in the 1830s, still based in Cuba, the Spanish-born Ruviroza y Urzellas reportedly arrived in Havana aboard a slave ship from Africa.[138] He would later be identified as one of the owners of the slave vessel named Segunda Rosario.[139] By the mid-1840s, however, he had moved to Rio de Janeiro, with the British identifying him as "formerly an extensive slave dealer at Havana" and the "owner of several vessels, and of barracoons (slave depots) at Cape Lopo, and a fort in the river Zaire."[140] His name would soon appear on a list of Rio's most prominent slave traders.[141]

In 1853, as Brazil intensified its crackdown on the slave trade, Ruviroza y Urzellas found himself detained in Rio de Janeiro, accused of association with the *Camargo*, a ship known to have recently transported captives from Mozambique to Brazil. While denying involvement in the transportation of captives to Brazil, the Spanish man would candidly admit to his participation in the Cuban slave trade.[142] According to him, his primary activities in Rio de Janeiro involved forming alliances with Brazilian coffee plantation owners, a tactic commonly employed in Cuba.[143] By making this argument, he sought to bypass Brazil's anti-slave trade legislation, which only prohibited the transportation of enslaved Africans to the country itself. Yet he was still expelled from Rio, leaving for Lisbon before returning to Havana a few years later.[144]

While Ruviroza y Urzellas's expulsion dealt a blow to the slave trade networks in Rio de Janeiro, it barely affected his collaborative ventures with Castro Jr. Five years later, the duo would collaborate on the voyage of the schooner *Cobra*, which transported enslaved Africans to Trinidad. This enterprise brought together Rio de Janeiro-based Joaquim da Fonseca Guimarães & Co. and close associates near the Congo River, showing that the syndicate founded in Rio de Janeiro in 1852 was still operational.[145] According to British officials, partnerships like this served "to confirm what is notorious already with regard to his [Castro Jr.'s] connection with the Portuguese and Brazilian slavers."[146]

This partnership's significance comes into focus when considering the broader context of connections between Brazil and Cuba through the slave trade. By 1846, Cuban slave dealers, facing rising labor demands and a significant price differential (slaves costing around $200 in Brazil compared to $400 in Cuba), considered sourcing slaves directly from Brazil.[147] By then, according to the British, some Cuban merchants owned "vessels engaged in the Brazilian slave trade."[148] A watershed moment came about, however, as the slave trade to Brazil came to an end in the early 1850s. Bahian slave dealers, reflecting a broader trend, were said to redirect their African agents to send captives to Cuba instead.[149] In Cuba, officials reported the "seizure of a vessel believed to be Brazilian" off the southern coast of their island.[150] According to historian Adriam Camacho Domínguez, some of these landings were orchestrated by key figures like Salvador de Castro Jr., along with Rodrigo José de Abreu, who had been dispatched to Havana following the establishment of the 1852 syndicate in Rio de Janeiro.[151]

José de Abreu would soon be joined in Cuba by other agents seeking to escape anti-slave trade repression in Rio de Janeiro. One such agent was

Antonio Severino Avellar, who had by then built a long resume in the slave trade. In an earlier phase of his career, as discussed earlier in this chapter, Avellar had arrived in Luanda as the captain of the ship *Paquete de Loanda*.[152] Settling in the Angolan capital as an agent of prominent Rio de Janeiro slave dealer José Bernardino de Sá, he struck a close partnership Arsenio de Carpo, one of Luanda's most prominent slave dealers.[153] Avellar would hold the rank of militia major in the Portuguese province and was honored with the habit of the Order of Conception by the local government.[154] He would be called back to Rio by his employers in 1844, remaining in the city for two years before returning to West Central Africa, this time bypassing growing anti-slave trade repression in Luanda by setting shop in Ambriz.[155]

Avellar's life took a pivotal turn in 1852 when he was recruited by the syndicate created in Rio de Janeiro to organize the slave trade to Cuba. This recruitment reflected the syndicate's strategic vision of leveraging global financial and industrial resources to sustain the illegal trade. Avellar's bosses directed him to embark on several trips beyond the familiar South Atlantic world, including a visit to England that exemplified their aim of tapping into the heart of the Industrial Revolution. In London, Avellar met with representatives from Knowles & Foster, a banking firm that played a crucial role in facilitating capital movement for slave traders across the Atlantic.[156] This meeting underscores the intricate financial networks that underpinned the illegal slave trade, enabling its continuation despite increasing international pressure.

Avellar's journey then took him to Liverpool and Manchester, where he toured textile factories at the epicenter of the Industrial Revolution. This leg of his trip, captured in a letter by his close associate Guilherme José da Motta, highlights the slave trade's deep entanglement with the global capitalistic economy. Motta noted that he was "determined to go to London and Liverpool, [where] he will wait for Avellar: they will [then] go to Manchester to visit [textile] factories."[157] By exploring these industrial hubs, Avellar and his associates sought to forge direct supply lines for the goods that would be exchanged for enslaved Africans, effectively integrating the illegal trade into the fabric of the global economy. This strategic move demonstrates the adaptability and resilience of slave trade networks in the face of mounting opposition, as they continuously sought new ways to circumvent barriers and maintain their profitable enterprise.

By 1854, Avellar had moved to Cuba, reflecting the island's status as one of the citadels for the illegal slave trade, much like New York City. As a Rio de Janeiro newspaper pointed out, "Havana is the point of rendezvous for smugglers" of enslaved Africans.[158] Yet Avellar's arrival in Cuba coincided with a series of measures aimed at curbing the importation of enslaved Africans into the island. These measures, exemplified by the arrest of Julian Zulueta, Cuba's most prominent slave dealer, after one of his sugar estates was used for the landing of 1,200 captives on a ship called the *Lady Suffolk*, demonstrate the increasing pressure on the illegal slave trade in Cuba.[159] Notably, Avellar himself would soon be arrested and expelled from the island.[160]

Cuba's anti-slave trade actions were not solely a response to external pressures but also a reflection of complex domestic dynamics. British officials in Rio de Janeiro had provided intelligence about Avellar's impending arrival, highlighting the transnational nature of anti-slave trade efforts.[161] Yet the crackdown was driven by two interrelated factors. On the one hand, appeasing Britain was crucial for Spain to secure support against US annexation plots, underscoring the delicate geopolitical balance the country had to maintain.[162] On the other hand, domestic pressures played an increasingly significant role. As early as 1851, some Cuban elites had "come to the conclusion that the importation of slaves and the continuance of slavery will, in the end, be productive of consequences which they had not foreseen."[163] These apprehensions were fueled by recent slave revolts that had shaken the Spanish island, with officials acknowledging that the slave trade was "damaging for the credit of the government and the tranquility of the residents" of Cuba.[164]

Cuba's intensified efforts against the slave trade led observers in Brazil to speculate that slave traders might redirect their attention back to Brazil.[165] Yet the island's push proved to be short-lived, with the importation of captives continuing for another eleven years. When it finally came about, the end of the Cuban slave trade would stem from factors as diverse as the increased deployment of American warships near the island and the prosecution of slave dealers by law enforcement officers in New York City. As one report stated, "The vigor which has characterized the proceedings of the federal officers at this port during the last 12 months in discovering and bringing to trial parties suspected of having been engaged in slave trading has been productive of very beneficial results."[166]

As these changes unfolded, the U.S. Civil War became a critical factor in shaping the end of Cuba's slave trade. This development played a dual role. On one hand, it helped reconcile lingering tensions between the U.S. and Britain over collaborative efforts to curb the slave trade. To secure British support against the Confederacy, the Union government signed a treaty granting British naval forces the right to visit and search all ships flying the American flag. This action effectively dismantled a legal shield that had allowed the continuation of the slave trade for several decades despite its official outlawing.[167] On the other hand, the prospect of emancipation in the United States raised concerns among Spanish officials regarding potential social unrest within Cuba's enslaved population. Cuban authorities noted, "The island cannot be considered under normal conditions as long as the [American] revolution has established emancipation as its central tenet, as long as military campaigns in the neighboring republic count on free blacks of that country as a central element for the invasion of this island, and chiefly when there is fear that it has taught and incited our black slaves."[168]

As in Brazil, the fear was that the introduction of African slaves could lead to more slave revolts on an island where several episodes of resistance by enslaved Africans had already taken place. As early as 1857, a report by Governor of Cuba asserted that the preservation of the institution of slavery necessitated the end of imports of African captives. He argued that "the non-suppression of the slave trade injures the slave property of the island, the basis and foundation of her wealth and prosperity."[169] Yet such fears clearly gained more credibility with the onset of the U.S. Civil War. In response to the potential spread of instability, Spanish officials censored newspapers and increased surveillance of people of color. "Those who lacked respect for the white class" could be jailed for up to 30 days.[170] British accounts suggest that these combined pressures ultimately compelled the Spanish government to recognize the necessity of ending the slave trade. In their words, the Spanish government had been "at last compelled to see the necessity of putting an end to the slave trade" due to the "pressure of circumstances, and especially by the liberation of the slaves in the United States."[171]

Conclusion

As the transatlantic slave trade entered its twilight decades, Africa was neither a passive bystander nor an isolated outpost cut off from interconnected webs of commerce that defined the period. Rather, the African coastline was intertwined with far-flung commodity and financial chains that sustained the illegal trafficking of human beings across the Atlantic. Traders like Augusto Garrido personified these links, journeying from West Central Africa to the banking houses of London and Manchester's textile factories before returning with goods to purchase enslaved Africans. The travels of Garrido and others like him were not anomalous—they forged ties of mobility and exchange that profoundly shaped the slave trade's operations on the ground in Africa.

This chapter highlights the value of examining the abolition of the slave trade through a multi-sited, transnational lens. By detailing developments in Brazil, Cuba, the United States, and Africa in tandem, the narrative underscores how anti-slave trade policy took shape within a globalized web of intersecting pressures and strategic interests. It reveals abolition as a process that defies neat categorization into distinct national contexts. Brazil's move to ban slave imports stemmed from a confluence of pressures both internal and external. Though British naval operations threatened Brazilian sovereignty, other factors such as economic shifts, fear of slave uprisings, elite attitudes, and nationalist political dynamics also pushed Brazil away from the slave trade.

The core argument is that Africa was an active agent woven into far-flung commodity and capital flows powering slaving. By using Garrido's story, the chapter addresses broader themes of globalization, capitalism, and the complex interplay between slave trading and anti-slavery efforts. Deeply rooted in a transnational context, the narrative illustrates how the slave trade was sustained by a web of relationships that extended across continents and oceans. Garrido's travels and activities demonstrate the ways in which slave traders adapted and responded to increasing international pressure and legal restrictions. His story is a window into the larger, global story of the slave trade's final decades.

As global capitalism expanded, British, French, and American merchants gained footholds along the African coast, forging direct supply links with slave dealers that bypassed Luso-Brazilian intermediaries. The establishment of foreign traders in places like Ambriz demonstrated that Africa's relationship with the slave trade can no longer be understood solely through the lens of ties with Portugal and Brazil. With traders of various nationalities competing and collaborating on shore, the African coast had become a profoundly globalized space by the 1850s.

The prominence of Cuba in this final phase further exemplifies Africa's multidirectional integration with a wider world. As the chapters show, West Central Africa's vital connection to Cuba took shape through a matrix of interlocking networks—spanning Luanda, Ambriz, Rio de Janeiro, and Havana—that were laid down over the preceding decades. This complex infrastructure belies simplistic center-periphery framings that would relegate Africa to the margins. The analysis reveals African polities and traders as indispensable agents within networks that were simultaneously local, regional, and global in their coordinates.

This global interconnection had significant ramifications for African societies along the coast. As foreign traders established feitorias and formed alliances with local rulers, they injected external pressure and influence into local political systems. Power dynamics mutated as positions became increasingly transactional, purchased through material wealth accrued from engaging in the slave trade and collaboration with foreigners. Traditional authority eroded while political structures grew more fractured under the strain of contending internal and external interests. The influx of global capital and goods also transformed local economies, making them more dependent on producing captives to exchange for imported merchandise. Hence the slave trade had wide-ranging impacts on African communities, from the configuration of their political power to the very fabric of their economic life.

CHAPTER FIVE

O Mueneputo é Dembo e Alala

IN OCTOBER 1847, Dona Ana Joaquina dos Santos Silva, the famed Luanda businesswoman who built a multicontinental commercial empire by shipping thousands of enslaved Africans to Brazil, dispatched four envoys to meet Nawej II, the Mwant Yav or ruler of the powerful Lunda empire at the heart of West Central Africa. Traveling almost six hundred léguas east from Luanda, the envoys' mission was to shut down an expedition led by Joaquim Rodrigues Graça, which had departed four years earlier to conduct trade talks with the Lunda ruler. Initially the expedition's financier, Ana Joaquina reacted angrily when Graça breached a contract with her by dispatching goods from the interior to other merchants in Luanda. She then sent envoys to persuade Nawej II to expel the explorer and establish a direct trade agreement with her instead. To "save his life," Graça was forced to leave the musumba (royal court) hastily.[1]

Three of the envoys Ana Joaquina dispatched to the Lunda Empire were enslaved Africans, including a woman named Eufrazina, who would go on to play a pivotal role in the highly sensitive mission. To navigate their way to Lunda's capital city, the envoys relied on the guidance of a mixed-race trader, Antonio Bonifacio Rodrigues, who was based in the interior region of Pungo Andongo. Part of Ana Joaquina's extensive network of agents in Luanda's backlands, Rodrigues likely served as the translator in multiple meetings with the Lunda ruler. Yet it was Eufrazina who led the trade talks with Nawej II, as a clearly humiliated Graça suggested himself. To impress the Lunda ruler, the enslaved woman described her mistress "as the only one to rule in Angola as Dembo Alala, Senhora de todos estes matos (mistress of all these lands)," effectively placing the successful businesswoman above Portuguese authorities in the colony.[2]

By referring to Ana Joaquina as Dembo Alala, Eufrazina used just one of the several monikers with which the powerful businesswoman was usually described.[3] Near the coast, the Luanda native was known as Angana

Dembo or Andembo-iá-Lala.[4] In Luanda itself, she was referred to as the Baroness of Bungo, in reference to the Luanda neighborhood where she lived in a majestic building, the largest private house in the city. She was also called the Baroness of Luanda, a testament to her extraordinary power and wealth in the city.[5] In Brazil—a country where she owned properties and visited at least twice—Ana Joaquina was known as Ana de Angola by a powerful Salvador-based slave dealer who once crossed the Atlantic to meet her in Luanda.[6] These various names reflect the life of a woman whose influence spanned the broader Atlantic world of Brazil and Portugal while also embodying Angola's evolving relationship with powerful African polities like the Lunda empire.

This chapter seizes upon Graça's expedition and Dona Ana Joaquina's assertive trade diplomacy to explore the broader ramifications of abolition in the heart of West Central Africa. Historian Vanessa de Oliveira has explored abolition through the lenses of Luanda's gender dynamics, offering valuable insights into the roles of powerful women like Ana Joaquina.[7] Scholar Esteban Salas argues that the abolition was marked by efforts to establish a plantation system in the African colony, highlighting attempts to transform Angola's economy through commercial agriculture.[8] Yet the existing literature still leaves gaps in our understanding of the internal impacts of efforts to end the transatlantic slave trade in West Central Africa.

In this chapter, I deploy the conflict between Dona Ana Joaquina and Joaquim Rodrigues Graça as a vantage point to explore various aspects of Angola's transition from the transatlantic slave trade. The paramount issues here are the nature of slavery within and beyond territories under Portuguese influence, women's business and political roles in Luanda and African kingdoms, agricultural initiatives aimed at restructuring Angola's economy, and the nature of political power in slave trade-dependent African polities such as the Lunda empire.

To meet the Lunda ruler, Graça had embarked on a logistically challenging journey from his home in Bango Aquitamba, approximately 180 kilometers from Luanda. Setting out in April 1843 with a caravan of five hundred people, he first sought to reach Lunda territory through Kasanje, near the Kwango River. Trade with the east was then controlled by the Mbundu kingdom of Kasanje, which promptly denied him passage. Redirecting southward, Graça traveled toward Bié, an important trading hub, where he arrived a year after his departure from Bango Aquitamba. He stayed in Bié for almost three years, allegedly waiting for supplies and porters from Luanda to replace those lost to theft by members of his caravan.[9] In September 1846, he finally reached the Lunda's royal court, engaging in trade talks with the Lunda ruler for nearly a year before his expedition was abruptly brought to an end in 1847.

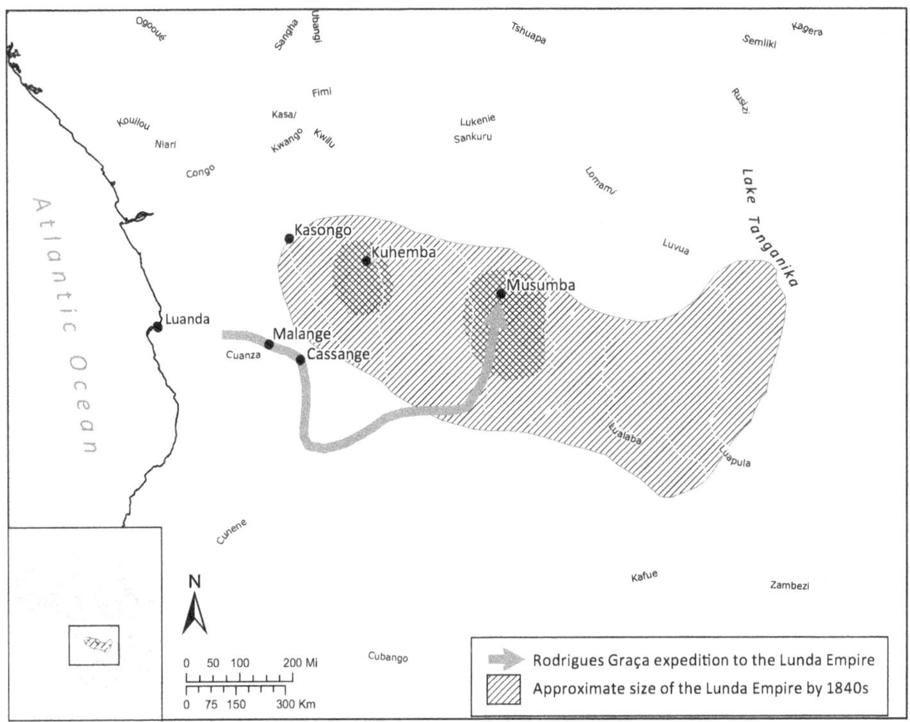

MAP 2. Joaquim Rodrigues Graça's Expedition

Graça's expedition received backing from a Luanda government then actively seeking ways to mitigate the impact of halting slave shipments from the city. The stakes could not be higher. Military commander Francisco Salles Ferreira declared that "the bulk of goods for Angola's trade" originated from Lunda.[10] Yet, while the potential benefits of a successful mission were evident, the challenges were daunting, largely due to Kasanje's opposition to attempts to loosen its grip on trade relations. Eastward into Lunda territory, Kasanje traders still played a crucial role in trade relations despite the emerging independent trade of the Chokwe, skilled in weaponry and hunting, and the Ambakista, traders from Portuguese-influenced regions who brought new concepts of slavery to Lunda society.[11]

Understanding Mwant Yav Nawej II's motives for engaging with the Portuguese is critical in this narrative. A man in his seventies who had been in power since the 1820s, the ruler had expanded the Lunda kingdom through military conquest and commercial growth, building upon the kingdom's earlier expansion in the previous century and transforming it into Africa's second-largest polity. Historian John Thornton notes that Lunda's influence extended "westward some 400 kilometers to the Kwango river in Angola, and

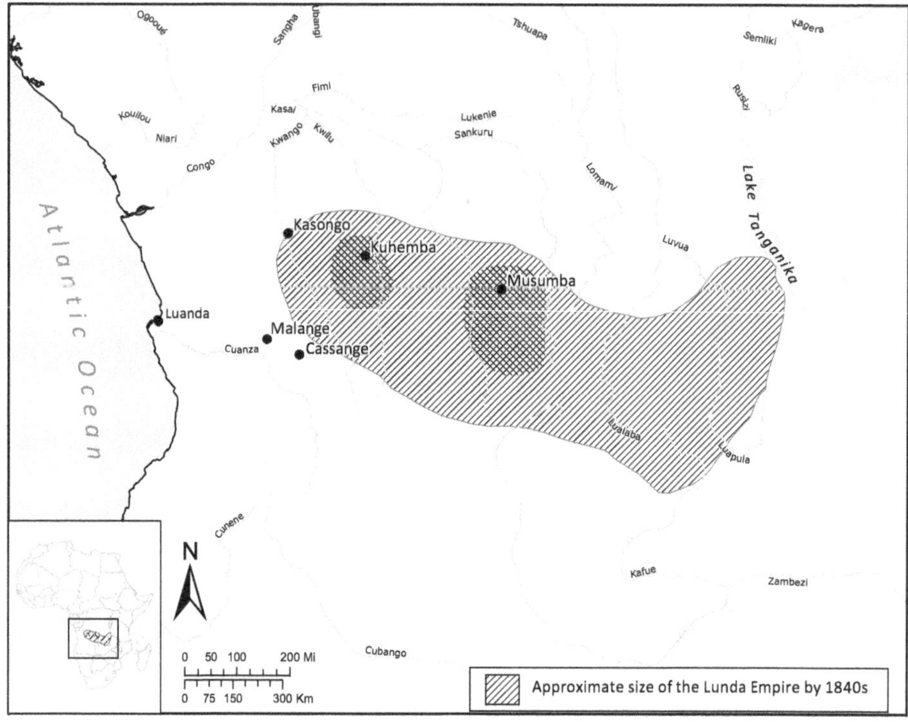

MAP 3. The Luanda Empire

then eastward to the shores of Lake Mweru another 400 or so kilometers."[12] In this expansive network, power was far from centralized, prompting scholars to debate whether they should call it a commonwealth, an alliance, or an empire.[13] For Graça, however, there was no debate: the Lunda ruler was "the emperor of the African chiefs in that immense sertões."[14]

For Nawej II, the potential alliance with the Portuguese was seen through the lens of growing political unrest within the Lunda kingdom, including a recent coup d'état attempt against him.[15] Signs of discontent were picked up by Graça himself on his journey through African territory. Regional leaders, or kilolos, expressed dissatisfaction over tributes (milambos) demanded from them by Nawej II, who would dispatch ruthless emissaries (tukwatas) to crush those who defied his power. A kilolo explicitly stated to Graça his willingness to "fulfill and take all orders [from the Luanda government]" and disregard those from the Lunda ruler.[16]

By engaging with the Portuguese, the Lunda ruler also sought to achieve leverage over independent trade then sweeping through West Central Africa. Scholars Joseph Miller and Jill Dias highlight the expansion of Ambakista and Cokwe traders east of the Kwango River into Lunda territory as significant factors in destabilizing the region's political balance.[17] The Cokwe, building upon expertise in weaponry and hunting, were a significant force behind the expansion of the ivory and wax trade. Ambakista traders spreading out of Portuguese-influenced regions further increased trade while bringing new conceptions of slavery into Lunda society. Taken together, these phenomena have been described by historian David Gordon as a "political economy of instability," where emerging leaders gained power at the expense of traditional political relationships.[18]

The relationship between the Lunda Empire and external actors—particularly the Portuguese colony of Angola, a major hub of the transatlantic trade in human captives—remains a contentious issue in West Central African history. Scholarly consensus long held that this commerce was pivotal in driving Lunda's eastward expansion, which profoundly impacted regional polities.[19] Recent scholarship has nuanced this view, suggesting that alternative factors beyond the Atlantic trade may have influenced Lunda's growth.[20] Yet the notion that Angola-Lunda relations were fundamentally rooted in the sale of enslaved Africans across the Atlantic has not faded away.[21]

This ongoing debate is closely intertwined with discussions about Angola's slaving frontier, a concept coined by historian Joseph Miller to describe the impact of the Atlantic demand for enslaved laborers generating waves of captivity that reached deep into the African interior, including the Lunda Empire. This view has come under scrutiny, with scholars arguing that the Lunda state "was probably much less important as a source of slaves" than previously thought.[22] The interactions between Ana Joaquina, Graça, and the Lunda Empire offer a unique lens through which to examine these scholarly debates. Notably, Lunda ruler Nawej II made a point of requesting the reopening of the transatlantic slave trade from Luanda, challenging emerging views about Lunda's diminished role in the slave trade while seemingly lending support to Miller's slaving frontier thesis.

After unceremoniously expelling Graça from his musumba, Nawej II dispatched several tukwatas (high-ranking officials) to meet Ana Joaquina in her house near Luanda. Historian Jan Vansina describes tukwatas as "traveling chiefs who would constantly travel with a militarized retinue to collect tribute or carry out orders in distant parts of the empire."[23] Journeying in a caravan with ivory and enslaved people, the Lunda emissaries hoped to trade them for "fazendas, weapons, powder, and beads." On returning to the musumba, they reported their awe at Joaquina's "opulence," with their accounts leading Lunda's people to regard the Luanda businesswoman as "the most important kilolo that Muene Puto [Portugal] had in Angola."[24]

Two sources provide further insights into the meeting between the Lunda emissaries and Ana Joaquina. Antonio Gil, a Portuguese lawyer then living in Luanda, left the only known account of the Lunda envoys' visit to Ana Joaquina's. According to Gil, "he had seen blacks from Lunda in the house of a lady who at the time was the woman who had the largest business with the sertão." He observed the envoys "prostrated themselves before her in the custom of their land, paying her a kind of adoration."[25] Gil's account underscores Ana Joaquina's extraordinary status, as the Lunda emissaries seemingly prioritized meeting her over the Governor of Angola, effectively recognizing her as the true power broker in the region.

More insights come from Henrique de Carvalho, a Portuguese explorer who visited the Lunda Empire several decades later, when the memory of Ana Joaquina's wealth and power was still alive. To lure her into sending goods inland, the Mwant Yav, communicating through his emissaries, said that he had large quantities of ivory to pay for them. The businesswoman then retorted that several of her traders were already in the interior but faced difficulties in being paid for goods sold to Lunda subjects. She cautioned the envoys that these pending debts would have to be settled for business to thrive. Otherwise, she warned, "no one would want to trade in his [Nawej II's] land."[26] This stern admonition to one of Africa's most formidable rulers vividly illustrates Ana Joaquina's unparalleled influence in shaping West Central African trade relations during this critical transition.

Eufrazina's Diplomacy: Gender and Slavery in Lunda

There is no doubt that what led to the debacle of Graça's trade talks with the Lunda ruler was the arrival of Ana Joaquina's envoys. According to Graça, "up to that point, the defendant (Ana Joaquina) had never had personal ties (*amizade*) or commercial ties" with the Mwant Yav. Yet the envoys brought a "valuable gift" from their mistress and asked the ruler to call off negotiations with Graça, which were well underway. They claimed that all the goods that Graça carried in his caravan belonged to Ana Joaquina, not him. With the ruler's tacit approval, the emissaries set fire to the compound where Graça stored a large amount of ivory intended for transport back to Luanda.[27]

While Eufrazina was just one of the four emissaries that Ana Joaquina dispatched to the Lunda Musumba, her role could not be overstated. In a meeting with the Lunda ruler, the envoys presented Graça as "a cangundo, an insignificant subordinate employee of their mistress."[28] According to them, the explorer could not be trusted, cared only about his own "business and fortune," and had no mandate to speak on behalf of the Luanda government.[29] To sow suspicion, they associated him with the Kasanje ruler, an avowed enemy of the Lunda ruler, arguing that "he was not even a white man, but merely a son or subject of the Cassanje ruler (jaga)." Yet, as Graça himself admitted, it was Eufrazina who ultimately convinced the ruler to expel him from the Musumba. According to her, "if he [Nawej II] sent his makotas to her master to receive her orders," Ana Joaquina "would provide him with a piece of artillery, which the Mwant Yav had so often requested to increase the greatness of his state."[30]

In the aftermath of his ill-fated expedition, Graça dismissively referred to the enslaved woman as a "mucama," a term widely employed in Angola and Brazil to denote enslaved domestic servants, as discussed in Chapter 2, and also used by Ambakista traders for women purchased as concubines in the colony's interior. Graça used the term in a derogatory way, expressing frustration with Eufrazina's leading role in his expedition's debacle. Decades later, Portuguese explorer Henrique de Carvalho, while conducting his own expedition to the Lunda empire, interviewed individuals who still remembered the arrival of Ana Joaquina's envoys at the musumba. Their account suggests some of them, including Eufrazina, had indeed performed tasks "at their owner's house (Ana Joaquina)," previously crossing paths with Graça.[31]

Yet, while the account collected by Carvalho seems on the face to corroborate Graça's dismissive portrayal of Eufrazina, it is highly unlikely that the shrewd Ana Joaquina, well-versed in the complex trade dynamics of West Central Africa, would assign such a critical diplomatic mission to a household servant. Most plausibly, Eufrazina was among the trusted deputies managing her extensive business interests across Angola and beyond. Her selection would likely have been based on proven expertise and a deep understanding of the intricate and often perilous world of diplomacy characteristic of the colony's hinterlands.

In a possible scenario, Eufrazina would have originally been one of many pumbeiros—traders who traveled in the interior on behalf of Luanda merchants—that Ana Joaquina employed to handle her sprawling business in West Central Africa, as Henrique Carvalho himself would suggest in another account.[32] In this role, she would have led caravans carrying a range of goods, including weapons, textiles, and gunpowder, for trade in areas beyond Portuguese influence. Her experience would have included treks back to Luanda, transporting commodities like wax and enslaved Africans. To better illustrate her responsibilities, a possible parallel would be the case of Helena Francisca, a free black woman who, in 1846, managed a small team including enslaved individuals and carriers, transporting goods between Calumbo and Quissama.[33]

Supporting this scenario is Ana Joaquina's regular use of enslaved Africans as pumbeiros, including a man named João José Ignácio, who had served as a sailor on one of her ships before being sent as a pumbeiro to trade near Kongo, where he eventually defected. According to Ignácio, it was "more convenient to trade on his account, seizing a great deal of goods he had in storage, without ever reporting on his whereabouts and business activities."[34] Another example is a mixed-race man named Frutuoso, who was once tasked with escorting forty-five enslaved Africans to Icolo, likely to work on one of Ana Joaquina's farms.[35] Like Eufrazina, some of these individuals would have been deployed in far-flung regions away from Luanda. In 1853, for example, two of her captives were arrested in Pundo Andongo, where they had likely been deployed as traders, due to "disorderly conduct, robbery, and violence."[36]

Whatever the case, it is unlikely that Eufrazina's status as an enslaved person would have necessarily seemed unnatural for the Lunda. By the time she arrived at Nawej II's court, Lunda slavery had undergone significant changes, becoming a complex institution that encompassed both traditional forms of dependence and new, commercially oriented practices. As historian David Gordon remarks, "Slavery and the trade in slaves became significant even in economic peripheries," with the employment of individuals on plantation-like estates, cultivating crops for caravans, serving as a notable example of this transformation.[37] This shift was likely influenced by Ambakista traders who, coming from Portuguese-influenced areas near the coast, brought with them familiarity with similar practices as they penetrated into Lunda territory.[38]

Yet, despite the emergence of new forms of slavery, traditional slavery still persisted. Under this system, some enslaved individuals had opportunities to shift owners or integrate into society, reflecting the relational nature of traditional slavery beyond mere market-driven dynamics. As scholar Jeffrey Hoover highlights, "A slave could be incorporated and potentially ascend to any level of status."[39] Given this context, the Lunda might have viewed Eufrazina through the lens of their traditional system, associating her with native individuals held under customary forms of servitude who were often deeply integrated into their society.

Gender dynamics represent another salient facet in examining Eufrazina's trajectory. While she serves as the only documented example of a female pumbeiro owned by Ana Joaquina, she was likely not an anomaly. Many of Ana Joaquina's contemporaries in the Angolan slave trade regularly employed women in such roles, illustrating the broader involvement of women in trade at the time. A case in point was Justiniano José dos Reis, a well-known slave dealer and former governor of Benguela. Like Ana Joaquina, Reis would regularly dispatch traders, including women, to the Benguela hinterland with a variety of goods to trade in slaves. One of his female pumbeiros, Bibiana, once petitioned the Benguela government to retrieve an enslaved person purportedly taken from her, likely intended for sale in Brazil.[40]

The records show that the experiences of these female pumbeiros varied, with some achieving greater independence and prominence than others. The most adept among them might be able to establish an inland base, from where they would send agents to the coast to transport captives and export goods, instead of making the journey themselves. For example, in 1826, Justiniano Jose Reis submitted a request to authorities in Benguela seeking permission to return to the Hambos hinterland the slaves who had delivered a shipment for Dona Lucrecia, suggesting that she had attained a level of autonomy in her trading activities.[41] However, despite the success achieved by some female pumbeiros, many faced significant risks in their trading activities. Dona Vitoria Pinheiro's story illustrates these dangers: she was once enslaved and nearly sent to Brazil after a failed transaction in the Benguela hinterlands. Pinheiro's freedom was secured only when João Batista Benites, a Benguela merchant who regularly employed her, vouched for her free status to the authorities.[42]

Eufrazina's success in swiftly accomplishing her diplomatic mission raises intriguing questions about how the Lunda dignitaries perceived her gender.

Remarkably, it took her far less time to achieve her goals than it had taken for Graça to be allowed to engage in negotiations after his arrival in the Lunda court. This contrast suggests that the Lunda elite might have drawn parallels between her and tukwatas, their own emissaries who leveraged diplomatic skills and military might to maintain the Lunda ruler's far-reaching influence. By evoking her mistress's authority and traveling with a small group of soldiers, as was customary for tukwatas, Eufrazina likely legitimized her position and facilitated her success in the eyes of the Lunda state. While gender dynamics undoubtedly played a role in how she was perceived, Eufrazina's effectiveness as a diplomat challenges simplistic assumptions about women's roles in African societies.

The Lunda dignitaries' apparent lack of concern about Eufrazina's gender may also be in part attributed to the prominent roles women played in Lunda society. This is exemplified by the Lunda origin story, which centers around Princess Lueji (also known as Ruwej, Luwej, or Lweji), who played a key role in the formation of the Lunda state. With the aid of a group of elderly nobles (atubung), Lueji governed the kingdom after her father relinquished power, having grown disillusioned with his sons and potential heirs, Kinguri and Kinyama. Lueji's marriage to a foreigner from the Luba kingdom, who would become the first Mwant Yav, triggered dissatisfaction among her siblings and led to several migrations that gave rise to the Imbangalas, Luvale, and Chokwe peoples.[43] This foundational narrative underscores the central role of women in Lunda politics and society, providing a context in which Eufrazina's gender might have been less of a barrier to her diplomatic mission than it would have been in Portuguese-controlled territories.

Beyond foundational myths, women also held paramount political positions, such as Nswan Murund and Lukuokexe, taking center stage in the fabric of Lunda politics. Selected from an independent royal lineage, the Nswan Murund reigned in a ceremonial fashion rather than ruling outright in day-to-day affairs. According to scholar Jeffrey Hoover, "the nswan murund reigns but does not rule."[44] Yet they played a pivotal role in approving or rejecting candidates to become the new Mwant Yav.[45] As the living symbol of ancestor Lueji, holders of the Nswan Murund position were exalted as "mothers of the Lunda," seeking to transcend factional interests to vet heirs to the throne. However, it is most likely that Eufrazina did not interact with these dignitaries during her mission to the Lunda court.

By contrast, she would almost certainly have interacted with the woman then holding the position of Lukuokexe, a titleholder who wielded significant political and administrative power in the Lunda kingdom. Known as "the mother of the first mwant yav," Lukuokexes were appointed from the king's immediate female kin and were actively involved in critical aspects of governance, such as the coronation of new rulers, influencing burial practices, and resolving disputes over royal succession.[46] According to reports reaching

Luanda (Angola's capital) around 1808, the Lukuokexe of that time resided independently from the Lunda ruler in her own domain. Demonstrating her autonomy, she even sent her own envoys on a trading mission to Luanda.[47] Recognizing her distinct political identity and influence, the Governor of Angola, Saldanha Gama, took the significant step of addressing a specific letter directly to her.[48]

Bypassing Kasanje?

The failure of Graça's expedition marked the end of a complex logistical undertaking that had taken four years to accomplish, involving the recruitment of approximately five hundred African porters. Although Graça seems to have conceived the idea of traveling to Lunda alone, he soon received support from José Xavier Bressane Leite, a newly appointed governor of Angola who had previously been a founding member and vice president of Lisbon's Geographical Society. "I casually told him that I was about to take a long trip to the interior of this country, and he immediately said that he would commission a mission from me."[49] Graça then asked for an honorary position in the colonial army "so that I could be seen as respectable by the gentio."[50]

Bressane Leite was eager to increase the flow of goods to Luanda at a time when the cessation of captive shipments was beginning to impact the city's economy. While appointing Graça as Sargento Mor of the residents of Golungo Alto, where he lived, the governor offered the merchant a piece of artillery, which Graça declined.[51] Support from the Luanda government continued after Pedro Alexandrino da Cunha succeeded Bressane Leite as the new governor of Angola. As the first governor to effectively combat the slave trade from the colony, Cunha was even more invested in reengineering trade terms with West Central Africa regions beyond Portugal's influence.[52]

In exchange for official support for the expedition, Governor Bressane Leite requested that Graça write an account of Africa's fauna, flora, and geography, even providing him with a report model.[53] This request reflected Portugal's drive to strengthen its presence in West Central Africa by increasing scientific knowledge about interior regions beyond coastal territory under its nominal control. About six years earlier, the government had already hired Swiss explorer J. C. Lang, who wrote a report on oil reserves in Dande published in 1886 but whose travels in Mossamedes were deemed a fiasco.[54] German explorer Georg Tams traveled to Luanda and Benguela in the early 1840s with some support from the Portuguese government of Angola.[55]

Two other explorers—Hungarian László Magyar and Austrian Friedrich Welwitsch—produced numerous reports on the African colony's people and geography. Magyar became involved with slave dealers in Benguela and eventually journeyed to the Benguela highlands.[56] However, his accounts largely remained unpublished despite reports to the Hungarian Academy of Science.

Welwitsch, on the other hand, had a significant impact in shaping views of Angola's economic potential at the time, frequently corresponding with Portuguese authorities and scientific outlets in Portugal.[57] A strong advocate for promoting commercial agriculture, he believed Angola could become a significant supplier of tropical commodities to Europe, including coffee and, primarily, cotton.[58]

In the case of Graça, his expedition's ramifications stretched beyond science. Luanda officials asked him to cross the continent to the headwaters of the Sena River, effectively connecting Angola to East Africa. This request was likely a response to recent reports that Portuguese Major Manoel José Correa Monteiro, traveling from Mozambique, had reached deep into West Central Africa. Relayed by an African trader (pumbeiro) who had visited the Lunda empire, the news prompted Governor of Angola Antonio Manoel de Noronha to pledge support for an expedition to link Angola to Mozambique.[59] When Graça departed Luanda, the Portuguese gave him letters of introduction to Portuguese authorities in East Africa.[60] However, whether the traveler ever seriously considered meeting this goal is unclear.

What he did pursue was a treaty of alliance with the Lunda emperor, which would have allowed pumbeiros and sertanejos (traders operating on behalf of Luanda merchants) to conduct business freely within his territory. This objective, if accomplished, would have dealt a blow to a long-standing arrangement in which the Mbundu kingdom of Kasanje acted as a middleman in trade exchanges between the Lunda Empire and Luanda since the early eighteenth century. In this arrangement, Kasanje greatly influenced the flow of goods (ivory, wax, and captives) to Angola's capital city. Traders who operated on behalf of Luanda sponsors had to conduct business in a market controlled by the Kasanje ruler, the feira de Casanje. While the market was governed by rules negotiated with Luanda officials and a director oversaw business on the ground, the ruler held a tight grip over the operation of the market.[61]

One of the key rules was that traders could not venture east on their own, which prevented direct trade exchanges between the Portuguese and the Lunda empire and thus safeguarded the kingdom's role. The ruler also employed psychological tactics, exaggerating the dangers of westward travel to discourage direct contact between Luanda and the Lunda empire. Lunda subjects and the Mwant Yav himself were told that "white people came from the ocean to eat black people," exploiting the widely held belief that white people were cannibals. To discourage the Lunda from sending military forces to break its grip over trade routes, the Jaga would warn them that Portugal would send military support if he were ever attacked.[62]

Kasanje's relationship with the Portuguese government in Luanda was far from smooth. As early as 1790, the Kasanje ruler (jaga) sent a letter to Luanda complaining about pumbeiros who violated existing rules by roaming outside the market and refusing to pay agreed-upon prices for captives and ivory.[63] By 1812, the relationship had deteriorated further when the Portuguese accused the jaga of refusing to turn over runaway slaves belonging to the Portuguese. The dispute led to the relocation of traders to another market in Mucari.[64] Two years later, Luanda officials expressed frustration after the jaga was accused of favoring an African trader over a feirante.[65] Recognizing that halting trade relations would be detrimental not only to the Portuguese but also to himself, the jaga dispatched an envoy to Luanda to negotiate an accord with the Luanda government in 1816.[66]

Against this backdrop, the rationale for establishing direct ties with the Lunda empire took on new urgency following Portugal's decision to curb the transatlantic slave trade from Luanda in the 1840s. The Lunda trade was viewed as pivotal for fostering a new economy in Angola, emphasizing ivory and other export goods. Governor Antonio Manoel de Noronha, a vocal opponent of the slave trade, arrived in Luanda to find the newly established Presídio de Duque de Bragança already operational. This fort was strategically located four to five days east of the Presídio de Ambaca, near the lands of Icolo, effectively bypassing Kasanje territory. Noronha recognized this new presidio as a crucial asset for developing direct trade relations with the Lunda, circumventing Kasanje's long-standing role as a middleman.[67]

Adaptative Strategies

Ana Joaquina's decision to fund Graça's expedition to the Lunda empire was a strategic move consistent with her established role in West Central Africa's complex trade dynamics. Born in 1789 to a Luso-African mother and a Portuguese military officer, her influence extended far and wide. According to Italian traveler Tito Omboni, the Luanda native was "obeyed by the most distant tribes. No one dares to oppose her will."[68] By the 1840s, just a few years prior to dispatching Graça and then her own envoys to the Lunda Empire, Ana Joaquina had been a prominent figure in commerce for over two decades, amassing wealth rumored to surpass tenfold Angola's colonial state revenue.[69] Her expedition to the Lunda Empire was part of a broader strategy to adapt her business operations to the declining transatlantic slave trade by securing new sources of commodities and labor for her expanding commercial ventures in Angola.

Ana Joaquina's business acumen extended beyond her trade ventures. Six years following her involvement in the Lunda expedition, she embarked on a journey to inspect her farms (arimos) in Icolo e Bengo, Dande, and Zenza do Golungo. This trip served not only as a display of her wealth but also as an assertion of her expanding influence in agricultural production. Her sizeable entourage, comprising over eighty individuals including at least seventy-eight enslaved people and several women of status known as donas, underscored her economic and social power. Notably, she was described as a "sixty-year-old white woman born in Luanda," a characterization that overlooked her mixed heritage but reflected her social ascension through wealth and cultural capital accumulation."[70]

Ana Joaquina had by then come a long way since the beginning of her career in Luanda. In the early nineteenth century, as historian Vanessa de Oliveira demonstrates, the Luanda businesswoman owned farms that supplied food to Luanda, which might have laid the foundation for her subsequent maritime ventures.[71] In one instance, a woman enslaved by her refused to declare three sacks of manioc flour and corn taken to Luanda's market (terreiro) in 1825.[72] By then, she was already an investor in the trade in African lives, the only woman among the twenty-four largest slave dealers shipping captives from Luanda between August 1819 and January 1822.[73] Eventually, the Luanda native would become the owner of at least ten slave vessels, purchasing four of them between 1824 and 1832.[74]

She would soon become the head of a business empire that extended from West Central Africa's hinterlands to various Atlantic cities, including Pernambuco, Rio de Janeiro, and Salvador. In Rio de Janeiro, one of her agents was José Fortunato da Cunha, who later joined a group of slave dealers (known as the Portuguese firm) that relocated to New York City to organize the final phase of the slave trade to Cuba.[75] In Salvador, she maintained connections with Joaquim Pereira Marinho, the city's primary slave dealer, who traveled to Luanda on October 31, 1835.[76] In their meetings in Luanda, the two likely focused on strategies to bypass a recently established ban on importing enslaved Africans to Brazil, possibly considering the use of Montevideo as a gateway for covertly smuggling captives into Brazil.[77] Tellingly, Joaquim Rodrigues Graça would later ship to Montevideo seventy-five captives to the city on a ship that belonged to Ana Joaquina.

Ana Joaquina was a key facilitator of the networks of the Atlantic trade, the backbone of her sprawling commercial empire, frequently sponsoring slave dealers seeking government-issued licenses to enter Luanda from Brazil and Ambriz. One of the beneficiaries of these maneuvers was a man named Joaquim Moreira da Costa, who arrived in Luanda as a passenger on a ship named Argo in 1846.[78] Another was Ignacio de Gouveia e Souza, a Brazilian slave dealer who kept his activities in Luanda shrouded in secrecy due to the outlawed nature of the slave trade. Tellingly, when he returned to his home country, Souza declared that although he believed he had no outstanding debts in Luanda, anyone who felt otherwise had eight days to make a claim— at Ana Joaquina's house.[79]

She also maintained extensive business ties with the Luanda hinterland and beyond, which provided access not only to enslaved people but also to a steady supply of export commodities like ivory and wax. In 1847, she requested 50 porters from the Ambaca district to transport goods from the Kasanje fair to Luanda.[80] That same year, she sought an additional 50 porters for one of his agents—Custodio de Lemos Soares—to move cargos of wax and ivory from

Kasanje to Luanda.[81] This request was immediately followed by another in which she petitioned the Luanda government to obtain 60 porters to carry ivory and wax from Pungo Andongo to Luanda.[82]

Graça was only one of several individuals who received financial backing from Ana Joaquina for commercial ventures. She frequently provided loans and credit to various individuals, including a man arrested for enslaving someone to repay a debt owed to her.[83] Manoel Antunes de Carvalho, a city battalion captain, passed away before fulfilling his financial obligations to her.[84] In 1852, Ana Joaquina was said to have lent "a large amount of money" to another woman, Dona Marina Rodrigues da Silva.[85] She also offered insurance coverage for ships transporting enslaved Africans to Brazil, an exceedingly risky investment. Reminiscent of her early ventures, however, she continued investing in food production near Luanda as well. In 1852, she and José Vaz Contreiras e Araújo were named as the only Luanda residents capable of meeting the government's request for flour and cattle, though they disagreed on proposed prices.[86]

While Ana Joaquina's dominance in business was pronounced, it is worth pointing out that she was not the only woman from Luanda involved in such endeavors. Despite her unparalleled success, other women also engaged in significant commercial activities. In 1822, Dona Maria Roza da Conceição appointed a representative in Rio de Janeiro to liquidate various assets, including a small house and three enslaved individuals she inherited from her deceased father.[87] In a different case, Dona Mariana da Piedade enlisted the help of Felix José dos Santos, who represented João Gomes Valle, a distinguished trader from Rio de Janeiro, to secure a bill of exchange valued at 1,000,000 réis.[88] Dona Ana Ubertali, another important slave dealer in Luanda, engaged in several economic activities near the city, becoming the owner of a sugar plantation in Bengo. Yet none of them ever came close to Ana Joaquina's level of entrepreneurship or the scope of her business empire.

Women's influence in business was also evident in Benguela. A case in point was Dona Tereza de Jesus Ferreira Torres Viana, who became wealthy after marrying Jose Luiz da Silva Viana, likely the most important slave dealer in Benguela in the 1840s. In a petition to the governor of Angola in 1855, while all the other male signers included their status as proprietors or merchants, Dona Tereza signed as Viana's widow.[89] By the time she married Vicente Barruncho, recently appointed governor of Benguela, she had likely already become perhaps the largest investor in commercial agriculture in Benguela. By 1861, she owned three plantations in the Dombe Grande, one with more than three hundred enslaved people, contributing to her becoming the leading exporter of cotton, wax, and orchil weed from the port of Benguela.[90]

The success of these businesswomen was often tied to the unique opportunities provided by Portuguese inheritance laws, which entitled widows to half of the couple's estate.[91] Beyond financial gains, these opportunities had broader social and political ramifications. One striking example is Maria da

Silva, a Luanda widow who had inherited a considerable fortune from her late husband. In 1799, she chose not to settle accounts with her father, Antonio Jose da Silva, a merchant who had spent forty years in Angola before relocating to Rio de Janeiro. According to Silva, he had "left his substantial trading house, valued at over one hundred thousand cruzados, in the hands of Alexandre de Mesquita e Almeida," who then married his daughter. Following Almeida's death, Maria da Silva's influence grew so substantially that "no one is willing to accept the powers of the petitioner [his father] to settle his accounts with his petitioned daughter."[92]

While Portuguese inheritance laws could significantly empower some women both economically and politically, it is important to note that for some women, like Dona Delfina de Miranda Brito Vieira, economic autonomy came before widowhood. In 1839, she wrote to the governor of Angola, protesting the confiscation of cows from her family's property near Luanda. Her husband, who had traveled to Rio de Janeiro and left his ship, the brig *Aventura*, docked in the port, explicitly entrusted his business affairs to Delfina. As the husband himself admitted, he had "gone to Rio de Janeiro at the end of last October and left his ship (brig *Aventura*) docked in this port under the care of his lady Delfina de Miranda Brito Vieira, as well as other business of his [commercial] house."[93]

As the transatlantic slave trade faced increasing opposition, Ana Joaquina began to explore new business opportunities that would allow her to adapt to the changing economic landscape in Angola. As early as 1836, she was the primary investor in a company that explored commercial agriculture in Angola, though its operations were short-lived.[94] She also transported supplies on her vessels to the newly established agricultural colony in Mossâmedes, where she owned a trading post for orchella and ivory as late as 1849.[95] These initiatives showcase Ana Joaquina's efforts to position herself at the forefront of Angola's economic transformation, as the colony sought to reduce its reliance on the slave trade and promote other sources of revenue.

None of these projects, however, came close to her investment in sugar production, which closely aligned with the Luanda government's economic goals for the colony. According to the British, she was responsible for "the only attempt to give capital a more wholesome direction," having "commenced erecting [sugar] mills which she expects to see come into operation in the course of the present year."[96] The scale of her investments undoubtedly gave commercial agriculture a strong impulse. It is important to note, however, that Africans had long been engaged in sugar production, as evidenced by the substantial quantities of sugarcane they brought daily to the Quitanda market in Luanda.[97] Nevertheless, Ana Joaquina's sugar mills represented a significant step toward the expansion of this sector, setting her apart from other producers.

For the Luanda government, Ana Joaquina's investments represented one of the most consequential attempts to create a post-slave trade economy in

Angola. Officials did not hesitate to support her, complying with policies that Portugal itself had long laid out. As early as 1838, Lisbon officials instructed the newly appointed Governor of Angola, Antonio Manoel de Noronha, to support the development of commercial agriculture in the colony. In 1846, officials stated that she "must receive protection due to its convenience for the province."[98] Four years later, after visiting her properties, Governor of Angola Adrião Accacio da Silveira Pinto reported that a sugar mill was near completion and that sugar and rum production would begin soon.[99]

While Ana Joaquina's investments in commercial agriculture were undoubtedly prominent, she was hardly the only woman to invest in agriculture in Luanda or Benguela. As early as 1797, a significant proportion, about one-third, of the agricultural estates (arimos) in Catumbela, near Benguela, were owned by women. Notably, donas (ladies of status) like Ana Joaquina held 17% of these properties.[100] Nor was she the only investor—man or woman—venturing into sugar production. In Benguela, by the mid-nineteenth century, there were at least four sugar mills located in areas like Equimina and Bumbo and along the Quicupangombe River.[101]

Yet no one could boost a commitment to sugar production as strong as Ana Joaquina's, which involved traveling to Brazil herself to learn about sugar cultivation techniques. According to British sources, "she has herself been in the Brazils and witnessed the process of cultivations and manufacturing sugar and expresses herself pleased and confident as to the result of her present endeavors."[102] While in Pernambuco, Ana Joaquina hired a French sugar specialist named Pedro Regaire to develop her farms near Luanda. In 1846, Regaire reportedly went to Icolo e Bengo to work on sugar farming and mills on Ana Joaquina's land.[103]

Ana Joaquina's decision to hire foreign sugar specialists was not unprecedented in Angola. The colonial government had previously recognized the potential benefits of foreign expertise in developing the sugar industry. In 1839, Governor of Angola Antonio Manoel de Noronha asked a Portuguese consul in Recife to facilitate the dispatch of two French specialists and an enslaved person to develop sugar production and Brazilian rum in Angola.[104] This initiative failed due to a lack of funding and difficulties locating proper soil for sugar cultivation in Angola. One of the individuals involved, José Augusto da Silva Neves, petitioned the Portuguese government in 1840, stating that he had gone to Angola from Rio de Janeiro but had not received a salary after five months.[105]

Despite the setbacks experienced with Pedro Regaire, the French sugar specialist Ana Joaquina had hired to develop her farms near Luanda, she soon contracted another specialist from Pernambuco, Manoel J. C. de Freitas, to continue the work. According to an 1847 account, Freitas was then living at Ana Joaquina's estate in Icolo, which featured a nearly completed sugar mill and distillery that he expected to begin manufacturing sugar and liquor that year. The estate also had an oven for lime and facilities for tile and brick production. This highlights Ana Joaquina's vertical integration and leverage of specialized expertise to further sugar production near Luanda.[106]

The impact of foreign specialists on the quality of sugar produced on Ana Joaquina's farms was notable. Portuguese traveler Jose Caldeira praised the sugar and rum from the farms as being of "excellent" quality.[107] However, not all assessments were as favorable; while two samples of sugar were deemed of poor and middling quality, a third was acknowledged as comparable to the prestigious sugar products of French and British colonies.[108] In 1857, Ana Joaquina herself contributed a note to a Luanda weekly, robustly defending her investments in sugar production. Despite not being "headed by a white person," she declared that her sugar mill had been a successful venture.[109]

Critically, Ana Joaquina's sugar investments played a significant role in growing the institution of slavery in Angola.[110] In 1846, officials described her as the "owner of several arrimos (farms) and many captives."[111] A year later, British reports indicated that nearly three hundred enslaved people worked on a recently established sugar farm near Luanda, owned by Ana Joaquina. This was indicative of the vast scale of her agricultural operations, which reportedly involved as many as 2,000 captives and freed slaves by the mid-1850s.[112]

Ana Joaquina's outreach to the Lunda empire gains further meaning in this context. By engaging this predominant regional power, she likely sought to secure not only ivory and wax but also enslaved laborers for her burgeoning sugar operations. Her adaptive maneuvers epitomized the calculations of merchants pursuing new profits as the transatlantic slave trade entered its twilight. Ultimately, Ana Joaquina redirected her networks to procure labor for commodity crop cultivation instead. Her vanguard role in pioneering plantation agriculture aligned with Portugal's vision for Angola, which was predicated on the growth of slavery in the colony. Yet this also reinforced the extractive and dehumanizing nature of Portuguese rule for countless African lives. The trajectory of this influential merchant-turned-planter encapsulates the shifting strategies—and enduring human toll—as colonial commerce confronted abolition's slow arrival.

Shared Interests

Without Ana Joaquina's backing, the expedition led by Graça would likely have never been launched. She provided two-thirds of the funds used by Graça to procure goods for the journey. These goods were acquired from three influential Luanda merchants, including Francisco Antonio Flores, a Brazilian newcomer representing a powerful Rio de Janeiro slave trade house. The remainder of the goods were sold by Antonio Lopes Silva and Manoel Francisco Alves de Brito, two of Luanda's most influential merchants. Brito retired to Brazil in 1854, but Lopes Silva was a fixture of Luanda's politics and economy well into the 1860s.[113] Graça also relied on a bill of exchange in Rio de Janeiro.[114]

According to the contract between Ana Joaquina and Graça, despite the fact that Graça was the expedition leader, he was a minority partner in the enterprise. The agreement stipulated that profits were to be split evenly between the two parties, likely reflecting the considerable risks involved in Graça's hazardous role of venturing into the interior. While Graça had the freedom to sell goods acquired from Luanda in the sertões, he was under strict obligation to ship all products, including wax, ivory, and enslaved people, exclusively to Ana Joaquina. The contract expressly prohibited him from shipping these items to any other Luanda merchant.[115] This restriction may have been the root cause of their eventual fallout, as it is likely that Graça violated the contract by shipping goods to another Luanda merchant. Given Ana Joaquina's extensive network of associates in both the city and the sertões, she would have almost certainly learned of this breach from one of her many contacts.

Graça and his sponsor shared interests beyond just the Lunda expedition. Both would draw on experience observing commercial agriculture in Brazil to seek to establish a plantation system in Angola. As detailed earlier, Ana Joaquina went as far as to travel to Brazil and hire individuals familiar with Brazil's agriculture to direct her farms in Angola. Graça, on the other hand, visited Rio de Janeiro in 1829 and 1830 to study cocoa cultivation near the city. He remarked, "I went to Rio de Janeiro, and once there, I examined cocoa plantations (plantações). What I learned has partly contributed to cocoa cultivation in Angola."[116]

Upon establishing himself in Angola, Graça initially focused on cocoa cultivation but later shifted his agricultural pursuits to coffee. He established a coffee farm in Golungo Alto, which became his primary residence and a pivotal site for anchoring coffee production in the colony. According to historian Alan de Carvalho Souza, Graça likely drew inspiration from his observations of coffee farming during his time in Brazil.[117] This strategic move aligned with Portugal's vision for agricultural development in Angola. Highlighting Brazil as a model, officials promoted Angolan coffee production as early as 1839, pointing out its competitive edge over Brazilian coffee due to the absence of Portuguese import duties.[118] Yet Graça would eventually become critical of the reliance on Brazilian techniques to grow coffee in Angola.[119]

The transfer of Brazilian agricultural knowledge and techniques to Angola was not an isolated phenomenon; it was part of a broader pattern of the spread of Brazilian coffee production practices across the South Atlantic. According to historian Marta Macedo, former slave traders who had traveled extensively between Angola, Brazil, and São Tomé played a key role in transferring knowledge and practices from burgeoning Brazilian coffee plantations to these regions in the 1850s. Much as in Angola, these individuals drew on their firsthand observations of coffee cultivation in Brazil to establish plantation systems in their respective destinations. João Maria de Sousa e Almeida, a prominent slave trader who had visited Brazilian coffee estates, was one of the pioneers who modeled his investments in São Tomé after Brazil. Similarly, José Velloso de Carvalho, another key figure in São Tomé's coffee industry, attempted to replicate Brazilian practices, such as planting coffee in aligned rows to facilitate visual control and surveillance of the workforce, although his efforts ultimately failed.[120]

Beyond his trip to Brazil, Graça was likely inspired by the example of João Guilherme Pereira Barboza, another individual whose trajectory illustrates how the mobility of people and ideas across the South Atlantic shaped the development of plantation economies in the wake of the transatlantic slave trade. A Portuguese man who had gone to Angola by way of Brazil with an eye on investing in coffee production, Barboza had "left Brazil for Africa with the firm intention of becoming a coffee grower."[121] By the early 1830s, he had purchased 25 enslaved Africans at a market in Dondo, a town in the Luanda hinterland. By 1845, Barboza had over 150 enslaved people working on his coffee farms in Cazengo, which would soon emerge as Angola's main coffee-producing region.[122]

Alongside Ana Joaquina and Graça, Barboza became a pivotal figure in Angolan commercial agriculture. By the early 1840s, his estates in Cazengo boasted approximately 60,000 coffee bushes, escalating production from 170 arrobas in 1838 to 600 by 1845.[123] He requested the creation of a district in Cazengo and was appointed its chief in 1840.[124] Described by officials as the "first and sole" resident in Angola to establish a significant coffee-based agricultural enterprise, Barboza was later honored with the title Cavalheiro da Ordem de Nossa Senhora da Conceição de Vila Viçosa by the Luanda government.[125] Largely due to his efforts, the growth of coffee farming was evident in export figures as well, with 110,656 pounds of the crop being shipped from Luanda in 1848–49.[126]

Agricultural efforts such as the ones carried out by Graça and Barboza would not have been possible without the support from the Luanda government. A telling example was the granting of libertos to coffee and sugar farms at the time, where these "former" slaves were to provide labor to Angola's emerging economy.[127] For the government, reflecting widely held views, adult men were perceived as "more difficult to tame and acclimate to the tasks of farming, which they found tedious and were more inclined to evade, . . . [it] being easier and more convenient to educate these younger individuals who were still relatively free from vices."[128] Yet this rationale soon lost ground as labor models influenced by Brazil's experience of coffee production did not discriminate between male and female unfree laborers.

After Barboza's passing in 1850, authorities voiced concern that coffee production might decline.[129] Yet thanks to his early investments, coffee production was by then on the way up. Between 1838 and 1856, the number of coffee bushes grew markedly from just 60,000 to 415,000.[130] While Cazengo accounted for only 4,200 bushes or about 5% of Angola's total output in 1849, production in the region grew substantially in subsequent years.[131] Equally important, Barboza's success inspired other investors to follow his example—Albino José Soares Magalhães owned a sizable farm with 400 enslaved laborers by the mid-1850s.[132] Another coffee farmer influenced was Antonio Jose Lopes Soeiro, who was active in Cazengo by 1851.[133]

By then, Graça's coffee farm had become a cornerstone of Angola's coffee production. In 1856, he proudly described his property as "the best, perhaps, of the province," noting his substantial investment and challenges, such as "slave flights and death."[134] In "favorable years," according to contemporary accounts, the farm produced approximately 400 arrobas of coffee, supplied to local shops in Luanda and exported to Portugal.[135] Recognizing his pioneering efforts, the Luanda government appointed Graça an honorary major in the colonial army in 1863, two years before his passing.[136]

While Brazilian farming techniques initially influenced Angola's coffee production, they were eventually deemed unsuitable for the local conditions. Some local farmers attributed early setbacks to the adoption of these Brazilian methods, asserting that success was only achieved when they embraced indigenous African techniques.[137] A significant increase in coffee production—about fifty percent from 1854 to 1855—was once attributed to "indigenous coffee."[138] According to British missionary David Livingstone, who traveled through Cazengo in the 1850s, the region's extensive coffee plantations "were not planted by the Portuguese."[139] Officials later emphasized that Angolan coffee production "differed significantly from what is done in Brazil."[140]

Still, the influence of Brazil's agricultural model on Angola, particularly when it comes to the reliance on enslaved labor, is undeniable. To begin with, it provided a counterpoint to those who doubted the viability of commercial agriculture in the African colony, citing the supposed "ineffectiveness" of African laborers. Advocates of commercial agriculture pointed to Brazil's success, which they attributed to the labor of people from Angola. They argued that, once the slave trade ended, these individuals would excel even more in their "mother country where they were used to the atmosphere [*sic*]."[141] This rhetoric not only justified the expansion of bonded labor but also led to tangible consequences: as agricultural activities expanded, the enslaved population in Golungo, the base for Graça's coffee investments, increased dramatically from approximately 1,400 individuals in 1849 to 4,260 in 1856, illustrating the direct link between commercial agriculture and the rise in unfree labor.[142]

A Legal Battle

Before they clashed over the expedition to the Lunda empire, Ana Joaquina had helped Graça set up his coffee farm, using her political connections to back his request to obtain one hundred receptive Africans to work on his Golungo

Alto farm.[143] Recaptives, as discussed in Chapter 7, were Africans who had been released from slave vessels apprehended by the Portuguese navy, which was then actively engaged in curbing the transatlantic slave trade. As pointed out earlier, the two individuals had once partnered on the slave trade to Montevideo, with Graça shipping seventy-five enslaved Africans on one of Ana Joaquina's ships.[144] Yet the expedition to the Lunda empire deeply damaged their relationship.

Before Graça returned to Luanda, and likely after learning that he had violated the contract with her by shipping goods to other merchants in Luanda, a militia stormed his house in Golungo Alto. Acting on behalf of Ana Joaquina, the men told domestic workers at the property that Graça had died.[145] According to Graça, they tried to enslave one of his daughters and sexually attacked one of his household servants. As a result of the upheaval caused by the operation ordered by Ana Joaquina, many of his captives fled the property. This incident marked the beginning of a long battle between the former commercial partners.

The clash intensified after Graça returned to Luanda, with Ana Joaquina leveraging her political influence to prevent him from returning to his house in Golungo Alto. Several lawsuits followed. A Luanda judge dismissed a first suit seeking to embargo Graça's assets.[146] The explorer then turned to the courts to demand financial compensation, claiming that one-third of the goods taken to the sertões belonged to him. Another lawsuit filed by the businesswoman stalled in Luanda's circuitous legal system. In 1853, several years after the former partners had turned on each other, Ana Joaquina complained that a local judge had refused to "decide a petition she had filed against Joaquim Rodrigues Graça."[147]

Graça was not the only business partner with whom Ana Joaquina had a falling out. Duarte José Monteiro Nunes, a merchant based in Pungo Andongo, once traveled to Luanda to terminate a partnership with her.[148] Ana Joaquina received the merchant and requested more time to examine the accounting books presented by Nunes. Yet their negotiation quickly soured after Duarte published a note in Luanda's weekly Gazette unilaterally announcing the partnership's end. According to him, he could no longer wait for his partner to finish reviewing the accounts he had submitted.[149] In response, Ana Joaquina retaliated by stating that the partnership could not be dissolved because Duarte's funds and personnel (enslaved Africans) belonged to her.[150]

This legal battle was not Ana Joaquina's first time turning to Luanda's courts to defend her commercial interests. In 1850, a man named Christovão Miranda da Nóbrega was ordered to pay her eighty pieces of gold after failing to pay for a piece of gold jewelry encrusted with diamond.[151] In another case, Dona Maria dos Reis Dionizia had assets (properties and captives) auctioned in public after failing to honor a debt with her.[152] Yet none of these suits came remotely close to the stakes involved in the judicial litigation with

Graça, which not only involved vast sums of goods borrowed from Luanda merchants but also arguably the future of Angola's economy.

Only one other legal battle in Ana Joaquina's life came close to rivaling her dispute with Graça: a protracted litigation with her daughter, Dona Thereza Luiza de Jesus Garrido. Dona Thereza's marriage to Elizio Guedes Coutinho Garrido went against Ana Joaquina's wishes, straining their relationship.[153] The crux of their dispute was Dona Thereza's claim that her mother had wrongfully taken control of her late father's estate. She contended that Ana Joaquina owed her a substantial sum, totaling eighty contos of réis, even going so far as to demand a sequestration of her mother's assets.[154] In a public rebuttal, Ana Joaquina announced in Luanda's weekly publication that she had already settled her daughter's inheritance and retained full ownership of all her possessions.[155] The bitter family feud cast a gloomy pall over her life, however. According to Governor José Rodrigues Coelho do Amaral, the suit had cost Ana Joaquina all her assets. As she left for Lisbon in 1859, a trip in which she would pass away before reaching Portugal, she complained about "violence" against her in Luanda due to the lawsuit.[156]

In the Lunda Court

While Ana Joaquina firmly established her influence in the Lunda court through her envoys, Graça's ill-fated expedition still offers insights into the Lunda ruler's motivations for engaging with Portuguese traders. Graça's prolonged stay—almost a year after arriving at the musumba—aligned with the customary at the time. According to scholar Beatrix Heintze, foreign traders were not simply "permitted to storm in and get to the point regarding the reason for their visit."[157] Through several meetings, Graça sought to build ties with the Mwant Yav, who "recognized him not only as a merchant but as an ambassador" of the Luanda government. The Lunda ruler more than once visited the Portuguese explorer with "all his family and dignitaries of his state to listen to him more attentively."[158]

In welcoming Graça, the Lunda ruler invoked a dream about the arrival of a trading caravan dispatched by Mueneputo (Portugal). "Muatiânvua Noéji had dreamed one night that a trading caravan of a white man was going to arrive at his capital, and days later Rodrigues Graça arrived."[159] Graça not only brought commerce but also introduced the Lunda ruler to new spiritual concepts, emphasizing the deep reverence and blessings associated with them. To honor the symbols brought by Graça, Nawej II designated a special area within his dwelling, which he decorated with gifts of crucifixes, believing them to be tangible representations of his dream.[160]

The Lunda ruler's next steps were grounded in conventional diplomacy that underscored his commitment to the negotiations with Graça. For one, he pledged to send one of his sons, aged sixteen or seventeen, to Luanda for education.[161] This was a goodwill gesture to signal a willingness to partner with the Portuguese, who were then engaging in cultural diplomacy elsewhere in West Central Africa. Just a year earlier, King of Kongo Henrique II had allowed the Portuguese to take one of his younger sons to Portugal for schooling. Yet Nawej II's commitments extended beyond this. He also vowed to dispatch one of his uncles as an envoy to Luanda, a noteworthy pledge considering his uncle's role in the Lunda kingdom's political structure.[162]

On a fundamental level, the Lunda ruler's engagement with Graça in trade talks was a strategic maneuver aimed at bolstering political power amidst the rise of independent trade within his territories. Until the emergence of Cokwe and Ambakista trade, trade with the West had been an extension of the state rather than a private sector activity. Goods acquired by Lunda rulers, such as beads, cloth, cowries, and guns, functioned not only as commodities but also played a key role in the kingdom's social and political fabric. Rulers distributed these items as a form of patronage to bolster their power through the formation of clientele. Thus, Nawej II's engagement with Graça was not merely economically driven but was a calculated step to reinforce his authority.[163]

Against this backdrop, the Lunda ruler would go to great lengths to maintain control over trade in his territory. He assigned an official to oversee the transit of traders, ensuring that they reached the royal court (musumba).[164] Additionally, he engaged in trade diplomacy to bolster the presence of foreign traders in his territory. Prior to Graça's arrival, the ruler had already welcomed a European trader named Romão into his royal court.[165] He had also dispatched an envoy to meet with a Chokwe leader, inviting him to hunt elephants in Lunda territory.[166] Even after expelling Graça from his musumba, the Lunda ruler contacted Lourenço Bezerra and affirmed his desire to have "white people coming to his royal court (Musumba) for trade."[167]

In this context, the Lunda ruler revealed himself particularly interested in Portugal's stance against the transatlantic slave trade. According to him, "due to the prohibition [of the transatlantic slave trade] we have suffered with lack of fazendas for our consumption," a statement that provides compelling evidence of how measures taken by the Luanda government to prohibit shipments of captives from Luanda reverberated inland.[168] The ruler then requested the reopening of the slave trade from Luanda, tying it to the deportation of individuals who had committed "crimes of murder, robbery, adultery, disobedience, and witchcraft."[169] Without the slave trade, the ruler observed, he would be left with only the death penalty "as an example to others."[170] According to Graça, the number of people executed every day for various crimes in the kingdom stood at more than sixty.[171]

In response, Graça pointed out that shipments of captives across the Atlantic were no longer allowed but that the sale of captives was still possible "in your land" for the benefit of "agriculture, fishing, and other activities useful to society."[172] This position was closely aligned with the Luanda government's policy of creating an export-oriented economy in Angola based on slave labor. As early as 1831, Governor of Angola Santa Comba Dão had informed the soba of Bié that exports of captives had been banned but that the sale and purchase of captives within Angola and nearby regions was still possible.[173] Almost twenty years later, the same policy found an echo in orders that the Luanda government issued to authorities in the city. According to them, the transit of captives via land and water was allowed within the colony.[174]

Yet Graça's trade talks were abruptly derailed with the "casual" arrival of Ana Joaquina's envoys, including Eufrazina. In what Graça described as a "perfid betrayal," the envoys convinced the ruler that he was merely a minor partner of Ana Joaquina. According to Graça's later report, the ruler's demeanor changed instantly, with a significant factor being Ana Joaquina's offer to provide him with a piece of artillery. From that point on, Nawej II not only treated the Portuguese explorer with disdain but also halted payments for goods already purchased. As Graça remarked, the envoys had successfully persuaded the ruler that he was nothing more than a "merchant from the Cuango."[175]

The sudden downfall culminated in Graça's compound being set on fire, destroying eight thousand libras of high-quality ivory. Further acts of violence ensued. As the explorer prepared to return to his base in Golungo Alto, Lunda nobles demanded that all arms and powder carried by members of the expedition be surrendered. They threatened to kill the expedition members if they did not comply, forcing Graça to make a hasty retreat. The Lunda ruler even ordered a blockage of the path back to the coast. Graça was forced to leave behind the equivalent in banzos of 418 pontas de marfim, which the ruler and his subjects still owed him.[176]

In a testament to one of the central tenets of the expedition, the Portuguese explorer managed to leave Lunda territory with almost four hundred captives. The enslaved Africans suffered immensely during the hurried return journey to the coast, facing severe casualties due to insufficient food supplies and harsh conditions. Graça reported that 174 people perished during the march to the coast, and another 128 captives succumbed to diseases contracted during the arduous journey from Lunda, dying upon arriving in Golungo Alto. The explorer attributed part of these losses to his detainment in Luanda by city officials following a lawsuit filed against him by Ana Joaquina.[177]

Conclusion

The complex web of relationships and ventures involving Ana Joaquina and Graça serves as a microcosm of the broader transformations in Angola as the transatlantic slave trade ended. Her commercial empire, trade diplomacy with the Lunda empire, and support of commercial agriculture reveal her significant influence on making a post-slave trade economy in Angola. She navigated and shaped these shifting dynamics by relying on networks and resources she had built up as one of Angola's largest slave dealers, leveraging her extensive network of connections and resources to diversify Angola's economy. Ana Joaquina's influence had far-reaching consequences for the lives of enslaved Africans and the region's long-term economic development, as her ventures helped to perpetuate and reshape systems of exploitation and control.

Eufrazina's vital role as an emissary in Lunda, despite her enslaved status, underscores the complex intersection of power, gender, and servitude within both the Lunda Empire and Portuguese Angola. It challenges traditional views of slavery and brings to light the fluidity of societal roles within these societies. Eufrazina's experience highlights the ways in which enslaved individuals could attain positions of influence and authority, even as they remained trapped within systems of oppression. Her story, along with those of others like her, represented only one of several types of slavery dynamics in West Central Africa, where commercial forms of slavery then on the rise coexisted with traditional forms of slavery in places like the Lunda empire. By examining these diverse experiences, we can develop a more nuanced understanding of the complexities of slavery in the region.

Ana Joaquina's negotiations with the Lunda empire not only highlighted her economic standing but also revealed a shrewd architect of Angola's transition away from the transatlantic slave trade. Her diplomatic efforts aimed to secure new sources of wealth and power in the changing economic landscape. Yet her investments in commercial agriculture, much like her nemesis's, reveal the continuing relevance of Angola's ties to Brazil even as the trade in enslaved Africans faded into a historical background. Ana Joaquina and Graça's experience in Brazil helped consolidate Angola's reliance on enslaved and forced labor for agricultural ventures, contributing to a trend that would inform the region's economy for decades to come.

The Lunda ruler engaged in a delicate balancing act while seeking to manage relations with the Portuguese, controlling trade routes and maintaining the stability of his vast empire. The arrival of Ana Joaquina's envoys signaled a shift in this balance. By negotiating a direct trade agreement with Ana Joaquina, the ruler sought to cut out middlemen like the kingdom of Kasanje while countering the destabilizing effects of independent trade, such as through the expansion of Cokwe traders. This engagement with Portuguese traders like Ana Joaquina and Graça highlights the Lunda Empire's active role in shaping the transition from the transatlantic slave trade, as the ruler sought to adapt to changing economic circumstances and preserve his power. As such, the Lunda ruler's actions offer a new perspective on the complex interplay between African polities and European colonial interests during this transformative period.

The nature of power in the Lunda Empire, as evidenced by these events, was deeply intertwined with the control and manipulation of trade relationships and the strategic use of tribute and alliances. The Lunda ruler's approach to governance thus reflected the continuing importance of wealth in people, a concept that undergirded political dynamics in West Central Africa. By insisting on tributes in various forms, whether from subordinate leaders or through trade partnerships, Nawej II sought not just to amass wealth but also to reaffirm loyalties and preserve power.

CHAPTER SIX

Fracturing African Sovereignty

IN 1856, Henrique II, an ailing octogenarian ruler of the Kingdom of Kongo, voluntarily "placed himself, the state, and his subjects under the immediate protection" of the Portuguese crown.[1] This decision, made following the arrival of Portuguese emissaries and troops aiming to occupy Bembe—a mining region located approximately 200 kilometers inland from the coast—marked a pivotal shift in the balance of power in West Central Africa. It gave Portugal key leverage in Kongo's internal affairs just as a succession crisis roiled the African kingdom and as Portugal found itself competing with Britain, France, and the US for influence in West Central Africa.

The Portuguese military expedition's primary objective had been to sever the supply of copper from Bembe to the coast of Ambriz, where British and US traders received the mineral and then exported it abroad. It was a thriving business, which the Portuguese sought to yank from foreign hands. Yet, as the commanders settled into their newly conquered territory, it became clear that the presence of the troops at a time of deep instability in the African kingdom presented Portugal with a unique opportunity to shape the impending political crisis. The potential consequences of this intervention would reverberate throughout the region, altering the course of Kongo's history and the balance of power in West Central Africa.

This chapter unravels the complex web of factors that contributed to Kongo's internal strife, examining how the abolition of the slave trade, coupled with intensifying territorial expansion and international competition for new trade prospects, destabilized the kingdom's political landscape. By focusing on the fractious relations between traditional authorities inland and commercially oriented coastal elites, the chapter demonstrates how external pressures intersected with local power dynamics. Kongo's experience is situated within the larger context of European empire-building in Africa and the Indian Ocean, revealing strategies employed by imperial powers to exert control and gain privileged access to expanding trades. This analysis underscores how the

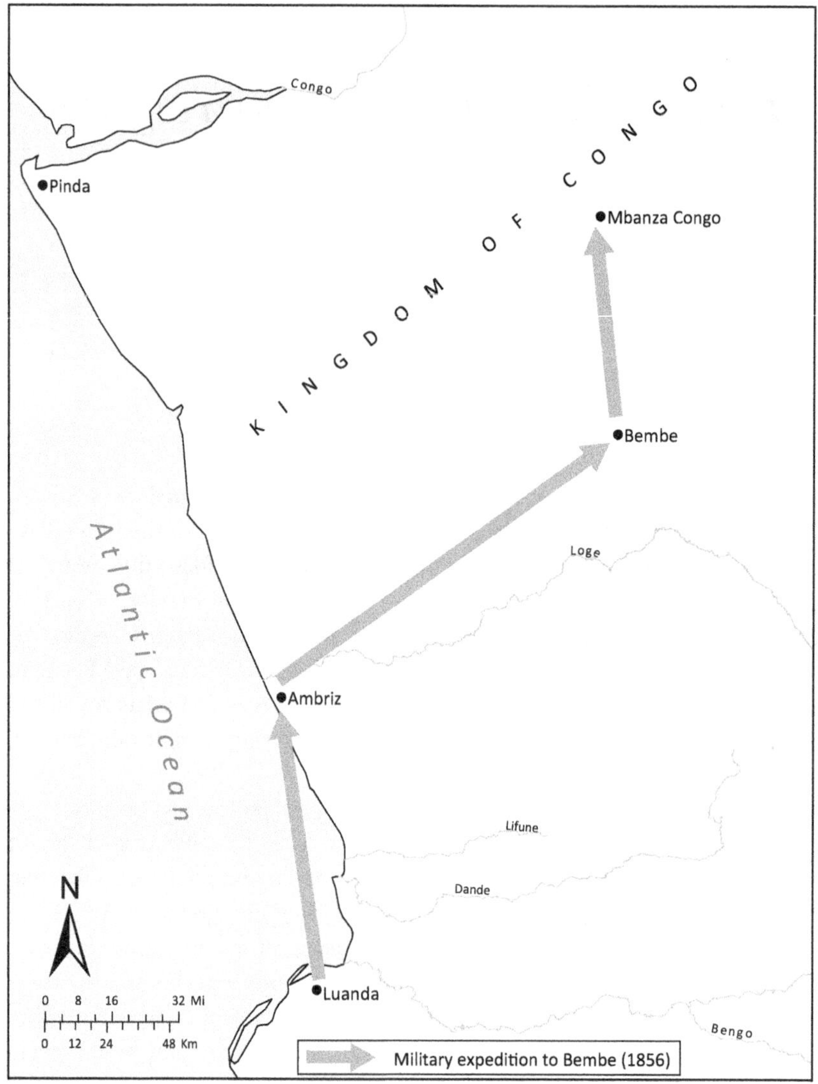

MAP 4. Bembe Expedition

end of the transatlantic slave trade did not signify the end of foreign exploitation, but rather its transformation into new forms of economic and political dominance.

Historically, it was not the first time the Portuguese deployed troops within the African kingdom. Back in the sixteenth century, Portugal had sent approximately six hundred soldiers to drive out invading jagas, foreign marauders, from the kingdom. In return, Kongo backed Portugal's efforts to establish an urban enclave on the coast, laying the foundation for what would later become the city of Luanda.[2] Kongo itself was no stranger to political instability aris-ing from power succession. An attempt to instill stability was made in the early eighteenth century by establishing a power rotation system.[3] By the early nineteenth century, however, chaotic power transitions were again a norm, bringing significant political instability to the African kingdom.

Nor was Henrique II's apparent acquiescence to Portuguese emissaries necessarily inconsistent with the kingdom's history. A long history of rulers or members of the elite leveraging outside backing to attain power or execute political maneuvers within the kingdom preceded his decision to place him-self under the protection of the Portuguese.[4] In 1803, members of the king-dom's elite reached out to the Portuguese in Luanda to seek support to expel a sitting king due to his "malevolent ways and diabolical customs."[5] As late as 1830, amid a deeply turbulent succession crisis, a contender for the king-dom's throne called upon the Luanda government to send in troops to help him.[6] A little over a decade later, Henrique II himself would request military assistance from Luanda, and a faction seeking to dethrone him would ask the Brazilian government to intervene in Kongo's internal politics.[7]

Yet Henrique II's 1856 alignment with Portugal still stands out as a signifi-cant inflection point in Kongo's history. Never before had a Portuguese interven-tion unfolded against a backdrop of so many global powers vying for influence in West Central Africa, driven by economic interests and the region's emerging strategic importance. France, which just a few years prior had deployed naval patrols to the coast to crush shipments of enslaved Africans, now spearheaded a new forced migration to take indentured laborers from Congo to the French Caribbean. Rather than ending exploitation, abolition catalyzed opportunities for empire-building and increased foreign interference in African politics as Europe scrabbled to gain access to Africa's resources.

Historians have long grappled with how Kongo found itself in a vortex of abolition that tore apart its political fabric. Jelmer Vos interprets the suc-cession crisis in Kongo as a struggle between factions: one involved in the slave trade and the other aligned with the Portuguese administration in Angola, which aimed to abolish the slave trade and expand its influence.[8] John Thornton suggests that Kongo's new ruler benefitted from the shift from the slave trade to legitimate commerce by taxing commodities like ivory, wax, and rubber.[9] Cecile Fromont argues that Kongo's elite's long experience with international trade and diplomacy endowed it with the tools to negotiate the transition beyond the transatlantic slave trade.[10]

Building upon this scholarship, this chapter tells the story of an African kingdom struggling to adjust to transformations brought about by abolition. The narrative begins by exploring how foreign powers leveraged their naval presence to challenge Portugal's territorial claims, protect their trading inter-ests, and intervene in local politics. Simultaneously, the growth of legitimate commerce, particularly copper, brought about new economic opportunities and shifts in power dynamics along the coast. Against this backdrop, the chapter traces fractious relations between traditional authorities and coastal elites in Kongo, uncovering how global forces collided with the governing structures of an African kingdom.

By situating Kongo within a broader context of imperial competition across Africa and the Indian Ocean, the chapter underscores the complex interplay of diplomacy, trade, and military power that marked the rise of European presence in the continent. By moving beyond Atlantic-focused studies of abolition to bridge the gap between the Atlantic and Indian Ocean regions, it reveals how Britain's assertive anti-slave trade policies extended across the Southwest Indian Ocean, challenging Portugal's territorial claims in East Africa and beyond. Simultaneously, the chapter places West Central Africa in the broader context of Atlantic Africa, drawing parallels between the fate of Kongo and the impact of European interventions in other regions such as Lagos and the Bight of Benin. Just as Kongo faced the strategic manipulation of its succession crisis by Portuguese and French forces, British naval power was leveraged to alter the landscape of politics and commerce in West Africa. These interconnected developments reveal how the end of the transatlantic slave trade catalyzed opportunities for empire-building and increased foreign interference in African politics, as Europe sought to gain access to Africa's resources and expand its influence across the continent.

Coastal Disputes

The deployment of troops to the lower Congo, including Bembe, in 1856 marked the culmination of two decades of disputes between Portugal and European powers for influence in regions such as Ambriz, Cabinda, and Molembo. Portugal's chief rival was Britain, whose opposition to Portuguese sovereignty in these areas was rooted in skepticism about its commitment to curbing the slave trade as well as concerns that Portuguese territorial claims could potentially hinder the growth of British commercial interests. A British naval commander succinctly expressed this: "A [Portuguese] jurisdiction over that part of the coast may in existing circumstances and without something definite as to the extent of their authority lead to serious inconvenience in the protection and extension of British commerce."[11]

The intensification of British anti-slave trade diplomacy in West Central Africa underscored the region's significant role in supplying enslaved labor to the Americas. By combining naval and diplomatic efforts, the British had managed to reduce shipments of captives in regions located north of the equator, including the Bight of Benin and Lagos. Yet the trade in enslaved Africans was much more challenging to tackle south of the equator. Following the closure of slave trade operations in Luanda and Benguela, African ports like Loango, Molembo, Cabinda, and Ambriz emerged as the principal sources for the Atlantic slave trade. Portugal had never permanently occupied these regions. Yet it claimed them under the "rights of discovery" from its fifteenth-century expansion into Africa.

These claims set Portugal at odds not only with Britain but also with France and the United States, all of which dispatched naval forces to the African coast to suppress the slave trade. Portugal viewed these naval deployments as direct challenges to its territorial ambitions. As early as 1838, newly appointed anti-slave trade Governor of Angola Antonio Manoel de Noronha recognized that "the continuation of that trade is now improper without exposing those provinces to insults by British cruisers and giving them the pretext to enter into direct negotiation with [African] neighbors on the coast."[12] At the time, Portuguese officials entertained the idea of founding a city near the mouth of the Congo river with the "well-founded hope that it will grow in commerce, wealth, and population, making it deserving of this denomination."[13] Yet these plans were eventually shelved due to "grave discord with France, Britain, and the United States."[14]

Against this backdrop, Portugal's primary concerns centered on Britain's push against the slave trade, which had by then become closely aligned with its aim to develop commercial enterprises in Africa, often under the guise of free trade.[15] This was coupled with Britain's increasingly more robust notions of territorial expansion that stood at odds with Portugal's geopolitical interest. As early as 1822, a British captain named Charles Phillips suggested the colonization of São Tomé, then a Portuguese colony, on the grounds that the island had economic potential similar to Jamaica's.[16] Shortly afterward, another British captain, John Adams, proposed the establishment of a colony in Molembo, one of the regions that Portugal claimed as hers, to resettle Africans liberated from slave vessels.[17]

While the British never created a colony near Portugal's territories in West Central Africa, naval forces deployed to end the slave trade undermined Portugal's geopolitical interest in the region. A particularly telling episode occurred in 1860 when the Portuguese government of Luanda launched a punitive expedition to the Kongo. When exhausted Portuguese troops reached the Ambriz region, their commander sought aid from British and American traders to care for fatigued men. Yet the British refused, claiming that assisting Portugal would suggest collusion in aggression and damage relations with local groups, underscoring how even indirect British interference posed challenges to Portuguese territorial authority in the region.[18]

Portugal's concerns escalated as Britain unilaterally passed a bill in 1839 authorizing its naval vessels to seize slave ships sailing under the Portuguese flag off the coast of Africa. According to historian Leslie Bethell, "for the first time, the British navy could operate effectively off the Congo, off the coasts of Angola and Mozambique and off the coast of Brazil."[19] In response, the government of Luanda ordered joint naval operations with the British,

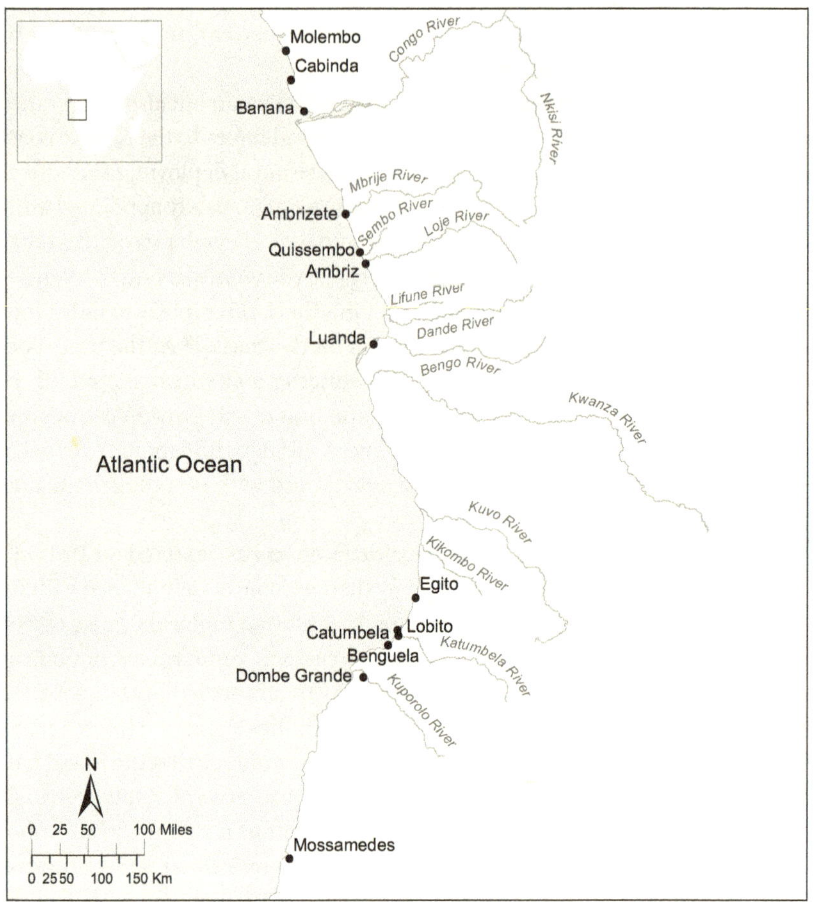

MAP 5. West Central African Regions

an appeasing move taken without the prior approval of Lisbon that did not address the underpinnings of an increasingly strained relationship.[20] Yet the futility of Portugal's efforts became evident when a British commander directly challenged its claims about regions north of Luanda: "The Portuguese claim, I believe, the sovereignty of the coast as far north as the Loango, but they have no possession of one foot of the country north of Cape Lagosta, and the native chiefs do not acknowledge any dependence on the Portuguese."[21]

A pivotal shift came about when Portugal was forced to sign an anti-slave treaty with Britain in 1842, leading to a dramatic escalation of British naval operations along the African coast. Over the next five years, British patrols increased from thirteen to thirty ships—comprising nearly one-third of Britain's entire navy.[22] In 1845 alone, intensified naval efforts led British forces to seize or destroy at least forty-three slave ships near the Angolan coast.[23] A single British cruiser, the *Styx*, was responsible for apprehending almost thirty slave vessels between June 1847 and January 1848.[24]

These mounting naval operations placed significant external pressure on Portugal, leading the country to take steps against the slave trade in territories under its jurisdiction such as Luanda and Benguela. The fear was that inaction would be perceived as complicity with the slave trade, which could then lead to a challenge to the country's territorial presence in West Central Africa. In 1844, Portuguese officials in Lisbon warned counterparts in Benguela, then embroiled in accusations of tolerance for or participation in the slave trade, by stating, "Any relaxation in this matter could be fatal to your government, given that on more than one occasion it has led British cruisers to violently seize ships within the harbor of the city with clear signs of being dedicated to the smuggling of slaves, thus making the fortresses and authorities of the district go through such a great affront."[25]

By 1847, in response to the new landscape, Portugal had deployed five warships to police Luanda—equal to one-third of its navy—playing a pivotal role in disrupting the slave trade in what had until then been the most significant slave port city in the Atlantic.[26] The new policy earned praise from British naval commanders: "The measures pursued by the present Governor-General of this province appear to have succeeded in suppressing all direct attempts at the slave trade in Portuguese vessels."[27] Yet tensions soon resurfaced as slave dealers shifted operations northwards to regions such as Ambriz, Cabinda, and Molembo, which Portugal claimed but had never occupied.

As early as 1846, Britain had already sought to curb the slave trade in these regions by pushing for an agreement with Portugal that would have allowed it to disembark "small detachments of their crews from time to time as occasion might require in order to destroy the barracoons (slave depots) on any part of territories belonging to or claimed to belong to Portugal on that part of the coast of Africa and being more than a given distance say ten or fifteen miles from any Portuguese establishment."[28] The proposal was in line with the characteristically military approach to its anti-slave trade campaign that Britain had adopted since the 1840s, which called for direct actions against the slave trade in Africa. Yet Portugal turned it down, promising instead to engage in joint anti-slave trade operations with Britain.[29]

Portuguese anxiety escalated when British naval commanders threatened to place Ambriz under a blockage after local people attacked warehouses that belonged to the Liverpool-based firm Hatton & Cookson. Reportedly, "the natives immediately attacked us with stones, sticks, and knives, severely wounding two white men who were attempting to save some ivory."[30] Initially, the "king" of Ambriz adopted a defiant stance, asserting his capability to resist the power of the British navy.[31] However, faced with threats from British naval commanders, he eventually caved in, agreeing that cargoes of goods could be landed free of customs and promising financial compensation.[32]

The complexity of the situation was further compounded by the fact that Britain was not alone in leveraging the campaign against the slave trade to advance its geopolitical interests in Africa. The United States and France also relied on naval forces and growing commercial interests to make strategic moves along the African coast. While their deployments were officially intended to support treaties suppressing the slave trade, both countries harbored significant doubts about Britain's true motives for seeking to end the trade. The prevailing criticism was that Britain's global anti-slave trade campaign was merely a guise for establishing commercial dominance worldwide.

As an alternative to granting Britain the right to visit and search American vessels or those sailing under the US flag, which had become instrumental in the operations of the slave trade, the US government deployed a squadron to the African coast in the 1840s.[33] Over the next two decades, US warships averaged the capture of only two ships per year, a rate significantly lower than that of British cruisers during the same period.[34] Yet the ships played a role in supporting the burgeoning US trade in Africa, which, at the time, surpassed the trade volumes of both France and Britain.[35] Recognizing the importance of maritime forces in protecting trade interests, a U.S. naval commander once stated: "I have previously endeavored to call the attention of the government to the need for United States vessels on this part of the coast to protect our commerce here and at Ambriz."[36]

The presence of US naval forces coupled with a burgeoning US trade activity was viewed as threatening by Portugal. An episode is illustrative. In 1841, the Luanda government dispatched a delegation to Ambriz to reassert the government's influence by cracking down on foreign trade. U.S. traders agreed to redirect their imports through Luanda and pay the necessary import duties, seemingly complying with Portuguese demands. However, they vehemently opposed any restrictions on their freedom to trade at the African port. In their words, "Portugal did not have more rights than other nations [trading] in that place [Ambriz], and because they paid [duties] to the local king, they were under no obligation to the provincial government of Angola."[37]

Similar geopolitical goals guided France's forays into West Central Africa. Unlike the United States, France had once granted Britain the right of search and visit, a key tool to inspect vessels suspected of engagement in the transatlantic slave trade. Yet this concession came under strain when the British seized a French ship leaving Brazil, prompting the French government to walk away from a proposed multinational treaty in 1841 that aimed to expand these search rights.[38] Tension escalated further when a British cruiser seized a vessel chartered by the French government to transport African recruits to French Guiana, accusing it of engaging in the slave trade.[39]

As a result of these tensions, the French were particularly cautious about ceding any maritime authority that could potentially give the British undue leverage over French shipping and trading operations.[40] Still, the country agreed to maintain a naval presence of approximately equal strength with Britain's. According to US naval commander A. H. Foote, "France at one time had equal force with Great Britain on the coast of Africa, say twenty-six vessels."[41] The goal was to prevent Britain from using the campaign against the slave trade to inspect France's vessels or those sailing under the French flag. As historian Raphael Cheriau points out, "Only French ships of war had the right to visit, search, and seize vessels flying the French flag."[42]

By 1846, Luanda's weekly gazette noted the presence of "six French warships patrolling the northern Coast" from the city, which would go on to capture eleven slave vessels.[43] The ships engaged in skirmishes against slave trade infrastructure in Liberia and Gabon, where France established a short-lived station for its naval force.[44] In 1847, France had between five and seven ships along the coast near Angola, which detained or destroyed twelve slave vessels, second only to the British.[45] By the early 1850s, the country had de-escalated its naval deployment along the African coast. French commander Edouard Bouët-Willaumez stated: "The French division, which amounted to 14 warships at the beginning of my command, has been reduced since that time."[46]

French anti-slave trade efforts extended to the Gabon Estuary, which had by then become a hub for Brazilian, Portuguese, and Spanish slave traders. By 1845, French commanders took steps to expel slave dealers and detained canoes carrying slaves for sale in the estuary, bringing individuals to face trial in French-controlled Gorée, Senegal. However, these measures proved largely ineffective since France did not have anti-slave trade agreements with Spain, Portugal, or Brazil. This prevented French cruisers from intervening against slave traders from these nations, who frequented Gabon most regularly. As a result, the slave trade persisted in the region into the 1850s.[47]

French engagement with West Central Africa was unique in two ways. First, the country leveraged its colonial enclave of Senegal to extend southwards, establishing missionary outposts in Gabon and founding Libreville as a settlement for Africans released from slave vessels.[48] This policy mirrored what Britain had once done in Fernando Po, where a British commander built a settlement to resettle recaptured Africans by relying on labor-drawn regions under their control in Sierra Leone and the Gold Coast.[49] By the 1850s, naval Commander Édouard Bouët-Willaumez, a former interim governor of Senegal and architect of France's early expansionism in West Africa, considered the Comptoir du Gabon as one of the "external dependencies" of Senegal.[50] Though merchant presence remained limited, new roads facilitated communication between the coast and the interior. "Since we have established ourselves in Gabon, large and good roads make communications between this point and the interior of the country easier every day, and vice versa."[51]

Second, France's policy toward Africa was marked by the influential role played by the Maison Régis, a commercial house that specialized in supplying Africa's plant-based commodities to Marseille's soap-making industry. Based in Marseille, the Régis firm built a network that stretched along West Africa (Senegal, Gabon, and Angola) to the East African coast (Mozambique and Zanzibar) and the Indian Ocean (Madagascar). Its success hinged on a model of integrated vertical operations, controlling the supply chain from African production sites to Marseille's manufacturing facilities. By the 1840s, the firm's primary trading posts were in the Bight of Benin, particularly in Dahomey, where its agents had secured deals with local rulers that granted it a monopoly on importing European goods and exporting palm oil.[52] The firm was recurrently accused of facilitating the slave trade by selling goods and ships to and from slave dealers.[53] As will be discussed later, the Régis firm would play a key role in the succession crisis in the kingdom of Kongo.

Imperiled Ambitions

It would be difficult to overstate the challenges posed by this complex landscape to Portugal's ambitions in West Central Africa. After losing Brazil, Portugal gradually shifted its imperial aspirations to the region, seeking to establish Angola as an alternative plantation economy. However, with the slave trade still thriving through networks beyond its control, implementing this vision proved challenging. More fundamentally, genuine doubts arose regarding Portugal's ability to successfully occupy territories like Ambriz, Molembo, and Cabinda, which it claimed but had not effectively controlled. As the slave trade continued to cast a deep shadow, the buildup of foreign commerce and naval forces along the coast meant that Portugal's territorial ambitions in West Central Africa faced daunting uncertainties.

According to the Portuguese government, Britain and France had twice recognized Portugal's sovereignty over these regions—in 1810 and 1817.[54] Yet, after deploying their naval forces to the African coast, both countries disputed these claims. British commander Foote, who arrived in Luanda in 1843 to implement an anti-slave trade treaty Britain had signed with Portugal the previous year, stated: The "British government had previously denied such claim."[55] Similarly, Bouët-Willaumez, the commander of French forces in Africa, stated unequivocally: "France has never recognized Portuguese claims of sovereignty rights over Cabinda."[56]

This situation was particularly challenging in terms of Portugal's long-held ambition of occupying Ambriz. As early as 1847, Portuguese officials acknowledged that occupying the African territory would only be viable "if the three main naval powers [Britain, France, and the United States] did not militarily oppose it."[57] In 1855, when the decision to finally occupy the African port was undertaken, a cautious approach shaped their decision-making process, underscoring the stakes for the Portuguese in the face of naval forces on the coast. At the time, the number of British cruises had declined because of the Crimean War. Yet Luanda officials acknowledged the possibility of "any military confrontation with the far more powerful naval forces of these countries."[58]

Portugal's concerns about military actions against its African territories were certainly not overblown. The rivalry between Portugal and Britain was not limited to West Central Africa; it extended to other regions, such as the Gulf of Guinea. As early as the 1820s, Britain's anti-slave trade campaign played a role in the country's expansion into the Gulf of Guinea, particularly the island of Fernando Po, then under Spanish control. Reflecting Britain's growing assertiveness in using its naval power to advance its abolitionist agenda, a settlement for enslaved Africans released from slave vessels was created. Notably, this settlement would form the core of a new African colonial elite that would eventually dominate the island. The case of Fernando Po illustrates how Britain's anti-slave trade campaign created the conditions for imperial activity, even if not always intentional or predictable.[59]

The rivalry between Portugal and Britain continued to manifest itself in other parts of the African coast. Just as tensions rose along the coast of West Central Africa, Portugal and Britain also clashed over control of the island of Bolama on the Upper Guinea Coast. Leveraging Portugal's inability to suppress the slave trade in territories it claimed, Britain sought to undermine Portuguese sovereignty claims and establish permanent settlements for producing tropical exports. Despite Portugal's appeals to prior agreements recognizing its territorial rights, Britain ultimately occupied Bolama in 1860, signaling its growing assertiveness in challenging Portuguese claims.[60]

Significantly, Britain's campaign against the slave trade extended beyond Africa to the Indian Ocean and Asia, taking on a global dimension that challenged Portugal's territorial claims in these regions as well. In East Africa, Britain made inroads in Portuguese-claimed territories in Mozambique as early as the 1820s, when they embarked on a five-year survey mission to map the entire East African coast from the Cape of Good Hope to the Horn of Africa.[61] These disputes gained further momentum as Britain's anti-slave trade campaign took a militaristic turn in the 1840s. A Portuguese Governor in Mozambique felt forced to grant the British permission "to enter all the rivers and secondary ports of the Portuguese possessions on the east coast of Africa."[62]

Britain's anti-slave trade campaign in the Indian Ocean faced the daunting task of confronting deeply entrenched systems of enslavement that had been ongoing for decades, with devastating impacts on local populations in Mozambique. One such example was the situation in Delagoa Bay, where the rising demand for slaves in Brazil and the Mascarene Islands led to intense slave raiding that decimated the Tembe population. Between 1823 and 1830, over 20,000 captives were shipped from Delagoa Bay to the Mascarenes or Brazil, with conservative estimates suggesting over 4,000 enslaved people per year on average. By the late 1820s, according to historians Linell Chewins and Peter Delius, systematic enslavement had left Tembe territory "almost depopulated."[63]

Britain's assertive anti-slave trade policies must be understood in the broader context of a campaign that extended across the Southwest Indian Ocean. A case in point was its attempt to crack down on the supply of enslaved people to the Mascarene islands of Mauritius and Réunion between 1811 and the early 1830s. Britain devoted naval resources to intercepting slave ships and pressured local rulers in Madagascar and Oman to ban slave exports, entangling the suppression of the slave trade with imperial competition and territorial claims.[64] According to historian Matthew Hopper, while Britain's anti-slave trade efforts in the Indian Ocean were at times limited or even contradictory in their effectiveness, they nonetheless contributed to the expansion of British influence and power in the region, with the suppression of the slave trade serving as a tool to justify policies of conquest and occupation.[65]

Notably, part of the supply of labor taken to the Mascarene islands came from regions under Portugal's jurisdiction, which further set the British at odds with the Portuguese. Scholar Leigh Muffet notes that the British "pushed for a colony in Mombasa in East Africa in a move to gain influence over Mozambique."[66] Against this backdrop, when Portuguese officials consented to British ships entering rivers and ports under their control in the 1840s, it underscored the coercive pressure of Britain's abolitionist interventions.[67]

It was in the Atlantic, however, where Britain likely more adeptly leveraged its campaign against the slave trade to advance its geopolitical interests, assertively supporting allies and undermining antagonistic local rulers. A telling example was the overthrow of the pro-slave trade Kosoko regime, replaced by an anti-slavery faction under Akitoye.[68] This episode was far from isolated. In 1848, a ruler had already been deposed in Bonny for backing slavery and defying British interests.[69] Following this pattern, Whydah faced a naval blockade in 1851, and by 1861, Lagos was annexed, becoming a British colony. These actions signaled Britain's expanding imperial footprint in West Africa.[70]

Britain's increasingly assertive actions in Africa and beyond did not go unnoticed in Luanda, the capital city of Portuguese Angola. The city's weekly gazette (BOGGPA) would occasionally feature reports on Britain's increasingly global imperial reach, including military triumphs in places as far away as India and a naval blockade in Canton.[71] This coverage likely colored Portuguese perceptions of British anti-slavery efforts along the West Central African coast as being driven by broader motives of territorial expansion. As Portuguese officials pointedly observed, "It is remarkable that the British government wants to prevent others from proceeding in Africa as they, with much less right, are proceeding in Asia."[72]

The BOGGPA's reporting on the bombardment of Lagos in 1851, which, according to the gazette, left the city "reduced to ashes," further underscored Britain's growing military leverage along the African coast.[73] This news likely prompted Portuguese officials to consider their disputes with Britain within broader geopolitical rivalries, heightening concerns over ceding influence to a rival seeking to build geopolitical hegemony in several corners of the globe, including West Central Africa. Strikingly, the British themselves made a point of showcasing their feats, once placing an article in the BOGGPA to announce that they had "raised the blockade of all the ports in the Bight of Benin, except Whydah," a thinly veiled reference to their growing military leverage along the African coast.[74]

Kongo's Fractured Politics

Against this backdrop, Portuguese officials in Luanda responded with suspicion when, in 1845, British naval commander John Foot suggested a joint mission to engage in anti-slave trade talks with the kingdom of Kongo's ruler Henrique II. On the surface, Foot's proposal seemed reasonable. "I think we could succeed in gaining this king over to our views to discuss the best way of getting rid of this new evil [the slave trade]," the commander suggested.[75] Most enslaved people shipped across the Atlantic were either captured or crossed territories that belonged to the kingdom of Kongo. Just a few days from the kingdom's capital city, Mboma was likely the greatest emporium of the trade in slaves in the region.[76] According to Hungarian traveler László Magyar, who visited Mboma in the late 1840s, a "multitude" of captives were taken to the market every day from multiple points deep into the African interior.[77]

However, the British assessment of the situation failed to account for the complex realities of Kongo's internal politics. Having overthrown King André I just a few years earlier and still facing opposition from the expelled ruler, Henrique II was then a relatively new ruler.[78] Troops under his command numbered about 12,000 warriors. Yet he faced fierce internal opposition, with adversaries once reporting the loss of two hundred lives in a single battle against him.[79] His enemies had once sought support from Luanda, pledging to implement anti-slave trade policies and proposing to reduce Ambriz's independence as a free coastal port. When their efforts were dismissed, they sought backing from Brazil, signaling the depth of the opposition then faced by the Kongolese ruler.[80]

Further weakening the power of Kongo's centralized power were centripetal forces unleashed by the Atlantic trade, which transformed social, political, and religious fabrics in territories under the control of Henrique II. Mboma is a case in point. Local chiefs built alliances with foreigners and leveraged access to imported goods to redirect wealth away from traditional centers of power like Mbanza Kongo, the kingdom's capital. Political power was achieved by associating with foreign merchants, as discussed in Chapter 4, with a myriad of kings and princes leveraging the economic gains of the slave trade to purchase titles of nobility that, in the past, would have been acquired through traditional means.

In this complex political landscape, the entrenched influence of the slave trade emerged as a decisive factor in shaping Kongo's governance and relations. The arrival of foreign traders and a larger inflow of imported goods into local societies gave rise to unprecedented political fragmentation. In 1845, a French naval commander reported the existence of "many [coastal] villages under the direction of chiefs whom all depend on the King of the Congo."[81] By then, however, Kongo's monarchs had long become vulnerable to the whims of prominent slave traders who held significant power. According to Hungarian traveler Ladislau Magyar, Kongo rulers "did not have effective power beyond a splendid title."[82]

Crucial to this landscape were religious institutions like Khimba and Lemba, which enabled the power of Mboma chiefs and other coastal brokers by giving them a tight grip over the internal trade. Khimba was a cult that created bonds among initiates that facilitated trade, travel, and mutual assistance in a region marked by political fragmentation and violence. As a governing institution in areas lacking centralized authority, Lemba kept trade routes peaceful and markets orderly by conferring prestige and immunity on adherents. Both institutions involved elaborate secret practices, including a language that nonmembers did not speak and religious protocols that made them exclusive. By policing commerce, restricting participation, and projecting spiritual potency, they allowed Mboma chiefs to shape governance around trade, monopolizing trade routes and acquiring significant political power derived from Atlantic wealth and association with foreign traders.

As these internal factors reshaped the political landscape in Kongo, Portuguese officials in Luanda were not entirely unaware of the shifting power dynamics at play. Governor of Angola Pedro Alexandrino da Cunha, a former naval commander with deep knowledge of the coast north of Luanda, once pointed out: "The king [of Kongo] has no power whatsoever because of more important and wealthier [coastal] potentates who do not respect him at all."[83] Portuguese officials knew about African chiefs who controlled and benefited from the transit of enslaved Africans through their territories, collecting duties and levies as they saw fit. "The chiefs of the principal towns and states of the interior profit by the transit of slaves through their territories, in removing them to the sea coast, duty or slave being levied on them by the chiefs of those independent tribes."[84]

For the Portuguese, however, what mattered the most were the geopolitical implications of the British naval presence along the African coast, not the deeply deleterious impact of the slave trade on Kongo's politics. Would the British use the campaign against the slave trade to challenge Portugal's territorial claims over regions such as Ambriz, Cabinda, and Molembo? In this context, the proposal for a joint mission to Kongo was seen as part of British maneuverings to advance their geopolitical interests. In the view of Portuguese officials, the mission might embed the British in a territory that had been in

Portugal's orbit of influence since the sixteenth century. In response, therefore, they not only rejected the proposal but also swiftly organized their own delegation to meet King Henrique II of Kongo. Their goal? To convince the king of Kongo to compel his subjects to abandon the slave trade, thus removing Britain's primary stated justification for engaging the African kingdom.[85]

The mission was highly sensitive due to a wider geopolitical context that saw not only the British forces but also French forces along the coast. In instructions to envoys dispatched to Kongo's capital Mbanza Kongo, Luanda officials emphasized the need to cautiously gauge Henrique II's stance on a potential treaty to abolish the slave trade entirely. The envoys were advised to proceed with discussions only if the initial reception from the Kongolese court was not overtly hostile, a cautious approach that seemed to implicitly recognize the relative fragility of a monarch who had just recently suffered a bloody coup d'état attempt.[86]

Henrique II, for his part, saw the envoys' overtures as an opportunity to subvert established power dynamics that had long favored coastal elites over monarchs like himself. Consequently, he boldly agreed to a treaty that not only prohibited the slave trade but also transferred control of Ambriz to Portugal.[87] This decision, which would soon prove to be a miscalculation, positioned him against coastal rulers who had prospered from the slave trade and viewed the treaty as a direct challenge to their interests. Tellingly, the Kongo king asked the Portuguese to station troops near his court to "defend [him] with their weapons and support" in the event he was attacked "in the [royal] court," underscoring that he anticipated a backlash following his alignment with Portugal's demands.[88]

The request proved to be prophetic as pressures from powerful subjects soon led Henrique II not only to renege the anti-slave trade treaty but also to lobby the Luanda government for the continuation of the trade in enslaved Africans. To justify the reversal, the ruler argued that African wealth was rooted in "slaves obtained through wars or as tribute paid by people who traded in slaves."[89] His inability to maintain his anti-slave trade stance in the face of pressure from powerful subjects underscored the extent to which the slave trade had eroded the monarch's traditional authority. In response, Portuguese authorities, unable to sway the ruler's decision, were reduced to a formal denunciation of the trade in enslaved Africans, asserting that "existing treaties between Portugal and European nations do not allow such an outrageous commerce."[90]

Ambriz's Takeover

In the wake of the diplomatic stalemate in Kongo, where Henrique II's vacillation reflected the entrenched power of the slave trade amid increasing British naval and diplomatic pressures, Portuguese authorities turned to a more direct assertion of control of Ambriz. Luanda officials still made efforts to manage the issue through diplomatic channels with the African kingdom. As late as 1853, a newly appointed governor of Angola sent a letter to the ruler urging him to crack down on local rulers who enabled the slave trade.[91] Yet it soon became clear that the Kongo's ruler's inability to rein in powerful coastal subjects not only undermined his power but now imperiled Portugal's aspirations of eventually occupying territories north of Luanda, including Ambriz.

Portugal's shift in strategy eventually led to the organization of an expedition to occupy the African port, signaling a transition from negotiation to military intervention that mirrored Britain's own endeavors elsewhere in Africa, as discussed earlier in this chapter. Led by Governor of Angola José Rodrigues Coelho do Amaral, an expedition comprised of 600 soldiers and three warships left Luanda in May 1855.[92] In a letter to a ruler in Mussulo, a coastal region on the way to Ambriz, the Luanda government requested approval for troops to march through his territory, justifying the launching of the expedition on the grounds that the Ambriz people were "rebels" because they had allegedly attacked Portuguese traders.[93]

With the occupation of the African port, Luanda officials sought to achieve two goals. Firstly, they aimed to crack down on the port's continuing role in the slave trade. Although Ambriz was only one of multiple shipping points along the coast, it played a key role in the logistics and financial framework of the slave trade. Troops thus left Luanda with specific orders to take measures to dismantle any infrastructure of the transatlantic slave trade. Upon arrival, they found some 150 captives then being held for shipment across the Atlantic. Aware of the influence of Luanda slave dealers in Ambriz, Lisbon officials had instructed their Angola counterparts to keep the expedition secret so it would not be sabotaged.[94] After the completion of the takeover, Luanda officials ordered Ambriz officials to track slave trade activities by "national and foreign vessels."[95]

Yet the expedition's aims were not confined only to the Atlantic trade in enslaved Africans. Equally important was Ambriz's role as a hub of a growing foreign trade. In 1850, a British consul in Luanda reported that British merchants had imported goods to Ambriz valued at £30,000, exporting ivory, copper, and gum cargoes worth between £50,000 and £60,000.[96] By comparison, the trade in the Gold Coast, which had long been under British influence, generated about three times more revenue at the time.[97] Similarly, in Lagos, where the British had established control in 1851, the export value by 1853 had reached an estimated £166,763.[98]

From the viewpoint of Luanda officials, the fear was that this trade would set back Portugal's plans to create a post-slave trade economy in Angola. Specifically, they worried that trade exchanges in Ambriz would redirect inland resources away from Angola's capital, Luanda. As early as 1851, officials estimated that "two-thirds or, perhaps one-fourth, of the provincial revenues were lost through [trade] in that port [Ambriz]."[99] Compounding concerns was

FIGURE 6.1. British palaver with the king of Ambriz

Ambriz's role as a primary entry point for foreign goods, which were then clandestinely distributed throughout Portuguese-controlled territories. According to a governor of Angola, "a great number of goods are freely unloaded by Americans, English and Brazilians and later clandestinely introduced in the sertões."[100] Once they were brought to Angola, these goods "could easily undersell the merchants of Angola and play mischief with the trade of the province."[101]

Against this background, the Portuguese expedition left Luanda with orders to amicably persuade the Ambriz ruler to relinquish his territory, offering a gift as a sign of Luanda's peaceful intentions. However, forewarned of the expedition's approach, the ruler staunchly refused their overtures, declaring that he "did not want anything, nor would he accept anything from the government of Angola." He "was and wanted to remain the king of Ambriz, both in the interior [sertões] and the coast."[102] Despite the ruler's firm stance, the military superiority of Luanda's forces ultimately overpowered African resistance.[103]

The ripple effects of the Portuguese takeover extended into neighboring territories, with African rulers in nearby Ambrizete demonstrating their willingness to even sign an anti-slave trade treaty with the British in exchange for protection against any invasion "by any foreign power"—a clear reference to Portuguese expansionism.[104] While forbidding Europeans from trading in Ambrizete, the treaty empowered the British to confiscate boats involved in the slave trade and hold local rulers responsible for any enslaved Africans shipped from the territory.[105] Portuguese authorities in Luanda quickly contested the treaty, challenging its legitimacy by asserting Ambrizete as part of Portuguese dominion and criticizing Britain's offer of protection to Africans against external threats.[106]

The Ambriz takeover was clearly part of a broader attempt to assert Portuguese territorial rights in regions north of the African port, including Molembo.[107] A year earlier, a six-person Molembo delegation had visited Luanda to pledge allegiance to Portugal during a public ceremony, which was intentionally held in the presence of foreign naval commanders.[108] This public ceremony drew a strong rebuttal from the British naval forces' commander, who refused to attend on the grounds that it would legitimize Portugal's territorial claims, stating, "My presence at such meeting would be an acknowledgment on my part of the right of Portugal to the sovereignty of a certain portion of this coast."[109] When a Portuguese warship arrived at Molembo to follow through with the treaty, however, a local ruler disavowed it.[110]

This was not the only setback that the Portuguese faced. While Britain did not immediately react militarily to the Ambriz occupation, it pointedly refused to acknowledge Portugal's territorial claims. British officials regarded it as an act of conquest rather than control over lands historically belonging to the Portuguese crown.[111] In response, authorities in Lisbon sought to placate Britain by pledging to end slavery in Ambriz, Cabinda, and Molembo.[112] Though eventually resigned to the Ambriz takeover as a fait accompli, Britain insisted that Portuguese territorial expansion must remain confined solely to Ambriz itself, effectively forcing the country to drop immediate plans to assert claims over Cabinda and Molembo.[113]

How did King Henrique II of Kongo, previously seen by the British and Portuguese as instrumental to ending the slave trade, react to the takeover of Ambriz—officially part of his territory? As historian Jelmer Vos observes, Henrique regarded the occupation as an opportunity to subjugate influential slave trading rivals active along the Atlantic coast, especially in Ambriz.[114] Despite not being consulted beforehand, the king endorsed the move as justified "punishment" against local rulers who had grown increasingly independent on wealth from selling captives across the Atlantic. "I direct my praises to you for the punishment you have given to the ruler of Ambriz, for although he was once a tributary of the kings of Congo, for some time now he has not paid tribute." Moreover, he vowed to "adopt appropriate measures to punish some of my subjects" involved in the Atlantic trade. To that end, he tellingly requested rifles from Luanda, signaling that such a measure would be met with resistance.[115]

This stance earned Henrique II praise in Luanda, with a newspaper publishing an obituary of the soon-to-be deceased king commending his decision to end the "inhumane slave trade."[116] Viewing the Ambriz takeover as a key strategic victory for Portugal, Governor of Angola José Rodrigues do Amaral capitalized on Kongo's newly found anti-slave trade policy to outline a new economic vision for the African kingdom. In his view, "the people taken from your kingdom could be employed in agriculture, the extraction of the country's resources, and in trade with civilized nations." At the same time, the Governor reminded Kongo's ruler that abandoning the slave trade offered not just economic gains, but political ones as well, suggesting that without trading in captives, "the kingdom's circumstances would be very different from the current situation."[117]

Yet, echoing his reversal ten years earlier, Henrique II would soon bow to the forces of the slave trade, distancing himself from Portuguese actions in Ambriz. Likely due to pressure from coastal rulers, the monarch would go as far as to request a written statement from the Luanda government to the effect that he had not transferred the African port to the Portuguese.[118] Shortly afterward, he would petition the Luanda government seeking clemency for the ousted ruler of Ambriz, a shift in position prompted by pressures from the coastal chieftains of Mussolo and Namboango.[119] At first, Governor of Angola Coelho do Amaral responded by saying that the Ambriz ruler and his subjects were free to return to their land, as long as they recognized Portuguese control of the territory.[120] Yet he adamantly refused to reconsider the Ambriz takeover, citing Portugal's "rights of conquest."[121]

Instead, to counter the influence exerted by coastal rulers on King Henrique II, the governor proposed a strategic alliance that would have empowered the Kongo ruler by ensuring the loyalty of its coastal subjects. "Be well convinced that the development of the prosperity of your states depends on the continuation of the closest alliance between us. The minor potentates who seek to induce you to loosen this alliance do so only for their ill purposes, and they want to compromise you."[122] Promising to restore Kongo's old glory around the kingdom's monarchy, the proposal hinted at Portugal's growing interest in a significant copper trade that connected Bembe, a mining region just ten days away from Kongo's capital, and foreign traders on the coast.[123]

Significantly, the alliance was proposed prior to the dispatch of the expedition that would take over the Bembe mines. According to Governor Coelho do Amaral, the mines must be freed from the grip of local rulers to unlock their economic potential. "Tell me, what interest does it serve you to have a minor potentate as the absolute and sole lord of the rich copper mines of the Bembe hills? Does he give you any share of its yield? No, he does not even allow those from Congo to go to the mines."[124] This initiative was presented not only as a response to the immediate challenges posed by the local chiefs but also as part of the economic foundation for a new partnership between Kongo and Portugal. "Ally with us frankly and truly, because this is where your real interest lies."[125]

Copper

Governor Coelho do Amaral's emphasis on the Bembe mines underscores their crucial role in Portugal's strategic interests in West Central Africa. In the sixteenth century, copper had already influenced Portugal's approach to the Kingdom of Kongo, yet now the issue had acquired new meaning due to the looming end of the slave trade and foreign participation in the copper trade. By 1855, British officials noted that "the trade in copper ore at [Ambriz] had increased significantly, and a much larger quantity of it had been shipped to England and the United States in the past year than in any previous year."[126] In that year alone, British exports reached an estimated 255 tons—nearly matching the average annual amount of copper brought to the coast during the fifteen years prior to Portugal's occupation of Ambriz.[127]

This trade was, however, halted with the takeover of Ambriz in 1855. According to British reports, the once significant copper ore trade at Ambriz ceased entirely following the military intervention: "The trade in copper ore, which was previously conducted on a significant scale between the British agents at Ambriz and the native Bembe-men, has come to a complete halt."[128] By 1856, British diplomats estimated that the value of British imports had been reduced to £25,913, representing half of the imports recorded five years before the Ambriz takeover.[129] The disruption of this thriving copper trade had far-reaching consequences, not only for the local economy and the livelihoods of the Bembe people who were directly involved in the trade but also for the strategic calculations of both the Portuguese and the British in the region.

Yet Portuguese efforts to consolidate control over the copper trade proved limited in scope and duration as foreign traders relocated to regions north of Ambriz like Kissembo, situated only about three miles north of the River Loje and outside Portuguese control. This new locale allowed foreign trading houses to tap into the same copper-rich interior region while evading Portuguese authorities in Ambriz. According to British accounts, prominent Liverpool and Salem firms, "which had engaged in a valuable commerce at Ambriz for several years," moved their bases of operation to Kissembo.[130] From their new stations, British observers reported, the traders were "quickly absorbing the entire trade of the former site."[131]

Faced with the failure of their efforts to consolidate control over the copper trade through the occupation of Ambriz alone, the Luanda government decided to take more drastic action. A second expedition was dispatched deep into the territory of Kongo. Leveraging amplified military might, including 250 soldiers from Portugal, the goal was to take over the Bembe mines, stopping the flow of the mineral to the coast.[132] This expedition would likely not have been possible without the previous occupation of Ambriz, as Portuguese officials acknowledged. "The point of Ambriz is perfect for all these goals. Its distance to the mines is similar to the distance between these and any of our

FIGURE 6.2. American and British factories in Ambrizete

districts in the north—even the district of Encoje. The trip between Ambriz and Luanda is short, by the ocean and land, and offers great convenience."[133]

Nor would these expeditions have been possible without the support of a Brazilian national named Francisco Antonio Flores. Flores, whose trajectory as a slave dealer was traced in Chapter 4, was now pivoting toward supporting Portugal's territorial ambitions in the lower Congo. He became instrumental in the success of both the Ambriz and Bembe expeditions by funding weaponry and underwriting the participation of an allied African ruler with a formidable force of five hundred warriors.[134] Tellingly, a Lisbon newspaper (Diário de Portugal) referred to the Ambriz expedition as the "expedition of the merchant Flores to Ambriz," underscoring the significance of his contributions in bolstering the Portuguese military efforts in the region.[135]

Flores's support was not altruistic. In return for logistical and financial support for the expeditions, he received a lifelong license to explore "copper, other minerals, and useful substances in mines that existed in the lands of Dembo Ambuela, in the district of Encoje (Ambriz) province of Angola."[136] This license was just one of many that the Brazilian would obtain for mining exploration across multiple regions of Angola, ultimately securing forty percent of the copper exploration licenses issued in the country.[137] In a telling sign, the expedition was delayed so the troops could take mining equipment sent from Lisbon by Flores. As Governor Amaral pointed out, "This is why I have postponed the expedition's launch," signaling the symbiotic relationship between Portugal's territorial expansionism and the former slave dealer's commercial interests.[138]

The Bembe expedition drew a strong backlash from African populations in the lower Congo. As the troops closed in on the mines, Africans "were busy, with great eagerness, filling the open pits with earth, stones, mats and everything that came to their hands, convinced that, by doing so, they made us lose track of the mines we were looking for."[139] According to German naturalist Adolph Bastian, widespread anger resulted in a near siege state in Bembe, with surrounding people uniting in opposition to the Portuguese. The unrest destabilized trade exchanges in several sections of the region, with Bastian stating that for three months, "only one copper caravan had managed to pass, and even that one, although escorted by all available troops, had suffered heavy losses." Other caravans en route from Loanda were also robbed.[140]

Yet African resistance was not enough to prevent the expedition from achieving its objective, with the Portuguese stationing approximately 700 soldiers, including cavalry and infantry units, in Bembe by the end of 1856.[141] The occupation dealt a crushing blow to the copper trade, with immediate consequences for exports of the mineral by US and British nationals on the coast. As the British stated in 1857, "their trade had been significantly injured by the Portuguese, who monopolized the inland commerce, thus preventing it from reaching the seacoast."[142]

Flores's exploits in the copper mines met with less success. He formed a partnership with the British firm John Taylor and Sons and Mrs. Pinto, Perez, and company to tap copper potential.[143] Yet, despite ambitious goals, the venture fell short of initial projections, as Flores himself admitted.[144] Although the mines produced over two thousand pounds of malachite monthly, earlier assessments had overestimated both the quality and feasible volume. The British mining team revealed that while some surveys gauged copper content as high as 60 percent, typical ore density was closer to 40 percent. Further hampering profitability, issues with copper quality and logistical transportation also posed considerable roadblocks.[145] At least one account stated that Flores wound up poor due to his substantial investments in the Bembe copper mining project.

Succession Crisis

While copper exploration in Bembe fell short of initial hopes, the military forces occupying the mines would soon become a significant factor in a succession crisis unfolding in the nearby Kingdom of Kongo. To consolidate their position, shortly after the Portuguese military forces arrived, a fort was built, with a governor of Ambriz being ordered to reside there to better influence the local population.[146] Emissaries were dispatched to Kongo's capital to meet King Henrique II, an ailing man whose reign was seen as ending soon. They reported that the ruler spoke "with interest in the occupation of this point [Bembe], showing me how satisfying such an important measure was for his States, not only because he could count on the Portuguese forces for assistance when needed, but because it was a great benefit for his people, as they could come here, without any fear, to exchange their goods."[147]

According to the emissaries, Henrique II had already chosen one of his nephews, a man named Pedro Katende, as his heir, a decision that would play a crucial role in the impending succession crisis. This choice was later echoed in an obituary in a Luanda weekly publication following the king's death in 1857.[148] By then, however, a fierce power struggle was already underway. Adolph Bastian, a German naturalist who visited Mbanza Kongo after Henrique II's death, learned while in Luanda that the provisional queen's eldest son, Dom Afonso, had been designated as the heir to the throne.[149] However, his candidacy was soon withdrawn because it violated the kingdom's matriarchal tradition of power succession.[150] More importantly, another contender, Alvaro Ndongo, had outmaneuvered Katende and Afonso to emerge as the most likely successor to Henrique II.[151]

As Pedro Katende and Alvaro Ndongo were nephews of the recently deceased Henrique II, the lineage issues that hindered Afonso's candidacy did not apply.[152] Katende viewed himself as the rightful successor, having been anointed by the late king, from whom he had received Kongo's most sacred royal objects, including the royal scepter, throne, and crown.[153] In practice, no ruler could ascend to power without these highly valued traditional symbols. The Katende faction contended that the late king's decision to bequeath these symbols of authority directly to him, sidestepping conventional succession protocols, underscored his explicit endorsement. While stressing this argument, they suggested that they had concealed some of the items as bargaining chips in the succession dispute.

As the succession struggle unfolded, it became increasingly intertwined with imperial competition playing out along the coast between the Portuguese, British, and French. The previously discussed occupation of Ambriz, for instance, had ignited strong resentment against the Portuguese while enhancing British stature among Africans.[154] Similarly, the takeover of Bembe destabilized the region by disrupting the copper trade, an economic lifeline not just for foreign traders along the coast but also for African chiefs who benefited from this commerce. Calls soon emerged for the new king of Kongo to retake the mines. According to one observer, "in Congo, it seemed that preparations were being made for a general attack [of Bembe], [the] waiting only for the young king to ascend the throne to settle the partisan struggles and rally under his banners."[155]

The situation contrasted sharply with Henrique II's likely goal when he anointed Katende as his successor. By doing so, the late king might have sought to prevent yet another of the many bloody transitions of power in Kongo's history. Such transitions were so disruptive that many in Mbanza Kongo would vacate their homes and only return after a new ruler was installed, thereby escaping violence.[156] However, the plan began unraveling even before the king's passing. As Portuguese envoys stated, "The king has come under significant pressure over the past two years by a relative named Dom Álvaro, who coerced him into declaring him his successor. He has sent a brother to visit us, and they have demonstrated the utmost amicability towards us."[157]

The unfolding crisis was, in part, of King Henrique II's own doing, as the ruler broke with tradition by naming his own successor. According to historian John Thornton, Katende, belonging to the same faction—Madimba—as the late king, was seen as a continuation of Henrique II's regime. Reportedly, the ruler would have asked Katende and his allies to "preserve the things of the kingdom as he had established them in life."[158] Yet the maneuver ran contrary to the long-standing tradition of rotating power among different families, prompting some to display "reluctance to have two kings of the same faction to succeed each other."[159]

While Henrique II's decision to appoint Katende as his successor was significant to the succession crisis, Ndongo's ties with coastal traders in Mboma arguably proved to be more crucial. Mboma was then a key hub of a French forced migration scheme recently established in the lower Congo. The schema was led by the Maison Régis, one of several firms contracted by France to transport forced workers to the Caribbean.[160] Several attempts were made to recruit Africans in regions of West Africa such as the Bight of Benin, yet the lower Congo became the primary hub of the forced migration, largely because of the networks of the still active transatlantic slave trade.[161]

The engagé system, a central feature of the French scheme, was first utilized by France in Senegal from 1818 to 1846. During this period, thousands of Africans were held under labor contracts for fourteen years after being "rescued" from slavery, with few becoming totally free after their apprenticeship period. Although the system was phased out, it was eventually revived to address labor shortages after France abolished slavery in 1848. Under this revived system, Africans held under the engagé system were transported across the Atlantic to the Caribbean. Consequently, about 27,000 forced workers were taken from West Central Africa between 1857 and 1861.[162]

The Régis firm's activities in Mboma were central to the success of the French forced migration scheme. By 1859, according to British reports, the Régis's agents would purchase significant numbers of slaves, paying "as much as 5l or 6l sterling each for them in well-assorted goods."[163] To facilitate business, they would build ties with African chiefs in Mboma, many of whom had long benefited from the slave trade. "I have been informed that the payments to the chiefs were usually made in kind, and consisted generally of cotton cloths of English manufacture, gunpowder, and arms".[164] Africans who refused to be recruited were forced to work ten years in French factories in Mboma as "compensation for refusing engagement."[165]

The Régis firm's operations were facilitated not only by their ties with Mboma chiefs but also by the support they received from the French state, including from its navy. According to historian Norm Schrag, the firm "transported workers from Mboma to the coast under safe conduct of the French navy."[166] France's naval power would be deployed against Mboma chiefs who might resist the firm's presence.[167] The French navy was also used to quash opposition from Portuguese authorities to the recruitment schema. In one notable incident, French commanders threatened military action against a Governor of Angola who questioned the legitimacy of forcibly moving thousands of Africans across the Atlantic to French Caribbean colonies.[168]

The French forced migration quickly drew criticism from British and Portuguese officials. The Portuguese accused the French of "rescuing" Africans from slavery, "teaching [them] how to say the word 'yes' in French, dressing [them] and then shipping [them] to French possessions as colonials."[169] British authorities characterized the scheme as a poorly disguised form of the slave trade.[170] Strikingly, French recruiters themselves at least once openly admitted recruiting Africans through the transatlantic trade networks in human beings.[171] Yet they dismissed criticism by pointing to low levels of mortality among Africans taken to the French Caribbean. While stating that Africans enlisted voluntarily in the "free" scheme, they implausibly argued that their forced migration contributed to ending the transatlantic slave trade and that slave dealers were their enemies.[172]

By lending support to the Ndongo, the Régis firm acted in line with a previous history of engagement with African rulers on several corners of the continent, frequently in support of France's overall geopolitical goals. A notable example was the firm's relationship with the Dahomey kingdom, where its agents frequently engaged with King Gezo to safeguard its commercial interests and even arranged for the education of Gezo's sons in Marseille.[173] These interactions had implications far beyond mere business dealings. By establishing strong connections with Dahomey's leadership, the Régis firm positioned France as a contender against British and Luso-Brazilian traders in an area transitioning from the slave to the palm oil trade. The firm's actions, as historian Robin Law points out, were central to a process that eventually led to French rule over Whydah forty-one years later.[174]

While the French played a significant role in supporting Ndongo, they were not the only ones backing his bid for the throne. Ndongo was said to be on good terms with slave dealers who had long operated in Mboma and other places. According to historian Jelmer Vos, a Portuguese commander pointed out that slave dealers "supplied the group of D. Alvaro Ndongo the gunpowder, arms, textiles, and beads [from] which they gain the favor of all Kongo people."[175] However, despite their influence, slave dealers lacked the military power that the French could muster through their naval forces. Nor could they ever contemplate establishing a territorial presence in West Central Africa that directly threatened Portugal's geopolitical aspirations. By contrast, the French considered military action to establish a stronghold in the Loango kingdom after envoys visited the kingdom's court, signaling their willingness to expand their influence in the region.[176]

By backing Ndongo, the Régis firm sought to empower a contender for Kongo's throne who would presumably be more amenable to its newly created forced migration. For Ndongo, French support proved crucial, enabling him to amass a formidable personal army and bolster his political profile. In contrast, his rival Katende lacked ties to international players and was initially unaware of the French migration activities along the coast, putting him at a significant diplomatic and strategic disadvantage.[177] To offset Ndongo's advantage and gain crucial external support, he would actively seek to cultivate ties with the Portuguese, paying two visits to their base in Bembe, once even attending mass with military officers—a clear attempt to align himself with Portugal.[178]

Portuguese officials, increasingly suspicious about Ndongo's connections with the French, became further worried when they learned about letters he had presumably sent to coastal rulers in Mussulo, calling on them to proclaim themselves "French" kings.[179] This alleged action exemplified how the succession crisis in Kongo had become inextricably linked with the broader imperial rivalries playing out along the African coast, with Ndongo's actions threatening to further embed French interests in the region at the expense of Portugal. In Luanda, officials viewed such an act as a direct threat to their geopolitical interests in regions that had long been under Portugal's influence.

Interestingly, Katende himself sought to exploit Portuguese fears of French encroachment by emphasizing Ndongo's ties with the French. This strategic move demonstrated Katende's understanding of the delicate geopolitical balance and his attempt to leverage international rivalries to his advantage in the succession crisis. According to Katende, Ndongo had "spent a great amount of goods to gain the support of electors of the kingdom's successor," promoting the notion that his rival could not be trusted due to his connections with the French.[180] By highlighting Ndongo's alleged French backing and his lavish spending to gain support, Katende aimed to present himself as the more reliable and less threatening option to Portuguese interests. This maneuvering underscored how deeply European imperial competition had become intertwined with internal Kongolese politics, with succession candidates actively exploiting international tensions to bolster their own positions.[181]

With French support, Ndongo easily outmaneuvered Katende, securing the endorsement of Kongo's council of elders. This council, a long-standing institution in Kongo's political system, held the ultimate responsibility for selecting the kingdom's rulers, acting as a check on royal power and ensuring some degree of consensus among the nobility. The French influence on this process was significant. According to historian David Birmingham, "the French provided Alvaro with enough good quality textiles to bribe the Kongo electors into choosing him, rather than Pedro, as their king."[182]

The election brought Ndongo to the brink of becoming the new ruler of Kongo. However, Kongo's political traditions dictated that he could not officially assume power until his predecessor, Henrique, was buried—a process that could take up to four months.[183] This extended interregnum period between a king's death and his successor's coronation was a common feature of Kongolese politics, rooted in complex funeral rites and power transfer ceremonies. While designed to ensure a smooth transition, in practice, this lengthy period of uncertainty often provided ample opportunity for Kongo's traditionally fractious politics to throw the kingdom into chaos, as rival factions could use this time to challenge the election results or build opposition to the chosen successor.

As the succession crisis unfolded and the interregnum period prolonged the uncertainty, Portuguese officials in Luanda coldly weighed their options for intervention. The presence of the Bembe military detachment, established after the expedition, had significantly changed the dynamics of Portugal's potential involvement in Kongo's internal politics. "Either Katenda wins [the election in Congo], and then we can intervene more unfailingly to support him, without using great means; or Prince Dongo prevails." Regarding Ndongo, they openly spoke about making him "respect what we have already conquered" and even discussed "attacking him in his own terrain."[184] These strategies reflected a Luanda government that was not only fully aware of the political leverage afforded by the Bembe military detachment but also willing to deploy it to shape Kongo's internal politics—a scenario that would have been highly unlikely prior to the Bembe expedition.

The Portuguese presence in Bembe had thus altered the balance of power and provided Portugal with new opportunities to assert its influence over the Kingdom of Kongo during this critical juncture. Initially, Luanda officials chose to leverage their newly found influence in a political instead of outrightly military way, informing Congolese electors that Ndongo was "hostile to our interests, as he has never engaged with us" and that their preferred candidate was the Marquis of Katende.[185] However, when the council still chose to elect Ndongo, they changed their approach, dispatching a 200-soldier military detachment supported by artillery to install Katende as the new king of Kongo.[186]

The installation of Katende came at a deep cost to Kongo's sovereignty. In exchange for Portuguese military backing, Katende took the unprecedented step of swearing vassalage to the Portuguese crown. This act marked a significant change in recent Kongo-Portuguese relations, effectively diminishing Kongo's political autonomy. The criticism this move earned from Nicolau da Agua Rosada, a member of the Kongolese nobility exiled in Luanda, highlighted the tensions created by this external intervention.[187] This development can be seen as part of a broader trend across Africa, where European powers increasingly sought to formalize their influence over African polities, often through treaties or, as in this case, acts of vassalage that significantly eroded African sovereignty while maintaining a facade of local rule.

The installation of Katende—now named Pedro V—as the new ruler of Kongo provided Portugal with what seemed like a compliant partner who would likely support its territorial and economic ambitions in Kongo's territory. This move was viewed as particularly important for countering the growing influence of other European powers in the region, especially the French, who had backed Ndongo's bid for the throne. However, for the African kingdom, the intervention ushered in a period of further turmoil. Ndongo refused to relinquish his claim to the royal throne, leading to a devastating civil war that consumed the kingdom and threatened the new ruler's grip on power.[188]

In response to the civil war and the threat posed by Ndongo's faction, the Luanda government found itself having to dispatch a force of five hundred soldiers to Kongo, "marching over that city [Mbanza Congo]."[189] The deployment of such a significant military force underscores the extent to which Portugal was willing to invest in securing its newly found influence over the kingdom. By 1861, Luanda authorities declared that the Portuguese flag was *flutuando* in the Congo, "where our troops had been able to expel the faction of the rebel prince and destroy their *banzas* and settlements."[190] Angolan Governor Sebastião Lopes de Carvalho e Menezes confidently declared, "We have stationed a garrison in Salvador of Congo, and the new king and his subjects are obedient to us."[191] This assertion of Portuguese authority, however, belied the precarious nature of their position, as they faced the constant threat of resistance from factions loyal to Ndongo and other discontented elements within Kongo society.

Conclusion

The historical narrative of the Kingdom of Kongo, as explored in this chapter, underscores the intricate interplay of global and local dynamics that shaped its fate. The arrival of a Portuguese military expedition in the nearby Bembe region in 1856 and its subsequent influence on Kongo's internal politics marked a significant turning point. While Kongo was no stranger to external interference, the context of abolition—marked by territorial expansion and international competition for new trade prospects in West Central Africa—introduced new complexities. Internal strife, a common occurrence in the kingdom's history, was aggravated by these external forces, leading to intensified power struggles. Faced with deeply destabilizing forces, the kingdom navigated geopolitical rivalries among Portugal, Britain, France, and the United States along the West Central African coast—each nation with its own vested interests.

Tracing the global pressures exerted by contending imperial powers, the chapter develops a granular analysis of Kongo's internal politics and the fractious relations between traditional authorities and coastal elites. As European imperial ambitions mounted along the coast, Kongo's centralized power had been weakened by trade and political dynamics that, though certainly not new, had been further catalyzed in the last decades of the slave trade. These dynamics came to a head during a succession crisis that roiled Kongo due to acute factionalism aided by foreign interference. By examining the relationship between Kongo's governance and competing networks of power, the chapter thus reveals how global forces collided with the governing structures of an African kingdom.

The chapter's exploration of abolition in multiple settings of Africa and the Indian Ocean seeks to offer a more nuanced perspective on the complex interplay between the end of the transatlantic slave trade, imperial competition, and the reshaping of political and economic landscapes across the globe. By situating West Central Africa within the broader context of Atlantic Africa and drawing parallels between Kongo's experience and the impact of European interventions in regions such as Lagos and the Bight of Benin, the chapter illuminates the far-reaching and often unintended consequences of abolition. The analysis reveals how the suppression of the slave trade, rather than signaling an end to foreign exploitation, instead catalyzed new forms of imperial expansion and intensified competition for resources and influence in Africa.

Moreover, the examination of Britain's assertive anti-slave trade policies in the Indian Ocean and their impact on territories claimed by Portugal in East Africa and beyond underscores the truly global nature of the abolition movement and its profound entanglement with imperial rivalries and the redrawing of territorial claims. By tracing the ripple effects of abolition across vast geographic expanses and multiple imperial spheres, the chapter offers a powerful reminder of the interconnectedness of global forces and local dynamics in shaping the trajectory of African polities like Kongo. This analysis also highlights the paradoxical nature of abolition, as the campaign to end the slave trade often served as a tool for imperial powers to justify policies of conquest and occupation, ultimately leading to new forms of domination and exploitation.

The integration of the Kingdom of Kongo into the Portuguese sphere of influence, marked by Henrique II's strategic alignment in 1856, can be seen as part of a broader contest over sovereignty and empire-making dynamics in West Central Africa. European firms and empires sought new modes of informal control and privileged access to expanding palm oil, copper, and other trades through partnerships with African authorities. Yet these delicate relations, underpinned by coercive diplomatic and military leverage, also contained destabilizing tensions that could erupt in disputes over sovereignty. In this context, African polities like Kongo found themselves ensnared in a web of overwhelming constraints arising from regional African rivals and ascendant European powers.

CHAPTER SEVEN

Making Forced Labor
(Locally and Globally)

IN 1857, three women—Cabundo, Camassa, and Ndembo—petitioned the government in Luanda, the capital of Portuguese Angola, to revoke a judicial decision listing them as part of a deceased guardian's estate. In their petition, the African women argued that a judge had allowed their late guardian's heirs to sell them as enslaved people in a public auction to settle their mother's debts despite their status as apprentices (libertos)—a status often seen as a pathway to freedom but in reality part of a continuum of human exploitation. While Camassa was granted freedom after paying money to be removed from the estate inventory, Cabundo and Ndembo's lack of financial means initially condemned them to slavery. Yet the women's fate was reversed after the Luanda government rebutted the judicial ruling and ordered them free. Not only must they not be sold, but officials also determined that their apprenticeship period had already ended.[1]

The experiences of the three African women serve as a reminder of the human dimension of abolition. Their story provides a poignant example of ordinary Africans pushing back against new structures of labor exploitation and oppression brought about by abolition itself. Their cases represent an example in which abolition principles were upheld and enforced. Others, however, found themselves trapped in apprenticeship, deprived of their rights, and treated merely as units of labor. Significantly, this pattern was not unique to Angola but reflected global processes where the legal framework of abolition became a breeding ground for creating new forms of unfree labor.

This chapter delves into the experiences of people like Cabundo, Camassa, and Ndembo to analyze the consequences of abolition efforts in regions of Angola under Portuguese influence, which led to the end of shipments of captives to the Americas but set the stage for the rise of unfree labor. Scholars have long recognized the prevalence of slavery and "modified forms of slavery" in the post-slave trade era. Mariana Candido notes that as the slave trade ended, slavery and colonialism became increasingly intertwined.[2] Miguel Bandeira Jerônimo echoes such a view by arguing that "the juridical codification of native labor in the Portuguese colonies, in its successive modulations and specifications, always operated as a support to legitimize Portuguese colonial activity."[3] What has remained unexamined is how exactly abolition itself—both in its local and in its global iterations—sustained slavery and enabled new forms of unfree labor in Angola.

Focusing on the coercive nature of abolition, this chapter unpacks this process by adopting a global perspective that traces the circulation of ideas and practices about labor between the British, French, and Portuguese empires. Central to this process were mechanisms such as Britain's apprenticeship and France's engagé system, which were ostensibly designed to provide a gradual transition to freedom but that often became vectors of unfreedom. Within Britain, apprenticeship, a system in which young people were bound to work for a master craftsman for a set period to learn a trade, had long been relied upon to care for poor and orphaned children.[4] The British also applied apprenticeship to transition their colonies out of slavery in 1834 and to regulate the labor of Africans rescued from slave ships after the 1807 abolition of the British slave trade.[5]

Similarly, France developed its own system of indentured labor, known as the engagé system, to address labor shortages in its colonies. Inspired by the practice of indentured servitude, which had been widely employed during colonial times, this system was adapted to address fears of labor shortage in Senegal following the end of the slave trade in 1817. While a small number of France's engagé Africans were released from slave vessels, as was the British practice, the vast majority were purchased from African traders and placed under long-term contracts, typically lasting several years. Between 1818 and 1846, the French acquired 3,225 engagés in Senegal, mostly from regions of the interior. The system was initially justified as a means to promote the emancipation and freedom of slaves without damaging slaveholders' interests, while also providing labor for new agricultural ventures.[6]

Notably, Portugal's forced migration practices were heavily influenced by and interconnected with those of other colonial powers as they all navigated the end of the slave trade and slavery. Drawing inspiration from British apprenticeship and French engagism, Portugal established its own system of labor exploitation, particularly in the forced migration route from Angola to the islands of São Tomé and Príncipe.[7] This mirrored similar practices across European empires: British colonies moved people from Sierra Leone and St. Helena to the Caribbean and South Africa; France relocated workers from Senegal to the Caribbean and the Indian Ocean; and both empires facilitated movement from Mozambique to Mauritius and the Réunion islands.[8] These systems played a crucial role in new forced migrations that took thousands of Africans across the Atlantic and Indian Oceans.

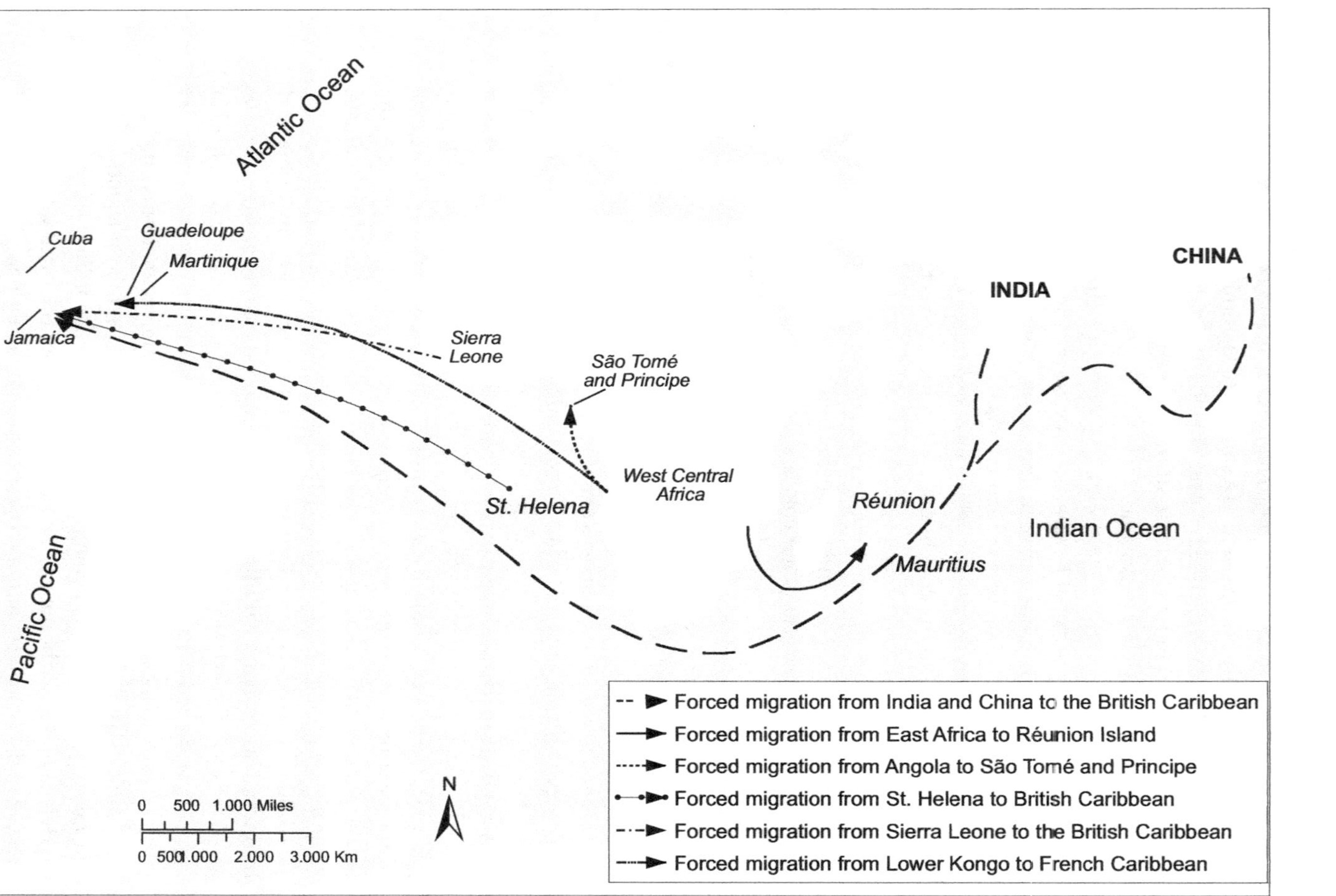

MAP 6. Forced Migrations (Atlantic and Indian Oceans)

In all these cases, African people forcefully removed from their homelands were placed under systems like the engagé system or apprenticeship. Portugal's adoption and adaptation of these practices demonstrates how colonial powers exchanged ideas and strategies to maintain labor control in the abolition era. The Portuguese government often justified its actions by referencing similar practices in British and French colonies, highlighting the interconnected nature of these exploitative systems. This circulation of ideas and practices across empires resulted in the creation of new forms of unfreedom under the guise of abolition, effectively perpetuating labor exploitation on a global scale.

By situating the local story of abolition in Angola within a broader global context, this chapter reveals not only the interconnected nature of labor exploitation in the age of abolition but also how abolition itself was a tool for the creation of new forms of unfreedom. While dismantling the slave trade, abolition transformed it into new systems of forced labor that perpetuated the exploitation of African labor. This dynamic was not unique to Africa. Historian Yesenia Barragan highlights how abolition in Latin America, characterized by a gradual approach, often recreated slavery and forced labor in new forms.[9] Both Barragan and historian Magdalena Candioti note that abolition laws, particularly those concerning the "free womb," spread across newly independent Spanish South American republics, underscoring the global interconnectedness of labor policy reforms during the abolition era.[10]

Yet it was in the African context that abolition-induced unfreedom emerged as central to the making of empires. As the Portuguese, British, and French extended their reach in Africa, they increasingly relied on mechanisms first devised to end the slave trade to foster new forms of labor exploitation and the creation of new forced migrations. This process can only be adequately understood through a global perspective acknowledging that labor practices circulated beyond local imperial and national contexts. France's decision to revive the engagé system in the 1850s was influenced by Britain's own experience with the removal of recaptive Africans to its colonies. Portugal, in turn, used both experiences to justify its own new forced migration from Angola to St Tomé and Príncipe.

A history of labor in post-slave trade Angola would be remiss without addressing how racial ideologies provided a justification for new forms of forced labor in the wake of the transatlantic slave trade. Maeve Ryan's observation that racism was deeply ingrained in British abolitionism can be similarly applied to the Portuguese context in West Central Africa.[11] Following Catherine Hall and Sonya Rose, I contend that ideas about race and racial differences were crucial in naturalizing the brutal exploitation of African labor amid hardening colonialism.[12] Echoing notions of white superiority that were then circulating globally, Portugal justified forced labor through portrayals of Africans as inferior and naturally idle. These racial ideologies provided a framework for reimagining labor exploitation in the wake of the slave trade's decline, shaping both policy and practice in colonial Angola.

This chapter is divided into three sections. The first section examines the British apprenticeship system and the French engagé system, tracing their origins and the ways in which they facilitated the exploitation of African labor. The second section explores how these systems gave rise to new patterns of forced migration across the Atlantic and Indian Oceans, connecting diverse regions under British, French, and Portuguese control. The third and final section delves into the specific case of Angola, examining how the legal framework of abolition served to maintain and legitimize the ongoing exploitation of African labor, and highlighting the role of racial ideologies in naturalizing this exploitation. By tracing these interconnected processes, this chapter argues that abolition itself became a tool for the creation and justification of new forms of unfreedom and labor exploitation in Angola and beyond.

Global Dynamics of Apprenticeship and Engagism

By the time Portuguese abolition got underway in the 1840s, anti-slavery had long provided tools for imperial powers to perpetuate labor regimes that either bore a strong resemblance to slavery or laid the groundwork for new forms of unfree labor. A case in point was apprenticeship. Historian Richard Anderson argues that apprenticeship "concealed a wide spectrum of experiences."[13] Bronwen Everill explores the lives of former apprenticed Africans who eventually became members of Sierra Leone's elite as "writers, managers, and other officials."[14] Ndubueze Mbah shows how those who migrated to Old Calabar defined freedom as mobility and generated "rebellion, self-fashioning, and anti-imperial ideologies of belonging."[15] Historian Allen Howard documents cases of recaptives who eventually became wealthy.[16] As Samuel Nyanchoga and Michelle Liebst note in coastal Kenya, some liberated Africans resisted unfree labor through cultural and ritual practices, asserting their agency within oppressive systems.[17] Yet much of the reality of apprenticed Africans was defined by labor exploitation. As historian Beatriz Mamigonian points out, "Whether formally or informally, their rights would be questioned, undermined, and revoked in practice."[18]

From early on, apprenticeship was fraught with legal ambiguities, exploitative practices, and the persistence of conditions akin to slavery. Britain established the legal framework for apprenticing Africans rescued from illegal slave ships in 1807, yet several key questions about their legal status and treatment remained unresolved.[19] As a result, across British colonies in the Caribbean, the Indian Ocean, and West Africa, the implementation of apprenticeship varied widely, often exposing Africans released from slave vessels to labor practices and economic imperatives.[20] In Trinidad, plantation and slave owners manipulated the distinction between apprentices and enslaved labor to serve their own interests.[21] Apprentices frequently found themselves subjected to harsh working conditions, physical abuse, insufficient provisions, and restrictions on their mobility, with colonial officials and private masters exploiting legal loopholes and resisting efforts to enforce protective measures.[22]

Like those held under apprenticeship in British territories, African engagés found themselves caught in a legal limbo between slavery and freedom in French colonies such as Senegal, Réunion, and Guadalupe, a status that enabled their ongoing exploitation under colonialism and plantation work. Echoing the rhetoric of their British counterparts, French officials justified this system by portraying it as a benevolent means of "redeeming" Africans from the cruelties of the slave trade and slavery. Yet, as historians Céline Flory, Juliana Farias and Kelly Brignac demonstrate, this rhetorical justification was often at odds with the lived experiences of African engagés, often marked by harsh labor conditions, the constant fear of never attaining promised freedom, and new forced migrations.[23]

The British, like the French, utilized apprenticeship as a means to secure labor and establish colonial control, particularly in Sierra Leone. Long envisioning apprenticeship as a pillar of their strategy to obtain labor and transform Sierra Leone into a viable colony, they pursued this vision despite the high cost it often imposed on recaptives.[24] The latter were sold, were auctioned off, or labored under conditions akin to slavery.[25] Many chose to escape to the African interior due to systemic mistreatment under British jurisdiction.[26] With tragic results, more than three thousand were deployed as a tool of empire-building in the Gambia between 1818 and 1838.[27] Many were also enlisted into the British army and deployed in the Caribbean and Africa.[28]

Similar dynamics of empire building drove the creation of the engagé system in the French empire. As Brignac points out, the goal was to restructure the economic foundations of France's empire after the loss of Haiti in 1804. Between 1818 and 1846, of the 3,225 Africans held as engagés in Senegal, only 102 became free after the required 14 years of labor. As Farias observes, colonial officials in Senegal acknowledged that engagistes frequently manipulated the system to transform engagés into de facto captives, further entrenching coercion under the guise of contractual labor.[29] While France abolished the system in 1844, it would later revive it to provide African workers for its colonies in the Caribbean and Indian Ocean.[30] From 1817 to 1861, around 70,000 workers were held under the engagé system in French colonies in the Atlantic and Indian Oceans.[31]

By the mid-1830s, around 700 engagés already toiled in French Ste. Marie, a small island off the eastern coast of Madagascar, as Brignac shows, under conditions of coercion and levels of exploitation similar to those of their counterparts in Senegal.[32] With the end of slavery in 1848, the system became further embedded elsewhere in the French empire. Between 1849 and 1859, an estimated 10,000 to 12,000 engagés, mainly from East Africa and Madagascar, were transported to Réunion Island under the guise of "free" labor, even though many had been purchased from slave traders or kidnapped.[33] This period saw a dramatic increase in recruitment, often through illegal means. Ships regularly engaged in dubious recruitment practices, with many workers embarked from ports known for slave trading on the East African coast, mostly Mozambique.[34]

Although the system was again phased out in the 1860s, it persisted through various subterfuges, often using French-controlled Nossi-Be as a laundering point for illegal recruits. Plantation owners and recruiters exploited loopholes, such as falsifying workers' origins, claiming they were from territories under French jurisdiction such as the Comoros or Madagascar.[35] Facing a suspension of indentured labor from British India, the system was again revived between May 1888 and the end of 1889, when 1,500 workers were taken from Mozambique to La Réunion.[36]

While the engagé system remained confined to regions under the influence of the French in Africa, the Americas, and the Indian Ocean, the apprenticeship system migrated to other imperial and national spaces. In Liberia, it paved the way for the government to control African labor, fundamentally shaping labor policies.[37] In places where slavery had not been outlawed, such as Brazil, apprenticed Africans were subjected to systematic labor exploitation.[38] Under Spanish colonialism in Cuba, they regularly toiled alongside captives and indentured workers from China, being sold as slaves and denied rights from which the enslaved could benefit, such as manumission and coartación.[39]

Similarly, recaptives in the Indian Ocean faced harsh labor conditions and exploitation, much like their counterparts in the Atlantic world. Individuals taken to Christian mission stations were forced to work on plantations, not only producing the food they consumed but also cultivating cash crops to offset the expenses of running the missions.[40] Others ended up in plantations in the Seychelles, Zanzibar, and Mauritius, where they labored alongside indentured workers from India or were later leased to the government.[41] According to Hopper, they were "highly valued for their labor and were sought after by plantation owners for fieldwork as well as by local notables to serve as domestic servants."[42] In Bombay, they worked on activities including "railway construction, apprenticed in workshops of the railway company, or employed in the port or by the police."[43]

This is the backdrop against which the Portuguese adoption of apprentices in Angola must be understood. By the end of the 1830s, the Portuguese navy had begun to sporadically capture slave vessels leaving regions under Portuguese jurisdiction, leading to a small apprenticed population in Luanda. As early as 1839, 59 Africans released from slave vessels were held in the Luanda battalion while awaiting assignment to the city's residents.[44] One was a woman named Zumbi, placed under the custody of a military officer with a child. A master promised to "educate, provide for, and dress" and return her to the government "as soon as required."[45]

Luanda's growing recaptive population soon became a flash point of global geopolitics, pitting Portugal against Britain. As early as 1840, the Portuguese government rejected a British proposal to adjudicate slave vessels apprehended by the Portuguese navy in their admiralty courts. Portugal argued that the proposal stemmed from Britain's desire to transport recaptives to their Caribbean colonies to compensate for the labor shortage caused by the abolition of slavery in the British Empire.[46] Nevertheless, Britain persisted in its efforts. In 1842, as it signed an anti-slave trade treaty with Britain, Portugal saw itself again having to refuse to transfer recaptives to the Caribbean.[47] A year later, a British judge in the Luanda's mixed commission stated that he had been "appointed at this place to effect the removal of recaptive Negroes to the West Indies."[48]

Similar frictions unfolded in Cuba and Brazil. In Cuba, where a mixed commission led to the release of approximately twenty-six thousand Africans, the local government first allowed the British to take formerly enslaved people to their colonies. In 1846, British officials reported a "total of 184 men, 108 women, and 102 children" removed to Jamaica.[49] The decision stemmed in part from the fear that recaptured Africans' presence would destabilize the institution of slavery.[50] Yet tensions arose after Spain opted to employ recaptives on the island to meet the demand for labor generated by sugar production.[51]

In Brazil, British allegations of recaptives being effectively re-enslaved ignited significant diplomatic tensions. A British commissioner remarked that "the government of Brazil has no sufficient control over the inhabitants to enable it to prevent the apprenticed blacks from being again fraudulently sold as slaves, and thenceforth more cruelly treated than if placed in a lawful and acknowledged state of slavery."[52] This observation was corroborated by recaptives themselves, who reported being "treated as slaves" or even "worse than dogs."[53] In response, British authorities began placing recaptives with "trusted" British nationals in Rio.[54] However, reflecting both the brewing tensions and the labor demands in British colonies, over two thousand recaptives were subsequently transported from Brazil to the British Caribbean.[55] Under mounting British pressure, the Brazilian government ultimately freed recaptives in 1853.[56] Nevertheless, this issue later contributed to the "Questão Christie," a diplomatic crisis in 1862 that resulted in Brazil severing diplomatic relations with Britain for two years.[57]

In Angola, a significant shift came with the anti-slave trade treaty signed by Britain and Portugal in 1842. This treaty led to the establishment of a mixed commission in Luanda tasked with adjudicating cases involving vessels apprehended with captives by both Portuguese and British navies. Alongside this initiative, a new authority called the Junta de Superintendência dos Negros Libertos was formed, assuming comprehensive control over recaptives released from ships seized beyond Portuguese territorial waters. According to Francisco Valdez, "enslaved people captured on board a slaver are declared free [*sic*] and immediately liberated. They are subsequently taken under the charge of the Junta de Superintendência dos Negros Libertos."[58]

However, the Luanda mixed commission would play a relatively minor role in the fate of recaptives, being responsible for the liberation of only about 137 Africans.[59] This low number was partly due to Britain's practice of redirecting captives to St. Helena, a British territory with a recently established vice-admiralty court, rather than taking them to Luanda. This strategic maneuver

FIGURE 7.1. St. Helena

allowed Britain to circumvent Luanda's lukewarm support for abolition while eventually gaining the authority to send thousands of recaptives to Caribbean colonies, a topic to be explored later. In this context, Portugal's decision to establish a Luanda tribunal in 1844 to adjudicate cases involving vessels apprehended by its navy proved more significant. With the Portuguese navy taking a more assertive role in curbing slave trade activities along the African coast, approximately two thousand individuals were released from slave vessels and barracoons (slave depots) between 1836 and 1861.[60]

From around one hundred individuals in 1844, Luanda's recaptive population grew to about five hundred in 1845, about ten percent of the city's overall population.[61] The growth of Luanda's recaptive population correlated with state measures to increase social control over the city's unfree population. In 1845, authorities ruled that any recaptive found on the street carrying weapons would be arrested.[62] An official overseeing libertos later mandated that "all blacks (males and females) were to bathe every day on a nearby beach at noon and before dinner" and issued specific instructions about where to procure the water.[63] Following attempts by Africans found on board the ship *Flor de Campos* to escape, Luanda authorities reported fear of "a concerted plot to seduce all the adults to do the same."[64] As a result, these Africans were deported to São Tomé and Príncipe, fueling a forced migration still in its early stages.

Those held in Angola were put to work in regions under Portuguese influence, helping propel Portugal's plans to drive the colony's economy away from the transatlantic slave trade. In 1848, for example, 20 of these Africans were sent to the commander of Cambambe, likely to serve in support of military operations.[65] Yet what was no doubt more important was the government allocation of recaptive Africans to work on agricultural projects, which helped propel Angola's economy away from the slave trade and set the stage for a deep reliance on forced labor. As early as 1844, one hundred enslaved people taken from the brig *Caçador* were sent to the newly created colony of Mossamedes "to be employed in agricultural work."[66]

New Forced Migrations

Although the British were vocal in criticizing the Portuguese treatment of recaptives, they did no better in their colonies and territories. In Trinidad, where naval commanders charged with enforcing anti-slave trade laws were also planters, "there was little room for the accommodation of apprentices who did not work in the fields," and many were re-enslaved.[67] In Tortola and Antigua, where many recaptives escaped brutal working conditions by running away, widespread abuse and coerced labor prompted the British government to dispatch an investigative commission.[68] In South Africa, where recaptive Africans' children were taken from their parents, "masters could continue to coerce labor from parents by holding apprenticeships over their children."[69] In the Mauritius and Seychelles islands, according to reports circulating in Britain, British officials would "sell" apprenticed Africans to local planters.[70]

Worse yet was Britain's invention of a brand-new forced migration of recaptives from Sierra Leone and St. Helena to the British Caribbean, which eventually inspired not only the French but also the Portuguese to create their own. According to scholar Maeve Ryan, the new forced migration "constituted the third-largest stream of coerced migrants in the nineteenth century."[71] The creation of this system was directly tied to the end of slavery in the British Empire in 1838, although the British had already begun this practice on a smaller scale even before the official abolition, having taken 5,969 apprenticed Africans from Sierra Leone to colonies in the Caribbean.[72] Between 1841 and 1867, about 32,000 recaptive Africans were taken from Sierra Leone to the British Caribbean (Jamaica, British Guiana, and Trinidad).[73]

Also noteworthy is how Britain's new forced migration of recaptives from St. Helena to the Caribbean loomed large as France debated its own labor policies. As early as 1842, the French considered the merits of Britain's approach to relocating recaptives, with a Minister of the Navy seeking to persuade the government to emulate Britain's example and going so far as to dispatch ships to Sierra Leone to observe British recruitment methods firsthand.[74] However, France's ability to emulate Britain's forced migration practices was limited by several factors. Although the French navy patrolled the African coast to curb the slave trade, it did not apprehend as many slave vessels as the British did, which meant that France had fewer recaptive Africans to relocate. Moreover, the abolition of slavery in French colonies in 1848 led to the temporary suspension of the engagé system, further restricting France's means of obtaining African workers.

After the abolition of slavery in 1848, however, France found itself having to revive the engagé system to address labor shortages in its colonies in the Caribbean and the Indian Ocean. They then transformed the system into a cornerstone for new forced migrations, shipping thousands of people across the Atlantic and Indian Oceans. Between 1857 and 1861, approximately 27,000 laborers were transported from the lower Congo to the French Caribbean.[75] In East Africa, the forced migration resulted in the relocation of more than 33,000 African engagés from Mozambique and Madagascar to the French-controlled Réunion island between 1851 and 1859.[76] As in the Caribbean, the demand for labor in Réunion was driven by a plantation economy heavily reliant on forced labor.[77]

FIGURE 7.2 African man taken into French forced migration

To justify its decision to create these forced migrations, French officials invoked England's own practices of removing recaptive Africans to the Caribbean and Mauritius islands. They argued that their actions were equivalent to Britain's transportation of individuals from seized slave vessels to its colonies in the Caribbean. As one French official stated, "England herself [. . .] gives us an example in this respect." They maintained that it was crucial for France to adopt a policy that had served as "a means of salvation for several English colonies after slave emancipation." When criticized by the British, a French commander riposted that the only difference between the engagé system and the removal of recaptives to British colonies was that the French bought their Africans on land while the English seized theirs at sea and forced them to emigrate.[78]

The British and French models of forced migration not only influenced each other but also had a profound impact on the labor policies of other European empires, such as Portugal. Seeking to expand its agricultural production in São Tomé and Príncipe, a Portuguese colony off the coast of Gabon that was experiencing the early stages of a coffee boom, Portugal developed its own system to remove recaptive Africans from Angola to the islands.[79] To justify their actions, officials invoked the migration that the British had established between Sierra Leone and their colonies in the Caribbean. As stated by them, all present and future recaptured Africans "should be conveyed to St. Thomé and Principe, in the same manner as Her Britannic Majesty's Government causes them to leave Sierra Leone for Jamaica or other ports of the West Indies."[80]

At first, the Portuguese forced migration did not reach voluminous numbers, yet a milestone was crossed when a trader named João Maria de Souza Almeida applied for a license to ship one hundred enslaved workers from Benguela to São Tomé in 1856.[81] Souza Almeida was a native of the Portuguese island who had once been a governor of Benguela, where he also made a name for himself in the slave trade. His trajectory embodies the circulation of knowledge about labor exploitation and empire-building in the South Atlantic. He had once lived in Rio de Janeiro, where he purchased a small farm and studied methods to cultivate coffee and cocoa production. Together with other slave dealers living in the city, he was then forced out of Brazil after the prohibition of the slave trade in the early 1850s. On the way back to Africa, he spent time in Lisbon, where he obtained the license to take African laborers from Benguela to the island.[82]

Further momentum for the Portuguese forced migration came through the actions of other influential individuals in the colonial system. Manoel José da Costa Pedreira, a farmer investing in coffee production in São Tomé, obtained a license to take up to one hundred libertos from Luanda to the island.[83] This development, following Souza Almeida's earlier initiative, signaled the emergence of a new trans-Atlantic migration system that exploited African labor for colonial agricultural enterprises in São Tomé and Príncipe. The involvement of established planters like Pedreira reflected a growing recognition of the potential for African labor to fuel the islands' nascent plantation economy.

However, as the Luanda government moved to approve another request by a Luanda resident named Manoel Antonio de Oliveira, British officials objected to the nascent forced migration, claiming that it was a façade for the transatlantic slave trade to Cuba. In response, while admitting that known slave dealers had previously sought to send "free" Africans to the islands, Governor of Angola José Rodrigues Coelho do Amaral defended the new forced migration by stating that the Africans taken to São Tomé and Príncipe were libertos, not enslaved people.[84] By laying out this argument, Governor Coelho do Amaral essentially used Portugal's newly issued abolitionist laws to justify the country's brand-new forced migration, thus mirroring Britain's justification for the shipment of thousands of apprenticed Africans from St. Helena and Sierra Leone to the British Caribbean.

To further back up their actions, the Portuguese claimed that Africans taken to São Tomé and Príncipe received treatment in conformity with an anti-slave trade treaty that Portugal had signed with Britain in 1842. Before leaving Luanda, African workers received a letter of freedom, and once in São Tomé and Príncipe, they were placed under the purview of the Junta Protetora dos Libertos. Theoretically, they were entitled to rights such as having a day off work per week, which they could sell back to their contractors, and were set free if a judge decided that they had been mistreated or their master did not provide for them.[85] These rights, however, were rarely enforced, underscoring the hollowness of Portugal's abolition efforts and drawing complaints from the British, who were themselves engaged in the forced migration of thousands of Africans to their Caribbean colonies.

For Portugal, what was at stake was the development of a robust colonial economy in São Tomé and Príncipe. The islands were dubbed "Portuguese Cuba," likening them to the Spanish colony in the Caribbean then known as an agricultural powerhouse. This moniker was justified by São Tomé and Príncipe's rising coffee production at the time. According to historian Marta Macedo, a single coffee plantation had "more than one million coffee plants and 250 workers" in 1861.[86] However, Portuguese officials believed that the sparsely populated territory would fail to reach its full productive potential without an influx of forced laborers from Angola.[87] Although coffee exports reached 54,000 arrobas between 1858 and 1861, they believed that this figure represented only a small fraction of the island's potential production if more workers were available.[88]

Propelling the forced migration from Angola to São Tomé and Príncipe were powerful underlying factors, including the fact that African workers contracted for twenty dollars in Angola could be sold for 100 dollars in São Tomé. The short length of the trip—only five days—made it an attractive prospect for farmers and investors, who sometimes traveled from São Tomé to Angola to purchase forced workers, with some making multiple trips. As historian Tracy Lopes shows, several members of the Luanda elite were involved in the forced migration as investors.[89] While Luanda and Benguela were the primary points of departure, people were also shipped from elsewhere in Africa, including Gabon. São Tomé investors, however, were said to prefer workers from Luanda, as those from Gabon were said to often escape back to their homeland in continental Africa.[90] Between 1876 and 1904, about 47,000 individuals were taken from Angola to São Tomé and Príncipe.[91]

The new forced migration strained Portugal's relationship with Britain. The British questioned official estimates of two thousand people shipped from Luanda, with one official stating, "I have no means of knowing with certainty the number that has been sent to the island during the current year [1861], but they must amount to many hundreds."[92] They alleged that many Africans were transported from regions outside Portuguese control, near and north of the Congo River, using documents issued by Luanda authorities and small boats owned by former or current Portuguese slave traders.[93] To curb these abuses, they proposed that those leaving Luanda appear before the mixed commission—a bilateral body established to adjudicate cases of suspected illegal slave trading—to declare whether they were departing Angola voluntarily.[94]

To deflect British criticism, the Portuguese drew parallels between their forced migration practices and other contemporary labor movements reshaping global markets. They contended that their actions in São Tomé and Príncipe mirrored those in Spanish Cuba, which had begun importing Chinese indentured laborers in the late 1840s, concurrent with a still ongoing influx of enslaved people from Africa. Between 1840 and 1875, approximately one hundred and fifty thousand Chinese workers were transported to Cuba. By 1861, Chinese indentured laborers constituted about ten percent of Cuba's unfree population.[95]

The Chinese forced migration to Cuba was part of a much wider surge of forced migration from China at the time, which was a response to escalating economic distress and social upheaval within China itself. Most Chinese migrants originated from the southern provinces of Guangdong and Fujian, with millions traveling to various destinations in Southeast Asia, the Pacific, and the Indian Ocean. Only a small percentage of these migrants, fewer than 750,000, signed indentured contracts with European employers. Chinese brokers, bypassing legal prohibitions on indentured emigration, delivered recruits to European firms. Strikingly, Macau, a Portuguese enclave, played a key role in forced Chinese migration, as pirates and brokers exploited vulnerable individuals, funneling them into indentured contracts under the guise of legality, as highlighted by historian Paulo Cesar Gonçalves.[96] The prevalence of kidnapping led to disputes between China and major European powers, each accusing the other of enabling this exploitative trade.[97]

For the Portuguese, their actions were part of a broader pattern of colonial labor exploitation that transcended national boundaries. They argued that Britain had forcefully removed recaptive Africans from Sierra Leone and St. Helena to its Caribbean colonies, where they were "employed in agricultural work and were subject to coerced labor." In their view, Britain's status as a global power shielded it from international criticism for these practices.[98] Portuguese officials also pointed to the forced migrations that France sponsored to its colonies to fend off charges against them. They contended that "if it is legitimate to contract blacks from Africa with the obligation of work for a certain amount of time and take them to French colonies, or employ coolies [sic] from India and China [. . .] and then take them to French, Spanish and English colonies, it is still more licit to take blacks who are obligated by law to work for a certain amount of time from one [Portuguese] colony to another."[99] These arguments underscore Portugal's efforts to legitimize its practices by situating them within a broader context of interconnected colonial labor exploitation that spanned European empires.

Forced Labor in Angola

Portugal's efforts to legitimize its forced migration practices by invoking the examples of other colonial powers were not limited to the forced movement of workers between colonies. The same legal frameworks and justifications that enabled forced migration also contributed to the emergence of forced labor within Angola itself, as the colony transitioned away from the slave trade and toward new forms of labor exploitation. Case in point: the introduction of the "liberto" status, which became a key tool for perpetuating labor exploitation under the guise of abolition.

The interconnection between abolition efforts and new forms of labor exploitation can be traced back to an 1842 anti-slave trade decree between Portugal and Britain. While ostensibly aimed at curtailing the transatlantic slave trade, the decree effectively repackaged forms of bondage under the guise of apprenticeship. This legal maneuver recategorized individuals released from slave vessels as libertos, or apprentices, often subjected to conditions scarcely distinguishable from those of slavery. The introduction of the "liberto" status thus pioneered a connection between abolition legal architecture and forced labor that would undergird Angola's transition beyond the slave trade and legal slavery.

This process of redefining labor relationships under the guise of abolition gained further momentum with Portugal's anti-slavery decree from 1854, which set in motion a gradualist process to end slavery that effectively extended the institution's life while also providing the means to create new forms of coerced labor. The decree gave slaveholders thirty days to register enslaved people already living in African territories under the control of the Portuguese. According to the official "census," the number of enslaved people in 1854 stood at 61,711 individuals.[100] Any slaveholder who failed to comply with that would have their enslaved laborers placed under the status of libertos. Moreover, any unfree African person brought into regions under Portuguese jurisdiction would be considered libertos, not enslaved people.[101]

Importantly, like apprenticed Africans released from slave vessels after the 1842 anti-slave treaty, these libertos were placed under an apprenticeship system. They were required to work for seven years before being considered free—a status achieved only by a small minority in the colony. Historians Edward Alpers and Daniel Domingues argue that the 1854 decree—particularly its registration facet—"was part of a larger effort by metropolitan Portugal to assert meaningful administrative control over its African colonies."[102] Yet other factors were at play.

As early as 1847, British Foreign Secretary Palmerston drew a direct connection between the continuation of the slave trade and the existence of slavery in Portuguese territories. In his view, "the Portuguese government would contribute most effectual and important assistance towards the abolition of the slave trade if it would prohibit its subjects in its possessions on the coast of Africa from purchasing or owning slaves."[103] Later, Luanda-based British diplomat Edmond Gabriel suggested that not only the sale of enslaved people but also slaveholding itself should be considered felonies. For Gabriel, "the suppression of the slave trade by Portugal can only be considered a nominal, and not a bona fide measure until she shall impose some restraint upon this system of buying and selling slaves in her African dominions."[104]

Portugal was not alone in its approach to abolition as an opportunity for new forms of labor exploitation. Similar patterns emerged in other European colonies, as discussed earlier, where the transition from slavery to "free" labor often involved the implementation of coercive labor practices under different guises. These strategies aimed to mitigate the economic impact of abolition on colonial and local economies while maintaining control over the labor of formerly enslaved individuals. The parallel experiences across European empires underscore the ways in which measures intended to end slavery frequently led to the perpetuation of exploitation and dominion over African labor.

In Angola, the 1854 decree revealed a complex interplay between abolition and economic interests, which is evident in statements by slaveholders in support of the legislation. According to slaveholders, "the primary goal of this provident and beneficial law [1854] was promoting emancipation and freedom of slaves without damaging or ruining slaveholders, since in this province there are many and important fortunes that consist of slaves."[105] Francisco Travassos Valdez, an officer in the Luanda mixed commission with firsthand knowledge of Angola, echoed these sentiments, noting that, "by these means, the final abolition of slavery will be consummated without any serious injury to the proprietors" of enslaved people and land.[106] These perspectives underscore a widespread understanding among Portuguese colonial elites that the abolition process was carefully crafted to safeguard their economic interests and only secondly transition the colony away from slavery.

The treatment of libertos following the decree bore out these priorities. Libertos were branded like enslaved people: "All slaves who enter this province are considered *libertos*, and as such are branded like slaves sent to São Tomé."[107] Furthermore, they could be bought and sold like captives, effectively reducing them to a fungible labor force. Austrian naturalist Fredcrico Welwitsch noted that it was more economical to purchase libertos than enslaved Africans.[108] Moreover, libertos were subject to severe punitive measures, mirroring the treatment of enslaved individuals. In one instance, a "liberto" employed at the Luanda city council was subjected to two hundred lashes.[109]

Despite the decree's apparent safeguards for slaveholders' interests and the continued exploitation of libertos, some sectors in Angola still viewed the legislation as a threat to the established economic order. This opposition was particularly evident in Luanda, where the city council held an extraordinary meeting "attended by about one hundred and fifty citizens" to voice opposition to the legislation. According to the council, "the power of slaveholders was already very insecure and precarious, even before the decree's publication."[110] They argued that the decree would undermine the "regular reproduction of the necessities of life" and disrupt Luanda's economic fabric, which heavily relied on slavery. Many slaveholders owned small numbers of captives, and "many females of this city" depended on their captives to earn a living.[111]

To further press against the new decree, the Luanda city council leveraged prevailing fears of slave flights and potential revolts, arguing that the decree might spur further escapes and potentially incite a catastrophic uprising. The council drew parallels to slave revolts and episodes of political and social unrest in Saint-Domingue (Haiti), Pará, and Bahia. In their view, the 1854 decree held the potential of triggering a similar uprising in the city, and rumors of its promulgation had already incited "excitement" among the enslaved population. Such an uprising, they argued, would be particularly dangerous if supported by members of nearby runaway communities, potentially resulting in a "scene of disasters like that of St. Domingo, Pará, and Bahia."[112]

While the new legislation never incited an uprising, it did instill a sense of empowerment among libertos. In Benguela, residents observed that apprenticed Africans no longer "want to work as slaves," becoming "as indolent and disrespectful as they had been diligent and submissive" in the past. In one particular incident, a master reported having to punish a black woman who, after telling an overseer she did not want to work, "came to me to request her letter of freedom."[113] In Luanda, five apprenticed Africans fled a construction site and, even after soldiers were sent to arrest them, refused to return, claiming that "they did not want to work in the quarry as the job was too heavy." As a result, authorities noted that libertos believed their status "granted them the right to act as they pleased without fear of punishment."[114]

This newfound assertiveness was not without legal foundation. With the 1854 decree, the colonial state took steps to codify previously informal practices within Angola's slavery system, particularly manumission, and endowed enslaved people with tools to challenge mistreatment by their owners. Prior to the decree, manumission was already part of slavery's fabric, yet it lacked legal validation. With the decree, however, the practice became part of the legal framework of slavery, enhancing the negotiating power of enslaved individuals before similar legal recognitions were made in Brazil, where the absolute right to manumission was not recognized until 1871.[115] Under the new Portuguese law, all slaves within the crown's territories could claim their "natural freedom," provided they compensated their owners, thereby introducing a more regulated approach to slavery.[116]

Tasked with overseeing manumission was a newly created *Junta dos Escravos e Libertos* (Board for the Protection of Enslaved and Freed People), which oversaw a fund designated for the manumission of those deemed "worthy of the royal bounty."[117] Enslaved Africans who had managed to save enough money could initiate the manumission process by petitioning the Junta. The procedure involved a judicial hearing to set the price for the enslaved person's freedom, requiring negotiations between the slaveholder and the enslaved individual. In cases where consensus could not be reached, a neutral party would take temporary custody of the enslaved person until a three-member panel could assess and agree on a fair price.[118] In 1856, Andreza Paulo Bartolomeu and Bernarda Manoel took advantage of the legislation, each paying considerable sums toward securing their freedom.[119] From 1856 to 1866, over 300 individuals, at least 195 men and 113 women, gained freedom through the Junta's auspices.[120]

The Junta also provided enslaved people with a tool to contest abuse and negotiate conditions, thus offering a measure of protection against slaveholders' abuses. As historian Tracy Lopes highlights, it "gave enslaved people a forum to seek protection against abuse and negotiate the conditions of their enslavement."[121] In 1856, a man named Vicente filed a complaint charging that a master "mistreated him, beating him, giving him little to eat, and overworking him."[122] In another case, the Junta ordered a master to prove that his captives had been registered in 1854 after a complaint about physical abuse.[123] However, the effectiveness of the Junta was limited. Many enslaved people lacked access to this legal recourse, particularly those in rural areas far from Luanda. The case of Cabundo, Camassa, and Ndembo, who had to petition the government to overturn a judicial decision that had allowed them to be sold as enslaved people despite their liberto status, further illustrates the Junta's limitations in protecting the rights of those it was meant to serve.

The Junta's limited effectiveness and libertos' ambiguous legal status helped perpetuate a system of labor exploitation that closely resembled slavery. This continued exploitation was particularly evident in Angola's expanding plantation economy, where major investors in commercial agriculture served as a microcosm for the broader economic trends. Ana Joaquina dos Santos Silva, a leading force in developing sugar production near Luanda, received two hundred apprenticed Africans to work on her farms.[124] Similarly, João Guilherme Pereira Barboza, another key figure in commercial agriculture, heavily relied on apprenticed African labor for his extensive coffee farms.[125] The enduring nature of this exploitation is evident in the fact that seven years after Barboza's death in 1855, 223 libertos were still reported as workers on one of his farms in Cazengo.[126]

The perpetuation of this exploitative labor system under the guise of abolition was further enabled by the support of colonial officials, who saw libertos as a crucial resource for Angola's economic development. As early as 1857, Governor Coelho do Amaral reported that while enslaved people still outnumbered libertos, the latter would soon become the dominant labor force in Angola.[127] This prediction was later echoed by Governor Sebastião Lopes de Carvalho e Menezes, who stated: "Slavery has been abolished by law, and it is not expected to revive; however, the law admits the condition of being a freed person, or a free black person, obliged to ten years of service in favor of the one who redeemed them from slavery."[128] These perspectives reveal how colonial officials deliberately used the new legal framework of abolition to maintain a steady supply of cheap labor, crucial for their economic plans in Angola.

To rationalize their position, officials argued that developing commercial agriculture under white control in Angola would be impossible without forced labor, claiming that harsh tropical conditions made white individuals incapable of handling agricultural work.[129] This reasoning reveals an interplay between economic imperatives, racial ideologies, and power structures. By framing forced labor as a necessity for economic development, officials legitimized the continued exploitation of African workers under the new legal framework, reflecting the broader colonial mindset that viewed African labor as a resource to be harnessed for the empire's benefit. The emphasis on the unsuitability of white labor for tropical conditions underscores how racial theories reinforced and justified existing power dynamics, naturalizing the exploitation of African workers within the colonial economic system.

Portugal's approach to abolition was by then marked by what could be characterized as a mix of calculated opportunism and cynicism. A revealing case in point was the abolition of slavery in the recently occupied Ambriz, just north of Luanda. After occupying the territory in 1855, in a bid to garner British support for their territorial expansion, the Portuguese declared freedom for captives recently brought from the interior.[130] However, they did not extend this benefit to Ambriz's existing enslaved population. While issuing directives to officials on the ground, the Luanda government declared that their role was "to tolerate the work by enslaved Africans, treating them as though they are free, and enforcing the [anti-slavery] law [only] when those affected by slavery requested official intervention" to end slavery.[131] As late as 1872, indeed, while still deliberately refusing to implement their own anti-slavery law, they vowed to keep forced laborers "uncertain about their actual [legal] status" as free people.[132]

The principles established by the 1854 decree were reinforced and expanded through a series of subsequent legislative measures and policies, culminating in an 1858 edict that further solidified Portugal's gradual abolition in Angola. To justify such an approach, Portuguese architect of abolition Sá da Bandeira invoked a financial rationale. In his words, "it is not possible for the time being to completely abolish slavery in all provinces as it is not practical to mobilize resources to compensate slaveholders for the value of their slaves financially."[133] Due to these financial constraints, the abolition of slavery would transpire gradually. This process would be facilitated by the natural decrease in the enslaved population over time (attrition of Africans held in captivity), the institutionalization of manumission following the 1854 decree, and the implementation of the 1856 Free Womb Law.[134]

The cumulative effect of abolition measures, including the 1854 decree and the 1858 edict, led to a significant increase in the liberto population in Angola.

From 1859 to 1863, the number of libertos more than doubled, increasing from approximately 14,000 to nearly 30,000 individuals.[135] The impact was particularly evident in specific regions of the colony. In Mossamedes, enslaved Africans (632) vastly outnumbered the liberto population (72) in 1856.[136] By 1864, however, the liberto population swelled to 1,200 individuals.[137] This shift reflected a broader trend across Angola, where libertos emerged as a new category of unfree laborers, barely distinguishable from a still robust slave population. As British traveler John Monteiro observed, "There are presently in Angola several sugar and cotton plantations worked by slaves, at present called libertos."[138]

While the cumulative effect of abolition measures led to a significant increase in the liberto population, the reality of their lived experiences often fell far short of the promised freedom. Despite the legal provision that libertos would gain complete freedom after ten years, this principle was routinely violated, underscoring the hollowness of the gradual abolition process. According to Watson Vredenburg, a British arbitrator on the Luanda mixed commission who had a unique vantage point to assess the implementation of anti-slavery measures, this provision was "totally disregarded" outside Luanda. Only a few libertos living in Luanda successfully obtained complete freedom. For others, life as a forced laborer became their destiny. On a visit to Benguela, Vredenburg encountered a judge who stated that most of the libertos in the city "ought by law to be free; but it appears to be nobody's business to see that they obtain their liberty."[139]

The erosion of rights guaranteed by anti-slavery legislation set the stage for further encroachments on the freedoms of libertos. A turning point came in 1869, when the Portuguese government recategorized all enslaved people in colonial territories as libertos. This legislation represented another step in the consolidation of labor exploitation under the guise of abolition, as it effectively perpetuated the subjugation of African workers while nominally granting them a new legal status. Under this system, the newly designated libertos were obligated to contract their services for two periods of time, each lasting two years, and were compelled to work.[140] The reclassification of enslaved people as libertos in 1869, coupled with the disregard for the legal provision granting libertos complete freedom after ten years, further underscored the hollowness of Portugal's gradual abolition process and the failure to protect the rights of these nominally free workers.

The grim reality of the libertos' situation did not escape the attention of contemporary observers, including Portugal's architect of gradual abolition Visconde de Sá da Bandeira. "As for the state of slavery, which was legally abolished, it still exists in reality under another name, as the legal provisions favorable to the freedmen have not been complied with, and they have been, and are, treated as if they were slaves."[141] Sá da Bandeira's critique situated the plight of the libertos within a broader pattern of labor exploitation that emerged as the legal categories of slave and liberto blurred and the promise of emancipation gave way to new forms of coercion and control. In this context, abolition was the antithesis of freedom and instead served as a tool for reconfiguring and legitimizing systems of oppression, ultimately perpetuating the subjugation of African laborers under the guise of legal reform and the rhetoric of progress.

The justification for extending liberto status to all enslaved people reveals a global cross-pollination of ideas and practices among colonial powers, as they sought to legitimize the ongoing exploitation of labor in the post-abolition era. According to Portuguese officials, "current slaves will be considered free people and under very similar circumstances to Chinos and Indian workers, who are contracted to work during a certain number of years in British and French colonies due to voluntary contracts."[142] The Portuguese government's rhetoric attempted to align the status of former slaves with that of indentured laborers, despite the stark differences in their origins and the circumstances of their recruitment. This strategy reflects a broader pattern among European empires of using the language of "free" labor and voluntary contracts to mask various forms of coercion and exploitation, whether applied to formerly enslaved Africans or to indentured workers from Asia.

The pattern of using legal frameworks to perpetuate coercive labor practices reached its apex with a decree passed in 1875. While reiterating that enslaved individuals would be considered libertos one year after the decree's publication, it subjected these individuals to a regime of public tutelage and mandatory two-year labor contracts. The decree meticulously regulated contracts, with articles dictating everything from the minimum wages and working hours to the acceptable grounds for transferring a liberto's contract to a new master. Failure to secure an approved contract was criminalized, with "vagrant" libertos being liable to up to two years of forced labor on public works projects. The decree thus exemplifies how abolition was not a genuine transition to freedom but rather the harnessing of the rhetoric of abolition to construct a new regime of labor exploitation.

To justify the coercion of apprenticed Africans into what effectively amounted to forced labor, Portuguese officials relied heavily on racial ideology, propounding the belief that "blacks from our Africa are in a state of almost total barbarism" and that "forced recruitment and servitude are our primary, most effective, and perhaps the only means to civilize them." In this perspective, Africans serving as forced laborers were merely repaying the Portuguese for their supposed rescue from "savagery" and slavery.[143] This viewpoint further suggested that Africans were inherently averse to work, necessitating forced labor to transform them into productive laborers. Some officials even advocated that manumitted Africans should continue to work under state supervision, arguing that failing to do so would set a poor example for other Africans whose labor was also deemed essential.[144]

The widespread use of racial ideology to justify forced labor was not lost on outside observers. As early as 1860, Edmond Gabriel, a British consul in

Luanda who had long lived in the colony, observed that "one of the arguments most prominently advanced in support of the system of enslaving of the Africans is that their intellectual faculties are of an inferior order; that they are an inferior race of beings."[145] Of course, the reliance on racial ideology to defend forced labor practices was not limited to the Portuguese context; it was part of a broader global pattern of justifying coercive labor systems in the aftermath of abolition. Across European colonial empires, intellectuals and officials drew upon similar racist assumptions to argue for the necessity of maintaining strict control over colonized populations and extracting their labor. These ideas circulated through transnational networks, influencing policies and practices across vast geographical distances.[146]

In the Portuguese context, the justification for forced labor is exemplified by the work of intellectuals like Felix Meyer, an unapologetic proponent of coerced African labor. Meyer's arguments, rooted in racist assumptions, considered Africans as lacking "intellectual and moral development" and afflicted by pervasive idleness due to Angola's tropical climate and the "spontaneous fertility of the soil."[147] By arguing that ending unfree labor would doom commercial agriculture in Angola, Meyer highlighted not only the racial underpinnings of Portugal's colonial project but also how Portuguese officials viewed their labor policies in Angola within a transnational context of colonial labor exploitation. He contended that Angola's farmers, unlike their counterparts in Spanish Cuba or France's colonies in the Indian Ocean, lacked the resources to import coolies from Asia, thus necessitating the continued reliance on coerced African labor.[148]

Just as the British and French had relied on systems like apprenticeship and engagism to maintain a supply of coerced labor in their colonies, Meyer argued that Portugal needed to embrace forced labor to ensure the viability of its colonial economy in Angola. His comparative analysis of labor practices across various colonial settings underscores the transnational nature of these debates and the global circulation of ideas about race, labor, and colonial development. More importantly, Meyer's arguments exemplify how abolition often led not to freedom, but to the reformulation of coercive labor practices under new guises. This dynamic reveals the true nature of nineteenth-century abolition efforts: rather than genuinely liberating African laborers, European powers used both the rhetoric and legal praxis of abolition to create new forms of unfreedom that sustained their colonial economies. Thus, Meyer's work serves as a potent illustration of how abolition itself became a tool for creating and justifying new forms of labor exploitation, shaped by racial ideologies, economic imperatives, and the legal frameworks of colonial rule.

The legal framework established during the colonial period played a crucial role in normalizing coercive labor practices that would persist in Angola and other Portuguese colonies well into the twentieth century. This legislation codified racialized notions of African labor, casting African workers as intrinsically lazy and in need of coercive discipline to be productive. Laws against "vagrancy" allowed colonial authorities to arbitrarily conscript Africans into contract labor if they were deemed insufficiently industrious. The indigenato system, fully established in Angola in 1926, created a stark legal divide between citizens and indígenas ("natives"), with indígenas subjected to specific obligations including forced labor, while white settlers were automatically classified as citizens and exempt from these impositions. Only a tiny number of "assimilated" Africans were able to escape indigenous status.[149] In this way, the legal system underpinning colonial rule racialized unfree labor as the presumptive norm for the African population.

The Angolan case serves as a powerful illustration of how abolition, far from being a straightforward path to emancipation, often functioned as a means for colonial powers to refashion and legitimize systems of labor exploitation, drawing upon a shared repertoire of legal frameworks, racial ideologies, and economic imperatives that circulated across imperial boundaries. The exploitative labor relations and racist ideologies embedded in abolition-era legislation provided a durable foundation for the even harsher forced labor regimes imposed as Portuguese colonial rule intensified in the early twentieth century. Although forced labor in twentieth-century Angola differed in scale and severity from its nineteenth-century antecedents, it was in many ways a direct consequence of the legal dehumanization of African workers set in motion by the gradual abolition process during the waning years of slavery.

Conclusion

The stories of Cabundo, Camassa, Ndembo, and countless other Africans lay bare the bitter irony at the heart of nineteenth-century abolition. While European powers congratulated themselves on ending the slave trade, they simultaneously constructed new forms of unfreedom that condemned African laborers to a life of exploitation and subjugation. The legal ambiguities, economic imperatives, and racist ideologies that shaped apprenticeship, engagism, and the liberto system reveal the hollowness of the era's emancipatory rhetoric. These systems, presented as pathways to freedom, instead functioned as insidious tools of control, denying Africans true autonomy and perpetuating their oppression under the guise of paternalistic protection.

Abolition, in practice, was less a path to liberation than a transition to new modes of coercion, justified by notions of African inferiority and the "civilizing mission" of European rule. The capture and transport of African laborers through old slave routes, the brutal conditions they endured, and the indefinite deferral of their freedom all echoed the horrors of the supposedly abolished slave trade. These parallels underscore the extent to which slavery's legacies were not erased but rather transmuted into new forms under the banner of abolition. The racist ideologies that had long underpinned slavery were not discarded but instead repackaged to legitimize the ongoing exploitation of African labor, now framed as a necessary step in the "civilizing" process.

Crucially, these developments cannot be understood in isolation but must be situated within the broader context of European colonial expansion. The emergence of intra-colonial migrant flows, from Angola to São Tomé and Príncipe, from Sierra Leone to the Caribbean, from Senegal to Réunion, reveals how the exploitation of African labor was inextricably tied to the consolidation of European power across Africa and the Indian Ocean. The circulation of ideas and practices between empires, exemplified by the Portuguese adoption of British apprenticeship and the French revival of engagism, underscores the global interconnectedness of these systems. This exchange of strategies and ideologies highlights the ways in which European powers collectively transformed abolition into a tool of oppression, using the language of emancipation to create new forms of subservient labor that served their imperial interests.

Tracing these connections challenges us to rethink the geographical and temporal boundaries of slavery and its afterlives. The experiences of Cabundo, Camassa, and Ndembo were not isolated incidents but part of a larger pattern of exploitation that spanned continents and oceans. By considering the Atlantic and Indian Ocean worlds together, we can better understand the global structures of power and oppression that emerged in the wake of abolition. The forced migration of African laborers to the Caribbean, the export of Indian indentured workers to the colonies, and the circulation of exploitative labor practices across imperial boundaries all reveal the interconnected nature of these systems. Recognizing these entanglements is crucial for grappling with the enduring legacies of slavery and unfreedom that shaped the colonial world well into the twentieth century.

Conclusion

WORLDS OF UNFREEDOM weaves the history of the slave trade and slavery into the core narrative of global history, unveiling their inextricable links and rupturing national frameworks to reveal vast transnational networks built on bondage and exploitation on a global scale. This approach transcends borders to illuminate the human toll and global reach of commodified bodies, coerced labor, and accumulated capital. In this history, the fates of enslaved Africans are bound together by violent threads of history transcending national borders on multiple continents. While situating the slave trade within narratives of global history, the book recenters the experiences of the enslaved, giving them their rightful place not just as a chapter, but as a foundational pillar in the story of abolition.

Crucially, *Worlds of Unfreedom* bridges the gap between the Atlantic and Indian Ocean worlds, revealing the interconnectedness of the processes that shaped the post-abolition era. It traces the emergence of new forms of forced labor and racialized exploitation across these vast oceanic spaces, from the Portuguese colonies in Africa to the British and French territories in the Caribbean and the Indian Ocean. This global perspective underscores the fact that the end of the transatlantic slave trade did not mark a clean break with the past, but rather a reconfiguration of the global economy and power structures on new terms.

Too often, history is still told from a standpoint that emphasizes the northern hemisphere, with economic pulses, anti-slavery forces, and the drive for empire-building radiating out of Europe to encompass the globe. In contrast, *Worlds of Unfreedom* shifts the focus to Africa and Africans by presenting a kaleidoscope of events unfolding on the ground. To tell a story of empire-building, geopolitical rivalries, and bottom-up forces that propelled abolition, this book pays very close attention to the minutiae of daily life, unveiling historical agency not only by ruling classes but also by marginalized and dispossessed historical subjects. Broad political and social geographies emerge from lived experiences and translocality, furnishing more nuanced accounts of large-scale processes full of richness, harrowing dramas, contradictions, heart-breaking violence, and contingencies.

Worlds of Unfreedom's analysis of the intricate webs of financial connectivity that sustained the slave trade in its twilight years underscores the deep entanglement of this heinous commerce with the emerging global capitalist economy. West Central Africa was not a passive periphery but an integral node in the sprawling networks of capital, goods, and labor that powered the illegal slave trade. The region's coastal enclaves, such as Ambriz and Cabinda, emerged as critical hubs where slave traders from various nations—including Cuba, Brazil, the United States, and European powers—converged to forge alliances and exploit African vulnerabilities.

These interlocking networks had profound social and political ramifications for African societies along the coast. The influx of foreign traders and their partnerships with local rulers transformed power dynamics, eroding traditional authority structures and fostering a growing dependence on the slave trade for access to imported goods. As political power became increasingly transactional, purchased through the material wealth accrued from collaborating with foreigners, African communities faced the strain of competing internal and external interests. An analysis of these transformations highlights the far-reaching impact of global capital on local social and political fabrics.

The complex geopolitical landscape that emerged from these entanglements underscores the multidimensional nature of the forces shaping abolition in West Central Africa. Beyond the well-documented rivalry between Portugal and Britain, the United States and particularly France played a crucial role in the region's political and economic affairs. French efforts to gain a foothold in West Central Africa, as well as the United States' tacit support for the illegal slave trade through its lax enforcement of anti-slave trade laws, added further layers of complexity to the geopolitical chessboard.

By delving into the granular details of everyday life and the complex web of relationships that connected African societies to global networks, *Worlds of Unfreedom* challenges the notion of a clear divide between the local and the global. The intricate power dynamics within the Lunda Empire and the Kingdom of Kongo, as well as their interactions with European powers, reveal a world in which the boundaries between local and global were increasingly blurred. The stories of individuals like Eufrazina, who navigated the complex terrain of diplomacy and power in the Lunda court, and Kongo's succession crisis, which was deeply entangled with the interests of Portuguese, British, and French actors, underscore the ways in which African societies were not only shaped by global forces but also actively participated in shaping them.

Worlds of Unfreedom's exploration of the Lunda Empire and the Kingdom of Kongo also highlights the importance of understanding African polities on their own terms, recognizing their unique political structures, cultural practices, and systems of meaning-making. By examining the intricacies of power and authority within these societies, such as the role of tukwatas in the Lunda Empire and the complex interplay between traditional authorities and coastal elites in Kongo, the book moves beyond simplistic binaries of "African" versus "European" or "local" versus "global." Instead, it reveals a world of fluid identities, shifting alliances, and contested spaces, where African actors navigated the challenges and opportunities presented by the globalizing forces of commerce and empire-building. This approach not only enriches our understanding of African history but also offers a more nuanced and dynamic view of global history, one that recognizes the agency and complexity of local societies in shaping the contours of an increasingly integrated world.

In tracing intricate webs of connectivity and the multiple forces at play, *Worlds of Unfreedom* ultimately presents a more comprehensive and nuanced understanding of the abolition of the transatlantic slave trade in West Central Africa. This approach, which combines granular analysis of individual lives and events with a broad, global perspective, offers valuable insights into the human dimensions of this transformative historical process. By foregrounding African agency and resistance, the book weaves a more inclusive and balanced narrative of abolition, one that recognizes the central role of those who suffered most under the yoke of slavery and the slave trade.

Whoever wants to understand the end of the infamous transatlantic trade in human beings cannot gloss over Africa, where it all started. This undertaking cannot be achieved without placing African history on a global frame, viewing it from many and complex sides. By focusing on entanglements between many different settings across the globe, *Worlds of Unfreedom* reveals the historical lines that connected them and the intricate knots and nodes they formed. While emphasizing permeability and connections, the book disrupts usual binaries by centering abolition, nascent colonialism, and forced labor on the lived experiences of individuals across multiple settings. This approach not only makes history more tangible but also accounts for Africa's contexts of exchange and adaptation in a global world.

In this narrative, everyday life becomes the backdrop where multiple histories unfold. This interpretation reveals an African world that was deeply integrated into global currents, full of threats, violence, and risks. A narrative that does not elide the violence and oppression of growing colonialism and labor regimes yet still places people at the center of the analysis restores history to its tenets. What emerges is a more complicated, nuanced, and pluralistic perspective of the past that considers how free and unfree Africans, and not only white Europeans, participated in the making of African history. In this narrative, Africa is a motor of history and not simply a region that felt the effects of external events.

The stories of individuals like Inbundo, Tabião, Eufrazina, and countless others illustrate the multifaceted ways in which Africans navigated the complex landscape of abolition and its aftermath. Their experiences, marked by resistance, adaptation, and creativity in the face of oppression, challenge traditional narratives that cast Africans as passive victims of historical forces beyond their control. Instead, we see how African agency, in its myriad forms, shaped the contours of abolition and the post-abolition world.

Importantly, the book does not shy away from the uncomfortable truth that colonial forces did not only emanate from Europe. The story of Dona Ana Joaquina dos Santos Silva is a case in point. Despite her remarkable success as a businesswoman and her influence in shaping Angola's post-slave trade economy, we cannot overlook the fact that she was also a notorious slave dealer whose wealth was predicated on the suffering and violence inflicted on thousands of human beings transported across the ocean to the Americas. Her investments in commercial agriculture and her trade diplomacy with the Lunda Empire were predicated on the exploitation of enslaved labor. What's more, her story serves as a stark reminder that the forces of colonialism and oppression were not solely the domain of white Europeans but could also be perpetuated by African elites who benefited from these systems.

In this narrative, granular details of everyday life—a gift of kola nuts between lovers, the songs and chants of street vendors, the intricate codes of courtship and mourning—take on new meaning when viewed through the lens of a global history deeply committed to attending to the intersection of the local and global. These quotidian practices were not merely a colorful backdrop but rather the very fabric of history, shaping and reflecting the broader currents of change that swept across African societies in this era. By closely examining these intimate moments and cultural expressions, *Worlds of Unfreedom* offers a rich and deeply textured portrait of African life in the age of abolition, one that restores a sense of humanity and complexity to history too often reduced to abstract forces and impersonal trends.

Inbundo's escape from a slave caravan and his decision to share intelligence with Portuguese forces highlight the critical role that enslaved Africans played in undermining the foundations of the slave trade. By leveraging their intimate knowledge of the inner workings of the trade, individuals like Inbundo struck blows against the system that sought to commodify their lives. Similarly, Tabião's actions in alerting authorities to an impending shipment of captives from Equimina underscore the ways in which enslaved Africans actively resisted their oppression, even at great personal risk. Their actions were so pivotal as to prompt changes to the very anti-slave trade legislation. These acts of defiance, often overlooked in traditional histories, were crucial in hastening the demise of the slave trade.

In this story, the connections that tied Angola to Brazil were not only about the brutal business of the slave trade per se, though this was no doubt the backbone of a highly complex system across the South Atlantic. José Ferreira Gomes's complex trajectory, straddling the worlds of Angola and Brazil, illuminates the ways in which ideas about race, identity, and political contestation circulated across the Atlantic, shaping the dynamics of power and resistance in both Angola and Brazil. The Benguela Revolt, in which Ferreira Gomes played a key role, underscores the deep-seated grievances that fueled African resistance to Portuguese colonial rule and the imposition of new economic orders as the transatlantic slave trade drew to an end.

Dona Francisca Joaquina do Amaral's harrowing experience of patriarchal violence and legal subjugation lays bare the gendered dimensions of power in Luanda's colonial society. Her story reveals how accusations of female transgression could be weaponized to serve political ends, as rival factions jockeyed for influence in the city's turbulent political landscape. At the same time, the rich tapestry of African cultural influences that shaped Dona Amaral's world, from the symbolic importance of kola nuts to the central role of quitandeiras in the city's economic and social life, underscores the enduring vitality of African traditions and practices, even in the face of increasing colonial encroachment. These granular details of everyday life, much like the stories of Inbundo and Tabião, offer a window into the complex interplay of power, resistance, and cultural resilience that characterized African experiences during the age of abolition.

These individual stories, woven together, form a rich tapestry that challenges Eurocentric narratives of abolition and its aftermath. They reveal an African world that was neither static nor insular, but rather deeply enmeshed in global networks of trade, politics, and culture. African actors, far from being mere pawns in a European game, actively shaped the course of history through their choices, actions, and resistance. By centering African experiences and agency, *Worlds of Unfreedom* thus reframes the history of abolition to restore Africa and Africans to their rightful place at the heart of this global story.

The notion that a proper comprehension of how the transatlantic trade in human beings came to an end can be achieved by focusing only on European macro-politics is, at the very least, misplaced, if not altogether wide of the mark. The struggle to end the trade was far from straightforward, and outcomes were determined by a complex interplay of decisions and actions by a wide range of actors. This complexity challenges simplistic narratives of abolition as a solely European-driven process. The full story was contingent on a vast array of actors—many with ambiguous loyalties and ambitious agendas—acting across national borders on Atlantic and global scales.

These actors included not only European policymakers and abolitionists, but also African rulers, enslaved individuals, free people of color, merchants, and countless others whose actions and choices collectively shaped the course of events. The alliances, rivalries, and negotiations between these diverse players created a complex web of interests and influences that defies easy categorization. Enslaved Africans like Tabião and Inbundo actively resisted their oppression, leveraging their knowledge and position to undermine the slave trade. African rulers like Mwant Yav Nawej II of the powerful Lunda Empire strategically engaged with European powers to bolster their own positions, while also grappling with the destabilizing effects of new forms of commerce and shifting power dynamics within their own societies.

By broadening our analytical lens to include these diverse perspectives, we gain a more nuanced understanding of the multifaceted and often contradictory forces that ultimately led to the dismantling of the transatlantic slave trade. This approach reveals abolition as a global process, deeply embedded in the economic, political, and social dynamics of the Atlantic world and beyond. It underscores the ways in which the struggle against the slave trade was intimately bound up with broader contestations over power, resources, and identity, both within Africa and on a global stage.

The global scope of abolition-induced forced labor is a crucial aspect of this history that cannot be overlooked. The phenomenon was not limited to a single country or region but rather played out across multiple continents, from the Portuguese colonies in Africa to the British and French territories in the Caribbean and the Indian Ocean. Nor can the connection between abolition and the rise of new forms of coerced labor be glossed over. In Angola, the end of the slave trade gave rise to new forms of bonded labor, as "liberated" Africans were pressed into service on plantations and public works projects under the guise of "apprenticeship" and "contract" labor. Similar systems took root in other parts of Africa and the colonized world, as imperial powers sought to maintain a supply of cheap, exploitable labor in the aftermath of abolition.

This global perspective highlights the interconnectedness of the processes that shaped the abolition era and the ways in which the legacies of slavery and abolition continued to reverberate across vast distances. It underscores the fact that the end of the transatlantic slave trade did not mark a clean break with the past, but rather a reconfiguration of the global economy and power structures on new terms, with abolition itself serving as a driving force behind these transformations. The persistence of forced labor and racialized exploitation in the post-abolition era was not an aberration or a localized phenomenon, but rather a defining feature of the emerging global order, one that was deeply rooted in the complex dynamics of abolition and its aftermath.

By tracing these connections, the book offers a powerful reminder of the need to understand the history of forced labor as a truly global phenomenon, one that was intimately bound up with the rise of modern capitalism, imperialism, and white supremacy. It challenges us to grapple with the deep and enduring links between the slave trade, abolition, and the forms of unfreedom and inequality that continue to shape our world today.

Spanning the globe, *Worlds of Unfreedom* unveils a world in which unfreedom ruled robustly and ubiquitously. Freedom, by contrast, was elusive and precarious, if not entirely absent. In this world, the edifice of abolition was fundamentally constructed on the perpetuation of labor exploitation, which was now more deeply entrenched than ever within the fabric of systemic racism and rising colonialism. With abolition, a fundamental link between unfreedom and colonialism came into being that further exploited and racialized non-white lives on a global scale. The current ramifications of these histories cannot be overlooked, as the enduring legacy of abolition-induced labor exploitation systems continues to define modern life in multiple ways.

Worlds of Unfreedom's critique of abolition offers a sobering counter-narrative to traditional portrayals of this era as a harbinger of freedom. The global legacy of empires—a global construct based on a doctrine of white supremacy—is its pioneering role in the transatlantic trade in human beings, which thrived on the suffering of millions of Africans until its dismantling in the nineteenth century. Yet what came after was far from liberating. With the end of the transatlantic trade, new ideologies came about to underpin imperial expansion and regimes of forced labor and modern slavery based on the racialized exploitation of low-paid workers, the denial of workers' rights, and discrimination on multiple levels. These regimes encapsulate deep structural inequalities that characterize current global capitalism.

Worlds of Unfreedom serves as a call for a more critical and expansive understanding of the history of abolition and its aftermath. It challenges us to look beyond simplistic narratives of progress and liberation and confront the ways in which the end of the transatlantic slave trade gave rise to new forms of unfreedom that continue to shape the modern world. By centering African experiences and perspectives, the book offers a powerful reminder of abolition's human costs. It invites us to see the world through the eyes of enslaved Africans, libertos, and others who were systematically excluded and exploited, recognizing their humanity, agency, and resilience in the face of unimaginable hardship. Their stories challenge us to unravel the complex threads of abolition that span continents and oceans, weaving them into a new narrative that honors the struggles and sacrifices of those who came before us. They remind us that even as abolition gave way to new systems of exploitation, people found ways to assert their humanity, resist oppression, and imagine a world beyond bondage—a legacy that continues to resonate in our ongoing struggles for justice and equality.

NOTES

Introduction

1. "Auto de Perguntas" on September 18, 1856, Arquivo Histórico Ultramarino (AHU), Angola, pasta 23-2.

2. "Cópia de Carta do Governador do Distrito do Bembe," undated, AHU, papéis de Sá da Bandeira, maço 827. See also John Monteiro, *Angola and the River Congo* (New York: Macmillan and Co., 1876), p. 107.

3. "Ofício do Governador Geral de Angola" on May 10, 1865, AHU, maço 824.

4. Dispatch by Gabriel on July 30, 1858, FO 84, 1043, fls. 359–366.

5. Marina Carter and Nira Wickramasinghe, "Forcing the Archive: Involuntary Migrants 'of Ceylon' in the Indian Ocean World of the 18–19th Centuries," *South Asian History and Culture*, 9, 2, 2019, p. 195.

6. Clare Anderson, *Subaltern Lives: Biographies of Colonialism in the Indian Ocean World, 1790–1920* (New York: Cambridge University Press, 2012).

7. Carlo Ginzburg, "Microhistory and World History," in Jerry Bentley, Sanjay Subrahmanyam, Merry E Wiesner-Hanks (eds.), *The Cambridge of World History* (NY: Cambridge University Press, 2015), vol. 6, p. 462. See also Francesca Trivellato, "What Differences Make a Difference? Global History and Microanalysis Revisited," *Journal of Early Modern History*, 27, 2023, pp. 7–31.

8. Jean-Paul Zuniga, "L'histoire Impériale à L´ Heure de L'Histoire Globale: Problèmes et Approches," *Revue d'histoire Moderne et Contemporaine*, 2007, 5, 54-4, pp. 54–68.

9. Nick Salvatore, "Biography and Social History: An Intimate Relationship," *Labour History*, 87, 2004, 187–193.

10. Benedetta Rossi, "The Abolition of Slavery in Africa's Legal Histories," *Law and History Review*, 42, 1, 2024, p. 3.

11. Michelle Liebst, "The Sultans of Zanzibar and the Abolition of Slavery in East Africa," *Law and History Review*, 42, 1, 2024, pp. 49–74.

12. Sandra Greene "Minority Voices: Abolitionism in West Africa," *Slavery & Abolition*, 36, 4, 2015, p. 648.

13. Becca De Los Santos, "Poor Souls" and "Dangerous Vagabonds": the Enslaved Pursuit of Liberation in Post-Abolition Senegal, 1848–1865," Honors Thesis (Department of French and Italian), Stanford University, 2024, p. 8.

14. Bronwen Everill, *Abolition and Empire in Sierra Leone and Liberia* (NYC: Palgrave Macmillan, 2013), pp. 119-125; Lisa Lindsay, *Atlantic Bonds: A Nineteenth-Century Odyssey from America to Africa* (Chapel Hill: University of North Carolina Press, 2017), pp. 89–90, 92–93.

15. Paul Lovejoy, "Diplomacy in the Heart of Africa: British-Sokoto Negotiations over the Abolition of the Atlantic Slave Trade," in Myriam Cottias and Marie-Jeanne Rossignol (eds.), *Distant Ripples of British Abolition in Africa, Asia and the Americas* (Trenton: Africa World Press, 2017), p. 89; Paul Lovejoy, *Jihad in West Africa during the Age of Revolutions* (Athens: Ohio University Press, 2016), chapter 7.

16. Philip Misevich, *Abolition and the Transformation of Atlantic Commerce in Southern Sierra Leone, 1790s to 1860s* (Trenton: African World Press, 2019), p. 197. For similar phenomena in the Caribbean, see Laurent DuBois and Richard Turits, *Freedom Roots: Histories from the Caribbean* (Chapel Hill: UNC Press, 2020), p. 114.

17. Aida Freudenthal, "Os Quilombos de Angola no Século XIX: A Recusa da Escravidão," *Estudos Afro-Asiáticos*, 32, 1997.

18. Mariana Candido, "The Expansion of Slavery in Benguela During the Nineteenth Century," *International Review of Social History*, 65, 28, 2020, p. 22.

19. Jose Curto, "Resistência à Escravidão na África: o Caso dos Escravos Fugitivos Recapturados em Angola, 1846–1876," *Afro-Ásia*, 33, 2005, pp. 67–86.

20. Robin Law, "Africa in the Atlantic World, c. 1760—c. 1840," Nicholas Canny and Philip Morgan (eds.), *The Oxford Handbook of the Atlantic World: 1450-1850* (Oxford: Oxford University Press, 2011), p. 595.

21. Adiele E. Afigbo, "Africa and the Abolition of the Slave Trade," *William and Mary Quarterly*, LXVI, 4, 2009, p. 707.

22. Clare Anderson, "After Emancipation: Empires and Imperial Formations," in Catherine Hall, Nicholas Draper and Keith McClelland (eds.), *Emancipation and the Remaking of the British Imperial World* (Manchester: Manchester University Press, 2014), pp. 113–130; Lisa Lowe, "History Hesitant," *Social Text*, 33, 4, 2015, p. 87; Indrani Chatterjee, "British Abolitionism from the Vantage of Pre-Colonial South Asian Regimes," in David Eltis, Stanley Engerman, Seymour Drescher and David Richardson (eds.), *The Cambridge World History of Slavery* (NYC: Cambridge University Press, 2017), pp. 441–465. See also Benjamin Lawrance, *Amistad's Orphans: An Atlantic Story of Children, Slavery, and Smuggling* (New Haven: Yale University Press, 2014), p. 5.

23. Antoinette Burton, "Not Even Remotely Global? Method and Scale in World History," *History Workshop*, 64, 2007, pp. 325–326.

24. Dispatch by Gabriel and Henry Huntley on October 10, 1861, FO 84, 1133, fls. 21–33v.

25. George Tams, *Visit to the Portuguese Possessions in South-West Africa* (London: T. C. Newby, 1845), vol. I, p. 134. For teeth-filing as a widespread practice in the lower Congo, see *Simmonds's Colonial Magazine and Foreign Miscellany* (London: Simmonds & Ward, Foreign & Colonial Office, 1845), vol. V, 18, p. 175; Alfredo de Sarmento, *Os Sertões d'Africa* (Lisboa: F. A. da Silva, 1880), p. 36; Monteiro, *Angola and the River Congo*, p. 144.

26. Tams, *Visit to the Portuguese Possessions in South-West Africa*, vol. I, pp. 132–133.

27. Francisco Antonio Pinto, *Angola e Congo* (Lisboa: Livraria Ferreira, 1888), p. 140.

28. *Simmonds's Colonial Magazine*, vol. V, p. 176. For the importance of body marks and tattooing in the diaspora, see Sharla Fett, *Recaptured Africans: Surviving Slave Ships, Detention, and Dislocation in the Final Years of the Slave Trade* (Chapel Hill: UNC Press, 2016), p. 74; Henry Lovejoy, *Prieto: Yorùbá Kingship in Colonial Cuba during the Age of Revolutions* (Chapel Hill: University of North Carolina Press, 2018), p. 104; João Reis, Flavio Gomes, and Marcus Carvalho, *The Story of Rufino: Slavery, Freedom, and Islam in the Black Atlantic* (NY: Oxford University Press, 2019), p. 149.

29. Adolph Bastian, *Ein Besuch in San Salvador, der Hauptstadt des Konigreichs Kongo* (Bremen: Druck und Verlag von H. Strack, 1859), p. 252. See also Megan Crutcher, "'For King and Empire': The Changing Political, Economic, and Cultural Identities of Kru Mariners in Atlantic Africa, 1460-1945," *The Journal of African History*, 64, 3, 2023, p. 442; Emma Christopher, "African Sailors in the Atlantic World," *Oxford Research Encyclopedia of African History*, 2023, p. 4.

30. *Simmonds's Colonial Magazine*, vol. V., pp. 175–176.

31. William Holman Bentley, *Dictionary and Grammar of the Kongo Language* (London: Trubner & Co, 1886), p. IX.

32. István Rákóczi, *O Planalto do Bié: Diários de Viagem de László Magyar (1848–1857)* (Lisboa: Edições Colibri, 2019), p. 37.

33. Norm Schrag, "Mboma and the Lower Zaire: A Socioeconomic Study of a Kongo Trading Community, c. 1785-1885" (PhD Dissertation, Indiana University, 1985), p. 90. See also Wyatt MacGaffey, "Kongo Slavery Remembered by Themselves: Texts from 1915," *International Journal of African Historical Studies*, 41, 1, 2008, p. 74.

34. Samba Mampuya, *Survivance et répression de la traite négrière du Gabon au Congo de 1840 a 1880* (Paris: Les Editions la Bruyere, 1990), p. 205.

35. *Simmonds's Colonial Magazine and Foreign Miscellany*, vol. VI, p. 156. See also Catarina Madeira-Santos, "Esclavage Africain et Traite Atlantique confrontés: Transactions Langagières et Juridiques," *Brésil(s)*, 1, 2012, p. 138.

36. Domingos José Franque, *Nós, Os Cabindas: História, Leis, Usos e Costumes dos Povos de N'goio* (Lisboa: Argo, 1940), p. 102.

37. Sarmento, *Os Sertões d'Africas*, pp. 94–96.

38. *O Americano*, October 2, 1850, 315, vol. IV, pp. 3–4. For a reference of sexual assaults against enslaved women on ships apprehended by the British and taken to St. Helena, see Andrew Pearson, *Distant Freedom: St. Helena and the Abolition of the Slave Trade, 1840–1872* (Liverpool: Liverpool University Press, 2016), p. 116. See also Randy Browne, Lisa Lindsay, John Wood Sweet, "Rebecca's Ordeal, from Africa to the Caribbean: Sexual Exploitation, Freedom Struggles, and Black Atlantic Biography," *Slavery & Abolition*, 43, 1, 2021, pp. 40–67.

39. *Simmonds's Colonial Magazine*, vol. VI, p. 264. For recaptives experience on St. Helena, see Pearson, *Distant Freedom*, Chapter 5; Manuel Barcia, *The Yellow Demon of Fever: Fighting Disease in the Nineteenth-Century Transatlantic Slave Trade* (New Haven: Yale University Press, 2020), Chapter 4; Maeve Ryan, *Humanitarian Governance and the British Anti-Slavery World System* (New Haven: Yale University Press, 2022), p. 112.

40. *Simmonds's Colonial Magazine*, vol. V, pp. 181–182.

41. *Simmonds's Colonial Magazine*, vol. V, pp. 181–182.

42. Wyatt MacGaffey, *Kongo Political Culture: The Conceptual Challenge of the Particular* (Bloomington: Indiana University Press, 2000), p. 27.

43. William Bentley, *Life on the Congo* (London: The Religious Tract Society, 1887), p. 72. For West Africa, see Robin Law, "West Africa's Discovery of the Atlantic," *The International Journal of African Historical Studies*, 44, 1, 2011, pp. 1–25; John Parker, *In My Time of Dying: A History of Death and the Dead in West Africa* (Princeton: Princeton University Press, 2021).

44. James Tuckey, *Narrative of an Expedition to Explore the River Zaire, usually called the Congo, in South Africa, in 1816* (London: J. Murray, 1818), p. 187.

45. Tuckey, *Narrative of an Expedition to Explore the River Zaire*, p. 187.

46. Schrag, "Mboma and the Lower Zaire," p. 94.

47. David Richardson, *Principles and Agents: The British Slave Trade and Its Abolition* (New Haven: Yale University Press, 2022), p. 94.

48. Sarmento, *Os Sertões d'Africa*, pp. 94–96.

49. William Bentley, *Appendix to the Dictionary and Grammar of the Kongo Language* (London: The Baptist Missionary Society, 1887), p. 345.

50. Wyatt MacGaffey, "Indigenous Slavery and the Atlantic Trade: Kongo Texts," in Stephanie Beswick and Jay Spaulding, *African Systems of Slavery* (Trenton: Africa World Press, 2010), p. 175. See also Jelmer Vos, "Child Slaves and Freemen at the Spiritan Mission in Soyo, 1880–1885," *Journal of Family History*, 35, 1, 2011, pp. 71–90; Benjamin Kala-Ngoma, "L'Esclavage Domestique chez les Bembe (Congo-Brazzaville) XVIIIe–XXe Siècles," *Cahiers d'Études Africaines*, 204, 2011, pp. 945–978; David Gordon, "Slavery and Redemption in the Catholic Missions of the Upper Congo, 1878–1909," *Slavery and Abolition*, 2017, pp. 577–600. For a classic statement, see Suzanne Miers and Igor Kopytoff, *Slavery in Africa: Historical and Anthropological Perspectives* (Madison: University of Wisconsin Press, 1979), p. 17.

51. Monteiro, *Angola and the River Congo*, p. 33. See also Jelmer Vos, "Slavery in Southern Kongo in the Late Nineteenth Century," in *Trabalho Forçado Africano: Experiências Coloniais Comparadas* (Porto: Campo das Letras, 2006), pp. 315–336; Esteban Salas, "Slavery and Resistance in West Central Africa," *Oxford Research Encyclopedia of African History*, 2023, pp. 1–19.

52. Schrag, "Mboma and the Lower Zaire," pp. 32–33, 127, 134.

53. Bastian, *Ein Besuch in San Salvador*, p. 70. For seventeenth-century dynamics, see Linda Heywood, "Slavery and Its Transformation in the Kingdom of Kongo: 1491–1800," *Journal of African History*, 50, 1, 2009, pp. 1–22. See also Susan Broadhead, "Slave Wives, Free Sisters: Bakongo Women and Slavery c. 1700–1850," in Claire Robertson and Martin Klein (eds.), *Women and Slavery in Africa* (Portsmouth, NH: Heinemann, 1983), pp. 160–181.

54. *Simmonds's Colonial Magazine and Foreign Miscellany*, vol. V., p. 176.

55. MacGaffey, *Kongo Political Culture*, p. 192.

56. Tony Ballantyne, "On Place, Space and Mobility Nineteenth-Century New Zealand," *New Zealand Journal of History*, 45, 1, 2011, pp. 50–70; Angelo Torre, "Micro/Macro: ¿Local/Global? El Problema de la Localidad en una Historia Espacializada," *Historia Crítica*, 69, 2018, pp. 37–67.

57. José Guadalupe Ortega, "Machines, Modernity, and Sugar: The Greater Caribbean in a Global Context, 1812–50," *Journal of Global History*, 9, 1, 2014, pp. 1–25; Dale Tomich,

"Commodity Frontiers, Spatial Economy, and Technological Innovation in the Caribbean Sugar Industry, 1783–1878," in A. B. Leonard and David Pretel (eds.), *The Caribbean and the Atlantic World Economy: Circuits of Trade, Money and Knowledge, 1650–1914* (New York: Palgrave Macmillan, 2015), pp. 184–217. For overviews of the Spanish and Cuban slave trade, see Alex Borucki, David Eltis, and David Wheat, "Atlantic History and the Slave Trade to Spanish America," *American Historical Review*, 2015, pp. 433–461; David Eltis and Jorge Felipe-Gonzalez, "The Rise and Fall of the Cuban Slave Trade: New Data, New Paradigms," in Alex Borucki, David Eltis, and David Wheat (eds.), *From the Galleons to the Highlands: Slave Trade Routes in the Spanish Americas* (Albuquerque: University of New Mexico Press, 2020), pp. 201–222.

58. María del Carmen Barcia, *Pedro Blanco, El Negrero. Mito, Realidad y Espacios* (Havana: Editorial Boloña, 2018); Jorge Felipe Gonzalez, "The Transatlantic Slave Trade and the Foundation of the Kingdom of Galinhas in Southern Sierra Leone, 1790–1820," *Journal of African History*, 62, 3, 2021, pp. 319–341; Lizbeth Chaviano Pérez, "Cuba, agent formel ou informel de l'impérialisme espagnol dans le Golfe de Guinée?," *Outre-Mers*, 410–411, 1, 2021, pp. 169–184, Martin y Alharilla, "Les factoreries négrières espagnoles des côtes africaines (1815–1860)," *Outre-Mers*, 1, 410–411, 2021, pp. 143–167; José Antonio Piqueras, *Negreros españoles en el tráfico y en los capitales esclavistas* (Madrid: Catarata, 2021).

59. For exceptions to the rule, see Gustau Nerín, *Traficants d'ànimes: Els negrers espanyols a l'Àfrica* (Barcelona: Editorial Pòrtic, 2015), Chapter 6; Manuel Barcia, *The Yellow Demon of Fever: Fighting Disease in the Nineteenth-Century Transatlantic Slave Trade* (New Haven: Yale University Press, 2020.

60. "Providencias requeridas a sua Majestade . . . por alguns Negociantes da Praça de Lisboa" on *Annaes Maritimos e Coloniaes*, 3, 4a Séria, 1844, pp. 121–143. For context, see Miguel Bandeira Jerónimo, "Portugal no Mundo," in António Costa Pinto and Nuno Gonçalo Monteiro (eds.), *A Construção Nacional, 1834–1890* (Lisboa: Fundación Mapfre, 2013), p. 92. See also Pedro Aires Oliveira, "Um Império Vacilante (c. 1820–c. 1870)," *História da Expansão e do Império Português*, in João Paulo Oliveira Costa, José Damião Rodrigues and Pedro Aires Oliveira (Lisboa: Esfera dos Livros, 2014), pp. 347–377.

61. "Relatório do Ministério do Ultramar" in 1840, *Annaes Maritimos e Coloniaes*, 4, 1841, p. 1.

62. Gabriel Paquette, *Imperial Portugal in the Age of Atlantic Revolutions: The Luso-Brazilian World, c. 1770–1850* (New York: Cambridge University Press, 2013), p. 316.

63. Leonor Freire Costa, Pedro Lains, and Susana Münch, *An Economic History of Portugal, 1143–2010* (NY: Cambridge University Press, 2016), p. 276. See also José Luís Cardoso and Francisco Comín, "Economic Policies and Institutions," in Pedro Lains et al. (ed.), *An Economic History of the Iberian Peninsula, 700–2000* (NYC: Cambridge University Press, 2024), pp. 519–545.

64. Paquette, *Imperial Portugal in the Age of Atlantic Revolutions*, p. 320. See also Pedro Tavares de Almeida, "As Chaves do Período, 1834–1890," in Pinto, Monteiro, *A Construção Nacional*, pp. 19–35; Valentim Alexandre, "The Portuguese Empire, 1825–1890: Ideology and Economics," in Olivier Pétré-Grenouilleau (ed.), *From Slave Trade to Empire: Europe and the Colonization of Black Africa, 1780s–1880s* (London and New York: Routledge, 2004), p. 113; Oliveira, "Um Império Vacilante," p. 367.

65. Paquette, *Imperial Portugal in the Age of Atlantic Revolutions*, pp. 347–348.

66. "Actas da Associação Marítima e Comercial," *Annaes maritimos e coloniaes*, n. 6, 1843, p. 70.

67. "Instruções para o Governador Antonio Manoel de Noronha" on October 3, 1838, AHA, cód. 259. See also Alan de Carvalho Souza, "Do Brasil para África: O Café na Viragem do Império Português (1807–1850)," PhD Dissertation, Programa Universitário de Doutoramento em História (Universidade de Lisboa, ISCTE, Universidade Católica Portuguesa, Universidade de Évora), 2020, pp. 238–239.

68. Antonio Joaquim Guimarães Junior, *Memória sobre a Exploração da Costa ao Sul de Benguela, na Africa Occidental, e Fundação do Primeiro Estabelecimento Comercial na Bahia de Mossamedes* (Lisboa: Typografia de F. C. A., 1842), p. i. See also José Tavares de Macedo, "Reflexões Tendentes à Formação de um Sistema Colonial," *Annaes Maritimo e Coloniaes*, 3, segunda series, janeiro de 1842, p. 131.

69. *Revista Universal* (Lisboa: Imprensa da Gazeta dos Tribunais, 1847), tomo. 6, p. 230.

70. Luiz Felipe de Alencastro, *O Trato dos Viventes. Formação do Brasil no Atlântico Sul* (São Paulo: Companhia das Letras, 2000); Mariana Candido, *An African Slaving Port and the Atlantic World: Benguela and its Hinterland* (New York: Cambridge. University Press, 2013); Charlotte de Castelnau-L'Estoile, *Páscoa et ses deux maris: Une esclave entre Angola, Brésil et Portugal au XVIIe siècle* (Paris: Presses Universitaires de France, 2019); Mariana Armond Dias Paes, "Shared Atlantic Legal Culture: The Case of a Freedom Suit in Benguela," *Atlantic Studies*, 17, 3, 2020, pp. 419–440; John Marquez, "Witnesses to Freedom: Paula's Enslavement, Her Family's Freedom Suit, and the Making of a Counterarchive in the South Atlantic World," *Hispanic American Historical Review*, 101, 2, 2021, pp. 231–263.

71. Tom McCaskie, "Cultural Encounters: Britain and Africa in the Nineteenth Century," in Philip D. Morgan and Sean Hawkins (eds.), *Black Experience and the Empire* (Oxford: Oxford University Press, 2004), 166–193; Martin Lynn, "The Imperialism of Free Trade and the Case of West Africa, c. 1830-c.1870," *The Journal of Imperial and Commonwealth History*, XV, 1, 1986, pp. 22–40.

72. Rebecca Shumway, "Exploiting British Ambivalence toward Africa: Fante Sovereignty in the Early 19th Century," in Kate Fullagar and Michael McDonnell (eds.), *Facing Empire: Indigenous Experiences in a Revolutionary Age, 1760-1840* (Baltimore: Johns Hopkins University Press, 2018), pp. 72–89; Rebecca Shumway, "West Africa in Global Trade and Empires." *The William and Mary Quarterly*, 77, 4, 2020, p. 675–681.

73. Seymour Drescher, "Emperors of the World: British Abolitionism and Imperialism," in Derek Peterson (ed.), *Abolitionism and Imperialism in Britain, Africa, and the Atlantic* (Athens: Ohio University Press, 2010), pp. 129–149.

74. John Darwin, "Imperialism and the Victorians: The Dynamics of Territorial Expansion," *The English Historical Review*, 112, 447, 1997, pp. 614–42; John Darwin, *The Empire Project: The Rise and Fall of the British World-System 1830-1970* (NYC: Cambridge University Press, 2009), pp. 23–63.

75. Robin Law, "Abolition and Imperialism: International Law and the British Suppression of the Atlantic Slave Trade," in Derek Peterson (ed.), *Abolitionism and Imperialism in Britain, Africa, and the Atlantic* (Athens: Ohio University Press, 2010), pp. 150–175.

76. Bronwen Everill, *Abolition and Empire in Sierra Leone and Liberia* (NY: Palgrave Macmillan, 2013), p. 3.

77. Richard Huzzey, *Freedom Burning: Anti-Slavery and Empire in Victorian Britain* (NY: Cornell University, 2012), p. 4.

78. Ryan, *Humanitarian Governance and the British Anti-Slavery World System*, p. 157. See also Lauren Benton and Lisa Ford, *Rage for Order: The British Empire and the Origins of International Law* (Cambridge: Harvard University Press, 2016), p. 124.

79. Sujit Sivasundaram, *Waves Across the South: A New History of Revolution and Empire* (Chicago: Chicago University Press, 2020); Fahad Ahmad Bishara, *A Sea of Debt: Law and Economic Life in the Western Indian Ocean, 1780-1950* (NYC: Cambridge University Press, 2017), p. 16.

80. Richard Allen, "Slave Trading, Abolitionism, and New System of Slavery in the Nineteenth-Century Indian Ocean World," in Robert Harms, Bernard Freamon, and David Blight (eds.), *Indian Ocean Slavery in the Age of Abolition* (New Haven: Yale University Press, 2013), p. 192.

81. Edward Alpers, "On Becoming a British Lake: Piracy, Slaving, and British Imperialism in the Indian Ocean during the First Half of the Nineteenth Century," in Harms, Freamon, and Blight, *Indian Ocean Slavery in the Age of Abolition*, p. 54.

82. Guillemette Crouzet, *Genèses du Moyen-Orient: le Golfe Persique à l'Âge des Impérialismes (c. 1800-c.1914)* (Ceyzerieux: Champ Vallon, 2015), pp. 225–280; Behnaz Mirzai, *A History of Slavery and Emancipation in Iran, 1800-1929* (Austin: University of Texas Press, 2017), Chapter 6. See also Behnaz Mirzai, "The Persian Gulf and Britain: The Suppression of the African Slave Trade," Hideaki Suzuki (ed.), *Abolitions as a Global Experience* (Singapore: NUS Press, 2015), pp. 113–130; Matthew Hopper, *Slaves of one Master: Globalization and Slavery in Arabia in the Age of Empire* (New Haven: Yale University Press, 2015).

83. M. Reda Bhacker, *Trade and Empire in Muscat and Zanzibar: Roots of British Domination* (London: Routledge, 1994); Beatrice Nicolini, *Makran, Oman, and Zanzibar: Three Terminal Cultural Corridor in the Western Indian Ocean (1799–1856)* (Brill: Leiden, 2004), pp. 111–131; Hideaki Suzuki, *Slave Trade Profiteers in the Western Indian Ocean: Suppression and Resistance in the Nineteenth Century* (NY: Palgrave, 2017), pp. 42–44; Raphaël Cheriau, *Imperial Powers and Humanitarian Interventions: The Zanzibar Sultanate, Britain, and France in the Indian Ocean, 1862–1905* (NYC: Routledge, 2020), pp. 101–117.

84. Tâmis Parron, "The British Empire and the Suppression of the Slave Trade to Brazil: A Global History Analysis," *Journal of World History*, 29, 1, 2018, p. 24.

85. Everill, *Abolition and Empire in Sierra Leone and Liberia*, pp. 109, 121.

86. Denise Bouche, *Histoire de la Colonisation Française* (Paris: Fayard, 1991), pp. 18, 20, 35.

87. David Todd, "Un passager clandestin: la colonisation informelle dans l'historiographie des empires français," *Outre-Mers*, 1, 410–411, 2021, p. 17–36. See also David Todd, *A Velvet Empire: French Informal Imperialism in the Nineteenth Century* (Princeton: Princeton University Press, 2021); Olivier Grenouilleau, *La révolution abolitionniste* (Paris: Gallimard, 2017), pp. 414-425.

88. Joseph-Pierre Diouf, "Le Sénégal des années 1860," in Éric Anceau et Dominique Barjot (eds.), *L'Empire Libéral: Essai d'Histoire Globale* (Paris: SPM, 2021), p. 269. See also Yves-Jean Saint-Martin, Le Sénégal sous le second Empire (Paris: Karthala, 1989). For the wider context, see C. Newbury and A. S. Kanya-Forstner, "French Policy and the Origins of the Scramble for West Africa," *Journal of African History*, 10, 2, 1969, pp. 253–276; Margaret McLane, "Commercial Rivalries and French Policy on the Senegal River, 1831–1858," *African Economic History*, 15, 1986, pp. 39–67; Lancelot Arzel, "Les Français en Afrique Central (des années 1830 aux années 1920). Occupations territoriales, exploitations économiques et contestations de l'ordre colonial," in Joëlle Alazard et Sihem Bella (eds.), *Nouveaux regards sur l'Afrique coloniale française: 1830–1962* (Paris: Bréal, 2021), pp. 41–42; Jenna Nigro, "Trading for Empire: Commerce and French Colonial Rule in Senegal, c. 1817–1860," *Journal of Colonialism and Colonial History*, 23, 1, 2022. See also Bernard Schnapper, *La Politique et le commerce français dans le Golfe de Guinée de 1838 à 1871* (Paris: Mouton, 1961).

89. Serge Daget, *La Répression de la Traite des Noirs au XIXè Siècle* (Paris: Éditions Karthala, 1997), p. 477; Lawrence Jennings, *French Anti-Slavery: The Movement for the Abolition of Slavery in France, 1802–1848* (New York: Cambridge University Press, 2000), p. 208.

90. Bouche, *Histoire de la Colonisation Française*, pp. 44–45. For references to Senegal as a template for France's pursuits in Gabon, see Testimony of le Baron Rodolphe Darricau on April 4 1845, *Accounts and Papers*, Slave Trade, vol. 67, 19 January–24 1847, p. 54. For context, see Hubert Deschamps, "Quinze ans de Gabon (les débuts de l'établissement français, 1839–1853)," *Revue Française d'Histoire d'Outre-Mer*, 50, 1963, pp. 283–345; Isabelle Surun, "Appropriations Territoriales et Résistances Autochtones. Entre Guerre de Conquête, Alliance et Négociation," in Pierre Singaravélou (ed.), *Les Empires Coloniaux, XIXe-XXe Siècle* (Paris: Points Seuil, 2013), pp. 37–75.

91. *Revista Universal Lisbonense*, 1a da 3a serie, n. 25, 1842, p. 295.

Chapter 1: Unraveling the South Atlantic

1. "Ofício do Secretário Geral da Província de Angola" on November 13, 1846, Arquivo Histórico Ultramarino (AHU), segunda seção de Angola, pasta 10-A.

2. "Ofício do Governador de Benguela" on June 5, 1845, Arquivo Histórico de Angola (AHA), cód. 459, fls. 1v.-2.

3. George Tams, *Visit to the Portuguese Possessions in South-West Africa* (London: T. C. Newby, 1845), v. I, p. 98.

4. John Purdy, *Laurie's Sailing Directory for the Ethiopic of Southern Atlantic Ocean* (London: J & W. Rider Printers, 1855), p. 504.

5. "Mapa Estatístico do Distrito de Benguela" in 1860, AHA, cx. 5568. For statistical data on Benguela's population in 1860, see BOGGPA, n. 27, 4 de julho de 1863, p. 213. See also Mariana Candido, "Women, Family, and Landed Property in the Nineteenth-Century

Benguela," *African Economic History*, 43, 2015, p. 140; Mariana Candido, "Strategies for Social Mobility: Liaisons between Foreign Men and Enslaved Women in Benguela, ca. 1770–1850," in Gwyn Campbell and Elizabeth Elbourne (eds.), *Sex, Power, and Slavery* (Athens: Ohio University Press, 2014), p. 273.

6. "Ofício do Governador de Angola" on November 14, 1846, AHU, segunda seção de Angola, pasta 10-A.

7. "Notas dos Crimes cometidos por José Ferreira Gomes," AHU, segunda seção de Angola, pasta 10-A.

8. Dona Leonor de Sousa e Almeida, "Agricultura em Benguela," in *Almanach de Lembranças Luso-Brasileiro para ano de 1860* (Lisboa: Typographia Franco-Portugueza, 1859), pp. 242–243; *Almanach de Lembranças Luso-Brasileiro para ano de 1860* (Lisboa: Typographia Franco-Portugueza, 1859), pp. 254–255. For background on Catumbela agricultural production, see Esteban Salas, "Women & Food Production: Agriculture, Demography & Access to Land in Late Eighteenth-Century Catumbela," in Mariana Candido and Adam Jones (eds.), *African Women in the Atlantic World: Property, Vulnerability & Mobility, 1660–1880* (Suffolk: Boydell & Brewer, 2019), pp. 55–69; José Curto, "Women along the Catumbela River, 1797: Land Ownership, Agricultural Production, Labour and Trade," *Canadian Journal of African Studies / Revue canadienne des études africaines*, 54, 3, 2020, pp. 373–393. See also Esteban Salas, "Making Portuguese Colonial Governance: Slavery, Forced Labor, and Racial Ideology in the Interior from Benguela, 1760–1860," PhD Dissertation, University of Notre Dame, 2021.

9. "Autos Cíveis de Embargo ou Arresto" in 1858, TCB, maço 1, num. 47.

10. "Ofício do Governador de Angola" on November 14, 1845, AHU, segunda seção de Angola, pasta 10-A.

11. "Ofício do Secretário de Governor de Angola" on November 22, 1847, AHA, cód. 241, fl. 52.

12. "Portaria do Ministério da Marinha e Negócios do Ultramar" on January 15, 1847, AHA, cód. 262, fl. 36.

13. Francisco Xavier Lopes, "O Dombe Grande da Quisamba," *Annaes do Conselho Ultramarino*, Parte Não Oficial, Junho 1861. See also "Ofício do Governador de Benguela" on December 20, 1820, IHGB, lata 76, pasta 2. For historical context, see Mariana Candido, "The Expansion of Slavery in Benguela During the Nineteenth Century," *International Review of Social History*, 65, 28, p. 15.

14. "Ofício do Regente da Feitoria Real do Dombe Grande" on January 14, 1812, AHA, cód. 445, fls. 131–134v.

15. "Ofício do Governador de Benguela" on June 5, 1845, AHA, cód. 459, fls. 1v.–2; "Ofício do Governador de Benguela" on December 11, 1845, AHA, cód. 455, fls. 132–132v.

16. Augusto Bastos, *Monographia de Catumbella* (Lisboa: Tip. Universal, 1912), p. 7. See also Armindo Jaime Gomes, "Mundombe do "Dombe" ou Ndombe do Mundombe?," *Mulemba*, 4, 8, 2014, pp. 77–100. For further context, see Mariana Candido, "Slave Trade and New Identities in Benguela, 1700–1860," *Portuguese Studies Review*, 19, 1–2, 2011, pp. 59–75.

17. "Requisição de Francisco José de Mello" on June 16, 1824, AHA, cx. 138, fl. 73.

18. "Ofício do Governador de Benguela" on December 11, 1845, AHA, cód. 455, fls. 132–132v.

19. Jill Dias, "A Sociedade Colonial de Angola e o Liberalismo Português (c. 1820–1850)," in Miriam Halpern Pereira, Maria de Fátima Sá e Melo Ferreira, and João Serra (eds.), *O Liberalismo na Península Ibérica na Primeira Metade do Século XIX* (Lisboa: Sá da Costa Editora, 1982), pp. 267–28.

20. Luiz Felipe de Alencastro, *O Trato dos Viventes. Formação do Brasil no Atlântico Sul* (São Paulo: Companhia das Letras, 2000); Estevam Thompson, "Negreiros in the South Atlantic: The Community of "Brazilian" Slave Traders in Late Eighteenth Century Benguela," *African Economic History*, 39, 2011, p. 73–128; Mariana Candido, *An African Slaving Port and the Atlantic World: Benguela and its Hinterland* (New York: Cambridge. University Press, 2013); Charlotte de Castelnau-L'Estoile, *Páscoa et ses deux maris: Une esclave entre Angola, Brésil et Portugal au XVIIe siècle* (Paris: Presses Universitaires de France, 2019); Mariana Armond Dias Paes, "Shared Atlantic Legal Culture: The Case of a Freedom Suit in Benguela," *Atlantic Studies*, 17, 3, 2020, pp. 419–440; John Marquez, "Witnesses to Freedom:

Paula's Enslavement, Her Family's Freedom Suit, and the Making of a Counterarchive in the South Atlantic World," *Hispanic American Historical Review*, 101, 2, 2021, pp. 231–263.

21. Gilberto Guizelin, "Província (de) um grande Partido Brasileiro, e mui pequeno o Europeu: a repercussão da Independência do Brasil em Angola (1822–1825)," *Afro-Ásia*, 52, 2015, pp. 81–106.

22. Pierre Verger, *Fluxo e Refluxo do Tráfico de Escravos entre o Golfo de Benim e a Bahia de Todos os Santos: dos Séculos XVII a XIX* (São Paulo: Corrupio, 1987); Robin Law e Kristin Mann, "West Africa in the Atlantic Community: The Case of the Slave Coast," *William and Mary Quarterly*, 56, 2, 1999, pp. 307–31; João Reis, *Domingos Sodré, um sacerdote africano: escravidão, liberdade e candomblé na Bahia do século XIX* (São Paulo: Companhia das Letras, 2008).

23. Colin Newbury, *The Western Slave Coast and its Rulers* (London: Oxford University Press, 1961), p. 37; Elisee Soumonni, "Trade and Politics in Dahomey, with Particular Reference to the house of Régis,1842–1892," PhD Dissertation, University of Ife, 1983, pp. 31–32; Robin Law, "The Politics of Commercial Transition: Factional Conflict in Dahomey in the Context of the Ending of the Atlantic Slave Trade," *Journal of African History*, 38, 2, 1997, pp. 213–33; Robin Law, *Ouidah: The Social History of a West African Slaving Port, 1727–1892* (Athens: Ohio University Press, 2004), p. 166.

24. Newbury, *The Western Slave Coast and its Rulers*, p. 47.

25. João Reis, *Rebelião escrava no Brasil. A história do levante dos Malês em 1835* (São Paulo: Companhia das Letras, 2003).

26. Lisa Castillo, "The Exodus of 1835: Àguda Life Stories and Social Networks," in Tunde Babawale, Akin Alao and Tony Onwumah (eds.), *Pan-Africanism and the Integration of Continental Africa and Diaspora Africa* (Lagos: Centre for Black and African Arts and Civilization, 2011), 2, pp. 27–51; Manuela Carneiro da Cunha, *Negros, Estrangeiros: Os Escravos Libertos e sua Volta à África* (São Paulo: Companhia das Letras, 2013); Linda Lindsay, "To Return to the Bosom of their Fatherland: Brazilian Immigrants in Nineteenth-Century Lagos," *Slavery and Abolition*, 15, 1, 1994, pp. 22–50; Lisa Castillo, "Mapping the Nineteenth-Century Brazilian Returnee Movement: Demographics, Life Stories and the Question for Slavery," *Atlantic Studies, Global Currents*, 13, 1, 2016, pp. 25–52; Luis Nicolau Parés, "Entre Bahia e a Costa da Mina, Libertos Africanos no Tráfico Ilegal," in Giuseppina Raggi, João Figueiroa-Rego e Roberta Stumpf (eds.), *Salvador da Bahia: interações entre América e África (séculos XVI-XIX)* (Salvador: Edufba/Lisboa: CHAM, 2017), pp. 13–49.

27. Tams, *Visit to the Portuguese Possessions in South-West Africa*, v. I, p. 168.

28. Domingos José Franque, *Nós, Os Cabinda. História, leis, usos e costumes dos povos de N'Goio* (Lisboa: Argo, 1940), p. 49. For context, see Phyllis Martin, "Family Strategies in Nineteenth-Century Cabinda," *Journal of African History*, 28, 1987, pp. 65–86; Alberto Oliveira Pinto, *Nós os Cabindas: Domingos José Franque e a história oral das linhagens de Cabinda* (Lisboa: Novo Imbondeiro, 2003), p. 73.

29. "Diário do Rio de Janeiro," October 15, 1840, n. 231, ano XIX, p. 2.

30. BOGGPA, 12, 1865, 57.

31. "Requerimento de Arsenio Pompilio Pompeu de Carpo" on July 2, 1849, ANTT, MNE, cx. 541; Lopes, "Punishing Crime," pp. 40–49. For more examples of members of the Luanda elite who travelled abroad, see Carlos Pacheco, *José da Silva Maia Ferreira: O Homen e a sua Época* (Luanda: União dos Escritores Angolanos, 1990), pp. 90, 110–111; Jacopo Corrado, *The Creole Elite and the Rise of Angolan Protonationalism: 1870–1920* (Amherst: Cambria, 2008), p. 49; Tracy Lopes, "Punishing Crime: Jails and Confinement in Luanda, Angola, from 1836 to 1899," PhD Dissertation, York University, 2022, pp. 40–49.

32. Olatunji Ojo, "Document 2: Letters Found in the House of Kosoko, King of Lagos (1851)," *African Economic History*, 40, 1, 2012, p. 53. For other examples, see Law, *Ouidah: The Social History of a West African Slaving Port*, p. 186.

33. Toby Green, *A Fistful of Shells: West Africa from the Rise of the Slave Trade to the Age of Revolution* (Chicago: University of Chicago Press, 2019), p. 378.

34. "Informação Semestral da Companhia de Henriques de Benguela" on July 1, 1830, AHU, Angola, cx. 167, doc. 45.

35. "Informação do Delegado" in 1839, AHA, cód. 722; "Ordem do Governador de Benguela" on November 21, 1839, AHA, cód. 522, fls. 34–35.

36. "Decreto" on June 3, 1843, AHA, cód. 261.

37. Francisco Xavier Lopes, "O Dombe Grande da Quissamba" on August 15, 1847, *Anais do Conselho Ultramarino*, parte não oficial, série II, julho 1861, p. 182.

38. "Carta de Manuel Freire" on May 21, 1846, AHA, cx. 5568.

39. "Processo do Navio Feliz (1838–1839)," AHI, Coleções Especiais, lata 15, maço 4, pasta 1.

40. Admiral Elliot to Mr. Wood on January 28, 1840, in *Correspondence with the British Commissioners*, p. 74.

41. "Requerimento de José Ferreira Gomes" on September 24, 1824, AHA, cx. 138, fl. 84.

42. "Requerimento de José Ferreira Gomes" on January 8, 1825, AHA, cx. 138, fl. 99; "Requerimento de José Ferreira Gomes" on January 29, 1825, AHA, cx. 138, fl. 101.

43. "Francisco Ferreira Gomes e José Ferreira Gomes" on January 24, 1827, AHA, cód. 7182, fl. 35.

44. "Requerimento de José Ferreira Gomes" on October 29, 1827, AHA, cód. 7182, fl. 70; "requerimento de José Ferreira Gomes" on December 2 1827, AHA, cód. 7182, fl. 73v.; "Requerimento de José Ferreira Gomes" on July 11, 1828, AHA, cód. 7182, fl. 97.

45. Joaquim de Carvalho e Menezes, *Demonstração Geographica e Politica do Territorio Portuguez na Guine Inferior que abrange o Reino de Angola, Benguella, e suas Dependências* (Rio de Janeiro: Typographia Classica de F. A. De Almeida, 1848), p. 200.

46. "Ordem do Governador de Benguela" on June 12, 1836, AHA, cód. 521, fl. 34. For the *brigue Nova Sorte*, see AHA, cód. 521, fls. 24–24v.

47. "Ofício do Governador de Angola" on October 4, 1834, AHA, cód. 2310, fl. 61.

48. *Jornal do Comércio*, December 9, 1834, ano VII, n. 275.

49. "Auto de Sentença Cível" in 1858, TCB, maço 2, num. 85.

50. "Inventário de Florinda Josefa Gaspar" in 1863, ANRJ, n. 1085, cx. 4089, gal. A. Historian Mariana Candido's analysis suggests that the Ferreira Gomes family's wealth was due to Florinda's inheritance from her father. See Candido, "Women, Family, and Landed Property," p. 144. Yet the father had not passed away when she married her Brazilian husband. Nor was Ferreira Gomes solely reliant on her wife's connections to become a wealthy man. His position in the Benguela administration—possibly even siphoning off public funds earmarked to buy food supplies in Dombe Grande—and slave trade activities cannot be overlooked. By the early 1820s, he had become so influential politically that he could arrange for his oldest son—the future rebel leader José Ferreira Gomes—to marry Maria Nunes Romão, an underage orphan and the heiress of a large fortune in Benguela. See also Mariana Candido and Monica Lima, "Dona Florinda Josefa Gaspar (c. 1791–1862)," *Oxford Research Encyclopedia of African History*, 2024.

51. Alex Borucki, "The 'African Colonists' of Montevideo: New Light on the Illegal Slave Trade to Rio de Janeiro and the Río de la Plata (1830–42)," *Slavery & Abolition*, 30, 3, 2009, pp. 427–444; Florencia Thul Charbonnier, "Traficantes y Saladeristas: los brasileños y sus prácticas continuadoras del tráfico de esclavos en Montevideo en el marco de la abolición, 1830–1852," in Florencia Guzmán and María de Lourdes Ghidoli (eds.), *El asedio a la libertad: abolición y posabolición de la esclavitud en el Cono sur* (Buenos Aires: Editorial Biblos, 2020), pp. 211–235.

52. *Jornal do Comércio*, November 2, 1837, XL, 243, p. 2.

53. "Autos Cíveis de Justificação de Francisco Ferreira Gomes" on October 17, 1855, TCB, maço 7, número 348.

54. "Auto de Sentença Cível" in 1858, TBC, maço 2, número 85. For further information on the judicial dispute that led to the sequester of Ferreira Gomes's assets, see BOGGPA, May 10, 1856, n. 554, p. 10.

55. "Ofício da Junta Governativa de Benguela" on January 22, 1835, AHA, cód. 2310, fls. 84v.–85v.

56. "Ofício do Governador de Benguela" on October 27, 1825, AHA, cód. 449, fl. 59.

57. "Petição de José Ferreira Gomes" on February 4, 1826, AHA, cx. 138, fl. 163v.; "Requerimento de Francisco Ferreira Gomes and José Ferreira Gomes" on January 24, 1827, AHA, cód. 7182, fl. 35.

58. "Diário Fluminense" on April 23, 1830, n. 89, vol. 15, p. 355. For his father's trip, see "Diário Fluminense" on July 8, 1829, n. 7, vol. 14, p. 28.

59. BOGGPA, October 27, 1849, 213, p. 5.

60. "Resposta de José Ferreira Gomes ao Libelo de Domingos Rodrigues Vianna" on July 9, 1855, número 2251.

61. "Autos Cíveis de Apelação" in 1856, TCB, 2251; "Libelo de Domingos José Vianna" on June 28, 1855, TCB, número 2251. For information about Oliveira, see "Requerimento de José Ferreira Gomes" on October 20, 1840, AHA, cx. 1602.

62. "Autos Cíveis de Embargo" in 1858, TCB, maço 7, número 47.

63. Paes, "Shared Atlantic Legal Culture," pp. 419–440. For similar dynamics in the eighteenth century South Atlantic, see Marquez, "Witnesses to Freedom," pp. 231–263.

64. BOGGPA, 180, March 10, 1849; BOGGPA, 266, November 2, 1850, p. 4. For Joaquim Ribeiro de Brito's career, see Amanda Barlavento Gomes, "A Trajetória de Vida do Barão de Beberibe, um Traficante de Escravos no Império do Brasil (1820–1855)," MA Thesis, Universidade Federal de Pernambuco, 2016, pp. 11, 39,

65. "Ofício do Secretário Geral da Província de Angola" on November 23, 1846, AHA, cód. 3440, fls. 183–183v.

66. AHA, cód. 521, fl. 48; AHA, cód. 522, fl. 70v.; "Ofício do Governador de Benguela" on August 28, 1847, AHA, cód. 462, fl. 9v.; "Ofício do Governador de Benguela" on October 4, 1848, AHA, cód. 462, fls. 134–134v.

67. Nielson Bezerra, "The Paquete de Benguela: Illegal Slave Trade and the Liberated Africans in Rio de Janeiro," in Richard Anderson and Henry Lovejoy, *Liberated Africans and the Abolition of the Slave Trade* (Rochester: University of Rochester Press, 2020), p. 259.

68. "Ordem do Governador de Benguela" on November 21, 1839, AHA, cód. 522, fls. 34–35.

69. *Jornal do Comércio* on November 23, 1835, LX, 260, p. 4.

70. "Ofício do Governador de Benguela" on March 26, 1844, AHA, cód. 455, fl. 51.

71. "Ofício do Secretário do Governo de Benguela" on July 24, 1846, AHA, cód. 461; "Ofício do Governador de Benguela" on July 5, 1848, AHA, cód. 722, fls. 253–254.

72. Bezerra, "The Paquete de Benguela," pp. 259–260.

73. "Ofício do Governador de Benguela" on December 5, 1853, AHA, cód. 459, fls. 22v.–25v.

74. Jornal do Comercio 1830–1839, July 7, 1835, n. 145, ano IX, p. 3.

75. "Ofício do Cônsul Brasileiro em Luanda" on April 27, 1859, Arquivo do Itamarati (AI), cota 238/2/1.

76. "Termo de Fiança" on June 11, 1831, AHA, cód. 2563, fl. 104.

77. "Termo de Fiança de Sebastião de Souza" on June 11, 1831, AHA, cód. 2563, fl. 101v.

78. "Termo de Fiança" on March 21, 1831, AHA, cód. 2563, fl. 99.

79. BOGGPA, 23, 1867, 247–248.

80. "Petição de Josefa Maria and Ana Maria" on March 16, 1825, AHA, cx. 138, fl. 109v.

81. "Diário Fluminense" on April 23, 1830, n. 89, vol. 14, p. 355.

82. "Termo de Fiança" on December 20, 1831, AHA, cód. 2563, fls. 122, 123v., 126.

83. "Termo de Fiança" September 20, 1850, AHA, cód. 1309, fls. 9, 10v.

84. BGGPA, September 18, 1847, n. 106.

85. "Ofício do Governador de Benguela" on April 10, 1853, AHA, cód. 467, fls. 12v.–14. See also "Ofício do Secretário Geral do Governo de Angola" on June 22, 1854, AHA, cód. 109, fl. 125.

86. "Ofício do Secretário do Governo de Benguela" on June 27, 1849, AHA, cód. 722, fl. 320v.

87. BOGGPA, 554, 1856, p. 10.

88. "Inventário de Veríssimo Lopes de Moura" in 1858, TCB, unnumbered.

89. AHA, cód. 66, f. 107.

90. BOGGPA, 285, March 15, 1851, p. 2.

91. AHA, cód. 3160.

92. "Portaria Régia" on June 3, 1843, AHA, cód. 261, fl. 22. While incongruously denying that Porto was involved in the Atlantic trade, Benguela authorities hesitantly complied with

the order. See "Ofício do Governador de Benguela" on December 11, 1845, AHA, cód. 455, fls. 132–132v; "Ofício do Governador de Angola" on March 17, 1846, AHU, pasta 10-A.

93. "Ofício do Secretário de Governo de Angola" on April 18, 1853, AHA, cód. 109, fl. 76v.

94. "Ofício do Governador de Benguela" on June 5, 1845, AHA, cód. 459, fls. 1v.–2.

95. "Registro de Requerimentos" on July 16, 1839, AHA, cx. 1602, fl. 51v.; "Requerimento de Jácomo Felipe Torres" on September 3, 1839, AHA, cx. 1602; "Portaria do Ministro da Marinha e Ultramar" on December 12, 1839, AHA, cód. 259, fls. 102v.–103; "Despacho do Requerimento de Jácomo Felipe Torres" on June 31, 1845, AHA, cx. 151; "Passaporte" on August 30, 1844, AHA, cód. 522, fl. 203; "Ofício do Secretário de Governo de Angola" on October 28, 1851, AHA, cód. 326, fls. 197–197v. Jácomo Felipe Torres was the owner of the ship *Onze de Março*. See "Requerimento de Jácomo Felipe Torres" on July 16, 1839, AHA, cx. 1602, fl. 51v.

96. "Inventário de Veríssimo Lopes de Moura" in 1858, TCB, unnumbered.

97. "Ofício do Governador Interino de Benguela" on August 7, 1844, AHA, cód. 455, fl. 64.

98. "Petição de José Ferreira Gomes" on June 10, 1840, AHA, cx. 1602; "Requerimento de José Ferreira Gomes" on July 17, 1840, AHA, cx. 1602.

99. "Ofício do Secretário de Governo de Benguela" on November 7, 1844, AHA, cód. 456, fls. 112v.

100. Carvalho e Menezes, *Demonstração Geographica e Politica do Territorio Portuguez*, p. 54. For background, see Carlos Pacheco, *O Nativismo na Poesia de José da Silva Maia Ferreira* (Évora: Editorial Pendor, 1996); Carlos Pacheco, "Leituras e Bibliotecas em Angola na Primeira Metade do Séc. XIX," *Locus*, 6, 2, 2000, pp. 21–41; Jacopo Corrado, "The Rise of a New Consciousness: Early Euro-African Voices of Dissent in Colonial Angola," *E-Journal of Portuguese History*, 5, 2, 2007, pp. 1–15.

101. Alexandre Barata, Maçonaria, sociabilidade ilustrada e independência do Brasil (1790–1822) (Juiz de Fora/São Paulo: Editora UFJF/Annablume/Fapesp, 2006). See also Pablo Iglesias Magalhães, "A cabala maçônica do Brasil: o primeiro Grande Oriente Brasileiro: Bahia e Pernambuco (1802–1820)," *Revista do IAHGP* (Instituto Arqueológico, Histórico e Geográfico de Pernambuco), 70, 2017, pp. 73–138, 2017.

102. "Ofício do Juiz de Direito de Luanda" on April 1, 1840, AHU, segunda seção de Angola, pasta 3B; "Ofício Confidencial do Governador de Angola" on April 12, 1840, AHU, segunda seção de Angola, pasta 3B. For earlier concerns, see Pacheco, *José da Silva Maia Ferreira*, p. 88.

103. "Ofício do Sub-Delegado Antonio Tavares da Silva Castelo Branco" on December 26, 1849, AHU, segunda seção de Angola, pasta 16 A.

104. BOPPA, 15, December 20, 1845. See also BOGGPA, 278, January 25, 1851. For background, see Jacopo Corrado, "The Rise of a New Consciousness: Early Euro-African Voices of Dissent in Colonial Angola," *e-JPH*, 5, 2, 2007, pp. 1–15; Corrado, *The Creole Elite and the Rise of Angolan Protonationalism*, p. 46; Andrea Marzano, "Filhos da Terra: Identidade e Conflitos Sociais em Luanda," in Alexandre Vieira Ribeiro and Alexsander Gebara, *Estudos Africanos: Múltiplas Abordagens* (Niterói: Editora de UFF, 2013), pp. 30–58.

105. "Ofício do Governador de Benguela" on February 26, 1850, AHA, cód. 459, fls. 3v.–5v.; "Ofício do Governador de Benguela" on September 9, 1850, AHA, cód. 459, fls. 16v.–17.

106. "Ofício do Governador de Benguela" on November 13, 1848, AHA, cód. 464; "Ofício do Governador de Benguela" on September 9, 1850, AHA, cód. 459, fls. 16v.–17. For the relocation of Maia Ferreira—then a teenager—from Luanda to Rio de Janeiro with his family, see *Jornal do Comércio* on December 17, 1834, n. 282, ano VIII, p. 4.

107. "Ofício do Governador de Benguela" on February 26, 1850, AHA, cód. 459, fls. 3v.–5v.; "Ofício do Governador de Benguela" on September 9, 1850, AHA, cód. 459, fls. 16v.–17.

108. "Ofício do Juiz Substituto de Direito de Angola" on January 27, 1840, AHU, segunda seção de Angola, pasta 3 A. For further background, see Dias, "A Sociedade Colonial de Angola," pp. 275–277.

109. "Ofício da Junta Provisória de Angola" January 16, 1836, AHU, segunda seção de Angola, pasta 2; "Ofício do Governador de Angola" on April 8, 1836, AHU, segunda seção de Angola, pasta 2.

110. Diário de Pernambuco, 28 de maio de 1839, n. 115, p. 2.

111. Leslie Bethell, "Britain, Portugal and the Suppression of the Brazilian Slave Trade: The Origins of Lord Palmerston's Act of 1839," *The English Historical Review*, 80, 317, 1965, pp. 761–84.

112. "Ofício do Governador de Angola" on April 8, 1835, AHA, cód. 13, fl. 17v.–19.

113. "Ofício do Governador de Angola" on April 8, 1835, AHA, cód. 13, fl. 17v.–19.

114. Magda Ricci, "Cabanos, Patriotismo e Identidades: Outras Histórias de uma Revolução," in Keila Grinberg and Ricardo Salles (eds.), *O Brasil Imperial* (Rio de Janeiro: Civilização Brasileira, 2009), vol. II, p. 202. See also Luís Balkar Sá Peixoto Pinheiro, "Cabanagem: Percursos Históricos e Historiográficos," in Monica Duarte Dantas (ed.), *Revoltas, Motins, Revoluções: Homens Livres Pobres e Libertos no Brasil do Século XIX* (São Paulo: Alameda, 2011), pp. 201–229; Magda Ricci, "Cabanagem, Cidadania e Identidade Revolucionária: o Problema do Patriotismo na Amazônia entre 1835 e 1840," *Tempo*, 11, 2006, pp. 15–40; Mark Harris, *Rebellion on the Amazon: The Cabanagem, Race and Popular Culture in the North of Brazil, 1798–1840* (NY: Cambridge University Press, 2010).

115. Marcus de Carvalho, "Movimentos sociais: Pernambuco, 1831–1848," Keila Grinberg e Ricardo Salles (eds.), *O Brasil Império (1808–1889)* (Rio de Janeiro: Civilização Brasileira, 2009), p. 121–183. See also Bruno Câmara, "O retalho do comércio: a política partidária, a comunidade portuguesa e a nacionalização do comércio a retalho, Pernambuco 1830–1870," PhD Dissertation, UFPE, 2012. See also Jeffrey Needell, *The Party of Order: The Conservatives, the State and Slavery in the Brazilian Monarchy, 1831–1871* (Stanford: Stanford UP, 2006), p. 39.

116. Sergio Guerra Filho, "As Câmaras e o Povo: A Crise Antilusitana de 1831 no Interior da Província da Bahia," *Clio*, 38, 2020, p. 185. For Pernambuco, see Marcus de Carvalho, "O Antilusitanismo e a Questão Social em Pernambuco, 1822–1848," in Miriam Halpern Pereira et alii (eds.), *Emigração e Imigração Portuguesa nos Séculos XIX e XX* (Lisboa, Fragmentos, 1993), pp. 145–160; Marcus de Carvalho, "O encontro da soldadesca desenfreada com os cidadaos de cor mais levianos no Recife em 1831," *Clio*, 1, 18, pp. 109–137, 1998; "The Commander of all Forests against the "Jacobins" of Brazil: The Cabanada, 1832–1835," in John Gledhill (ed.), *New Approaches to Resistance in Brazil and Mexico* (Manchester: University of Manchester Press, 2012), pp. 81–99. For an overview, see Jeffrey Mosher, "Political Mobilization, Party Ideology, and Lusophobia in Nineteenth-Century Brazil: Pernambuco, 1822–1850," *Hispanic American Historical Review*, 80, 4, 2000, pp. 881–912.

117. Flávio Gomes, "Experiências transatlânticas e significados locais: idéias, temores e narrativas em torno do Haiti no Brasil Escravista," *Tempo*, 13, 2002, pp. 209–246.

118. Correio Mercantil da Bahia, March 17, 1843, 61. I would like to thank João José Reis for sharing this information.

119. "Ofício da Junta de Governo de Angola" on February 7, 1835, AHU, Angola, DGU, 585; "Ofício do Governador de Angola" on June 11, 1836, AHA, cód. 13, fl. 35; BOGGPA, 146, July 15, 1848.

120. BOGGPA, July 15, 1848, 146, p. 3; BOGGPA, March 31, 1849, n. 183, p. 4; BOGGPA, November 23 1848, 169, p. 4.

121. "Ofício do Governador de Angola" on March 19, 1837, AHU, segunda seção de Angola, pasta 3.

122. "Ofício do Governador de Angola" on May 30, 1839, AHA, cód. 14.

123. "Ofício do Governador de Angola" on November 21, 1839, AHU, segunda seção de Angola, pasta 5.

124. Marcello Basile, *Ezequiel Corrêa dos Santos: um jacobino na corte imperial* (Rio de Janeiro: Editora FGV, 2001).

125. Marcello Basile, "Revolta e cidadania na Corte regencial," *Tempo*, 11, 22, 2007, pp. 31–57; Marcello Basile, "O Laboratório da Nação: A Era Regencial (1831–1840)," in Keila Grinberg and Ricardo Salles (eds.), *O Brasil Imperial, 1831–1889* (Rio de Janeiro: Civilização Brasileira, 2009), vol. II, pp. 55–119. For further background on subaltern people politics at the time, see Gladys Sabina Ribeiro, "O desejo de liberdade e a participação de homens livres pobres e 'de cor' na independência do Brasil," *Cadernos Cedes*, 22, 58, 2002, pp. 21–45; Gladys

Sabina Ribeiro, *A liberdade em construção: identidade nacional e conflitos antilusitanos no primeiro reinado* (Rio de Janeiro: Relume Dumará, 2002). See also Hendrik Kraay, *Days of National Festivity in Rio de Janeiro, 1823–1889* (Palo Alto: Stanford University Press, 2013), pp. 55, 106, 107.

126. Guerra Filho, "As Câmaras e o Povo," pp. 188–189. For further background, see Ubiratan Araújo, "A Política dos Homens de Cor no Tempo da Independência," *Estudos Avançados*, 18, 50, 2004, pp. 253–259; João José Reis and Hendrik Kraay, "'The Tyrant Is Dead!' The Revolt of the Periquitos in Bahia, 1824," *Hispanic American Historical Review*, 89, 3, 2009, pp. 399–434.

127. Daniel Afonso da Silva, "Na Trilha Das 'Garrafadas': A Abdicação de D. Pedro I e a Afirmação da Identidade Nacional Brasileira na Bahia," *Análise Social*, 47, 203, 2012, pp. 268–97; Sergio Guerra Filho, "O Joio e o Trigo: Debates Antilusitanos e as (in) definições Nacionais na Bahia de 1831," in Dilton de Araujo and Maria José Rapassi Mascarenhas (eds.), *Sociedade e Relações de Poder na Bahia* (Salvador: Edufba, 2014), pp. 113–132; Daniel Afonso da Silva, "O 13 de Abril de 1831: A Bahia de Cipriano Barata e o Brasil de D. Pedro I no Final do Primeiro Reinado," *Análise Social*, 51, 218, 2016, pp. 146–68. For further background, see Sérgio Armando Diniz Guerra Filho, "O Antilusitanismo na Bahia (1822–1831)," PhD Dissertation, UFBA, 2015.

128. Hendrik Kraay, "'As Terrifying as Unexpected': The Bahian Sabinada, 1837–1838," *The Hispanic American Historical Review*, 72, 4, 1992, pp. 501–527; Monica Duarte Dantas and Roberto Saba, "The Sabinada Rebellion," *Oxford Research Encyclopedia of Latin American History*, 2020.

129. Monica Duarte Dantas, "Popular Revolts in the Empire of Brazil," *Oxford Research Encyclopedia of Latin America History*, 2020, p. 2. See also Mundinha Araújo, *Em busca de Dom Cosme Bento das Chagas, Negro Cosme: Tutor e imperador da liberdade* (Imperatriz: Ética, 2008); Matthias Röhrig Assunção, *De Caboclos a Bem-te-vis: Formação do Campesinato numa Sociedade Escravista: Maranhão 1800–1850* (São Paulo: Annablume, 2018).

130. "Ofício de Vicente Jose Moreira Lima" on April 20, 1849, AGM, Audaz, cx. 468-2.

131. Marcus de Carvalho, "Os Nomes da Revolução: Lideranças Populares na Insurreição Praieira, Recife, 1848–1849," *Revista Brasileira de História*, 23, 45, 2003, p. 233. For Mossamedes foundation, see Laila Brichta, "Mocâmedes: Fluxos entre Brasil, Angola e Portugal na Década de 1850," in Manuel-Reyes García Hurtado and Ofelia Rey Castelao, *Fronteras de Agua Las Ciudades Portuarias y su Universo Cultural (Siglos XIV–XXI)* (Santiago de Compostela: Universidade de Santiago de Compostela, 2016), pp. 453–467; Laila Brichta, "Economía y Actividad Pesquera en el Atlántico Sur: El Caso de Moçâmedes en el Siglo XIX," *Almanack*, *Guarulhos*, 21, 2019, p. 273–309; Frederico Ferreira, "Açúcar Brasileiro na África Portuguesa: O Caso dos Recifenses de Moçâmedes," *Faces de Clio*, 6, 11, 2020, pp. 223–249; Maria Luiza Ferreira Oliveira, "Dimensões do governo colonial em Moçâmedes e suas conexões com o Brasil: trabalho, negócios e conflitos, 1840–1860," *Revista Mundos do Trabalho*, 12, 2020, p. 1–27.

132. BOGGPA, 210, October 6, 1849, p. 3. See José Antonio Lopes da Silva and Antonio Romano França, *Anais do Município de Mossamedes (anos de 1839 a 1849)*, *Anais do Conselho Ultramarino*, parte não oficial, série I, julho 1858, p. 484. See also Simão José da Luz Soriano, *Revelações da Minha Vida* (Lisboa: Typographia Universal, 1860), p. 563.

133. "Ofício do Juiz de Direito de Luanda" on April 1, 1840, AHU, segunda seção de Angola, pasta 3B. For the memory of Brazil's independence in Angola, with a focus on the 1880s, see Eduardo Estevam Santos, "Imprensa, Raça e Civilização: José de Fontes Pereira e o Pensamento Intelectual Angolano no século XIX," *Afro-Ásia*, 61, 2020, p. 123.

134. "Carta de Jácomo Felipe Torres" on November 6, 1835, AHU, segunda seção de Angola, pasta 5.

135. "Ofício de Justiniano José dos Reis" on December 18, 1836, AHU, segunda seção de Angola, pasta 2. See also "Ofício da Junta Governativa de Benguela" on February 17, 1835, AHA, cód. 2310, fls. 85v.–86.

136. "Carta para o Juiz do Crime Interino" on August 11, 1835, AHA, cód. 163, fls. 10–10v.; "Bando contra o Uso de Armas de Fogo em Benguela" on August 20, 1835, AHA, cód. 521, fl. 4v.–5.

137. "Ofício de Justiniano José dos Reis" on December 18, 1836, AHU, segunda seção de Angola, pasta 2.

138. "Carta de José Ferreira Nunes dos Santos" on December 18, 1835, AHU, segunda seção de Angola, pasta 2.

139. "Ofício da Junta Governativa de Angola" on December 6, 1837, AHU, segunda seção de Angola, pasta 2.

140. "Sentença de João da Paixão Nogueira" on February 14, 1839, AHU, segunda seção de Angola, pasta 3 A.

141. AHU, segunda seção de Angola, pasta 2.

142. "Ofício do Governador de Angola" on October 24, 1839, AHU, segunda seção de Angola, pasta 5.

143. "Ofício do Governador de Angola" on October 24, 1839, AHU, segunda seção de Angola, pasta 5.

144. "Carta de Jácomo Felipe Torres" on November 6, 1835, AHU, segunda seção de Angola, pasta 5.

145. Candido, "Women, Family, and Landed Property," pp. 144–145.

146. "Portaria do Governador de Benguela" on November 7, 1814, AHA, cód. 519, fl. 155; "Portaria do Governador de Benguela" on April 19, 1817, AHA, cód. 519, fl. 230.

147. "Ordem do Governador de Benguela" on September 3, 1811, AHA, cód. 519, fl. 86.

148. "Portaria do Governador de Benguela" on January 9, 1811, AHA, cód. 519, fl. 58.

149. "Portaria do Governador de Benguela" on September 13, 1814, AHA, cód. 519, fl. 152v.; "Portaria do Governador de Benguela" on July 17, 1816, AHA, cód. 519, fl. 202v.

150. "Carta do Governador de Angola" on January 29, 1829, AHA, cód. 97, fl. 1. For succession rules in Ambaka, where matrilineality prevailed, see Jan Vansina, "Ambaca Society and the Slave Trade c. 1760–1845," *The Journal of African History*, 46, 1, 2005, p. 1–27.

151. "Carta do Governador de Angola" on January 29, 1829, AHA, cód. 97, fl. 1.

152. "Ofício do Governador de Benguela" on January 21, 1854, AHA, cód. 467, fl. 129v.

153. "Portaria do Governador de Benguela" on November 8, 1826, AHA, cód. 520, fls. 123–123 v.

154. "Petição de Francisco Ferreira Gomes" on July 14, 1824, AHA, cód. 138, fl. 76v.

155. "Ofício do Governador de Benguela" on December 11, 1845, AHA, cód. 455, fls. 132–132v.

156. Mariana Candido, *Wealth, Land, and Property in Angola: A History of Dispossession, Slavery, and Inequality* (NYC: Cambridge University Press, 2022), p. 74.

157. "Ofício do Conselho de Governo de Angola" on February 4, 1843, AHA, cód. 15, fls. 150–151. For further context, see Candido, *Wealth, Land, and Property*, p. 74.

158. "Carta de Manuel Freire" on May 21, 1846, AHA, cx. 5568.

159. "Ofício do Governador de Benguela" on September 10, 1846, AHA, cód. 455, fls. 211–211v.

160. "Ofício do Comandante da Escuna Ninfa" on December 26, 1845, AHA, cód. 7183, fl. 84.

161. "Requerimento de José Ferreira Gomes" on August 3, AHA, cód. 2788, fl. 127v.

162. "Ofício do Secretário Geral do Governo" on September 23, 1846, AHA, cx. 1412; "Ofício de Rodovalho" on October 12, 1846, Arquivo Geral da Marinha (AGM), cx. 471-1 (Brigue Mondego).

163. "Ofício do Governador de Benguela" on September 10, 1846, AHA, cód. 455, fls. 210–212.

164. "Ofício da Estação Naval" on October 21, 1847, AGM, Brigue Mondego, cx. 471-1.

165. "Ofício do Secretário Geral da Província de Angola" on September 23, 1846, AHA, cód. 3440, fls. 183v.–184; "Ofício do Governador de Benguela" on March 24, 1847, AHA, cód. 455, fl. 359–360v; "Ofício do Governador de Benguela" on December 25, 1848, AHA, cx. 5426; "Ofício do Governador de Benguela" on October 7, 1846, AHA, cód. 460, fls. 12–12v. For context, see René Pelissier, *História das Campanhas de Angola: Resistência e Revoltas, 1845–1941* (Lisboa: Editorial Estampa, 1986), pp. 64–66.

166. Menezes, *Demonstração Geographica e Politica do Territorio Portuguez*, p. 111.

167. "Ofício do Governador de Benguela" on January 17, 1825, AHA, cód. 520, fl. 29. For a reporto f insecutiry in Dombe Grande, see "Portaria do Governador de Benguela" on May 22, 1817, AHA, cód. 519, fls. 232v.–233.

168. "Ofício do Governador de Benguela" on November 20, 1843, AHA, cód. 455, fls. 21v.–22.

169. Menezes, *Demonstração Geographica e Politica do Territorio Portuguez*, p. 108; "Ofício do Governador de Benguela" on January 9, 1847, AHA, cód. 455; "Ofício do Governador de Benguela" on March 24, 1847, AHA, cód. 455, fl. 359–360v.

170. "Bando" on January 27, 1847, AHA, cód. 523, fls. 20v.–21v.; Ofício do Secretário da Província de Angola on June 2, 1847, AHA, cód. 167.

171. Francisco Xavier Lopes, "O Dombe Grande da Quissamba" on August 15, 1847, *Anais do Conselho Ultramarino*, parte não oficial, série II, julho 1861. See also Candido, *Wealth, Land, and Property in Angola*, pp. 81–82.

172. Menezes, *Demonstração Geographica e Politica do Territorio Portuguez*, pp. 117–122.

173. Menezes, *Demonstração Geographica e Politica do Territorio Portuguez*, p. 110.

174. BOGGPA, 498, 1855, 2.

175. "Ofício do Governador de Benguela" on March 20, 1847, AHA, cód. 7183, fls. 121.

176. Candido, "Women, Family, and Landed Property," pp. 143; Mariana Candido, "Conquest, Occupation, Colonialism and Exclusion: Land Disputes in Angola," in José Vicente Serrão, Bárbara Direito, Eugénia Rodrigues, and Susana Münch Miranda (eds.), *Property Rights, Land and Territory in the European Overseas Empires: Direitos de Propriedade, Terra e Território nos Impérios Ultramarinos Europeus* (Lisbon: CEHC-IU, 2014), p. 228. See Aida Freudenthal, *Arimos e Fazendas: a Transição Agrária em Angola, 1850–1880* (Luanda: Chá de Caxinde, 2005), pp. 90–91, 134, 143; Salas, "Making Portuguese Colonial Governance," pp. 62–65. See also Joana Dias Pereira, "Colonialism and Customary Land Tenure in Africa: Portuguese Representations and Policies During the 19th and 20th Centuries," *African Studies*, 82, 3–4, 2023, pp. 332–347.

177. BOGGPA, 85, April 24, 1847. See "Instruções para o President e Membros da Comissão de Lançamentos de Dízimos do Dombe Grande" on December 1, 1847, AHA, cód. 463, fls. 34–35v. See Maria Alexandra Aparício, "Dombe Grande. A Implantação dos Dízimos e suas Consequências na Região: Os Conflitos Militares 1852–1859," *Fontes & Estudos*, 1, 1994, pp. 49–61. See also Candido, "Women, Family, and Landed Property," p. 149.

178. BOGGPA, 432, January 7, 1854, p. 2. See BOGGPA, 110, October 16, 1847, p. 2; BOGGPA, 131, March 11, 1848. See also Freudenthal, *Arimos e Fazendas*, pp. 108–109.

179. BOGGPA, December 13, 1856, 585, pp. 3–6.

180. "Ofício do Governador de Benguela" on October 30, 1862, AHU, papéis de Sá da Bandeira, maço 825; "Carta do Governador de Benguela" on October 31, 1864, AHU, papéis de Sá da Bandeira, maço 827. For further background, see Candido, *Wealth, Land, and Property in Angola*, pp. 85–86.

181. Ofício do Delegado do procurador da coroa e fazenda on April 16, 1847, AHA, cód. 2788, fl. 85.

182. Requerimento de Jose Ferreira Gomes on May 8, 1847, AHA, cod. 2788, fl. 94.

183. "Requerimento de Jose Ferreira Gomes" on August 20, 1847, AHA, cód. 2788, fl. 135v.

184. "Ofício do Governador de Benguela" on September 27, 1847, AHA, cód. 722, fl. 195v.; "Ofício do Governador de Angola" on March 14, 1848, AHA, cód. 510, fl. 70.

185. "Requerimento de José Ferreira Gomes" on August 17, 1857, TBC, maço 1, número 40.

186. "Procuração de José Ferreira Gomes" on February 26, 1864, in "Inventário de Florinda Josefa Gaspar" in 1863, ANRJ, n. 1085, cx. 4089, gal. A.

187. "Autos Cíveis de Embargo ou Arresto" in 1858, TCB, maço 1, num. 47. For information on Francisco Geraldo Ferreira de Souza Guimarães, see "ofício do Secretário de Governo de Benguela" on July 3, 1849, AHA, cód. 722, fls. 321–321. Guimarães was the owner of 22 slaves in Benguela in 1854. See AHA, cód. 3160.

Chapter 2: *Makèzú*

1. "Auto de Querela" on December 12, 1846, Arquivo Histórico Ultramarino (AHU), Angola, pasta 13.

2. "Petição de Joaquim Gamboa" on December 11, 1826, AHU, Angola, pasta 13.

3. António Manuel Hespanha, *Como os juristas viam o mundo, 1550-1750. Direitos, estados, pessoas, coisas, contratos, ações e crimes* (Lisboa: Amazon Distribution GmbH, 2015), pp. 257-258, 620. I am grateful to Cristina Nogueira da Silva for this reference.

4. Tony Ballantyne and Antoinette Burton, *Empires and the Reach of the Global, 1870-1945* (Cambridge: Belknap Press, 2014), p. 144.

5. José Curto, "A Família Fortunato da Costa: De Portugal a Angola, via São Tomé, c. 1808 a 1859," *Afro-Ásia*, 67, 2023, pp. 97-141. See also José Curto, "'That Abominable Practice': Child Marriage in Two Slaving Ports (Luanda and Benguela), c. 1797-1846," *International Journal of African Historical Studies*, 54/2, 2021, p. 138.

6. Sophie Rose and Elisabeth Heijmans, "From Impropriety to Betrayal: Policing Non-Marital Sex in the Early Modern Dutch Empire," *Journal of Social History*, 55, 2, 2021, pp. 315-344.

7. Marisa Fuentes, *Dispossessed Lives: Enslaved Women, Violence, and the Archive* (Philadelphia: University of Pennsylvania Press, 2016), pp. 7-16.

8. Natalie Zemon Davies, "Decentering History: Local Stories and Cultural Crossings in a Global World," *History and Theory*, 50, 2011, p. 190.

9. Anjali Arondekar, "What More Remains: Slavery, Sexuality, South Asia," *History of the Present*, 6, 2, 2016, p. 147.

10. "Testemunho de Manoel Martins Cardozo" on February 24, 1847, AHU, Angola, pasta 13). Vanessa Oliveira, "Notas Preliminares sobre a Punição de Escravos em Luanda (Século XIX)," in *O Colonialismo Português: Novos Rumos da Historiografia dos PALOP* (Porto: Centro de Estudos Africanos da Universidade do Porto, 2013), pp. 155-175; Trabalho Escravo e Ocupações Urbanas em Luanda na Segunda Metade do Século XIX," in Selma Pantoja and Estevam Thompson (eds.), *Em Torno de Angola: Narrativa, Identidades e as Conexões Atlânticas* (SP: Intermeios, 2014), p. 260; Vanessa Oliveira, "Slavery and the Forgotten Women Slave Owners of Luanda (1846-1876)," in Paul Lovejoy and Vanessa Oliveira (eds.), *Slavery, Memory, Citizenship* (Trenton: Africa World Press, 2016), p. 141.

11. "Testemunho de Manoel Martins Cardozo" on February 24, 1847, AHU, Angola, pasta 13).

12. BOGGPA, 1858, 652, 11.

13. BOGGPA, 12, 1865, 57.

14. BOGGPA 150, August 12, 1848. Dona Maria Joaquina do Amaral's lawsuit and case are also examined in Vanessa de Oliveira, "Spouses & Commercial Partners: Immigrant Men & Locally Born Women in Luanda 1831-1859," in Mariana Candido and Adam Jones (eds.), *African Women in the Atlantic World: Property, Vulnerability & Mobility, 1660-1880* (Suffolk: Boydell & Brewer, 2019), p. 231.

15. Report on the Slave Trade by Gabriel and Jackson on February 14, 1848, FO 84, 719, fls. 61-74.

16. "Ofício do Governador de Angola" on October 31, 1828, AHU, Angola, cx. 160, doc. 43. For the impact of Brazil's first attempt of ending imports of slaves on Luanda, see "Carta do Governador de Angola" on June 22, 1830, AHA, cód. 160, fls. 150v.; "Ofício do Governador de Angola" on December 14, 1830, AHA, cód. 12, fls. 64-64v.

17. "Cópia de representação de negociantes do Porto" on January 14, 1840, AHA, cód. 259.

18. "Ofício do Ministro e Secretário de Estado dos Negócios de Marinha e Ultramar" on January 9, 1839, AHU, papéis de Sá da Bandeira, maço 824.

19. "Ofício do Comandante das Forças Navais Britânicas" on January 28, 1840, AHA, cód. 259. See also Mário António Fernandes de Oliveira, *Alguns Aspectos da Administração de Angola em Época de Reformas (1834-1851)* (Lisboa: Universidade Nova de Lisboa, 1981), p. 86; Valentim Alexandre, *Velho Brasil, Novas Áfricas: Portugal e o Império 1808-1975* (Porto: Afrontamento, 2000), pp. 99-101; João Pedro Marques, *The Sounds of Silence:*

Nineteenth Century Portugal and the Abolition of the Slave Trade (New York: Berghahn Books, 2006), p. 112.

20. "Ofício do Governador de Angola" on February 23, 1838, AHA, cód. 13, fl. 70–70v.

21. Dispatch by Edmond Gabriel and George Jackson on May 1, 1847, FO 84, 672, fls. 43–48.

22. Dispatch by Edmond Gabriel and George Jackson on May 1, 1847, FO 84, 672, fls. 43–48.

23. Dispatch by Edmond Gabriel and George Jackson on February 8, 1847, FO 84, 671, fls. 60–65. For further information about Câmara and Garrido's business activities, see BOGGPA, 1851, 320. See also Tracy Lopes, "Continuities between the Slave Trade, "Legitimate" Commerce, and the Serviçal Trade: a Look at Four Families in Angola in the Mid- to Late Nineteenth Century," *Canadian Journal of African Studies*, 58, 3, 2024, p. 563.

24. "Ofício do Governador de Angola" on May 26, 1847, AHU, Angola, pasta 13. For further context on the rivalry between Governor Pedro Alexandrino da Cunha and Judge José Maria Gonçalves, see Anne Stamm, "La Societé Créole à Saint-Paul de Loanda dans les Annés 1838–1848," *Revue Française d'Histoire d'Outre Mer*, 217, 1972, p. 591; Oliveira, *Alguns Aspectos da Administração de Angola em Época de Reformas*, pp. 91–92.

25. For further background on Carpo, see also João Pedro Marques, "Arsénio Pompílio Pompeu de Carpo: Um Percurso Negreiro No Século XIX," *Análise Social*, 36, 160, 2001, pp. 609–38; Carlos Pacheco, "Arsénio Pompílio Pompeu de Carpo: Uma Vida de Luta contra as Prepotências do Poder Colonial em Angola," *Revista Internacional de Estudos Africanos*, 16–17, 1992–1994, pp. 52–80; Jacopo Corrado, "The Rise of a New Consciousness: Early Euro-African Voices of Dissent in Colonial Angola," *E-Journal of Portuguese History*, 5, 2, 2007, pp. 1–15; Tracy Lopes, "Punishing Crime: Jails and Confinement in Luanda, Angola, from 1836 to 1899," PhD Dissertation, York University, 2022, pp. 40–49. For further context on the flow of foreigners into Luanda, see Vanessa Oliveira, "The Business of Self-Endowment: Women Merchants, Wealth and Marriage in Nineteenth-Century Luanda," in Jennifer Aston and Catherine Bishop (eds.), *Female Entrepreneurs in the Long Nineteenth Century: A Global Perspective* (NYC: Palgrave, 2020), p. 224.

26. "Representação da Câmara Municipal de Luanda" on October 9, 1839, AHU, segunda seção de Angola, pasta 5.

27. "Portaria do Ministro da Marinha e Ultramar" on January 29, 1840, AHA, cód. 259, fls. 113–113v.

28. "Ofício do Governador de Angola" on February 22, 1839, AHU, segunda seção de Angola, pasta 4.

29. "Bando sobre o Tráfico de Escravos" on May 11, 1839, AHA, cód. 522, fl 7v.

30. "Portaria do Governador de Benguela" on July 7, 1840, AHA, cód. 522, fls. 63–63v.

31. "Carta do Comandante do Navio Urania" on October 10, 1839, FO 84, 322, fls. 135–136v.; "Relatório do Ministério do Ultramar" in 1840, in *Annaes Marítimos e Coloniaes* (Lisboa: Imprensa Nacional, 1841), p. 161. See also Manuel Pinheiro Chagas, *As Colônias Portuguezas no Século XIX: 1811 a 1890* (Lisboa: Livraria de A. M. Pereira, 1891), p. 81.

32. AHA, cx. 148.

33. "Relatório do Ministério do Ultramar" in 1840, in *Annaes Marítimos e Coloniaes* (Lisboa: Imprensa Nacional, 1841), p. 161.

34. "Carta do Governador de Angola" September 6, 1843, AHU, maço 825.

35. "Ata da Sessão do Conselho de Governo de Angola" on August 21, 1844, AHA, cód. 2856.

36. "Ofício do Governador de Angola" on November 5, 1846, AHA, cód. 65, fls. 84–92; "Relatório do Comandante da Escuna Tâmega" on September 3, 1847, AGM, cx. 311.

37. Tracy Lopes, "Punishing Crime," p. 59.

38. BOGGPA, 342, 1852, 2. See also "Portaria do Governador de Angola" on April 1, 1851, AHA, cód. 280, f. 80v.

39. Alfredo de Sarmento, *Os Sertões d'Africa* (Lisboa: F. A. da Silva, 1880), p. 43.

40. BOGGPA, 644, 1858, 1; BOGGPA, 655, 1858, 7; BOGGPA, 1859, 719, 8.

41. "Ofício do Governador de Angola" on March 9, 1846, AHA, cód. 66, fls. 33–35.

42. George Tams, *Visit to the Portuguese Possessions in South-West Africa* (London: T. C. Newby, 1845), vol. I, p. 8. For an overview of theaters in Luanda, see José de Almeida Santos, *A Velha Loanda nos Festejos, nas Solenidades, no Ensino* (Luanda: Câmara Municipal de Luanda, 1972), vol. IV, pp. 108–119. See also Lopes, "Punishing Crime," p. 57.

43. John Monteiro, *Angola and the River Congo* (New York: Macmillan and Co., 1876), p. 193.

44. Saturnino de Souza e Oliveira, *Relatório Histórico da Epidemia de Varíola que grassou em Loanda em 1864* (Lisboa: Typographia Universal, 1866), pp. 91–92. For the relationship between midwives and abortion practices, see Londa Schiebinger, *Plants and Empire: Colonial Bioprospecting in the Atlantic World* (Cambridge: Harvard University Press, 2004), p. 121.

45. Zeb Tortorici, "Sexual Violence, Predatory Masculinity, and Medical Testimony in New Spain," *Osiris*, 30, 2015, pp. 272–294.

46. "Autos de Querela" on December 19, 1846, AHU, Angola, pasta 13.

47. "Petição de Joaquim Gamboa" on January 7, 1847, AHU, Angola, pasta 13.

48. "Testemunho de Sebastião Rodrigues de Moura" on April 23, 1847, AHU, Angola, pasta 13.

49. "Testemunho de Sebastião Rodrigues de Moura" on April 23, 1847, AHU, Angola, pasta 13.

50. "Testemunho de Joaquim Jose Cardozo da Silva" on February 24, 1847, AHU, Angola, pasta 13.

51. "Testemunho de Manuel Martins Cardozo" on February 24, 1847, AHU, Angola, pasta 13.

52. "Testemunho de José Ferreira" on February 24, 1847, AHU, Angola, pasta 13.

53. Roza José on April 24, 1847, AHU, Angola, pasta 13.

54. Tito Omboni, *Viaggi nell'Africa Occidentale* (Milano: Civelli, 1846), p. 91.

55. Omboni, *Viaggi nell'Africa Occidentale*, p. 91.

56. Ladislau Batalha, *A Língua de Angola* (Lisboa: Companhia Nacional Editora, 1897), p. 10.

57. "Ofício do Governador de Angola" on May 26, 1847, AHU, Angola, pasta 13. See also Stamm, "La Societé Créole à Saint-Paul de Loanda dans les Annés 1838–1848," p. 591; Oliveira, *Alguns Aspectos da Administração de Angola em Época de Reformas*, pp. 91–92.

58. Alfred Hauenstein, "La Noix de Cola. Coutumes et Rites de Quelques Ethnies de Côte d'lvoire," *Anthropos*, 69, 3/4, 1974, pp. 468–469. See also Paul Lovejoy, "Kola in the History of West Africa," *Cahiers d'Études Africaines*, 20, 77/78, 1980, pp. 97–134; Paul Lovejoy, "Kola Nuts: The 'Coffee' of the Central Sudan," in Jordan Goodman, Paul E. Lovejoy, and Andrew Sherratt (eds.), *Consuming Habits: Drugs in History and Anthropology* (London: Routledge, 1995), p. 112; Jean-Paul Colleyn, "L'alliance, le dieu, l'objet," *L'Homme*, 170, 2004, pp. 61–77; Philip Havik, "Hybridizing Medicine: Illness, Healing, and the Dynamics of Reciprocal Exchange on the Upper Guinea Coast (West Africa)," *Med. Hist.*, 60, 2, 2016, pp. 190, 192–193. See also Kalle Kananoja, *Healing Knowledge in Atlantic Africa: Medical Encounters, 1500–1850* (NYC: Cambridge University Press, 2021), p. 106.

59. Alfred Hauenstein, "La Noix de Cola. Coutumes et Rites de Quelques Ethnies de Côte d'lvoire," Anthropos, 69, 3/4, 1974, pp. 466–469; Paul Lovejoy, "Kola Nuts: The 'Coffee' of the Central Sudan," in Jordan Goodman, Paul E. Lovejoy, and Andrew Sherratt (eds.), Consuming Habits: Drugs in History and Anthropology (London: Routledge, 1995), pp. 112–113.

60. Dora de Lima, "Les descriptions d'un banquet royal au Ndongo (Angola) en 1560 par le jésuite António Mendes: l'ambivalence des sources colonials," *Afriques*, 5, 2014.

61. H. Boukoulou et P. Mbete, "Role social de la noix de cola au Congo," *Annales de l'Université Marien Ngouabi*, 11, 1, 2010, pp. 1–14.

62. Judith Carney and Richard Nicholas Rosomoff, *In the Shadow of Slavery: Africa's Botanical Legacy in the Atlantic World* (Berkeley: University of California Press, 2010), p. 71.

63. Robert Voeks, *Sacred Leaves of Candomblé: African Magic, Medicine, and Religion in Brazil* (Austin: University of Texas Press, 2003); Luis Nicolau Parés, *The Formation of Candomblé: Vodun History and Ritual in Brazil* (Chapell Hill: UNC Press, 2013); Flávio Gonçalves dos Santos, *Economia e cultura do candomblé na Bahia: O comércio dos objetos litúrgicos afro-brasileiros, 1850-1937* (Ilhéus: Editora Uesc, 2013).

64. João Reis, "De escravo a rico liberto: a trajetória do africano Manoel Joaquim Ricardo na Bahia oitocentista," *Revista História*, 174, 2016, pp. 15–68. See also Case Watkins, *Palm Oil*

Diaspora: Afro-Brazilian Landscapes and Economies on Bahia's Dendê Coast (NYC: Cambridge University Press, 2021), p. 105.

65. Edmund Abaka, "'Eating Kola': The Pharmacological and Therapeutic Significance of Kola Nuts." *Ghana Studies*, vol. 21, 2018, p. 150.

66. Frederico Welwitsch, *Synopse Explicativa das Mostras de Madeiras e Drogas Medicinaes e de Outros Objectos Mormente Ethnographicos* (Lisboa: Imprensa Nacional, 1862), p. 45. For a similar remark, see Monteiro, *Angola and the River Congo*, p. 188.

67. "Medicinal Products which the Inhabitants of West Africa, principally Angola and its Interior use," in William J. Simon, "A Luso-African Formulary of the Late Eighteenth Century: Some Notes on Angola Contributions to European Knowledge of Materia Medica," *Pharmacy in History*, 18, 3, 1976, p. 113. I would like to thank Kalle Kananoja for bringing this article to my attention.

68. Óscar Ribas, *Izomba: Associativismo e Recreio* (Luanda: Tip. Angolana, 1965), p. 38; Óscar Ribas, *Dicionário de Regionalismos Angolanos* (Luanda: Ministério da Cultura, 2014), p. 105; Óscar Ribas, *Alimentação Regional Angolana* (Lisboa, 1989), p. 12. See also Ana de Sousa Santos, "Quitandas e Quitandeiras de Luanda," *Boletim do Instituto de Investigação Científica de Angola*, 4, 2, 1967, p. 99.

69. Elias Alexandre da Silva Corrêa, *História de Angola* (Lisboa: Editorial Ática, 1937), vol. 1, p. 142.

70. J. D. Cordeiro da Matta, *Ensaio de Diccionario Kimbundu-Portuguez* (Lisboa: Typographia e Setereotypia Moderna, 1893), p. 104.

71. Óscar Ribas, *Uanga Feitiço: Romance Folclórico Angolano* (Lisboa: Edições 70, 1981), pp. 12–13. See also Monteiro, *Angola and the River Congo*, p. 188.

72. Corrêa, *História de Angola*, vol. 1, p. 142.

73. Welwitsch, *Synopse Explicativa das Mostras de Madeiras e Drogas Medicinaes*, p. 45. See also Adolph Bastian, *Ein Besuch in San Salvador, der Hauptstadt des Konigreichs Kongo* (Bremen: Druck und Verlag von H. Strack, 1859), p. 238.

74. Omboni, *Viaggi nell'Africa Occidentale*, p. 88.

75. Ribas, *Alimentação Regional Angolana*, pp. 12–13.

76. Ana de Sousa Santos, "Aspectos de Alguns Costumes da População Luandense," *Boletim do Instituto de Investigação Científica de Angola*, 7, 2, 1970, p. 57.

77. "Medicinal Products which the Inhabitants of West Africa, principally Angola and its Interior use," p. 113. See also Ribas, *Alimentação Regional Angolana*, pp. 12–13.

78. Corrêa, *História de Angola*, vol. 1, p. 142.

79. Corrêa, *História de Angola*, vol. 1, p. 142.

80. Welwitsch, *Synopse Explicativa das Mostras de Madeiras e Drogas Medicinaes*, p. 45.

81. Monteiro, *Angola and the River Congo*, p. 188.

82. Ladislau Batalha, *Costumes Angolenses* (Lisboa: Companhia Nacional Editora, 1890), p. 31.

83. Silva Corrêa, *História de Angola*, vol. 1, p. 142

84. "Alistamento do Bairro Nossa Senhora do Rosário, 1823–1832," Biblioteca Municipal de Luanda (BML), cód. 45.

85. "Alistamento do Bairro Nossa Senhora do Rosário, 1823–1832," BML, cód. 45.

86. José Curto, "Whitening the 'White' Population: An Analysis of the 1850 Censuses of Luanda," in *Em Torno de Angola: Narrativa, Identidades e as Conexões Atlânticas*, pp. 225–247.

87. "Alistamento do Bairro Nossa Senhora do Rosário, 1823–1832," BML, cód. 45.

88. AHU, sala 12, maços de Angola, maço 1107, 1851. For lower numbers for Luanda's population, see Charles Philippe de Kerhallet, *Manuel de la Navigation à la Côte Occidentale d'Áfrique* (Paris: Imprense Administrative de P. Dupont, 1851), p. 120.

89. José Curto, "The Anatomy of a Demographic Explosion: Luanda, 1844–1850," *The International Journal of African Historical Studies*, 32, 2/3, 1999, pp. 381–405.

90. AHA, cód. 2524.

91. Vanessa Oliveira, "Baskets, Stalls, and Shops: Experiences and Strategies of Women in Retail Sales in Nineteenth Century Luanda," Canadian Journal of African Studies/Revue canadienne des études africaines, 54, 3, 2020, p. 11.

92. Oliveira, *Relatório Histórico da Epidemia de Varíola*, p. 93.

93. Vanessa Oliveira, "Slave Labour and the Vulnerability of Enslaved Women in Mid-Nineteenth Century Luanda," in José Curto (ed.), *New Perspectives on Angola: From Slaving Colony to Nation State* (Peterborough: Baywolf Press/Éditions Baywolf, 2021), p. 153.

94. Oliveira, "Trabalho Escravo e Ocupações Urbanas em Luanda," pp. 255–259.

95. "Mapa do Número de Filhos e Filhas de Mulheres e Batizadas como Livres" on July 24, 1856, AHU, papéis de Sá da Bandeira, maço 824. For Mossamedes, see José Curto, "Uma Vila Esclavagista: Proprietários e seus Cativos em Moçâmedes, 1855," *Revista Brasileira de História*, 43, 93, 2023, p. 232.

96. Oliveira, "Slavery and the Forgotten Women Slave Owners of Luanda," pp. 133–135.

97. Oliveira, "Donas, Pretas Livres e Escravas em Luanda (Séc. XIX)," p. 453.

98. Oliveira, *Relatório Histórico da Epidemia de Varíola*, p. 228. See also Oliveira, "Trabalho Escravo e Ocupações Urbanas em Luanda na Segunda Metade do Século XIX," pp. 255–259.

99. Oliveira, "Slave Labor and the Vulnerability of Enslaved Women in Mid-Nineteenth Century Luanda," p. 157. See also Mariana Candido and Vanessa Oliveira, "The Status of Enslaved Women in West Central Africa, 1800–1830," *African Economic* History, 49, 1, 2021, p. 133.

100. J. D. Cordeiro da Matta, *Ensaio de Diccionario Kimbundu-Portuguez* (Lisboa: Typographia e Setereotypia Moderna, 1893), p. 104. See Mariana Candido and Vanessa de Oliveira, "Slavery in Luanda and Benguela," *Oxford Research Encyclopedia of African History*, 2022, pp. 15–17.

101. Lorena Telles, *Teresa Benguela e Felipa Crioula estava grávidas: Maternidade e escravidão no Rio de Janeiro (1830–1888)* (Franca: Unifesp, 2023), pp. 132–139.

102. Marcus de Carvalho, "De Portas Adentro e de Portas Afora: Trabalho Doméstico e Escravidão no Recife, 1822–1850," *Afro-Ásia*, 29–30, 2003.

103. "Declaração de Celestina" on December 12, 1846, AHU, Angola, pasta 13.

104. "Declaração de Jesuína" on December 12, 1846, AHU, Angola, pasta 13.

105. Testimony of Manoel Martins Cardozo, February 24, 1847, fls. 10v–11r.

106. Testimony of Antonio Pinto, February 24, 1847, fls. 11r–12r. For analyses of the structural violence of Luanda slavery, see Vanessa Oliveira, "Notas Preliminares sobre a Punição de Escravos em Luanda (Século XIX)," in *O Colonialismo Português: Novos Rumos da Historiografia dos PALOP* (Porto: Centro de Estudos Africanos da Universidade do Porto, 2013), pp. 155–175; Oliveira, "Trabalho Escravo e Ocupações Urbanas em Luanda na Segunda Metade do Século XIX," p. 260; Oliveira, "Slavery and the Forgotten Women Slave Owners of Luanda (1846–1876)," p. 141.

107. "Ofício do Secretário de Governo de Angola" on May 5, 1846, AHA, cód. 104, fl. 268v.

108. "Ofício do Secretário de Governo de Angola" on May 14, 1846, AHA, cód. 105, fl. 3.

109. "Ofício do Secretário Geral da Província" on March 1, 1847, AHA, cód. 167, fls. 15v.–16.

110. "Ofício do Secretário Geral da Província de Angola" on March 1, 1847, AHA, cód. 167, fls. 15v.–16.

111. "Portaria do Governador de Angola" on October 3, 1853, AHA, cód. 281, fls. 39–39v. See Anônimo, *Quarenta e Cinco Dias em Angola*, p. 112. See also Margarida Seixas, "Escravos e Libertos no Boletim Oficial de Angola (1845–1875)—I parte," E-REI, 2, 2014, p. 3; Lopes, "Punishing Crime," p. 84; Tracy Lopes, "Slave "Corrections" in Luanda, Angola from 1836 to 1869," *Punishment & Society*, 24, 5, 2022, p. 9.

112. "Ofício do Secretário Geral do Governo de Angola" on March 21, 1854, AHA, cód. 178, fls. 98–98v.; "Ofício do Secretário Geral de Angola" on January 31, 1855, AHA, cód. 112, fls. 162.

113. "Ofício do Secretário Geral do Governo de Angola" on January 28, 1854, AHA, cód. 178, fls. 39v.–40. For further examples of slave punishment, see "Ofício do Secretário Geral do Governo de Angola" on November 10, 1854, AHA, cód. 179, fl. 49; "ofício do Secretário de Angola" in February 1855, AHA, cód. 179, fl. 132.

114. "Ofício do Secretário Geral do Governo de Angola" on February 9, 1854, AHA, cód. 178, fl. 59–59v.

115. Oliveira, "Notas Preliminares sobre a Punição de Escravos em Luanda," pp. 155–175.

116. "Ofício do Juiz de Direito Substituto da Comarca de Luanda" on July 28, 1857, AHU, pasta 23 (2). For an argument about women being more vulnerable to private punishment, see Lopes, "Punishing Crime," p. 107.

117. Lopes, "Punishing Crime," pp. 104–106. See also Lopes, "Slave 'Corrections' in Luanda," pp. 11–12.

118. *Annaes Maritimos e Coloniaes* (Lisboa: Imprensa Nacional, 1845), parte official, quinta série, p. 234. See also Oliveira, "Baskets, Stalls, and Shops," p. 8.

119. Ladislau Batalha, *Angola* (Lisboa: Companhia Nacional Editora, 1889), p. 47.

120. Ribas, *Izomba*, p. 134.

121. Santos, "Quitandas e Quitandeiras de Luanda," p. 89.

122. Domingos Van-Dúnem, "Sobre o vocábulo quitandeira, Luanda," apud Orlando Santos, "Mamãs quitandeiras, kínguilas e zungueiras: trajectórias femininas e quotidiano de comerciantes de rua em Luanda," *Revista Angolana de Sociologia*, 8, 2011, p. 3.

123. Vanessa Oliveira, "The Gendered Dimension of Trade: Female Traders in Nineteenth Century Luanda," *Portuguese Studies Review*, 23, 2, 2015, pp. 113–114.

124. "Baskets, Stalls, and Shops," p. 9.

125. Oliveira, "Donas, Pretas Livres e Escravas em Luanda," p. 454.

126. Batalha, *Angola*, p. 47. See also Selma Pantoja, "Imagens e Perspectivas Culturais: o Trabalho Feminino nas Feiras e Mercados Luandenses," in Clara Sarmento (ed.), *Condição Feminina no Império Colonial Português* (Porto: Politema, 2008), v. 1, pp. 125–139; Selma Pantoja, "A Dimensão Atlântica das Quitandeiras," in Júnia Ferreira Furtado (ed.), *Diálogos Oceânicos. Minas Gerais e as Novas Abordagens para Uma História do Império Ultramarino Português* (Belo Horizonte: UFMG, 2001), v. 1, pp. 45–67; For Rio de Janeiro, see Melina Teubner, "Street Food, Urban Space, and Gender: Working on the Streets of Nineteenth-Century Rio de Janeiro (1830–1870)," *International Review of Social History*, 2019, pp. 1–26; Patricia Acerbi, *Street Occupations: Urban Vending in Rio de Janeiro, 1850-1925* (Austin: University of Texas Press, 2017), Chapter 1.

127. AHU, sala 12, maços de Angola, maço 1107, Administração de Angola, 1851. See Charles Thomas, *Adventures and Observations on the West Coast of Africa, and its Islands* (New York: Derby & Jackson, 1860), pp. 280–281. See also Selma Pantoja, "Quitandas e Quitandeiras: História e Deslocamento na Nova Lógica do Espaco de Luanda," *II Reunião Internacional de História da África*, v. 1. 2000, p. 179; Oliveira, "Baskets, Stalls, and Shops," p. 6.

128. Oliveira, "Baskets, Stalls, and Shops," pp. 7, 9.

129. "Ofício do Secretário Geral de Governo" on May 6, 1849, AHA, cód. 171, fl. 148.

130. Batalha, *Angola*, p. 47.

131. Batalha, *Angola*, p. 47. For Benguela, see Mariana Candido, "Strategies for Social Mobility: Liaisons between Foreign Men and Enslaved Women in Benguela, ca. 1770–1850," in Gwyn Campbell and Elizabeth Elbourne (eds.), *Sex, Power, and Slavery* (Athens: Ohio University Press, 2014), p. 276.

132. Anônimo, *Quarenta e Cinco Dias em Angola* (Porto: Typographia de Sebastião José Pereira, 1861), p. 51.

133. "Hipoteca entre Engrácia Antónia Fernandes Ribeiro e Antonio Luis Pereira de Lemos" on November 6, 1855, AHA, cód. 7741.

134. "Escritura de Venda e Compra" on January 7, 1864, AHA, cód. 12-3-3, fls. 84v–89v.

135. Ribas, *Izomba*, p. 131. See also Ana de Sousa Santos, "Prensas de Mandioca nos Musseques dos Arredores de Luanda," *Boletim do Instituto de Investigação Científica de Angola*, 5, 2, 1968, pp. 153–166.

136. *Iris: Periódico de Religião, Bellas Artes, Sciencia, Lettras, História, Poesia, Romance, Notícias e Variedade* (Rio de Janeiro: Typographia de L. A. Ferreira de Menezes, 1849), vol. II, pp. 132–139.

137. "Escritura de Venda e Compra" on January 7, 1864, AHA, cód. 12-3-3, fls. 84v–89v.

138. *Almanak Statistico da Província d'Angola e suas Dependências para o ano de 1852* (Luanda: Imprensa do Governo, 1851), p. 2. See also Santos, "Quitandas e Quitandeiras de Luanda," p. 89.

139. Charles Thomas, *Adventures and Observations on the West Coast of Africa, and its Islands* (New York: Derby & Jackson, 1860), pp. 280–281.

140. Monteiro, Angola and the River Congo, pp. 181–182.

141. Monteiro, *Angola and the River Congo*, p. 182.

142. Batalha, *Costumes Angolenses*, pp. 8–9.

143. Thomas, *Adventures and Observations on the West Coast of Africa*, p. 286.

144. Omboni, *Viaggi nell'Africa Occidentale*, p. 92.

145. F. A. Pinto, *Angola e Congo* (Lisboa: Livraria Ferreira, 1888), p. 126. See also Andrea Marzano, "Cantigas desaforadas e outras injúrias: o português e o quimbundo em Luanda (1870–1930)," in Ivana Stolze Lima and Laura do Carmo (eds.), *História Social da Língua II. Diáspora Africana* (Rio de Janeiro: Nau, 2014), p. 110.

146. Anônimo, *Quarenta e Cinco Dias em Angola*, p. 80.

147. Batalha, *A Língua de Angola*, p. 11.

148. Saturnino de Souza e Oliveira and Manuel de Castro Francina, *Elementos Grammaticaes da Lingua Mbundu* (Loanda: Imprensa do Governo, 1864), p. 2. For other Kimbundo words borrowed from Portuguese, see Francisco Salles Ferreira, *Explicações de Doutrina Christã em Portuguez e Angolense* (Lisboa: Typographia de Castro & Irmão, 1855), pp. 96–100. For background on the history of Kimbundo, see Jean-Pierre Angenot, Catherine Barbara Kempf, and Vatomene Kukanda, "Arte da Língua de Angola de Pedro Dias (1697) sob o Prisma da Dialetologia Kimbundu," *Papia*, 21, 2, 2011, pp. 231–252; Elisa Dias Ferreira de Azevedo, "Língua Ambunda em Foco: nos Rastros de Bernardo Maria de Cannecattim," *Fundação Casa Rui Barbosa*, 2015; Ivana Stolze Lima, "Escravidão e Comunicação no Mundo Atlântico: Em Torno da "Língua de Angola," Século XVIII," *História Unisinos*, 21, 1, 2017, pp. 109–121; Maria Carlota Rosa, "O Quimbundo em Cinco Testemunhos Gramaticais," *Confluência: Revista do Instituto de Língua Portuguesa*, 56, 2019, pp. 56–113.

149. Ribas, *Izomba*, p. 96.

150. Souza e Oliveira & Francina, *Elementos Grammaticaes da Lingua Mbundu*, p. X.

151. Oliveira & Francina, *Elementos Grammaticaes da Lingua Mbundu*, p. X. See also Amélia Mingas, *Interferência do Kimbundo no Português falado em Lwanda* (Lisboa: Campo das Letras, 2000).

152. Oliveira, *Relatório Histórico da Epidemia de Varíola*, p. 76.

153. Pinto, *Angola e Congo*, p. 136.

154. Ribas, *Uanga Feitiço*, pp. 65–81.

155. Francisco Travassos Valdez, *Six Years of a Traveller's Life in Western Africa* (London: Hurst & Blackett, 1861), p. 281; AHU, sala 12, maços de Angola, maço 1107, 1851.

156. Batalha, *Angola*, p. 61.

157. For a definition of pirão, see Ribas, *Izomba*, p. 132.

158. Valdez, *Six Years of a Traveller's Life in Western Africa*, pp. 279–281.

159. Oliveira, *Relatório Histórico da Epidemia de Varíola*, pp. 80–81; Joaquim de Carvalho e Menezes, *Demonstração Geographica e Politica do Territorio Portuguez na Guine Inferior que abrange o Reino de Angola, Benguella, e suas Dependências* (Rio de Janeiro: Typographia Classica de F. A. De Almeida, 1848), pp. 204, 206.

160. Batalha, *Angola*, p. 62. See also Batalha, *Costumes Angolenses*, pp. 52–54. For an analysis of reverie during funereal ceremonies, see Ribas, *Dicionário de Regionalismos Angolanos*, p. 53.

161. Batalha, *Angola*, pp. 59, 60, 61. See also Óscar Ribas, *Sunguilando: Contos Tradicionais Angolanos* (Luanda: União dos Escritores Angolanos, 1989).

162. Óscar Ribas, *Ilundo: Espírito e Ritos Angolanos* (Luanda: Museu de Angola, 1958), p. 28.

163. Batalha, *Costumes Angolenses*, p, 16.

164. Ribas, *Ilundo*, p. 29. See also Batalha, *Angola*, pp. 59, 60, 61. See also Ribas, *Sunguilando*.

165. Oliveira, *Relatório Histórico da Epidemia de Varíola*, pp. 84, 104. For a description of *quimbandas* in the interior of Angola, see Batalha, *Costumes Angolenses*, pp. 30–31. See BOGGPA, 319, November 8, 1851, p. 4. For the late nineteenth century, see Azevedo, "O Complexo Cultural Luandense Oitocentista," p. 113.

166. AHU, sala 12, maços de Angola, maço 1107, 1851. For the relationship between midwives and contraception, see Jaffary, *Reproduction and its Discontents in Mexico*, p. 77; Nora

Jaffary, "Reconceiving Motherhood: Infanticide and Abortion in Colonial Mexico," *Journal of Family History*, 37, 1, p. 5. See also Michele Reid-Vazquez, "Tensions of Race, Gender, and Midwifery in Colonial Cuba," in Sherwin Bryant and Rachel O'Toole (eds.), *Africans to Spanish America: Expanding the Diaspora* (Champaign: University of Illinois Press, 2012), pp. 186–205.

167. Welwitsch, *Synopse Explicativa das Mostras de Madeiras e Drogas Medicinaes*, p. 29.

168. Welwitsch, *Synopse Explicativa das Mostras de Madeiras e Drogas Medicinaes*, p. 55; "Medicinal Products which the Inhabitants of West Africa, principally Angola and its Interior use," p. 113. See Kalle Kananoja, "Bioprospecting and European Uses of African Natural Medicine in Early Modern Angola," *Portuguese Studies Review*, 23, 2, 2015, pp. 45–71. For Ghana, see Abena Dove Osseo-Asare, *Bitter Roots: The Search for Healing Plants in Africa* (Chicago: The University of Chicago Press, 2014), p. 98; Tom C. McCaskie, "'The Art or Mystery of Physick'—Asante Medicinal Plants and the Western Ordering of Botanical Knowledge," *History in Africa*, 44, 2017, pp. 27–62.

169. F. A. Pinto, *Angola e Congo* (Lisboa: Livraria Ferreira, 1888), pp. 108–109

170. "Alistamento do Bairro Nossa Senhora do Rosário, 1823–1832," BML, cód. 45.

171. Ribas, *Ilundo*, p. 45–46. For the key role that *quimbanda* played in *entambes*, see also Ribas, *Uanga Feitiço*, pp. 109–124.

Chapter 3: *Agents of Abolition*

1. "Ofício do Governador de Benguela" on November 16, 1854, Arquivo Histórico de Angola (AHA), cód. 459, fls. 51–52; "Ofício do Governador de Angola" on February 7, 1855, AHA, cód. 21, fls. 183–183v.

2. "Ofício de João Maximo da Silva Rodovalho" on November 21, 1854, Arquivo Histórico Ultramarino (AHU), DGU, 3a repartição, pasta 2760.

3. "Ofício do Governador de Benguela" on November 16, 1854, AHA, cód. 459, fls. 51–52; "Ofício do Governador de Angola" on February 7, 1855, AHA, cód. 21, fls. 183–183v.

4. "Certidão de Pedro Ferreira de Andrade" on February 19, 1855, AHU, Angola, DGU, pasta 2760, 3a Repartição.

5. Dispatch by Gabriel and Jackson on December 1, 1854, FO 84, 932, fls. 294–297.

6. Francisco Travassos Valdez, *Six Years of a Traveller's Life in Western Africa* (London: Hurst & Blackett, 1861), p. 116.

7. "Ofício de João Maximo da Silva Rodovalho" on November 21, 1854, AHU, Angola, DGU, pasta 2760, 3a Repartição.

8. "Ofício de João Maximo da Silva Rodovalho" on November 21, 1854, AHU, Angola, DGU, pasta 2760, 3a Repartição.

9. Michael Odijie, "Exploring African Abolitionism: Fante Perspectives on Domestic Slavery in the Nineteenth-Century Gold Coast," *Law and History Review*, 42, 1, 2024, p. 78.

10. Robert W. Slenes, "Malungu Ngoma vem!: África Coberta e Descoberta do Brasil," *Revista USP*, 12, 1992, pp. 48–67; Dale T. Graden, "An Act 'Even of Public Security': Slave Resistance, Social Tensions, and the End of the International Slave Trade to Brazil, 1835–1856," *Hispanic American Historical Review*, 76, 2, 1996), pp. 249–282; Dale Graden, "The Cape Lopez Africans at Maranhão: Geo-Political Literacy, British Consuls, and the Demise of the Transatlantic Slave Trade to Brazil," *Atlantic Studies*, 17, 3, 2020, pp. 302–326.

11. Consul Vines to Clarendon on January 28, 1854, in *British and Foreign State Papers (1853–1854)* (London: Ridgway, 1865), vol. XLIV, p. 1242.

12. Isadora Mota, "On the Verge of War: Black Insurgency, the 'Christie Affair,' and British Antislavery in Brazil," *Slavery & Abolition*, 43,1, 2021, pp. 122.

13. Robin Law, "Africa in the Atlantic World, c. 1760–c. 1840," Nicholas Canny and Philip Morgan (eds.), *The Oxford Handbook of the Atlantic World: 1450–1850* (Oxford: Oxford University Press, 2011), p. 595.

14. Rebecca Shumway, "Anti-Slavery in Nineteenth Century Fanteland," in Rebecca Shumway and Trevor Getz (eds.) *Slavery and its Legacy in Ghana and the Diaspora* (NY: Bloomsbury, 2017), p. 85.

15. "Periódico dos Pobres" on May 15 1855, n. 27, ano VI, p. 2.

16. "Ofício do Secretário Geral do Governo de Angola" on November 30, 1854, AHA, cód. 179, fls. 68v.–69.

17. "Ofício do Secretário do Governo de Benguela" on December 11, 1855, AHA, cód. 468, fl. 6v.

18. "Ofício do Governador de Benguela" on February 21, 1855, AHA, cód. 459, fls. 55v.–56. For a British account of the arrival of the Africans in Luanda, see dispatch by Gabriel and Jackson on February 28, 1855, FO 84, 906, 1855, fls. 107–110.

19. "Ofício do Governador de Angola" on January 7, 1851, AHU, segunda seção de Angola, pasta 17 A.

20. "Autos Crimes por Contravenção do Decreto de 10 de Dezembro de 1836" in 1854, TCB, maço 2, número 89.

21. "Ofício de João Maximo da Silva Rodovalho (Comandante do Brigue Serra Pilar)" on January 16, 1855, AHU, Angola, DGU, pasta 2760, 3a Repartição.

22. BOGGPA, 612, 1857, 7. See also John Monteiro, *Angola and the River Congo* (New York: Macmillan and Co., 1876), p. 267.

23. Report on the slave trade by Gabriel and Jackson on February 1855, FO 84, 906, 1855, fls. 95–99.

24. "Ofício do Governador de Benguela" on October 11, 1852, AHA, cód. 465, fls. 119–120v.

25. Charles Philippe de Kerhallet, *Manuel de la Navigation à la Côte Occidentale d'Afrique* (Paris: Imprense Administrative de P. Dupont, 1858), troisième tome, p. 139; Louis Edouard Bouët-Willaumez, *Commerce et Traite des Noires aux Côtes Occidentales d'Afrique* (Paris: Imprimerie Nationale), 1848, pp. 177–178.

26. "Ofício do Comandante da Escuna Conde do Tojal" on June 3, 1854, AHA, cód. 459, fls. 37v.–38. For earlier evidence of the resumption of the slave trade, see "Ofício do Secretário Geral do Governo" on January 7, 1853, AHA, cód. 176, fl. 93; "Ofício do Governador de Benguela" on January 19, 1853, AHA, cód. 465, fls. 140v.–141v.

27. Report on the State of the Slave Trade by Gabriel on February 25, 1858, FO 84, 1043, fls. 121–150. See also Discussion on the report to the project of law for the repression and punishment of the slave trade on April 18, 1866, in *Accounts and Papers* (London: Harrison and Sons, 1867), vol. LXXIII, p. 139. For an analysis of prices of enslaved Africans in Angola as it relates to Cuba, see Martín Rodrigo y Alharilla, "Beneficios y beneficiarios del comercio de esclavos en Cuba (1815–1867)," *Ayer: Revista de Historia Contemporánea*, 128, 4, 2022, pp. 112–113.

28. "Ofício do Governador de Angola" on September 21 1857, AHA, cód. 114, fls. 83v–84.

29. "Ofício do Governador de Benguela" on November 14, 1846, AHA, cód. 455, fls. 248–248v.

30. "Diário do Rio de Janeiro" on April 12 1834, n. 11, p. 4.

31. *Jornal do Comércio* on February 21 1839, n. 43, ano XIV, p. 4.

32. "Diário do Rio de Janeiro" on March 26 1838, n. 68, ano XVII, p. 4.

33. "Jornal do Comércio" on September 30, 1828, vol. IV, 234, p. 2.

34. Charles Thomas, *Adventures and Observations on the West Coast of Africa, and its Islands* (New York: Derby & Jackson, 1860), p. 277.

35. "Ofício do Governador de Angola" on May 30, 1840, AHA, cód. 15, fls. 7–7v.

36. October 19, 1827, AHA, cód. 7182, fl. 69; "Despacho do Requerimento de Caetano José" on February 21, 1829, AHA, cód. 7182, fl. 134. For other cases, see AHA, cód. 7182, fls. 117v., 146, 169; 173v. See also Mariana Candido, "Different Slave Journeys: Enslaved African Seamen on Board of Portuguese Ships, c. 1760–1820s," *Slavery & Abolition*, 31, 3, 2010, pp. 395–409; Jaime Rodrigues, "Circulação Atlântica: Idade, Tempo de Trabalho e Funções de Escravos e Libertos na Marinha Mercante Luso-Brasileira, Séculos XVIII e XIX," *História*, 34, 2, 2015, pp. 128–145; Reis, Gomes, and Carvalho, *The Story of Rufino*.

37. "Petição of Inacio Jose Silva" on April 2, 1823, AHA, cx. 138, fl. 27v.

38. "Petição de Manoel Joaquim de Noronha" on November 14, 1828, AHA, cód. 7182, fl. 116v.

39. "Ofício do Governador de Benguela" on August 29, 1829, AHA, cód. 449, fls. 171–171v.

40. Herbert Gilliland, *Voyage to a Thousand Cares: Master's Mate Lawrence with the African Squadron, 1844–1846* (Annapolis: Naval Institute Press, 2003), pp. 150–152.

41. Dispatch by Gabriel and Jackson on February 28, 1855, FO 84, 906, 1855, fls. 107–110. For further context, see Maria Cristina Wissenbach, "As Feitorias de Urzela e o Tráfico de Escravos: Georg Tams, José Ribeiro dos Santos e os Negócios da África Centro-Ocidental na Décade de 1840," *Revista Afro-Ásia*, 43, 2011, pp. 43–90.

42. "Ofício de João Maximo da Silva Rodovalho" on November 21, 1854, AHU, DGU, 3a repartição, pasta 2760. See also Mariana Candido, "The Expansion of Slavery in Benguela During the Nineteenth Century," *International Review of Social History*, 65, 28, 2020, p. 8.

43. Dispatch by Gabriel and Jackson on February 28, 1855, FO 84, 906, 1855, fls. 107–110.

44. "Ofício de João Maximo da Silva Rodovalho" on November 21, 1854, AHU, DGU, 3a repartição, pasta 2760.

45. "Carta de G. J. da Motta a Avellar [in Trindade]" on February 5, 1855, Arquivo Nacional do Rio de Janeiro (ANRJ).

46. A controversial decision, Xavier's release set Angolan officials at odds with their superiors in Lisbon. By the time Lisbon authorities directed their Angolan counterparts to issue a new warrant for Xavier's arrest, he had escaped to Ambriz. See "Ofício do Secretário Geral do Governo de Angola" on November 30, 1854, AHA, cód. 179, fls. 68v.–69; "Ofício do Governador de Benguela" on December 5, 1853, AHA, cód. 459, fls. 22v.–25v.; "Ofício do Governo de Angola" on December 4, 1854, AHA, cód. 109, fls. 138v.–139; "Ofício do Secretário do Governo de Benguela" on February 8, 1855, AHA, cód. 459; "Ofício de João Maximo da Silva Rodovalho" on May 5, 1855, AHU, Angola, DGU, pasta 2760, 3a Repartição.

47. "Ofício do Governador de Benguela" on March 11, 1854, AHA, cód. 467, fls. 153–155. See John Harris, "Circuits of Wealth, Circuits of Sorrow: Financing the Illegal Transatlantic Slave Trade in the Age of Suppression, 1850–66," *Journal of Global History*, 11, 2016, p. 415.

48. Dispatch by Gabriel and Jackson on January 22, 1856, FO 84, 985, fls. 120–122v.; "Translado de Autos Crimes" in 1857, TCB, maço 1, número 15; "Relação dos Réus Pronunciados" on September 9, 1856, AHU, segunda seção de Angola, pasta 22 A.

49. Dispatch by Gabriel and Jackson on January 22, 1856, FO 84, 985, fls. 120–122v.

50. "Ofício do Governador de Angola" on November 26, 1856, AHA, cód. 68, fls 3v.–4v.

51. Francisco Tavares de Almeida, *Memoria Justificativa do Ex-Governador de Benguella Francisco Tavares de Almeida* (Lisboa: Typographia da Revista Universal, 1852), p. 20. See also "Ofício do Comandante da Escuna Conde do Tojal" on June 3, 1854, AHA, cód. 459, fls. 37v.–38.

52. "Passaporte de José Luis Vianna" on April 26, 1839, AHA, cód. 522. In 1853, Vianna's age was recorded as 44. See "Autos Crimes por Furto" in 1853, TCB, maço 1, número 73. For an earlier trip to Rio by Vianna, see "Petição de José Luiz da Silva Vianna" on November 10, 1828, AHA, cód. 1233, fl. 116.

53. "Ofício do Governador de Benguela" on August 26, 1846, AHA, cód. 455; "Ofício do Governador de Benguela" on September 10, 1846, AHA, cód. 455.

54. BOGGPA, 204, August 25, 1849; BOGGPA, 384, 1852; BOGGPA, 384, 1853, p. 3.

55. AHA, cx. 1602.

56. "Translado de Autos Cíveis" in 1856, TCB, maço 51; "Autos Cíveis de Justificação" in 1855, TCB, maço 7, número 322.

57. "Ofício do Secretário Geral da Província de Angola" on November 23, 1846, AHA, cód. 3440, fls. 183–183v.; "Ofício do Governador de Benguela" on October 4, 1848, AHA, cód. 462, fls. 134–134v.

58. Dispatch by Gabriel and Jackson on May 21 1852, FO 84, 872, 1852, fls. 112–114; "Ofício do Governador de Benguela" on January 28, 1853, AHA, cód. 465, fls. 159v.–161; "Ofício do Governador de Benguela" on April 8, 1852, AHA, cód. 465, fls. 35–35v.

59. "Ofício do Delegado do Procurador da Fazenda Régia" on March 27, in "Autos de Tomadia" in 1854, TCB, maço 2, número 14.

60. "Ofício do Secretário de Governo de Angola" on March 7, 1854, TCB, maço 1, número 86.

61. "Auto de Corpo de Delito" on February 28, 1848, AHU, maço 888.

62. Passport on October 2, 1841, AHA, 522.

63. BOGGPA, 120, December 25, 1847.

64. "Ofício do cônsul português" in Rio de Janeiro on June 30 1849, ANTT, MNE, cx. 374.

65. "Translado de Autos Crimes," Translado dos Autos Crimes in 1857, TCB, maço 1, número 11.

66. George Tams, *Visit to the Portuguese Possessions in South-West Africa* (London: T. C. Newby, 1845), vol. I, p. 151.

67. *Almanak Statistico da Província d'Angola e suas Dependências para o ano de 1852* (Luanda: Imprensa do Governo, 1851), p. 49.

68. "Relatório de José Luiz da Silva Vianna" on January 2, 1848, BOGGPA, 131, 1848, 2; "Ofício do Secretário do Governo de Benguela" on November 3, 1846, AHA, cód. 461.

69. "Inventário de José Luis da Silva Vianna" in 1855, TCB, maço 1, num. 25.

70. "Ofício do Governador Interino de Benguela" on February 9, 1847, AHA, cód. 7183. For information on Vianna, see also Tams, *Visit to the Portuguese Possessions in South-West Africa*, vol. I, pp. 150–152.

71. "Autos Crimes" in 1851, TCB, maço 1, número 32.

72. "Petição de José Luiz da Silva Vianna" in 1854, TCB, maço 1, número 26.

73. "Relatório do Juiz de Direito da Comarca de Luanda Luiz Jose Mendes Affonso" on December 18, 1849, AHU, Pasta 16.

74. BOGGPA, 613, 1857, 7; Dispatch by Edmond Gabriel on February 23, 1859, FO 84, 1075, fls. 35–45.

75. "Sentença de Luiz José Mendes Affonso" on January 15, 1855, AHU, Angola, DGU, pasta 2760, 3a Repartição.

76. "Mapa da População Escrava de Angola" on August 18, 1849, AHU, papéis de Sá da Bandeira, maço 779; "Relatório do Governador Geral de Angola" on March 30, 1859, AHU, papéis de Sá da Bandeira, maço 825.

77. Report on the State of the Slave Trade on April 15, 1859, FO 84, 1075, fls. 94–116; "Mapa Estatístico do Distrito de Benguela" in 1860, AHA, cx. 5568. For the rise of the slave population in Benguela, see Esteban Salas, "Making Portuguese Colonial Governance: Slavery, Forced Labor, and Racial Ideology in the Interior from Benguela, 1760–1860," PhD Dissertation, University of Notre Dame, 2021, p. 106.

78. AHA, cód. 3160. See also Mariana Candido, *Wealth, Land, and Property in Angola: A History of Dispossession, Slavery, and Inequality* (NYC: Cambridge University Press, 2022), p. 146.

79. Report on the Slave Trade by Edmond Gabriel and George Jackson on February 18, 1847, FO 84, 671, 1847, fls. 99–111.

80. Ladislau Magyar, *Viagens no Interior da África Austral nos anos de 1849 a 1857*, Chapter Seven.

81. Carta de Frederico Welwitsch on August 20, 1861, in Frederico Welwitsch, "Cultura do Algodão em Angola" on August 20, 1861, *Jornal da Sociedade Agricola do Porto*, 10, 1861, pp. 31–39.

82. "Ofício do Governador de Angola" on March 19, 1838, AHA, cód. 13, fl. 38.

83. Carlos José Caldeira, *Apontamentos d'Uma Viagem de Lisboa à China*. Lisboa, Typographia de Castro & Irmão, 1853, p. 219.

84. *Revista Universal Lisbonense*, 11a da 3a série, n. 35, 1842, p. 417.

85. Report of Edmond Gabriel in 1850, PRO, FO 84/792, p. 191.

86. Report on the slave trade by Gabriel on February 11, 1857, FO 84, 1013, fls. 130–150. See also *Almanach de Lembranças Luso-Brazileiro para ano de 1860* (Lisboa: Typographia Franco-Portugueza, 1859), p. 204.

87. BOGGPA, January 15 1859, 694, 5.

88. BOGGPA, 43, 1864, 368.

89. "Ofício do Governador de Angola" on December 9, 1850, AHU, segunda seção de Angola, pasta 17 A. For further evidence on the establishment of orchella factories along the Benguela coast, see Tribunal da Comarca de Benguela (TCB), livro número 5 (tabelião Pedro Ferreira de Andrade), segundo ofício, fls. 102–102v.

90. "Ofício do Delegado do Procurador Régio" on May 24, 1856, AHA, cód. 469, fl. 39.

91. G. de Amaral (Benguela) to José Valentim Oliveira Menezes on May 12, 1858, AHA, cx. 2537.

92. "Ofício do Governador de Angola" on October 11, 1830, AHA, cód. 12, fls. 39–41.

93. José Joaquim Lopes de Lima, *Ensaios sobre a Statistica das Possessões Portuguezas na Africa Occidental e Oriental; na Asia Occidental; na China e na Oceania* (Lisboa: Imprensa Nacional, 1846), p. 74.

94. "Ofício do Governador de Angola" on October 3, 1833, AHA, cód. 12, fls. 145–145v.

95. "Ofício do Governador de Angola" on April 8, 1836, AHA, cód. 13, fls. 1–3; "Carta de Manoel da Cruz" on October 20, 1837, Biblioteca Nacional de Lisboa (BNL), cód. 600.

96. "Cópia de Representação de Negociantes do Porto" on January 14, 1840, AHA, cód. 259.

97. Antonio Joaquim Guimarães Junior, *Memória sobre a Exploração da Costa ao Sul de Benguela, na Africa Occidental, e Fundação do Primeiro Estabelecimento Comercial na Bahia de Mossamedes* (Lisboa: Typografia de F. C. A., 1842), p. ii.

98. Carlos José Caldeira, *Apontamentos d'Uma Viagem de Lisboa à China* (Lisboa: Typographia de Castro & Irmão, 1853), p. 219. For commercial relations between Portugal and African colonies, see Jorge Pedreira, "O Processo Econômico," in António Costa Pinto, Nuno Gonçalo Monteiro (eds.), *A Construção Nacional, 1834–1890* (Lisboa: Fundación Mapfre, 2013), pp. 149, 151.

99. Report on the State of the Slave Trade by Gabriel on February 25, 1858, FO 84, 1043, fls. 121–150.

100. "Portaria ao Governador de Angola" on January 10, 1844, *Annaes Maritimos e Coloniaes* (Lisboa: Imprensa Nacional, 1844), quarta série, 2, Parte Oficial, p. 18; "Ofício do Governador de Angola" on December 23, 1844, AHA, cód. 16, fls. 77–77v. "Providencias requeridas a sua Majestade por alguns Negociantes da Praça de Lisboa" in 1844, in *Annaes Marítimos e Coloniaes* (Lisboa: Imprensa Nacional, 1844), 4ª série, 3, parte oficial, p. 100; "Decreto" on July 5, 1844, *Annaes Maritimos e Coloniaes*, 9, segunda série, pp. 320–321.

101. "Requerimento dos Negociantes de Luanda" on October 17, 1848, BOGGPA, 162, 1848, 3; "Ata da Sessão do Conselho de Governo" on October 25, 1848, AHA, cód. 2856, fls. 110–112; BOGGPA, 161, October 28, 1848. "Decreto do Governo de Angola" on November 2, 1848, AHU, segunda seção de Angola, pasta 14. See also Mário António Fernandes de Oliveira, *Alguns Aspectos da Administração de Angola em Época de Reformas (1834–1851)* (Lisboa: Universidade Nova de Lisboa, 1981), p. 130.

102. Report on the slave trade by Gabriel on February 11, 1857, FO 84, 1013, fls. 130–150.

103. *Representação dos Principaes Moradores do Districto de Benguella* (Lisboa: Typographia, 1855), p. 10.

104. Monteiro, *Angola and the River Congo*, p. 267. For specific cases of individuals who owned large numbers of captives working on orchella extraction, see "Ofício do Secretário Geral do Governo de Angola" on April 24, 1850, AHA, cód. 511, fls. 218–218v.; "Ofício do Governador de Benguela" on April 15, 1852, AHA, cód. 465, fls. 54v.–55. For Mossamedes, see José Curto, "Uma Vila Esclavagista: Proprietários e seus Cativos em Moçâmedes, 1855," *Revista Brasileira de História*, 43, 93, 2023, p. 235.

105. "Auto de Corpo de Delito" on February 28, 1848, AHU, maço 888.

106. Tracy Lopes, "Punishing Crime: Jails and Confinement in Luanda, Angola, from 1836 to 1899," PhD Dissertation, York University, 2022, p. 104.

107. Tracy Lopes, "Slavery and Prison: Cases of Imprisonment in Luanda, 1857–1877," *Portuguese Studies Review*, 23, 2, 2015, p. 136.

108. Lopes, "Punishing Crime," p. 104; Tracy Lopes, "Free, Enslaved, and "Liberated" Women Imprisoned in Luanda, 1857 to 1884," *Historiæ*, 10, 2, 2020, p. 72; For Mossamedes, see Curto, "Uma Vila Esclavagista," p. 247.

109. Herbert Gilliland, *Voyage to a Thousand Cares: Master's Mate Lawrence with the African Squadron, 1844–1846* (Annapolis: Naval Institute Press, 2003), p. 161. For policing in Luanda, see Lopes, "Punishing Crime," pp. 57–58.

110. Francisco Tavares de Almeida, *Memoria Justificativa do Ex-Governador de Benguella Francisco Tavares de Almeida* (Lisboa: Typographia da Revista Universal, 1852), p. 19.

111. "Relatório de José Luiz da Silva Vianna" on January 2, 1848, BOGGPA, 131, March 11, 1848.

112. "Certidão de Pedro Ferreira de Andrade" on February 19, 1855, AHU, Angola, DGU, pasta 2760, 3a Repartição.

113. "Ofício do Governador de Benguela" on November 28, 1857, AHA, cód. 471, fl. 64.

114. *Relatório do Governador Geral da Província de Angola Sebastião Lopes de Carvalho e Menezes referido ao Ano de 1861* (Lisboa: Imprensa Nacional, 1867), pp. 82–83.

115. "Ofício do Governador de Angola" on October 15, 1850, AHU, pasta 16A.

116. "Autos Crimes," Tribunal da Comarca de Benguela, maço 1, número 67.

117. "Certidão de Pedro Ferreira de Andrade" on February 19, 1855, AHU, Angola, DGU, pasta 2760, 3a Repartição.

118. Raquel Gomes, "Códice 3256, Governo Geral de Luanda, 1854–1858, Registro de Escravos Fugidos: Problems and Possibilities," *Portuguese Studies Review*, 23, p. 27–41, 2015, p. 34.

119. "Petição dos Membros da Associação Comercial e Agrícola de Angola" on October 30, 1839, AHU, pasta 2C.

120. Petição de Manoel Joaquim Teixeira on May 29, 1839, AHA, cx. 1602.

121. "Ofício do Secretário de Governo" on June 5 1848, AHA, cód. 461, fls. 71v–72.

122. AHA, cód. 3160.

123. "Autos Crimes por Aliciar Escravos" in 1855, TCB, maço 2, número 118. For similar dynamics elsewhere in Africa, see Philip Misevich, *Abolition and the Transformation of Atlantic Commerce in Southern Sierra Leone, 1790s to 1860s* (Trenton: Africa World Press, 2019), p. 204.

124. "Ofício do Governador de Benguela" on March 7, 1852, AHA, cód. 465, fls. 21–22.

125. "Ofício do Governador de Benguela" on March 7, 1852, AHA, cód. 465, fls. 21–22.

126. "Certidão em Pública Forma" on May 23, 1857, AHU, pasta 23.

127. "Autos Crimes por Furto de Três Escravos" in 1857, TCB, maço 2, número 17.

128. José Joaquim Geraldo Amaral to José Valentim de Oliveira Menezes on August 20, 1857, AHA, cx. 2737.

129. "Requerimento dos pretos Carusombo e Antonio" on July 29, 1826, AHA, cód. 7182, fl. 6v.

130. "Ofício para o Diretor do Trem Real" on March 3, 1833, AHA, cód. 1433.

131. "Ofício do Secretário Geral da Província de Angola" on October 21, 1847, AHA, cód. 325, fl. 226.

132. Ladislau Magyar, *Viagens no Interior da África Austral nos anos de 1849 a 1857*, unpublished manuscript, Chapter 7, 13. See Éva Sebestyén, "A Sociedade Ovimbundu nos Relatórios de Viagens do Húngaro László Magyar: Sul de Angola, meados do século XIX," *Revista História: Debates E Tendências*, 15, 1, 2015, pp. 83–100. For a similar custom in Congo, see Linda Heywood, "Slavery and its Transformation in the Kingdom of Kongo: 1491–1800," *Journal of African History*, 50, 2009, p. 17.

133. "Memorial de Mucanos" on January 15, 1845, Sociedade de Geografia de Lisboa (SGL), reservado 1, pasta E (n. 2), estante 45, fls. 4–5. See also Salas, "Making Portuguese Colonial Governance," pp. 165–166.

134. "Ofício do Governador de Angola" on June 4, 1860, AHA, cód. 23, fls. 339–340.

135. "Ofício do Secretário Geral do Governo de Angola" on May 27 1856, AHA, cód. 181, fls. 34v–35; "Ofício do Secretário Geral do Governo de Angola" on July 9 1856, AHA, cód. 181, fl. 51v.

136. "Ofício do Secretário de Governo de Angola" on January 12 1859, AHA, cód. 184, fl. 26. See also *Archivo Universal: Revista Hebdomadaria*, July 11, 1859, 10 ano, 2a serie, no 2, p. 29.

137. "Carta de Eduardo" on October 3, 1866, AHU, papéis de Sá da Bandeira, maço 827. See also Sebastião Lopes de Calheiros e Menezes, *Relatório do Governo Geral da Província de Angola para o ano de 1861* (Lisboa: Imprensa Nacional, 1867), p. 19.

138. "Ofício do Governador de Angola" on June 4, 1860, AHA, cód. 23, fls. 339–340.

139. "Certidão de Pedro Ferreira de Andrade" February 19, 1855, AHU, Angola, DGU, pasta 2760, 3a Repartição.

140. "Ofício do Governador de Angola" on June 4, 1860, AHA, cód. 23, fls. 339–340.

141. "Ofício do Secretário Geral da Província de Angola" on October 14, 1847, AHA, cód. 325, fls. 220–221.

142. "Relatório da Administração da Província de Angola relativo ao ano de 1850," AHA, cód. 20, fls. 2–6.

143. Lopes, "Punishing Crime," pp. 61, 94.

144. "Ofício do Governador de Angola" on January 24, 1854, AHU, segunda seção de Angola, pasta 20. For more information about these fortifications, which had been finalized by the end of 1854, see "Ofício do Governador de Angola" on December 28, 1854, AHA, cód. 21, fls. 166v.–167. For the establishment of a pass, see Lopes, "Punishing Crime," p. 109.

145. For operations against quilombos in Icole and Calumbo, see Lopes, "Punishing Crime," p. 94.

146. Esteban Salas, "Making Portuguese Colonial Governance: Slavery, Forced Labor, and Racial Ideology in the Interior from Benguela, 1760–1860," PhD Dissertation, University of Notre Dame, 2021, p. 108.

147. "Ofício do Governador de Angola" on October 23, 1858, AHU, segunda seção de Angola, pasta 24 (1).

148. BOGGPA, 764, 1860.

149. Menezes, *Relatório do Governo Geral da Província de Angola para o ano de 1861*, p. 67.

150. José Vieira da Silva (Lucira) to Menezes on December 12, 1858, AHA, cx. 2537.

151. José Vieira da Silva (Lucira) to Soares and Narciso on December 12, 1858, AHA, cx. 2537.

152. José Vieira da Silva (Lucira) to José Valentim Oliveira Menezes on January 1, 1859, AHA, cx. 2537.

153. "Ofício do Governador de Benguela" on March 27, 1850, AHA, cód. 459, fls. 6–7v.

154. "Autos Crimes" in 1860, TCB, maço 1, número 39.

155. "Autos Cíveis" in 1859, TCB, maço 1, número 57.

156. "Ofício do Governador de Benguela" on September 6, 1856, AHA, cód. 459, fls. 84–84v.

157. "Ofício da Estação Naval" on April 17, 1854, AGM, cx. 319; Report on the Slave Trade by Jackson and Gabriel on February 21, 1854, FO 84, 932, fls. 45–53.

158. "Ofício do Governador de Angola" on January 31, 1856, AHA, cód. 22, fls. 88–89v.

159. "Ofício do Governador de Angola" on January 31, 1856, AHA, cód. 22, fls. 88–89v.

160. Report on the slave trade by Gabriel on February 11, 1857, FO 84, 1013.

161. Antonio Joaquim Guimarães Junior, *Memória sobre a Exploração da Costa ao Sul de Benguela* (Lisboa: Typografia de F. C. A, 1842), p. 7.

162. "Carta de Pedro Alexandrino da Cunha para o Visconde de Sá da Bandeira" on June 4, 1839, AHU, papéis de Sá da Bandeira, maço 825.

163. "Ofício do Secretário de Governo de Benguela" on December 3, 1853, AHA, cód. 459, fls. 20–22.

164. Campbell to Clarendon on March 27, 1858, *Accounts and Papers*, session 2, May 31–August 13, 1859, vol. XXXIV, p. 12

165. "Circular aos negociantes de Benguela" on March 19, 1850, AHA, cód. 461, fls. 22v.–23v.

166. "Ofício do Governador de Benguela" on March 12, 1854, AHA, cód. 459, fls. 32v.–34v.

167. "Ofício do Secretário do Governo de Benguela" on March 15, 1857, AHA, cód. 468, fl. 190–190v.; "Ofício do Secretário de Governo de Benguela" on May 9, 1855, AHA, cód. 459, fls. 61–62.

168. "Ofício do Governador de Mossamedes" on November 19, 1860, AHU, segunda seção de Angola, pasta 26.1.

169. Manoel Jose Correa, January 3, 1861, BOGGPA, 808, pp. 6/7; "Ofício do Governo Geral de Angola" on February 6, 1861, AHU, Angola, pasta 28; "Ofício do Governador de Angola" on April 27, 1861, AHU, Angola, pasta 28.

170. "Representação dos Produtores de *urzela* de Mossamedes" on March 24, 1860, AHU, Angola, pasta 29.

171. "Ofício do Governo Geral de Angola" on February 6, 1861, AHU, DGU-Angola, pasta 28.

172. "Representação dos Produtores de *urzela* de Mossamedes" on March 24, 1860, AHU, Angola, pasta 29.

173. Instructions sent to the Governor-General of Angola on June 14, 1855, *British and Foreign State Papers (1855–1856)* (London: William Ridgway, 1865), vol. XLVI, pp. 1021–1022.

174. Ward to Clarendon on July 28, 1855, *British and Foreign State Papers (1855–1856)* (London: William Ridgway, 1865), vol. XLVI, p. 1021.

175. Report on the Slave Trade by Jackson and Gabriel on February 21, 1854, FO 84, 932, fls. 45–53.

176. Jackson and Gabriel on January 29, 1856, in *Correspondence with the British Commissioners* from April 1, 1856 to March 31, 1857 (London: Harrison and Sons, 1857), p. 53.

177. Dispatch by H. V. Huntley on January 21, 1861, PP, *House of Commons*, vol. 61, p. 28.

178. BOGGPA, 780, 1860, p. 5.

179. "Ofício do Governador Geral de Angola" on September 12, 1860, AHU, DGU-Angola, pasta 27.

180. BOGGPA, 780, 1860, pp. 5–6.

181. "Ofício do Secretario de Governo de Benguela" on May 11, 1855, AHA, cód. 459, fls. 62–62v.

182. "Ofício do Secretário de Governo de Benguela" on May 9, 1855, AHA, cód. 459, fls. 61–62.

183. "Portaria do Governador de Angola" on January 28, 1856, BOGGPA (supplement to number 539), January 28, 1856, p. 1. See also "Portaria" of José Rodrigues Coelho do Amaral on January 28, 1856, *Correspondence with British Commissioners* from April 1, 1856 to March 31 1857 (London: Harrisons and Sons, 1857), p. 53.

184. "Decreto do Visconde de Sá da Bandeira" on September 27, 1856, BOGGPA (Suplemento), February 12, 1857, 593, p. 2.

185. "Translado de Autos Crimes" in 1857, TCB, maço 1, número 11.

186. "Ofício do Comandante da Escuna Conde do Tojal" on June 3, 1854, AHA, cód. 459, fls. 37v.–38.

187. Crabbe to the Secretary of the Navy on February 14 1857, in *The Executive Documents printed by the Order of the Senate of the United States* (first session, thirty-fifth congress) (1857–1858) (Washington: William Harris, 1858), p. 61.

188. Dispatch by Gabriel and Jackson in November 1856, fls. 395–397, FO 84, 985.

189. Miriam Herrera Jerez, "Fondeados en Sagua: el paisaje del tráfico ilegal de esclavos (1852–1858)," in María del Carmen Barcia, Miriam Herrera Jerez, Adriam Camacho Domínguez and Oilda Hevia Lanier (eds.), *Una sociedad distinta: espacios del comercio negrero en el occidente de Cuba* (1836–1866) (Havana: Editorial UH, 2017), p. 73; Adriam Camacho Domínguez, "La trata ilegal en el espacio trinitario: alijos, redes y emancipados (1852–1862)," in María del Carmen Barcia, Miriam Herrera Jerez, Adriam Camacho Domínguez and Oilda Hevia Lanier (eds.), *Una sociedad distinta: espacios del comercio negrero en el occidente de Cuba* (1836–1866) (Havana: Editorial UH, 2017), pp. 267–269.

190. Monteiro, *Angola and the River Congo*, p. 338.

191. "Ofício do Secretário do Governo de Benguela" on September 13, 1856, AHA, cód. 468, fl. 129v.; "ofício do Governador de Benguela" on September 19, 1856, AHA, cód. 469, fls. 110v.–111; "ofício do Governador de Benguela" on November 13, 1856, AHA, cx. 5443; Report on the slave trade by Gabriel on February 11, 1857, FO 84, 1013, fls. 130–150.

192. "Ofício do Juiz de Direito da Comarca de Benguela" on September 10, 1856, AHU, pastas de Angola, 22-A.

193. Dispatch by Gabriel and Jackson on November 5, 1856, FO 84, 985, fls. 398–400; "Ofício do Secretário de Governo Manoel da Silva Franco" on October 9, 1856, AHA, cód. 469, fls. 120v.–121.

194. "Ofício do Governador de Angola" on November 26, 1856, AHA, cód. 68, fls 3v.–4v.

195. "Relatório de Vicente Ferrer Barruncho" on November 26, 1856, BOGGPA, December 13, 1856, 585, pp. 3–6. See also Marques, 179.

196. "Ofício do Governador de Angola" on June 9, 1862, AHU, pasta 30, 1862. See also "Ofício do Governador de Angola" on April 24, 1862, AHU, pasta 30, 1862.

197. "Ofício do Governador de Angola" on March 18, 1857, AHU, segunda seção de Angola, pasta 23 (2). See also "Ofício do Governador de Angola" on October 23, 1858, AHU, segunda seção de Angola, pasta 24 (1)

198. "Ofício do Governador de Angola" on June 20, 1860, AHU, pasta 27; BOGGPA, 1860, 750, 5.

199. United States Ship Cumberland, December 8, 1858, in Executive Documents, printed by order of the House of Representatives (1860–1861) (Washington: Government Printing Office, 1861), p. 533.

200. Report on the slave trade by Gabriel on February 25, 1860, FO 84, 1104, fls. 234–260v.

201. "Ofício do Secretário de Governo Manoel da Silva Franco" on October 13, 1856, AHA, cód. 469, fl. 123; AHA, cód. 469, fls. 125v.–126; "Ofício do Governador de Benguela" on October 17, 1856, AHA, cód. 469, fls. 126–126v.

202. "Ofício do Governador de Benguela" on October 17, 1856, AHA, cód. 469, fls. 126v.–127; "Ofício do Governador de Benguela" on October 27, 1856, AHA, cód. 469, fls. 150v.

203. *Memoria acerca da Extincção da Escravatura* (Lisboa: Typografia Castro Irmão, 1889), p. 89.

Chapter 4: *Interlocking Networks*

1. "Ofício do Governador de Angola" on September 11, 1856, Arquivo Histórico de Angola (AHA), cód. 225, fls. 17–21. For Garrido's departure from Luanda in September 1853, when he stated that he would return to the city six or eight months later, see *Boletim Oficial do Governo Geral da Província de Angola* (BOGGPA), September 21, 1853, n. 417, p. 4.

2. BOGGPA, 674, 1858, 11.

3. BOGGPA, 1866, 7, 32.

4. Dispatch by Henry Huntley on January 24, 1861, FO 84, 1132, fls. 35–37.

5. "Ofício do Governador de Angola" on September 11, 1856, AHA, cód. 225, fls. 17–21.

6. Letter by George Jackson on September 25, 1854, FO 84, 932, fls. 219–219v.

7. Sven Beckert and Seth Rockman (eds.), *Slavery's Capitalism: A New History of American Economic Development* (Philadelphia: University of Pennsylvania Press, 2016), p. 12; Rafael Marquese, "A História Global da Escravidão Atlântica: Balanço e Perspectivas," *Esboços*, 26, 41, 2019, p. 28. For how scholars of capitalism and slavery have failed to properly credit Eric Williams's scholarship, see Harvey Neptune, "Throwin' Scholarly Shade: Eric Williams in the New Histories of Capitalism and Slavery," *Journal of the Early Republic*, 39, 2, 2019, pp. 299–326.

8. Gerald Horne, *The Deepest South: The United States, Brazil, and the African Slave Trade* (NY: NYU Press, 2007); Dale T. Graden, *Disease, Resistance, and Lies: The Demise of the Transatlantic Slave Trade to Brazil and Cuba* (LSU: Baton Rouge, 2014); Leonardo Marques, *The United States and the Transatlantic Slave Trade to the Americas, 1776–1867* (New Haven: Yale University Press, 2016); Dale Tomich, "The Second Slavery and World Capitalism: A Perspective for Historical Inquiry," *International Review of Social History*, 63, 3, 2018, pp. 477–501; John Harris, *The Last Slave Ships: New York and the End of the Middle Passage* (New Haven: Yale University Press, 2020).

9. Manuel Barcia, "Fully Capable of Any Iniquity: The Atlantic Human Trafficking Network of the Zangroniz Family," *The Americas*, 73, 3, 2016, pp. 303–324; Luis Nicolau Parés, *Joaquim de Almeida: A história do africano traficado que se tornou traficante de africanos* (SP: Companhia das Letras, 2023), pp. 176–186.

10. Jorge Gonzalez, "The Transatlantic Slave Trade and the Foundation of the Kingdom of Galinhas in Southern Sierra Leone, 1790–1820," *Journal of African History*, 62, 3, 2021, pp. 319–341.

11. Lizbeth Chaviano Pérez, "Cuba, agent formel ou informel de l'impérialisme espagnol dans le Golfe de Guinée?," *Outre-Mers*, 410–411, 1, 2021, pp. 169–184.

12. Martin Rodrigo y Alharilla, "Les factoreries négrières espagnoles des côtes africaines (1815–1860)," *Outre-Mers*, 1, 410–411, 2021, pp. 143–167. For the presence of Spanish and Cuban-born traders in Gallinas, see Gustau Nerín, *Traficants d'ànimes: Els negrers espanyols a l'Àfrica* (Barcelona: Editorial Pòrtic, 2015), chapter IV.

13. Dispatch by Gabriel and Henry Huntley on October 10, 1861, FO 84, 1133, fls. 21–33v.

14. Marques, *The United States and the Transatlantic Slave Trade to the Americas*, p. 184; Harris, *The Last Slave Ships*, p. 7; Sean Kelley, *American Slavers: Merchants, Mariners, and the Transatlantic Commerce in Captives, 1644-1865* (New Haven: Yale University Press, 2023), p. 364.

15. Harris, *The Last Slave Ships*, p. 55; Kelley, *American Slavers*, p. 365.

16. "Diário do Rio de Janeiro" on January 18, 1858, 16.

17. AHA, cód. 167, fl. 14; AHA, cód. 2570, fl. 103.

18. "Passaporte de Francisco Antonio Flores" on November 18, 1846, AHA, cód. 2514, fls. 18v.–19.

19. "Lista de Negociantes Pessoas com Circunstâncias de poderem assinar e endossar Letras" on April 23, 1846, AHA, cx. 1668.

20. "Registro de Concessão de Passaportes" on September 7, 1849, AHA, cx. 1736, fl. 18.

21. Dispatch by Brand on January 13, 1851, FO 84, 841, fls. 169–172.

22. "Diário do Rio de Janeiro" on January 18, 1858, 16.

23. Draft of Letter of Palmerston on May 19, 1852, FO 84, 876, fls. 176–178; draft of Dispatch from London to Packenham in Lisbon on May 19, 1852, FO 84, 875, fls. 22–23v.; "Circular Confidencial do Ministério dos Negócios da Marinha e Ultramar" on July 2, 1852, AHA, cód. 264, fls. 103–103v.

24. "Ofício do Governador Interino Antonio Sérgio de Souza" on September 1, 1852, AHA, cód. 20, fls. 170–170v.

25. Dispatch by Jackson on May 23, 1853, FO 84, 902, fls. 473–478v.

26. Jorge Felipe González, "Foundation and Growth of the Cuban-Based Transatlantic Slave Trade, 1790–1820," PhD Dissertation, Michigan State University, 2019, pp. 103–106.

27. Manuel Barcia and Effie Kesidou, "Innovation and Entrepreneurship as Strategies for Success among Cuban-based Firms in the Late Years of the Transatlantic Slave Trade," *Business History*, 60, 4, 2018, p. 547.

28. María del Carmen Barcia, *Pedro Blanco, El Negrero. Mito, Realidad y Espacios* (Havana: Editorial Boloña, 2018), p. 95; Parés, *Joaquim de Almeida*, pp. 178–179. See also José Antonio Piqueras, *Negreros españoles en el tráfico y en los capitales esclavistas* (Madrid: Catarata, 2021), p. 74; Alharilla, "Les factoreries négrières espagnoles des côtes africaines," p. 149.

29. María de los Ángeles Meriño Fuentes, Aisnara Perera Díaz, "Nascer Livre na Bahia de Todos-os-Santos: Um Pretexto para Reclamar a Liberdade em Cuba, 1817–1819," *Afro-Ásia*, 54, 2016, p. 300. For numbers for ships arriving in Havana from Salvador between 1811 and 1814, see González, "Foundation and Growth of the Cuban-Based Transatlantic Slave Trade, 1790–1820," p. 105. See also Parés, *Joaquim de Almeida*, p. 179.

30. María del Carmen, *Intereses en pugna: España, Gran Bretaña y Cuba ante la trata ilegal de africanos* (Aranjuez: Ediciones Doce Calles, 2021). See also Alain Yacou, *Essor des Plantations et Subversion Antiesclavagiste à Cuba* (1791–1845) (Paris: Karthala, 2010), pp. 429–443, 460–472; Rahma Jerad, *Les États-Unis et Cuba au XIXe Siècle: Esclavage, Abolition et Rivalités Internationales* (Rennes: Éditeur Presses Universitaires de Rennes, 2014), chapter 3; Karim Ghorbal, "Presión Abolitionista en Cuba: Inglaterra en el Centro de los Debates," in Aurelia Martín Casares (ed.), *Esclavitud, Mestizaje y Abolicionismo en los Mundos Hispánicos* (Granada: Universidad de Granada, 2015), pp. 63–81.

31. Graden, *Disease, Resistance, and Lies*, pp. 26–27; Michael Zeuske and Orlando García Martínez, "La Amistad: Ramón Ferrer in Cuba and the Transatlantic Dimensions of Slaving and Contraband Trade," in Josep Fradera and Christopher Schmidt-Nowara (eds.), *Slavery and Antislavery in Spain's Atlantic Empire* (New York: Berghahn, 2013), p. 216; Adriam Camacho Domínguez, "La trata ilegal en el espacio trinitario: alijos, redes y emancipados (1852–1862)," in María del Carmen Barcia, Miriam Herrera Jerez, Adriam Camacho Domínguez, and Oilda Hevia Lanier (eds.), *Una sociedad distinta: espacios del comercio negrero en el occidente de Cuba* (1836–1866) (Havana: Editorial UH, 2017), pp. 263–264; Parés, *Joaquim de Almeida*, p. 178.

32. Dispatch from Lacleay to Palmerston on January 1, 1832, in Michéle Guicharnaud-Tollis, *La Correspondence des Agents Britanniques en Poste à la Havane* (1820–1850)

(Paris: Université de Paris VIII, 1988), p. 29. For further background, see Graden, *Disease, Resistance, and Lies*, p. 118.

33. Randy Sparks, "Blind Justice: The United States' Failure to Curb the Illegal Slave Trade," *Law and History Review*, 35, 1, 2017, pp. 68–69. For further examples of ships sailing between Cuba and Brazil, see Graden, *Disease, Resistance, and Lies*, p. 27. For evidence of Spanish or Cuban born agents operating in West Africa, see Piqueras, *Negreros españoles en el tráfico y en los capitales esclavistas*, p. 156; Silke Strickrodt, *Afro-European Trade in the Atlantic World: The Western Slave Coast, c. 1550–c. 1885* (London: James Currey, 2015), p. 201.

34. Nerín, *Traficants d'ànimes*, p. 190; Barcia, "Fully Capable of Any Iniquity," p. 315. For Zangroniz in Whydah, see Robin Law, *Ouidah: The Social History of a West African Slaving Port, 1727–1892* (Athens: Ohio University Press, 2004), p. 173.

35. Barcia, *Pedro Blanco, El Negrero*, p. 95; Piqueras, *Negreros españoles en el tráfico y en los capitales esclavistas*, p. 191.

36. Luis Nicolau Parés, "Afro-Catholic Baptism and The Articulation of a Merchant Community, Agoué 1840–1860," *History in Africa*, 42, 2015, pp. 171–172. See also Parés, *Joaquim de Almeida*, pp. 183–186.

37. Nerín, *Traficants d'ànimes*, pp. 265–269.

38. Luiz Fernando Saraiva, Rita Almico, and Thiago Campos Pessoa, "Vida, Fortuna e Morte: A Trajetória de José Bernardino de Sá—Barão e Visconde de Villa Nova do Minho," in Luiz Fernando Saraiva, Silvana Andrade dos Santos, and Thiago Campos Pessoa (eds.), *Tráfico e Traficantes na Ilegalidade* (São Paulo: Hucitec, 2021), pp. 25–70. See also Walter Luiz Carneiro de Mattos Pereira, and Thiago Campos Pessoa, "Silêncios Atlânticos: Sujeitos e Lugares Praieiros no Tráfico Ilegal de Africanos para o Sudeste Brasileiro (c.1830–c.1860)," *Estudos Históricos*, 32, 66, 2019, pp. 79–100; Walter Luiz Carneiro de Mattos Pereira, "A 'Vasta Máquina' do Atlântico: O Iate Rolha na Costa Fluminense, em 1850," *Afro-Ásia*, 2022, p. 176. For Bernardino de Sá's ties with Pernambuco slave dealers, see Aline Emanuelle de Biase Albuquerque, "De "Angelo dos Retalhos" a Visconde de Loures: A Trajetória de um Traficante de Escravos (1818–1858)," MA Thesis, Universidade Federal de Pernambuco, 2016, pp. 84–86. See also João Reis, Flavio Gomes, and Marcus Carvalho, *The Story of Rufino: Slavery, Freedom, and Islam in the Black Atlantic* (NY: Oxford University Press, 2019), p. 133.

39. Report on the State of the Slave Trade on December 31, 1845, FO 84, 572, 1845, fls. 358–375.

40. Mary Karasch, "The Brazilian Slavers and the Illegal Slave Trade, 1836–1851," MA Thesis, University of Wisconsin, 1967, p. 17.

41. For Martínez's background, see Nerín, *Traficants d'ànimes*, pp. 139–145; María del Carmen Cósar Navarro, "Entre Cádiz y la Habana. Pedro Martínez y Compañia: la gran casa de comercio de esclavos en el reinado de Isabel II," in Martín Rodrigo y Alharilla and María del Carmen Cósar Navarro, *Cádiz y el Tráfico de Esclavos: de la Legalidad a la Clandestinidad* (Madrid: Sílex Universidad, 2018), pp. 229–262.

42. Report on the State of the Slave Trade on December 31, 1845, FO 84, 572, 1845, fls. 358–375. For background on Manoel Pinto da Fonseca, see Karasch, "The Brazilian Slavers and the Illegal Slave Trade, 1836–1851," pp. 13–17; José Capela, *Conde de Ferreira & Ca. Traficantes de Escravos* (Lisboa: Afrontamento, 2012), pp. 161–180; José Capela, *Dicionário de Negreiros em Moçambique (1750–1897)* (Porto: Centro de Estudos Africanos da Universidade do Porto, 2007), pp. 224–230; Arlindo Caldeira, *Escravos e Traficantes no Império Português: O Comércio Negreiro Português no Atlântico durante os Séculos XV a XIX* (Lisboa: Esfera dos Livros, 2013), pp. 307–311; João Marcos Mesquita, "O Comércio Ilegal de Escravos no Atlântico: A Trajetória de Manoel Pinto da Fonseca, c. 1831–c. 1850," MA Thesis, UNIRIO, 2019; João Marcos Mesquita, "'Comerciante par Excellence': O Mercado Ilegal de Escravos de Manoel Pinto da Fonseca," in Henrique Espada Lima, Waldomiro Lourenço da Silva Junior, and Beatriz Mamigonian (eds.), *Histórias da Escravidão e Pós-Emancipação no Atlântico (séculos XVIII ao XX)* (São Leopoldo: Casa Leiria, 2022), pp. 123–140.

43. Annual report on the slave trade by Gabriel and Jackson on February 5, 1850, FO 84, 793, fls. 91–108.

44. *The St. Helena Herald*, November 30, 1854.

45. Anne Stamm, "La Société Créole à Saint-Paul de Loanda dans les Annés 1838–1848," *Revue Française d'Histoire d'Outre Mer*, 217, 1972, p. 600.

46. Letter by George Jackson on September 25, 1854, FO 84, 932, fls. 219–219v.

47. "Bilhete de Guilherme José Correia da Silva" on April 2, 1854, ANRJ, IJ6 472; "Bilhete de Guilherme José Correia da Silva" on October 14, 1854, ANRJ, IJ6 472.

48. Dispatch by Brand on January 13, 1851, FO 84, 841, fls. 169–172. See also Henry Matson, *Remarks on the Slave Trade and African Squadron* (London: James Ridgway, 1848), p. 76.

49. Report of Edmond Gabriel in 1850, PRO, FO 84/792, p. 116; "Ofício do Governador de Angola" on October 25, 1846, AHA, cód. 66.

50. "Edital do Governador de Angola" on August 4, 1840, AHA, cód. 317, fl. 25.

51. Susan Broadhead, "Trade and Politics on the Congo Coast: 1770–1870," PhD Dissertation, Boston University, 1971, pp. 144–145; Susan Herlin, "Brazil and the Commercialization of Kongo, 1840–1870," in José Curto and Paul Lovejoy (eds.), *Enslaving Connections: Changing Cultures of Africa and Brazil during the Era of Slavery* (New York, Humanity Books, 2004), p. 262. See also Norm Schrag, "Mboma and the Lower Zaire: A Socioeconomic Study of a Kongo Trading Community, c. 1785–1885" (PhD Dissertation, Indiana University, 1985), p. 81.

52. Ana Lucia Araujo, *The Gift: How Objects of Prestige Shaped the Atlantic Slave Trade and Colonialism* (NYC: Cambridge University Press, 2023), p. 28.

53. Report on the State of the Slave Trade on December 31, 1845, FO 84, 572, 1845, fls. 358–375. See also Schrag, "Mboma and the Lower Zaire," p. 95.

54. Draft of letter by Palmerston on November 11, 1846, FO 84, 630, 1846, fls. 99–101.

55. István Rákóczi (ed.), *O Planalto do Bié: Diários de Viagem de László Magyar (1848–1857)* (Lisboa: Edições Colibri, 2019), p. 30.

56. George Tams, *Visit to the Portuguese Possessions in South-West Africa* (London: T. C. Newby, 1845), vol. II, p. 111.

57. George Slacum to Forsyth on October 16 1839, Correspondence with Spain, Portugal, Brazil, the Netherlands, and Sweden relative to the Slave Trade from January 1, 1840, to May 10th 1840 (London: William Clowes and Sons, 1840), p. 41.

58. "Registro de Feitorias pelo Brigue Vila Flor" between April 25 and June 7, 1857, AHU, segunda seção de Angola, pasta 23 (3).

59. Hugh Dyer, *The West Coast of Africa as seen from the Deck of a Man-of-War* (London: J. Griffin & CO, 1876), p. 113.

60. "Ofício do Secretário do Governo Geral de Angola" on November 11, 1856, AHA, cód. 225, fl. 85v.

61. John Monteiro, *Angola and the River Congo* (New York: Macmillan and Co., 1876), p. 267. For similar intermingling of legitimate and slave trades on the Bight of Benin, see Colin Newbury, *The Western Slave Coast and Its Rulers* (London: Oxford University press, 1961), p. 42.

62. Monteiro, *Angola and the River Congo*, pp. 84–85.

63. Schrag, "Mboma and the Lower Zaire," p. 97. See also Samba Mampuya, *Survivance et répression de la traite négrière du Gabon au Congo de 1840 a 1880* (Paris: Les Editions la Bruyere, 1990), p. 149.

64. Extract of Letter to Antonio José Moreira Pinto on May 12, 1840, *Correspondence with the British Commissioners* at Sierra Leone, the Havana, Rio de Janeiro, and Surinam relating to the Slave Trade from May 11 to December 31, 1840 (London: Clowes and Sons, 1841), p. 220.

65. Report by Jackson and Gabriel on January 25, 1853, in The Sessional Papers Printed by Order of the House of Lords (1854) (London: George Edward Eyre and William Spottiswoode, 1854), vol. XV, 79.

66. Wise to Buchanan on February 18, 1846, in *Executive Documents, Printed by Order of the House of Representatives (1849)* (Washington: Government Printing Office, 1849), p. 215.

67. Schrag, "Mboma and the Lower Zaire," pp. 64–65.

68. Lieutenant Pike to Commodore Wise on June 20, 1859, Class A, *Correspondence with the British Commissioners and Reports from British Vice-Admiralty Courts and from British Naval Officers relating to the Slave Trade from April 1, 1859, to March 31, 1860* (London: Printed by Harrison and Sons, 1860), pp. 112–113.

69. Commodore Wise to Rear Admiral Sir F. Grey on August 6 in *Correspondence with the British Commissioners* at Sierra Leone, Havana, the Cape of Good Hope, and Loanda from April 1 to March 31, 1859 (London: Harrison and Sons, 1859), p. 179.

70. Mampuya, *Survivance et répression de la traite négrière du Gabon au Congo de 1840 a 1880*, p. 215.

71. Schrag, "Mboma and the Lower Zaire," p. 82.

72. Schrag, "Mboma and the Lower Zaire," p. 83.

73. Martín Rodrigo y Alharilla, "Spanish sailors and the illegal slave trade to Cuba, 1845–1867," *Journal of Iberian and Latin American Studies*, 27, 1, 2021, p. 102.

74. St. Helena Herald, April 28, 1853.

75. Gilberto Guizelin, "De poeta a agente consular da mal-afamada 'companhia portuguesa': os vínculos entre José da Silva Maia Ferreira e a comunidade mercantil luso-brasileira em Nova York na década de 1850," in Francisco Topa (eds.), *Minha terra não tem salgueirais: o poeta angolano Maia Ferreira e a sua época* (Porto: Cátedra Agostinho Neto, 2024), pp. 31–61.

76. Félix Goizueta-Mimó, *Bitter Cuban Sugar: Monoculture and Economic Dependence from 1825–1899* (New York: Garland, 1987), p. 80; Louis Perez, *Cuba and the United States: Ties of Singular Intimacy* (Athens: University of Georgia Press, 2003), p. 13. See also Marques, *The United States and the Transatlantic Slave Trade to the Americas*, p. 109.

77. "Ofício do Secretário Geral de Angola" on September 23, 1855, AHA, cód. 113, fls. 4v.–5. See also *Tratado de Comércio e Navegação entre sua Majestade a Rainha de Portugal e dos Algarves e os Estados Unidos da América* (Lisboa: Imprensa Nacional, 1844).

78. "Tractado de Comercio entre o Governo de sua Majestade Fidelissima e o dos Estados Unidos" on January 20, 1841, *Annaes Maritimo e Coloniaes*, 7, segunda series, junho de 1842, p. 291.

79. "Diario do Rio de Janeiro" on February 5, 1838, n. 3, p. 4.

80. AHA, cód. 2359. For the entanglements of licit and illicit US trade with Africa, see Horne, *The Deepest South*, pp. 143–144.

81. Letter from Luanda on September 3, 1860, in *The African Repository* (Washington: C. Alexander, 1860), vol. XXXVI, p. 372. See also BOOGPA on April 18, 1857, n. 603, p. 11.

82. George Brooks, *Yankee Traders, Old Coasters & African Middlemen. A History of American Legitimate Trade with West Africa in the Nineteenth Century* (Boston: Boston University Press, 1970), p. 287.

83. "Diario do Rio de Janeiro" on February 5, 1838, n. 3, p. 4. See also John Guy Vassar, *Twenty Years around the World* (New York: Rudd & Carleton, 1861), p. 592.

84. BOGGPA, 1857, 599, p. 5; BOGGPA, 603, 1856, p. 11.

85. Appleton to McKeon on May 4, 1857, in *Executive Documents, printed by Order of the House of Representatives during the Second Session of the Thirty-Sixth Congress (1860–1861)* (Washington: Government Printing Office, 1861), p. 66.

86. Brooks, *Yankee Traders, Old Coasters & African Middlemen*, p. 287.

87. "Carta de Guilherme Jose da Silva Correia (Luanda) para João José Vianna (New York City)" on April 21, 1855, ANRJ, IJ6 472; "Interrogatório feito a João José Vianna" on March 7, 1856, ANRJ, IJ6 468.

88. BOGGPA, 33, 1864, p. 280.

89. The African Repository, vol. XXXII, n. 8, 1856, pp. 241–243. See also Robert Vinson, "The Law as Lawbreaker: The Promotion and Encouragement of the Atlantic Slave Trade by the New York Judiciary System, 1857–1862," *Afro-Americans in New York Life and History*, 20, 2, 1996, pp. 35–58; Sylviane Diouf, *Dreams of Africa in Alabama: The Slave Ship Clotilda and the Story of the Last Africans brought to America* (NY: Oxford University Press, 2007), p. 16; Sharla Fett, *Recaptured Africans: Surviving Slave Ships, Detention, and Dislocation in the Final Years of the Slave Trade* (Chapel Hill: UNC Press, 2016), p. 105; Kelley, *American Slavers*, pp. 360–362.

90. Appleton to McKeon on June 9, 1857, in African Slave Trade, Message from the President of the United States on December 6, 1860 (Government Printing Office, Washington, D.C., 1860), p. 67.

91. Dispatch of Parks [American Consul in Rio de Janeiro] on 4 December 1848, Americas Collection, 1811–1920, MS 518, box 5, folder 11, Woodson Research Center, Fondren Library, Rice University. See also Horne, *The Deepest South*, p. 63.

92. "Ofício do Secretario de Governo de Angola" on September 7, 1848, AHA, cód. 170, fls. 72v.–73.

93. "Ofício do Secretário do Governo Manoel da Silva Franco" on August 22, 1856, AHA, cód. 459, fls. 82–83.

94. John Machado to Lewis Cass on June 23, 1858, in *Executive Documents printed by Order of the House of Representatives* (1860–1861) (Washington: Government Office, 1860–1861), p. 110.

95. Alan Booth, "The United States African Squadron, 1843–1861," *Boston University Papers in African History*, 1, 1964, p. 86–87; Dennys Lypka, "The Slave Trade Department of the British Foreign Office and the Suppression of the Transatlantic Slave Trade, 1819–1854," MA Thesis, University of Calgary, 1977, p. 55; Marco Perry Basile, "The Slave Trade and the Foundations of U.S. International Legal Thought, 1808–1870," PhD Dissertation, Harvard University, 2016, p. 161.

96. Richard Huzzey, *Freedom Burning: Anti-Slavery and Empire in Victorian Britain* (NY: Cornell University, 2012), p. 56; Don E. Fehrenbacher, *The Slaveholding Republic: An Account of the United States Government's Relations to Slavery* (New York: Oxford University Press, 2002), pp. 168–169; John Oldfield, *Transatlantic Abolitionism in the Age of Revolution: An International History of Anti-Slavery, c. 1787–1820* (NY: Cambridge University Press, 2013), Chapter 7.

97. Andrew Foote, *Africa and the American Flag* (NY: D. Appleton & Co., 1854), p. 301. For context, see Matthew Karp, "Slavery and American Sea Power: The Navalist Impulse in the Antebellum South," *The Journal of Southern History*, 77, 2, 2011, pp. 283–324; Fett, *Recaptured Africans*, p. 21; Marques, *The United States and the Transatlantic Slave Trade to the Americas*, pp. 114–115, 128. For French opposition to the right of search, see Lawrence Jennings, "France, Great Britain, and the Repression of the Slave Trade, 1841–1845," *French Historical Studies*, 10, 1, 1977, pp. 101–125.

98. Edward Rugemer, "Slave Rebels and Abolitionists: The Black Atlantic and the Coming of the Civil War," *The Journal of the Civil War Era*, 2, 2, 2012, pp. 191–192. See also Huzzey, *Freedom Burning*, pp. 54–55.

99. Wise to Calhoum on January 12, 1845, Americas Collection, 1811–1920, MS 518, box 5, folder 11, Woodson Research Center, Fondren Library, Rice University. See also Matthew Karp, *This Vast Southern Empire: Slaveholders at the Helm of American Foreign Policy* (Cambridge: Harvard University Press, 2016), chapters 3 and 4.

100. "Despacho Reservado" on November 26 1856, ANTT, Ministério dos Negócios Estrangeiros, cx. 967, maço 5.

101. "Resumo da Fala do Ministro dos Negócios Estrangeiros de sua Majestade Britânica, Lord Palmerston" on July 14, 1851, BOGGPA, 330, 1852, p. 3. See also Beatriz Mamigonian, *Africanos livres: a abolição do tráfico de escravos no Brasil* (São Paulo: Companhia das Letras, 2017), p. 228, describing Palmerston statement as far more nuanced.

102. Jerningham to Clarendon on July 7, 1855, *British and Foreign State Papers, 1855–1856* (London: William Ridgway, 1865), p. 956.

103. Russell to Lyons on July 11, 1860, in African Slave Trade, Message from the President of the United States on December 6, 1860 (Government Printing Office, Washington, D.C., 1860), p. 441.

104. *Jornal do Comércio* on September 28, 1829, vol. IX, n. 579, p. 2. For the wider historical context, see Jaime Rodrigues, "The Abolition of the African Slave Trade in Brazil," *Oxford Research Encyclopedia* (Latin American History), 2020.

105. "Nota do Cônsul Português" on October 18, 1831, ANTT, MNE, Correspondências das Legações Portuguesas, cx. 534; "Ofício do Encarregado de Negócios de Portugal no Rio de Janeiro" on April 15, 1834, ANTT, Correspondências das Legações Portuguesas, cx. 535. See also *Diário de Pernambuco* on May 9, 1833, n. 102, p. 411. See also Tâmis Parron, "Vale Expandido: Contrabando Negreiro e a Construção de uma Política Nacional no Império do Brasil," *Almanack*, 7, 2014, pp. 145–146.

106. Mr. Fox to Viscount Palmerston on October 15, 1834, in *Correspondence with the British Commissioners* at Sierra Leone, Havana, Rio de Janeiro, and Surinam relating to

the Slave Trade (London: William Clowes and Sons, 1835), p. 35. See also Mamigonian, *Africanos Livres*, pp. 79–80.

107. Tâmis Parron, *A Política da Escravidão no Império do Brasil, 1826–1865* (Rio de Janeiro: Civilização Brasileira, 2011), Chapter 3; Sidney Chalhoub, *A Força da Escravidão. Ilegalidade e Costume no Brasil Oitocentista* (São Paulo: Companhia das Letras, 2012). For changes in politics as reflected on newspapers from Rio de Janeiro, see also Alain Youssef, "A Imprensa e a Reabertura do Tráfico Transatlântico de Africanos para o Brasil, 1831–1840," *Tempo*, 27, 2, 2021, pp. 229–246.

108. Report by João Batista Moreira on July 8, 1850, ANTT, MNE, cx. 374. For context, see Jaime Rodrigues, *O infame comércio: propostas e experiências no final do tráfico de africanos para o Brasil* (1800–1850) (Campinas: UNICAMP, 2000), pp. 171–184.

109. Palmerston to Hudson on October 15 1850, *British and Foreign State Papers (1850–1851)* (London: James Ridgway, 1863), vol. XL, pp. 366–367. For slave dealers social and political clout in Brazil, see Thiago Campos Pessoa, "Aristocracia negreira: a formação da nobreza imperial e o comércio clandestino de africanos em meados do oitocentos," *Almanack*, 35, 2023, pp. 13–23.

110. Marcus de Carvalho, "O Desembarque nas Praias: O Funcionamento do Tráfico de Escravos depois de 1831," *Revista de História*, 167, 2012, pp. 223–260. For Rio de Janeiro, see Thiago Campos Pessoa, "A Indiscrição como Ofício: O Complexo Cafeeiro Revisitado (Rio de Janeiro, c. 1830–c.1888)," PhD Dissertation, Universidade Federal Fluminense, 2015, Chapter 2. See also Marcus de Carvalho, "O Patacho Providência, um Navio Negreiro Política, Justiça e Redes depois da Lei Antitráfico de 1831," *Varia Historia*, 30, 54, pp. 777–806; Silvana Andrade dos Santos, "Nestas costas tão largas: o tráfico transatlântico de escravizados e a dinamização de economias regionais no Brasil (c. 1831–c. 1850)," *Revista de História*, 177, 2018, pp. 3–36.

111. Dispatch from Edmond Gabriel and George Jackson on August 22, 1848, FO 84, 719, fls. 254–259. See also Marques, *The Sounds of Silence*, p. 169.

112. E. L. Jackson, *St. Helena: The Historic Island from its Discovery to the Present Date* (New York: Thomas Whittaker, 1905), p. 278.

113. "Ofício" on September 25, 1848, MNE, cx. 541. See also Leslie Bethell, *The Abolition of the Brazilian Slave Trade: Britain, Brazil and the Slave Trade Question, 1807–1869* (New York: Cambridge University Press, 1970); Jeffrey Needell, "The Abolition of the Brazilian Slave Trade in 1850: Historiography, Slave Agency and Statesmanship," *Journal of Latin America Studies*, vol. 33, 4, 2001, pp. 681–711. For further context, see Jeffrey Needell, *The Party of Order: The Conservatives, the State and Slavery in the Brazilian Monarchy, 1831–1871* (Stanford: Stanford UP, 2006), pp. 138–155.

114. Hudson to Palmerston on August 5, 1848, in *British and Foreign State Papers, 1848–1849* (London: Harrison and Sons, 1862), pp. 394–395. See also Dale Graden, "An Act 'Even of Public Security': Slave Resistance, Social Tensions, and the End of the International Slave Trade to Brazil, 1835–1856," *Hispanic American Historical Review*, 76, 2, 1996), pp. 249–282; Graden, *Disease, Resistance, and Lies*, pp. 120–149; Dale Graden, "The Cape Lopez Africans at Maranhão: Geo-Political Literacy, British Consuls, and the Demise of the Transatlantic Slave Trade to Brazil," *Atlantic Studies*, 17, 3, 2020, pp. 302–326. For fear of slave revolts in Rio, see also Horne, *The Deepest South*, pp. 80–81.

115. Howden to Palmerston on March 20, 1848, in *British and Foreign State Papers, 1848–1849* (London: Harrison and Sons, 1862), p. 381. See also Thiago Leitão de Araujo, "Desafiando a Escravidão: Fugitivos e Insurgentes Negros e a Política da Liberdade nas Fronteiras do Rio da Prata (Brasil e Uruguai, 1842–1865)," PhD Dissertation, Unicamp, 2016. For overview of slave revolts preceding the abolition of the transatlantic slave trade, see Keila Grinberg, Magno Fonseca Borges, and Ricardo Salles, "Rebeliões Escravas antes da Extinção do Tráfico," in Keila Grinberg and Ricardo Salles (eds.), *O Brasil imperial* (Rio de Janeiro: Civilização Brasileira, 2009), vol. I, pp. 235–270.

116. *O Brasil: Vestra res Agitur* on August 31, 1850, n. 1647, Vol. XII, p. 2. See also *Grito Nacional* on November 29, 1848, n. 17, p. 4. See also Sidney Chalhoub, "The Politics of Disease Control: Yellow Fever and Race in Nineteenth-Century Rio de Janeiro," *Journal of Latin American Studies*, 25, 3, 1993, pp. 441–63; Chalhoub, *A Força da Escravidão*, p. 125.

117. *O Americano* on January 13, 1848, n. 36, vol. I, p. 3. See Hudson to Palmerston on August 5, 1848, in *British and Foreign State Papers, 1848–1849*, vol. XXXVII (London: Harrison and Sons, 1862), p. 392. See also Jaime Rodrigues, "O Fim do Tráfico Transatlântico de Escravos para o Brasil: Paradigmas em Questão," in Keila Grinberg and Ricardo Salles, *O Brasil Império* (Rio de Janeiro: Civilização Brasileira, 2009), vol. II, pp. 297–337.

118. Hudson to Palmerston on August 5, 1848, in *British and Foreign State Papers, 1848–1849* (London: Harrison and Sons, 1862), pp. 394–395.

119. Aline Emanuelle De Biase Albuquerque, "De Vendedor de Pão com Cesta na Cabeça" a Visconde de Loures: A Carreira Atlântica do Traficante Ângelo Francisco Carneiro," in Luiz Fernando Saraiva, Silvana Andrade dos Santos, and Thiago Campos Pessoa (eds.), *Tráfico e Traficantes na Ilegalidade* (São Paulo: Hucitec, 2021), p. 91.

120. *O Americano* on May 17, 1848, n. 72, vol. II, p. 3; *Grito Nacional* on May 4, 1850, n. 152, p. 1; *O Americano* on July 20, 1850, n. 294, vol. IV, p. 2; *Grito Nacional* on May 4, 1850, n. 152, p. 1; *O Americano* on July 31, 1850, n. 297, vol. IV, p. 3.

121. Hesketh to Hudson on September 7, 1850, *British and Foreign State Papers, 1850–1851* (London: James Ridgway and Sons, 1863), vol. XL, p. 452. For context, see Pessoa, "Aristocracia negreira," p. 10.

122. Gilberto Guizelin, "No Rastro dos Traficantes Retornados e Foragidos para Portugal: A 'Intelligencia Saquarema' no Combate ao Tráfico Atlântico de Escravos depois de 1850," *Almanack*, 30, 2022, p. 5. For intelligence gathering and anti-slave trade policies in the US, see Harris, *The Last Slave Ships*, pp. 137–183.

123. Consul Smith to Viscount Palmerston on March 19, 1851, FO 84, 841, fls. 75–77; Dispatch by the British consul in Lisbon on October 28, 1853, FO 84, 908, fls. 237–239. See also Marques, *The United States and the Transatlantic Slave Trade to the Americas*, pp. 181, 191.

124. Dispatch by the British consul in Lisbon on October 28, 1853, FO 84, 908, fls. 237–239; "Ofício de José de Vasconcellos e Souza" on July 16, 1850, ANTT, MNE, cx. 541. See Walter Carneiro de Mattos Pereira, "José Gonçalves da Silva: traficante e tráfico de escravos no litoral norte da província do Rio de Janeiro, depois da lei de 1850," *Tempo*, 16, 31, 2011, p. 288. For general context, see Gilberto Guizelin, *Comércio de Almas e Política Externa: A Diretriz Atlântico-Africana da Diplomacia Imperial Brasileira, 1822–1856* (Londrina: Eduel, 2013), p. 217; Marques, *The United States and the Transatlantic Slave Trade to the Americas*, pp. 181, 191.

125. Gilberto Guizelin, *Dois cônsules de sua majestade imperial em Luanda (1822–1861)* (São Paulo: Edusp, 2022), p. 226.

126. Extract of a dispatch of Ignacio Jose de Moraes to Edmond Gabriel on January 11, 1857, in *The Executive Documents printed by Order of the Senate of the United States (1857–1858)* (Washington: William Harris, 1858), p. 20.

127. "Ofício do chanceler servindo de consul geral brasileiro em Luanda" on February 27, 1857, Arquivo do Itamarati, 238/2/1.

128. Dispatch by Gabriel on January 29, 1858, FO 84, 1043, fls. 111–112. For further context, see Guizelin, *Dois cônsules de sua majestade imperial em Luanda*, pp. 277–289.

129. Dispatch by Gabriel on October 10, 1858, FO 84, 1043, fls. 444–446; Draft of letter to Edmond Gabriel on January 22, 1859, FO 84, 1074, fls. 1–2.

130. Harris, *The Last Slave Ships*, p. 54.

131. "Circular Confidencial do Ministério dos Negócios da Marinha e Ultramar" on July 2, 1852, AHA, cód. 264, fls. 103–103v.

132. Dispatch by Jackson on May 23, 1853, FO 84, 902, fls. 473–478v.

133. Dispatch by Jackson on May 23, 1853, FO 84, 902, fls. 473–478v.

134. Senhor de Castro to don Francisco Ruviroza, Trinidad de Cuba, on December 29, 1852, *Accounts and Papers*, Slave Trade, session 31, May 13–August 1859, vol. XXXIV, p. 33.

135. Harris, *The Last Slave Ships*, p. 96.

136. "Auto de Perguntas e Interrogatório feito a D. Francisco de Ruvirosa y Urzellas" on May 12, 1853, ANRJ, IJ6 468.

137. Memorandum in 1857, *Correspondence with the British Commissioners (Sierra Leone, Havana, the Cape of Good Hope, Loanda, and New York) and Reports from British*

Naval Officers relating to the Slave Trade from April 1, 1857, to March 31, 1858 (London: Harrison and Sons, 1858), p. 203.

138. Havana Commissioner on June 17, 1834, in *Correspondence with the British Commissioners at Sierra Leone, the Havana, Rio de Janeiro, and Surinam relating to the Slave Trade 1834* (London: William Clowes, 1835), p. 114; For Ruvirosa y Urzellas's background and earliest investments in the slave trade in Cuba, see Nerín, *Traficants d'ànimes*, pp. 247–258; Gustau Nerín, "Falsos Brasileños: las Trayectorias Africanas y Americanas de los Negreros Españoles Derizans y Rovirosa (1831–1863)," *Relea*, 1, 1, 2016, pp. 69–85. See also Pessoa, "A Indiscrição como Ofício," pp. 119–120; Guizelin, "No Rastro dos Traficantes Retornados e Foragidos para Portugal," p. 29.

139. *Her Majesty's commissioners to Viscount Palmerston on February 26, 1841, Correspondence with the British Commissioners at Sierra Leone, the Havana, Rio de Janeiro, and Surinam relating to the Slave Trade from January 1 to December 31, 1841* (London: William Clowes, 1842), p. 186.

140. List of principal slave dealers at Rio de Janeiro in 1845, *Accounts and Papers*, Slave Trade, vol. 67, 19 January–24 1847, p. 191. In Africa, his coastal establishments were run by his own brother. See "Her majesty's consul and arbitrator to the Earl of Aberdeen" on March 11, 1846, in *Accounts and Papers*, Slave Trade, vol. 67, 19 January–24 1847, p. 184.

141. Howden to Palmerston on March 20, 1848, in *British and Foreign State Papers, 1848–1849* (London: Harrison and Sons, 1862), p. 381. See Nerín, "Falsos Brasileños," p. 76.

142. "Interrogatório de Francisco Ruviroza y Urzellas" on May 11, 1853, ANRJ, IJ6 468; "Auto de Perguntas e Interrogatório feito a D. Francisco de Ruvirosa y Urzellas" on May 12, 1853, ANRJ, IJ6 468; "Carta de Francisco Ruviroza (Lisboa) para José Baptista de Souza (Rio de Janeiro)" on January 31, 1855, ANRJ, IJ6 468.

143. For the connection between coffee farms and the slave trade in Rio de Janeiro, see Pessoa, "A Indiscrição como Ofício," pp. 119–120. For such connections in the context of sugar mills in Pernambuco, see Marcus de Carvalho, "Os senhores de engenho-traficantes de Pernambuco, 1831–1855," in Luiz Fernando Saraiva, Silvana Andrade dos Santos, and Thiago Campos Pessoa (eds.), *Tráfico e Traficantes na Ilegalidade* (São Paulo: Hucitec, 2021), pp. 127–153. For similar dynamics in Cuba, see Miriam Herrera Jerez, "Fondeados en Sagua: el paisaje del tráfico ilegal de esclavos (1852–1858)," in María del Carmen Barcia, Miriam Herrera Jerez, Adriam Camacho Domínguez, and Oilda Hevia Lanier (eds.), *Una sociedad distinta: espacios del comercio negrero en el occidente de Cuba (1836–1866)* (Havana: Editorial UH, 2017), pp. 187–248.

144. "Carta de Francisco Ruviroza (Lisboa) para José Baptista de Souza (Rio de Janeiro)" on January 31, 1855, ANRJ, IJ6 468. See Nerín, "Falsos Brasileños," pp. 69–85.

145. Mr Scarlett to the Earl of Clarendon on March 26, 1858, *Accounts and Papers*, Slave Trade, session 31, May 13–August 1859, vol. XXXIV, p. 32.

146. Consul general Crawford to the Earl of Malmesbury on June 25, 1858, in Class A, *Correspondence with the British Commissioners and Reports from British Vice-Admiralty Courts and From British Naval Officers relating to the Slave Trade from April 1, 1858 to March 31, 1859* (London: Printed by Harrison and Sons, 1859), p. 170.

147. Her Majesty's Commissioners (Kennedy and Dalrymple) to Viscount Palmerston on October 7, 1846, *Minutes of Evidence taken before the Duke de Broglie* (London: T. R. Harrison, 1847), p. 171.

148. Commissioners to Palmerston on September 9, 1846, *Minutes of Evidence taken before the Duke de Broglie* (London: T. R. Harrison, 1847), p. 166.

149. Drake to Reynolds on April 23, 1851, in *Accounts and Papers (1852–1853)* (Washington: Harrison & Son, 1853), vol. 47, p. 222.

150. Crawford to Palmerston on November 15, 1851, *British and Foreign State Papers, 1851–1852* (London: William Ridgway, 1864), vol. XLI, p. 534.

151. Domínguez, "La trata ilegal en el espacio trinitario," p. 265.

152. *Jornal do Comercio*, April 13, 1837, n. 81, ano XI, p. 4.

153. Saraiva, Almico, and Pessoa, "Vida, Fortuna e Morte," p. 42. For Avellar's ties with Arsenio de Carpo, see Tracy Lopes, "Punishing Crime: Jails and Confinement in Luanda, Angola, from 1836 to 1899," PhD Dissertation, York University, 2022, p. 41.

154. Gazeta10 de julho de 1847, n. 7544, ano XXVI, p. 4.

155. Gazeta10 de julho de 1847, n. 7544, ano XXVI, p. 4.

156. "Carta de Guilherme José da Motta para Antonio Severino de Avellar (Trindade)" on October 8, 1854, ANRJ, IJ6 522.

157. "Carta de Guilherme José da Motta" on October 24, 1854, ANRJ, IJ6 522.

158. *Grito Nacional*, 19 de dezembro de 1855, n. 804, p. 2.

159. "Ofício de la Chefatura Principal de Policia" on June 21, 1853, Archivo Nacional de Cuba, Asuntos Politicos, leg. 48, numero 43. For background on the Zulueta family, see José Cayuela Fernández, "Transferencias de Capitales Antillanos a Europa. Los Patrimonios de Pedro Juan de Zulueta y Ceballos y de Pedro José de Zulueta y Madariaga (1823–1877)," *Estudios de Historia Social*, 44–47, 1988, pp. 191–211. For the *Lady Suffolk* incident, see José Antonio Piqueras, *La Esclavitud en las Españas* (Madrid: Catarata, 2011), pp. 112–114.

160. "Interrogatório de Antonio Severino de Avellar" on November 16, 1855, ANRJ, IJ6 522; "Ofício" on January 25, 1854, Archivo Nacional de Cuba, Gobierno General, leg. 427, no. 20575; "Nota" on January 28, 1854, Archivo Nacional de Cuba, Gobierno General, leg. 427, no. 20575.

161. Dispatch from the British consul in Havana on January 11, 1854, Gobierno general, leg. 427, no. 20575. See Domínguez, "La trata ilegal en el espacio trinitario," p. 265.

162. Julia Moreno Garcia, "Espanã y Gran Bretaña durante el Siglo XIX: La Abolicion de la Trata y La Esclavitud" (PhD Dissertation, Universidad Complutense de Madrid, 1984), pp. 696–733; José Gregorio Cayuela Fernández, "Los Capitanes Generales ante la Cuestion dela Abolicion (1854–1862)," in Francisco de Solano and Agustín Guimerá (eds.), *Esclavitud y Derechos Humanos* (Madrid: Consejo Superior de Investigaciones Científicas, 1990), p. 441; José Gregorio Cayuela Fernández, *Bahía de ultramar: España y Cuba en el siglo XIX* (Madrid: Siglo XXI de España, 1993); Piero Gleijeses, "Clashing over Cuba: The United States, Spain and Britain, 1853–55," *Journal of Latin American Studies*, 49, 2, 2016, pp. 229–238.

163. Crawford to Palmerston on November 22, 1851, in *British and Foreign State Papers, 1851–1852*, vol. XLI (London: William Ridgway, 1864), p. 535. See also Fernández, *Bahía de ultramar*, p. 239.

164. "Circular de la Secretaria de Gobierno" on May 28, 1856, Archivo Nacional de Cuba, Gobierno General, Asuntos politicos, leg. 220, no. 15; "Relatorio do Regente de la Audiencia Pretorial" on June 20, 1857, Archivo Nacional de Cuba, Gobierno General, Asuntos politicos, leg. 220, no. 15. For context, see María de los Ángeles Meriño Fuentes and Aisnara Perera Diaz, *Contrabando de Bozales en Cuba: Perseguir el Tráfico y Mantener la Esclavitud (1845–1866)* (Mayabeque: Ediciones Montecallado, 2015), pp. 104–127; Jesús Sanjurjo, *In the Blood of Our Brothers: Abolitionism and the End of the Slave Trade in Spain's Atlantic Empire, 1800–1870* (Tuscaloosa: The University of Alabama Press, 2021), pp. 100–108.

165. *Grito Nacional* on April 8 1853, n. 528, p. 1.

166. Consul Archbald to Earl Russell on November 17, 1862, p. 1439. For further historical background, see Marques, *The United States and the Transatlantic Slave Trade to the Americas*, Chapter 7; Harris, *The Last Slave Ships*, Chapter 5.

167. Huzzey, *Freedom Burning*, p. 57. See also A. Taylor Milne, "The Lyons-Seward Treaty of 1862," *American Historical Review*, 38, 3, 1933, pp. 511–525. For an argument that the Lyons-Seward Treaty also stemmed from internal pressures by abolitionist forces in the US, see Basile, "The Slave Trade and the Foundations of U.S. International Legal Thought," pp. 303–309. For the larger context of Anglo-American relations, see Robert Bonner, "Free Soil, Free Labor, Free Seas?: Civil War Statecraft and the Liberal Quest for Oceanic Order," in Jörg Nagler, Don Doyle, and Marcus Gräser (eds.), *The Transnational Significance of the American Civil War* (NY: Palgrave Macmillan, 2016).

168. "Ofício" on November 27, 1866, Archivo Nacional de Cuba, Gobierno General, leg. 439, no. 21267; "Expediente [written by Cuban representative in New York]" on December 29, 1865, Archivo Nacional de Cuba, Gobierno General, Asuntos Politico, leg. 227, no. 19; "Ofício" on January 8, 1866, Archivo Nacional de Cuba, Gobierno General, Asuntos Politico, leg. 227, no. 19. See also Iacy Mata, *Conspirações da Raça de Cor: Escravidão, Liberdade e Tensões*

Raciais em Santiago de Cuba (1864–1881) (Campinas: Unicamp, 2015), pp. 95–98. For the impact of the US civil war on Brazil's enslaved population, see Isadora Moura Mota, "Other Geographies of Struggle: Afro-Brazilians and the American Civil War," *Hispanic American Historical Review*, 100, 1, 2020, pp. 35–62. See also Samantha Payne, "A General Insurrection in the Countries with Slaves: The US Civil War and the Origins of an Atlantic Revolution, 1861–1866," *Past & Present*, 257, 1, 2022.

169. Circular of Governor of Cuba on May 2, 1857, in Executive Documents printed by Order of the House of Representatives (1860–1861) (Washington: Government Office, 1860–1861), p. 68.

170. "Circular Reservada" on December 20, 1866, Archivo Nacional de Cuba, Gobierno General, Asunto Politico, leg. 228, no. 1; "Ofício Reservado" on December 28, 1866, Archivo Nacional de Cuba, Gobierno General, Asunto Politico, leg. 228, no. 1.

171. Her majesty's acting commissary judge to Lord Stanley on September 30, 1868, in *Accounts and Papers*, Slave Trade, 10 December 1868–11 August 1869, 1868–1869, vol. LVI.

Chapter 5: *O Mueneputo é Dembo e Alala*

1. "Conta de Joaquim Rodrigues da Graça" in 1854, AHA, cx. 2856.

2. Joaquim Rodrigues Graça, "Expedição ao Muatayanvua: Diário de Joaquim Rodrigues Graça," in *Boletim da Sociedade de Geografia de Lisboa* (Lisboa, Imprensa Nacional, 1890), p. 368. See also Carlos Alberto Lopes Cardoso, "Ana Joaquina dos Santos Silva, Industrial Angolana da Segunda Metade do século XIX," *Boletim Cultural da Câmara Municipal de Luanda*, Luanda, 32, 1972, p. 8.

3. Francisco Travassos Valdez, *Six Years of a Traveller's Life in Western Africa* (London: Hurst and Blackett Publishers, 1861), vol. II, p. 118.

4. Carlos José Caldeira, *Apontamentos d'Uma Viagem de Lisboa à China* (Lisboa: Typographia de Castro & Irmão, 1853), p. 192; Carvalho, 568.

5. Valdez, *Six Years of a Traveller's Life in Western Africa*, vol. II, pp. 174–75; Caldeira, *Apontamentos d'Uma Viagem de Lisboa à China*, p. 192.

6. Cristiana Lyrio Ximenes, "Joaquim Pereira Marinho: Perfil de um Contrabandista de Escravos na Bahia, 1828–1887," MA Dissertation, UFBA, 1999, p. 60.

7. Vanessa Oliveira, *Slave Trade and Abolition: Gender, Commerce, and Economic Transition in Luanda* (Madison: University of Wisconsin Press, 2021), p. 35.

8. Esteban Salas, "Making Portuguese Colonial Governance: Slavery, Forced Labor, and Racial Ideology in the Interior from Benguela, 1760–1860," PhD Dissertation, University of Notre Dame, 2021.

9. Henrique de Carvalho, *O Jagado de Cassange* (Lisboa: Typographia de Christovão Augusto Rodrigues, 1898), p. 114. Historian Maria Emilia Madeira dos Santos argues his stay was so he could recover debts that the Bié ruler had with Ana Joaquina. See Maria Emília Madeira dos Santos, *Nos Caminhos de África: Serventia e Posse* (Angola—Século XIX) (Lisboa: IICT, 1998), p. 64.

10. "Memória Histórica sobre o Sertão do Cassanje pelo major Francisco de Salles Ferreira" on April 20, 1853, AHU, maço 823.

11. Joseph Miller, *Way of Death: Merchant Capitalism and the Angolan Slave Trade, 1730–1830* (Madison: University of Wisconsin Press, 1988), p. 145; Beatrix Heintze, "Translocal "Kinship" Relations in Central African Politics of the 19th Century," in Ulrik Freitag and Achim von Oppen (eds.), *Translocality: The Study of Globalising Processes from Southern Perspective* (Leiden: Brill, 2010), p. 181.

12. John Thornton, "The Expansion of Lunda: A New Look at Motivations," Jose Curto (ed.), *New Perspectives on Angola: From Slaving Colony to Nation State* (Peterborough: Baywolf Press, 2021), p. 11. See also John Thornton, *A History of West Central Africa to 1850* (NYC: Cambridge University Press, 2020), pp. 312–313

13. David Gordon, "Kingdoms of South-Central Africa: Sources, Historiography, and History," *Oxford Research Encyclopedia* (African History), 2021, p. 3.

14. "Conta de Joaquim Rodrigues da Graça" in 1854, AHA, cx. 2856.

15. Henrique de Carvalho, *Ethnographia e Historia Tradicional dos Povos da Lunda* (Lisboa: Imprensa Nacional, 1890), p. 564.

16. Graça, "Expedição ao Muatayanvua," pp. 419, 422. See Valdez, *Six Years of a Traveller's Life in Western Africa*, p. 185. See also Alfredo Margarido, "Processus de domination fondant un empire: Cas des Lunda," *Présence Africaine*, 55, p. 111.

17. Joseph Miller, "Cokwe Trade and Conquest in the Nineteenth Century," in Richard Gray and David Birmingham (eds.), *Pre-Colonial African Trade: Essays on Trade in Central and Eastern Africa before 1900* (New York: Oxford University Press, 1970), pp. 175–201; Jill Dias, "Angola," in Valentim Alexandre and Jill Dias (eds.), *Nova História da Expansão Portuguesa: O Império Africano* (Lisboa, Editorial Estampa, 1998), vol. X, p. 339; Jill Dias, "Caçadores, Artesãos, Comerciantes, Guerreiros: Os Cokwe em Perspectiva Histórica," Armando Coelho Ferreira da Silva and António Custódio Gonçalves (eds.), *A Antropologia dos Tshokwe e Povos Aparentados* (Porto: Faculdade de Letras da Universidade do Porto, 2003), pp. 17–49.

18. David Gordon, "Wearing Cloth, Wielding Guns: Consumption, Trade, and Politics in the South Central Africa Interior during the Nineteenth Century," in Robert Ross, Marja Hinfelaar, and Iva Pesa (eds.), *The Objects of Life in Central Africa: The History of Consumption and Social Change* (Leiden: Brill, 2013), p. 19. See also Jeffrey Hoover, "The Seduction of Ruwej: Reconstructing Ruund History (The Nuclear Lunda; Zaire, Angola, Zambia)," PhD Dissertation, Yale University, 1978, pp. 351–354.

19. John Thornton, "The Chronology and Causes of Lunda Expansion to the West, ca. 1700–1852," *Zambia Journal of History*, 1, 1981, p. 6; Miller, *Way of Death*; Jan Vansina, "It Never Happened: Kinguri's Exodus and Its Consequences," *History in Africa*, 25, 1998, pp. 387–403; Jan Vansina, "Du Nouveau sur la Conquête Lunda au Kwango," *Congo-Afrique*, 341, 2000, pp. 45–58; Jan Vansina, *How Societies Are Born: Governance in West Central Africa before 1600* (Charlottesville: University of Virginia Press, 2004), p. 258; Beatrix Heintze, "Translocal Kinship Relations in Central African Politics of the 19th Century," in Ulrike Freitag and Achim von Oppen (eds.), *Translocality: The Study of Globalising Processes from a Southern Perspective* (Leiden: Brill, 2010), p. 180.

20. Thornton, "The Expansion of Lunda," p. 12.

21. Thornton, *A History of West Central Africa to 1850*, p. 323.

22. Daniel Domingues da Silva, David Eltis, Philip Misevich, and Olatunji Ojo, "The Diaspora of Africans Liberated from Slave Ships in the Nineteenth Century," *Journal of African History*, 55, 2014, p. 352. See also Badi Bukas-Yakabuul and Daniel Domingues da Silva, "From beyond the Kwango—Tracing the Linguistic Origins of Slaves Leaving Angola, 1811–1848," *Almanack*, 12, p. 40. For an example of what is today a long list of scholars challenging Miller's slave frontier thesis, see José Curto, "Rethinking the Origin of Slaves in West Central Africa," in Awet Weldemichael, Anthony Lee, and Edward Alpers (eds.), *Changing Horizons of African History* (Trenton: African World Press, 2017), pp. 23–47. See also Estevam Thompson, "The Making of Quilengues: Violence, Enslavement and Resistance in the Interior of Benguela, 1600–1830," PhD Dissertation, York University, 2021.

23. Jan Vansina, *Kingdoms of the Savanna* (Madison: University of Wisconsin Press, 1966), p. 81. For tukwatas, see Jean-Luc Vellut, "Notes sur le Lunda et la Frontière Luso-Africaine (1700–1900)," *Études d'Histoire Africaine*, 3, 1972, p. 82; Thornton, "The Chronology and Causes of Lunda Expansion to the West," pp. 8–9.

24. Carvalho, *Ethnographia e Historia Tradicional*, p. 568. See also Cardoso, "Ana Joaquina dos Santos Silva, Industrial Angolana da Segunda Metade do século XIX," p. 8.

25. Antonio Gil, *Considerações sobre Alguns Pontos mais Importantes da Moral Religiosa e Sistema de Jurisprudência dos Pretos do Cosntinente da Africa Occidental Portugueza alem do Equador* (Lisboa: Typographia da Academia, 1854), p. 14.

26. Carvalho, *Ethnographia e Historia Tradicional*, p. 568. See also Vellut, "Notes sur le Lunda et la Frontière Luso-Africaine," p. 91.

27. "Libelo de Ação Comercial" in 1854, AHA, cx. 2856.

28. Carvalho, *O Jagado de Cassange*, p. 117.

29. Graça, "Expedição ao Muatayanvua," p. 368.

30. Graça, "Expedição ao Muatayanvua," p. 464; "Conta de Joaquim Rodrigues da Graça" in 1854, AHA, cx. 2856.

31. Carvalho, *Ethnographia e Historia Tradicional*, p. 571.

32. Carvalho, *O Jagado de Cassange*, p. 117. For pumbeiros, see Willy Bal, "Portugais Pombeiro: Commerçant Ambulant du Sertão," *Annali*, 7, 2, 1965, pp. 128–61.

33. "Passaporte de Helena Francisca" on October 20, 1846, AHA, cód. 2514, fl. 11.

34. Alfredo de Sarmento, *Os Sertões d´Africa: Apontamentos de Viagem* (Lisboa: Editor Proprietário, 1880), p. 33. See also Douglas Wheeler, "An Angolan Woman of Means: D. Ana Joaquina dos Santos e Silva, Mid-Nineteenth Century Luso-African Merchant-Capitalist of Luanda," *Santa Bárbara Portuguese Studies*, 3, 1996, p. 293; David Birmingham, "Slave City: Luanda through German Eyes," *Portuguese Studies Review*, 19, 2011, p. 84.

35. "Ofício do Secretário Geral de Angola" on July 1, 1847, AHA, cód. 325, fls. 171v.–172.

36. "Ofício do Secretário Geral de Governo" on January 12, 1853, AHA, cód. 176, fls. 98v.–99.

37. David Gordon, "The Abolition of the Slave Trade and the Transformation of the South-Central African Interior during the Nineteenth Century," *The William and Mary Quarterly*, 66, 4, 2009, pp. 928.

38. Vellut, "Notes sur le Lunda et la Frontière Luso-Africaine," pp. 77–78

39. Jan Vansina, "Government in Kasai before the Lunda," *The International Journal of African Historical Studies*, 31, 1, 1998, p. 8. See also Gordon, "The Abolition of the Slave Trade and the Transformation of the South-Central African Interior," p. 929.

40. "Petição de Bibiana" on May 9 1825, AHA, cx. 138, fl. 118v.

41. "Requerimento de Justiniano José dos Reis" on September 16, 1826, AHA, cód. 7182, fl. 18.

42. February 4, 1828, AHA, cód. 7182, fl. 81v.

43. David Gordon, "The Quotidian Politics of a Love Story: Researching, Assembling, and Mobilizing the Lunda Legend in the Late Nineteenth Century," *Journal of African History*, 64, 2, 2023, pp. 209–228. See also Vansina, *Kingdoms of the Savanna*, pp. 78–79.

44. Hoover, "The Seduction of Ruwej," pp. 112–113, 237.

45. Manuela Palmeirim, "Of Alien Kings and Ancestral Chiefs: An Essay on the Ideology of Kingship among the Aruwund" (London: SOAS, 1994), p. 44.

46. Carvalho, *Ethnographia e Historia Tradicional*, pp. 540, 550, 586.

47. J. C. Feo Cardozo de Castello Branco e Torres, *Memoria Contendo a Biographia do Vice Almirante Luiz da Motta Feo e Torres. A Historia dos Governadores e Capitaens Generaes de Angla, desde 1575 até 1825. Descripção Geographica e Politica dos Reinos de Angola e de Benguella* (Paris: Fantin, Paris, 1825), pp. 300–301. See also François Bontinck, "Le voyage des pombeiros: essai de reinterpretation," *Cultures au Zaire et en Afrique*, 5, 1974, p. 46.

48. "Carta do Governador de Angola" on January 22, 1808, AHA, cód. 240, fls. 60–61; "Carta do Governador de Angola" on December 5, 1808, AHA, cód. 240, fls. 69v–70v.

49. "Conta de Joaquim Rodrigues da Graça" in 1854, AHA, cx. 2856.

50. "Conta de Joaquim Rodrigues da Graça" in 1854, AHA, cx. 2856.

51. "Ofício do Governador de Angola" on March 7, 1843, AHA, cód. 16, fl. 4v.

52. "Conta de Joaquim Rodrigues da Graça" in 1854, AHA, cx. 2856. For Graça's appointment as Sargento Mor of Golungo Alto, see "Portaria do Ministério da Marinha e Ultramar" on June 21, 1843, AHA, cód. 521, fl. 20.

53. "Ofício do Governador de Angola" on March 7, 1843, AHA, cód. 16, fl. 4v.

54. For Lang's appointment, see Decreto Régio on August 17, 1838, AHA, cód. 259, fl. 6. See also "Relatório do Ministério do Ultramar" in 1840, in *Annaes Marítimos e Coloniaes* (Lisboa: Imprensa Nacional, 1841), p. 157.

55. George Tams, *Visit to the Portuguese Possessions in South-West Africa* (London: T. C. Newby, 1845).

56. Lászlo Magyar, *O Planalto do Bié: Diários de Viagem (1848–1857)* (Lisboa: Edições Colibri, 2019). For an assessment, see Manuel Pinheiro Chagas, *As Colónias Portuguezas no Século XIX: 1811 a 1890* (Lisboa: Livraria de A. M. Pereira, 1891), p. 116. See also N. de Kun, "La vie et le voyage de Ladislas Magyar dans l'intérieur du Congo en 1850–1852," *Bulletin des Sceances de l'Académie Royale des Sciences d'Outre-Mer*, 6, 1960, pp. 605–636; Éva Sebestyén,

"A Sociedade Ovimbundu nos Relatórios de Viagens do Húngaro László Magyar: Sul de Angola, meados do século XIX," *Revista História: Debates E Tendências*, 15, 1, 2015, pp. 83–100.

57. For Welwitsch's appointment, see "Decreto do Conselho Ultramarino" on August 1 1853, in *Annaes do Conselho Ultramarino*, parte official, 1854, vol. I, p. 125. For Magyar's appointment, see Annaes do Conselho Ultramarino, parte official, 1854, vol. I, p. 169. For contemporaneous assessments of Welwitsch's explorations, see *Archivo Universal: Revista Hebdomadaria*, August 29 1859, 10 ano, 2a serie, no 9, p. 137; Annaes do Conselho Ultramarino, parte não oficial, serie IV, junho 1863, p. 49–50. See also Bernardino Antonio Gomes, "As Explorações Phyto-Geographicas da Africa Tropical, e em Especial as da Guiné Inferior, ordenadas pelo Governo Portuguez e Executadas pelo Dr. Friederich Welwitsch nos annos 1854 a 1863," *Jornal de Sciencias Mathematicas, Physicas e Naturaes* (Lisbon: Typographia da Academia, 1884), pp. 151–194. For a recent assessment, see Diogo Ramada Curto, *O Colonialismo Português em África de Livingstone a Luandino* (Lisboa: Edições 70, 2020), pp. 33–34.

58. Frederico Welwitsch, *Synopse Explicativa das Amostras de madeiras e Drogas Medicinaes e de Outros Objectos mormente Ethnographicos colligidos na Provincia de Angola* (Lisboa, Imprensa Nacional, 1862); Frederico Welwitsch, "Cultura do Algodão em Angola" on August 20, 1861, *Jornal da Sociedade Agricola do Porto*, 10, 1861, pp. 285–294; *O Archivo Rural: Jornal de Agricultura, Artes e Sciencias Correlativas* (Lisboa: Typ. da Sociedade Typographicas Franco-Portugueza, 1862), vol. IV, p. 268; Frederico Welwitsch, "Jardins d'acclimatação na Madeira e Angola na Africa Austro-Occidental," in *O Instituto: Jornal Scientifico e Litterario* (Coimbra: Imprensa da Universidade, 1855), vol. III, p. 126; "Ofício de Frederico Welwitsch para o Prelado da Universidade de Coimbra" on January 15, 1859, in *O Instituto: Jornal Scientifico e Litterario* (Coimbra: Imprensa da Universidade, 1859), pp. 178–179.

59. "Ofício do Governador de Angola" on April 30, 1839, AHA, cód. 14, fls. 16v–17v. See also Maria Emília Madeira dos Santos, *Viagens de Exploração Terrestre dos Portugueses em África* (Lisboa: Centro de Estudos de História e Cartografia Antiga, 1988), p. 231.

60. "Ofício do Governador de Angola" on March 7, 1843, AHA, cód. 16, fl. 4v.

61. Vellut, "Notes sur le Lunda et la Frontière Luso-Africaine," p. 94; Jean-Luc Vellut, "Relations Internationales du Moyen-Kwango et de l'Angola dans la Deuxième Moitié du XVIIIe Siècle (c. 1750–1810)," *Études d'histoire africaine*, 1, 1970, p. 94. See also Miller, *Way of Death*.

62. Castello Branco e Torres, *Memoria Contendo a Biographia do Vice Almirante Luiz da Motta Feo e Torres*, p. 299. See also Ilídio do Amaral and Ana Amaral, "A Viagem dos Pombeiros Angolanos Pedro João Baptista e Amaro José entre Mucari (Angola) e Tete (Moçambique), em Princípios do Século XIX, ou a História da Primeira Travessia da África Central," *Garcia da Orta*, 9, 1–22, 1984, p. 19. For the enduring impact of such stories as late as the second half of the nineteenth century, see Carvalho, *O Jagado de Cassange*, p. 107; Beatrix Heintze, "Long-distance Caravans and Communication beyond the Kwango (c. 1850–1890)," in Beatrix Heintze and Achim von Oppen (eds.), *Angola on the Move: Transport Routes, Communications and History* (Frankfurt: Verlag Otto Lembeck, 2008), pp. 144–163.

63. "Carta do Governador de Angola" on November 17 1790, cód. 12289, fls. 38–41v. For further background, see Jean-Luc Vellut, "Le Royaume de Cassange et les Reseaux Luso-Africains (ca. 1750–1810)," *Cahiers d'Études Africaines*, 57, 1975, pp. 117–136; Thornton, *A History of West Central Africa to 1850*, p. 329.

64. "Carta do Governador de Angola" on August 17 1812, AHA, cód. 240, fls. 87–87v.

65. "Carta do Governador de Angola" on December 24 1814, AHA, 104, fl. 53.

66. "Carta do Governador de Angola" on November 8 1816, AHA, cód. 93, fls. 10–10v.

67. "Oficio do Governador de Angola" on April 20, 1839, AHA, cód. 14, fls. 10v.–11.

68. Tito Omboni, *Viaggi nell'Africa Occidentale* (Milano: Civelli, 1846), p. 101.

69. David Birmingham, "Slave City: Luanda through German Eyes," *Portuguese Studies Review*, 19, 2011, p. 83.

70. "Registro de Concessão de Passaporte" on September 21, 1849, AHA, cx. 1736, fl. 19v.–20. See also Vanessa Oliveira, "Donas, Pretas Livres e Escravas em Luanda (Séc. XIX)," *Estudos Ibero-Americanos*, 44, 3, 2018, p. 450.

71. Oliveira, *Slave Trade and Abolition*, p. 34 Vanessa Oliveira, "Gender, Foodstuff Production and Trade in Late-Eighteenth Century Luanda," *African Economic History*, 43, 2015, pp. 57–81.

72. "Carta do Governador de Angola" on September 10 1825, AHA, cód. 157, fls. 192–192v.

73. José Curto, "Um olhar sobre o mercado Luandense de escravizados, 1819–1822," *Portuguese Studies Review*, 30, 2, 2022, p. 79. For Santos Silva's early career, see also Arlindo Caldeira, *Escravos e Traficantes no Império Português: O Comércio Negreiro Português no Atlântico durante os Séculos XV a XIX* (Lisboa: Esfera dos Livros, 2013), p. 281.

74. Oliveira, *Slave Trade and Abolition*, p. 34.

75. "Ofício do Vice-Cônsul Português no Rio de Janeiro" on April 24, 1843, AHA, cx. 1479.

76. For Marinho's trip to Luanda, see APEB, seção colonial e provincial, polícia, registro de passaportes (1834–1837), maço 5883, fl. 118v. I thank Carlos Francisco da Silva Júnior for sharing this document with me.

77. Alex Borucki, "The 'African Colonists' of Montevideo: New Light on the Illegal Slave Trade to Rio de Janeiro and the Río de la Plata (1830–42)," *Slavery & Abolition*, 30, 3, 2009, pp. 427–444; Florencia Thul Charbonnier, "Traficantes y Saladeristas: los brasileños y sus prácticas continuadoras del tráfico de esclavos en Montevideo en el marco de la abolición, 1830–1852," in Florencia Guzmán and María de Lourdes Ghidoli (eds.), *El asedio a la libertad: abolición y posabolición de la esclavitud en el Cono sur* (Buenos Aires: Editorial Biblos, 2020), pp. 211–235.

78. "Ofício do Secretário Geral da Província de Angola" on January 17, 1846, AHA, cód. 104, fls. 132–132v.

79. BOGGPA, January 27, 1849, 174, p. 4.

80. "Ofício do Secretário Geral da Província de Angola" on July 23, 1847, AHA, cód. 325, fl. 180.

81. "Ofício do Secretário Geral da Província de Angola" on September 17, 1847, AHA, cód. 325, fl. 207v.

82. "Ofício do Secretário Geral da Província de Angola" on September 17, 1847, AHA, cód. 325, fl. 207.

83. "Carta do Governador de Angola" on June 25 1829, AHA, cód. 97, fls. 16v–17. For other female money-lenders in Luanda, see Vanessa Oliveira, "The Gendered Dimension of Trade: Female Traders in Nineteenth Century Luanda," *Portuguese Studies Review*, 23, 2, 2015, p. 119; Oliveira, "The Business of Self-Endowment," p. 230.

84. "Ofício do Secretário Geral da Província de Angola" on August 8, 1846, AHA, cód. 325, fl. 16.

85. BOGGPA, July 10, 1852, 354, fl. 6.

86. "Ofício do Secretário Geral da Província de Angola" on May 28, 1855, AHA, cód. 179, fl. 213v. For other cases of businesswomen supplying foods to the Luanda market, see Oliveira, "The Gendered Dimension of Trade," p. 110.

87. "Diário do Rio de Janeiro" on January 9, 1822, n. 7, p. 1.

88. "Diário do Rio de Janeiro" on February 20, 1822, n. 16, p. 64.

89. *Representação dos Principaes Moradores do Districto de Benguella* (Lisboa: Typographia, 1855), p. 72.

90. BOGGPA, 1862, n. 894, November 22, 1862, fl. 333–4; and BOGGPA, 1864, n. 6, Fevereiro 6, 1864, fl. 55. For further background on Tereza Barruncho, see Candido, *Wealth, Land, and Property in Angola*, p. 86. For Barruncho's properties in Benguela, see Aida Freudenthal, *Arimos e Fazendas: a Transição Agrária em Angola, 1850–1880* (Luanda: Chá de Caxinde, 2005), p. 213.

91. Vanessa Oliveira, "The Business of Self-Endowment: Women Merchants, Wealth and Marriage in Nineteenth-Century Luanda," in Jennifer Aston and Catherine Bishop (eds.), *Female Entrepreneurs in the Long Nineteenth Century: A Global Perspective* (NYC: Palgrave, 2020), p. 228. For inheritance laws in the Portuguese colonial world, see Mariana Dantas, "Succession of Property, Sales of Meação, and the Economic Empowerment of Widows of African Descent in Colonial Minas Gerais, Brazil," *Journal of Family History*, 39, 3, 2014, p. 223; Vanessa Oliveira, "Spouses & Commercial Partners: Immigrant Men & Locally Born Women in Luanda 1831–1859," in Mariana Candido and Adam Jones (eds.), *African Women in the Atlantic World: Property, Vulnerability & Mobility, 1660–1880* (Suffolk: Boydell & Brewer, 2019), p. 225.

92. "Cópia de Carta Régia dirigida ao Governador de Angola" on June 18, 1799, AHA, cód. 255, fls. 16v.–17.

93. Petition by Delfina de Miranda Brito Vieira on May 10, 1838, in José Antonio de Miranda Vieira, *Exposição dirigida a sua Majestade a senhora D. Maria I* (Lisboa: A. J. C. Da Cruz, 1839), p. 48; Vieira, *Exposição dirigida a sua Majestade a senhora D. Maria I*, p. 41. For further information on Dona Delfina's background, see Anne Stamm, "La Societé Créole à Saint-Paul de Loanda dans les Annés 1838–1848," *Revue Française d'Histoire d'Outre Mer*, 217, 1972, p. 601.

94. "Ofício do Governador de Angola" on April 8, 1836, AHA, cód. 13, fls. 10v.–12v.

95. "Ofício do Conselho de Governo de Angola" on December 22, 1842, AHA, cód. 15, fls. 143–144; "Ofício do Secretário Geral da Província de Angola" on May 15, 1849, AHA, cód. 171, fl. 156v.; "Ofício do Secretário Geral da Província de Angola" on October 16, 1850, AHA, cód. 174, fl. 126v. See also Wheeler, "An Angolan Woman of Means," p. 291; José Manuel de Azevedo, "A Colonização do Sudoeste Angolano: do Deserto do Namibe ao Planalto da Huíla, 1849–1900," PhD Dissertation, University of Salamanca, 2014, pp. 68, 70, 73.

96. Report on the slave trade by Edmond Gabriel and George Jackson on February 18, 1847, FO 84, 671, fls. 99–11.

97. Caldeira, *Apontamentos d'Uma Viagem de Lisboa à China*, p. 211.

98. BGGPA, September 12, 1846, n. 53. See also Wheeler, "An Angolan Woman of Means," p. 294.

99. BOGGPA, 254, August 10, 1850, p. 3; "Relatório da Visita feita aos Distritos do Bengo, Icolo, Barra do Dande e Alto Dande" on August 28, 1850, AHU, papéis de Sá da Bandeira, maço 823; "Ofício do Governador de Angola" on August 8, 1851, AHA, cód. 20, fls. 62v.–63. See also Oliveira, "The Gendered Dimension of Trade," p. 117.

100. José Curto, "Women along the Catumbela River, 1797: Land Ownership, Agricultural Production, Labour and Trade," *Canadian Journal of African Studies*, 54, 3, 2020, p. 8. See also Esteban Salas, "Women & Food Production: Agriculture, Demography & Access to Land in Late Eighteenth-Century Catumbela," in Mariana Candido and Adam Jones (eds.), *African Women in the Atlantic World: Property, Vulnerability & Mobility, 1660–1880* (Suffolk: Boydell & Brewer, 2019), pp. 55–69.

101. Annaes do Conselho Ultramarino, Parte Official, Serie 1, fevereiro de 1854 a dezembro de 1858 (Lisboa: Imprensa Nacional, 1867), p. 293.

102. Report on the slave trade by Edmond Gabriel and George Jackson on February 18, 1847, FO 84, 671, fls. 99–11.

103. "Ofício do Secretário de Governo de Angola" on September 10, 1846, AHA, cód. 325, fls. 38–38v.

104. "Ofício do Governador de Angola" on July 5, 1839, AHA, cód. 14, p. 1v.–2v. See also "Relatório do Ministério do Ultramar" in 1840, in *Annaes Marítimos e Coloniaes* (Lisboa: Imprensa Nacional, 1841), p. 157.

105. "Representação de José Augusto da Silva Neves" on October 30, 1840, AHU, segunda seção de Angola, pasta 3 C. See also Francisco Salles Ferreira, "Memória sobre o Presidio de Pungo Andongo," in *Annaes Maritimos e Coloniaes*, n. 4, 6 série, 1846, p. 115.

106. BOGGPA, 254, August 10, 1850, p. 3. See also Cardoso, "Ana Joaquina dos Santos Silva, Industrial Angolana da Segunda Metade do século XIX," p. 6.

107. Caldeira, *Apontamentos d'Uma Viagem de Lisboa à China*, p. 211.

108. BOGGPA, February 9, 1856, 541, p. 4.

109. BOGGPA, April 4, 1857, 601, 9.

110. For women's investment in commercial agriculture as a catalyst for the growth of slavery in Benguela, see Mariana Candido, "The Expansion of Slavery in Benguela During the Nineteenth Century," *International Review of Social History*, 65, 28, p. 23.

111. "Ofício do Governador de Angola" on November 14, 1846, AHA, cód. 16, fls. 239–239v.

112. Valdez, *Six Years of a Traveller's Life in Western Africa*, p. 277. See also Tracy Lopes, "The "Mine of Wealth at the Doors of Loanda": Agricultural Production and Gender in the Bengo," in Ana Cristina Roque e Maria Manuel Torrão (eds.) *O Colonialismo Português: Novos Rumos da Historiografia dos PALOP* (Porto: Ediçõs Húmus, 2013), pp. 181, 190.

113. For a brief sample of the multiple positions that Antonio Lopes Silva and Manoel Francisco Alves de Brito held in Angola's colonial society, see AHA, cód. 2856, fls. 93–96; "Ata da Sessão do Conselho do Governo" on October 25, 1847, AHA, cód. 2856, fls. 110–112. For Brito's return to Brazil, see BOGGPA, July 15, 1854, 459, p. 1.

114. "Conta de Joaquim Rodrigues da Graça" in 1854, AHA, cx. 2856.

115. "Contrato entre Ana Joaquin dos Santos Silva e Joaquim Rodrigues da Graça" on March 20, 1843, cx. 2856.

116. "Carta de Joaquim Rodrigues Graça" on March 2, 1864, BOGGPA, 11, 1864, 97. See also BOGGPA, May 9, 1863, 19. For the quality of cocoa produced in Angola, see the analysis of German naturalist Frederic Welwitsch, then working for the Angolan government, in BOGGPA, May 16, 1863, 20, p. 156.

117. Alan de Carvalho Souza, "Do Brasil para África: O Café na Viragem do Império Português (1807–1850)," PhD Dissertation, Programa Universitário de Doutoramento em História (Universidade de Lisboa, ISCTE, Universidade Católica Portuguesa, Universidade de Évora), 2020, p. 282.

118. "Portaria Circular do Conselho do Governo" on April 3, 1839, AHA, cód. 101, fls. 90v–91.

119. Souza, "Do Brasil para África," p. 282. See Freudenthal, *Arimos e Fazendas*, p. 176.

120. Marta Macedo, "Coffee on the move: technology, labour and race in the making of a transatlantic plantation system," *Mobilities*, 16, 2, 2021, pp. 262–272.

121. BGGPA, November 1, 1845.

122. José de Almeida Santos, "Perspectivas da Agricultura de Angola em Meados do Século XIX: Pedro Alexandrino da Cunha e o Pioneiro do Cazengo," *Anais da Academia Portuguesa de História*, 36, 2, 1998, pp. 135–138; Freudenthal, *Arimos e Fazendas*, pp. 168–169; Souza, "Do Brasil para África," pp. 238–239, 258–269.

123. "Carta de Boaventura de Lemos Simeão" on February 29, 1840, AHA, cód. 101, fls. 141v–142; "Ofício" on September 2 1845, AHA, cx. 146, frag. de códs; BGGPA, January 17, 1846, 19, p. 1. See also Freudenthal, *Arimos e Fazendas*, p. 169.

124. Freudenthal, *Arimos e Fazendas*, p. 170.

125. BGGPA, June 19 1847, n. 3; "Ofício" on September 2 1845, AHA, cx. 146, frag. de códs. See also Souza, "Do Brasil para África," p. 257.

126. Report of Edmond Gabriel in 1850, PRO, FO 84/792, p. 142. See also Freudenthal, *Arimos e Fazendas*, p. 178.

127. Freudenthal, *Arimos e Fazendas*, p. 169.

128. "Ofício do Secretário Geral do Governo de Angola" on December 8, 1846, AHA, cód 325, fls. 87v.–88. See also Lopes, "The 'Mine of Wealth at the Doors of Loanda,'" p. 186.

129. "Portaria Régia" in 1850, AHA, cód. 1178, fls. 116v.–129.

130. "Instruçãos para o Governador de Angola" on November 4, 1838, AHA, cód. 259, fls. 225–231v. See also BOGGPA, January 26 1856, 539, pp. 4–5.

131. "Ofício do Secretário de Governo de Angola" on November 10, 1849, AHA, cód. 107, fl. 151.

132. Freudenthal, *Arimos e Fazendas*, p. 174.

133. "Ofício do Secretário de Governo de Angola" on January 7, 1851, AHA, cód. 108. For other coffee investors in Cazengo, see Souza, "Do Brasil para África," pp. 276–280.

134. BOGGPA, March 15, 1856, 546, pp. 5–7.

135. BOGGPA, June 18, 1853, 403, p. 4; BOGGPA, April 26, 1857, 656, p. 4.

136. BOGGPA, July 4, 1863, 27, p. 210.

137. BOGGPA, January 13, 1855, 485, pp. 5–8.

138. BOGPPA, January 26, 1856, 539, pp. 4–5.

139. David Livingstone, *Missionary Travels and Researches in South Africa* (New York: Harper & Brothers Publishers, 1858), p. 435.

140. BOGGPA, May 30, 1863, 22, p. 174. For background, see Souza, "Do Brasil para África," p. 253; Jelmer Vos, "What Angolans got for their coffee: connecting histories of labour and consumption in colonial Africa, c. 1860–1960," in Devyani Gupta & Purba Hossain (eds.), *Across Colonial Lines: Commodities, Networks and Empire Building* (London: Bloomsbury Academic, 2023), p. 160.

141. "Instruções para o governador Antonio Manoel de Noronha" on October 3, 1838, AHA, cód. 259.

142. "Mapa da População Escrava de Angola" on August 18, 1849, AHU, papéis de Sá da Bandeira, maço 779; "Nota demonstrativa" on February 11, 1856, AHU, papéis de Sá da Bandeira, maço 822. See also Jelmer Vos and Paulo Teodoro de Matos, "The Demography of Slavery in the Coffee Districts of Angola, c. 1800–70," *Journal of African History*, 2021, p. 14. For similar dynamics elsewhere in Angola, see Lopes, "The 'Mine of Wealth at the Doors of Loanda,'" p. 184.

143. "Ofício do Secretário Geral da Província de Angola" on August 29, 1846, AHA, cód. 325, fls. 30v.–31.

144. "Petição de Joaquim Rodrigues Graça" in 1854, AHA, cx. 2856.

145. "Conta de Joaquim Rodrigues da Graça" in 1854, AHA, cx. 2856.

146. "Despacho de Juiz de Paz" on April 24, 1854, AHA, cx. 2856. See also BOGGPA, November 23, 1850, n. 269, p. 1.

147. "Ofício do Secretário Geral da Província de Angola" on May 18, 1853, AHA, cód. 177, fl. 43v.

148. BOGGPA, March 18, 1848, 132.

149. BOGGPA, June 17, 1848, n. 142, p. 4.

150. BOGGPA, April 8, 1848, 135, p. 4.

151. BOGGPA, June 25, 1849 (suplemento), p. 4; BOGGPA, January 12, 1850, n. 224, p. 2.

152. BOGGPA, March 3, 1849, n. 179, p. 4; BOGGPA, December 8, 1849, n. 219, p. 4. See also Candido, *Wealth, Land, and Property in Angola*, p. 130.

153. Cardoso, "Ana Joaquina dos Santos Silva, Industrial Angolana da Segunda Metade do século XIX," p. 9.

154. BOGGPA, January 26, 1856, 539, fl. 6. For further details about the dispute between Ana Joaquina and her daughter, see Tracy Lopes, "Continuities between the Slave Trade, "Legitimate" Commerce, and the Serviçal Trade: a Look at Four Families in Angola in the Mid- to Late Nineteenth Century," *Canadian Journal of African Studies*, 58, 3, 2024, p. 561.

155. BOGGPA, February 2, 1856, 540, fl. 8.

156. "Ofício do Governador de Angola" on June 4, 1860, AHA, cód. 23, fls. 339–340.

157. Heintze, "Translocal "Kinship" Relations in Central African Politics of the 19th Century," p. 193.

158. Graça, "Expedição ao Muatayanvua: Diário de Joaquim Rodrigues Graça," p. 368.

159. Carvalho, *Ethnographia e Historia Tradicional*, p. 519.

160. Graça, "Expedição ao Muatayanvua," p. 432; Carvalho, *Ethnographia e Historia Tradicional*, p. 519. See also Thornton, *A History of West Central Africa*, pp. 18–21.

161. Graça, "Expedição ao Muatayanvua," p. 368.

162. Graça, "Expedição ao Muatayanvua," p. 444; "Conta de Joaquim Rodrigues da Graça" in 1854, AHA, cx. 2856. See also Valdez, *Six Years of a Traveller's Life in Western Africa*, vol. II, p. 202.

163. Hoover, "The Seduction of Ruwej," p. 341.

164. Carvalho, *Ethnographia e Historia Tradicional*, p. 567.

165. Henrique Dias de Carvalho, *A Lunda: ou os Estados do Muatiânvua* (Lisboa: Adolpho, Modesto & Ca, 1890), p. 16.

166. Carvalho, *Ethnographia e Historia Tradicional*, p. 556.

167. Carvalho, *Ethnographia e Historia Tradicional*, pp. 577–578. See Carvalho, *A Lunda: ou os Estados do Muatiânvua*, p. 16. See also Beatrix Heintze, "Between Two Worlds: The Bezerras, a Luso-Africa Family in Nineteenth-Century Western Central Africa," in Philip Havik and Malyn Newitt (eds.), *Creole Societies in the Portuguese Colonial Empire* (Bristol: University of Bristol, 2007), p. 132. See also Vellut, "Notes sur le Lunda et la Frontière Luso-Africaine," p. 133.

168. Graça, "Expedição ao Muatayanvua," p. 443.

169. Graça, "Expedição ao Muatayanvua," p. 443. For similar rationale being laid out several decades earlier, Branco e Torres, *Memoria Contendo a Biographia do Vice Almirante Luiz da Motta Feo e Torres*, p. 301.

170. Graça, "Expedição ao Muatayanvua," p. 443.

171. Graça, "Expedição ao Muatayanvua," p. 458.

172. Graça, "Expedição ao Muatayanvua," p. 444.

173. "Ofício do Governador de Angola" on October 6, 1831, AHA, cód. 2310, fl. 31.

174. "Ofício do Secretário do Governo de Angola" on November 19, 1853, AHA, cód. 177, fl. 174.

175. Graça, "Expedição ao Muatayanvua," p. 368.

176. Graça, "Expedição ao Muatayanvua," pp. 465-466. See Madeira dos Santos, *Nos Caminhos de África*, p. 89

177. "Conta de Joaquim Rodrigues da Graça" in 1854, AHA, cx. 2856.

Chapter 6: Fracturing African Sovereignty

1. François Bontinck, "Pedro V, Roi de Kongo, Face au Partage Colonial," *Africa*, 37, 1/2, 1982, p. 6. See also Alfredo de Sarmento, *Os Sertões d'Africa: Apontamentos de Viagem* (Lisboa: Editor Proprietário, 1880), pp. 55, 64.

2. John Thornton, *A History of West Central Africa to 1850* (NYC: Cambridge University Press, 2020), p. 76.

3. Thornton, *A History of West Central Africa to 1850*, pp. 244, 278.

4. Thornton, *A History of West Central Africa to 1850*, p. 58.

5. "Carta Régia" on July 6, 1803, AHA, cód. 9, fls. 40-42.

6. Thornton, *A History of West Central Africa to 1850*, pp. 160-185, 342, 344.

7. "Carta dos Príncipes do Congo" on March 19, 1842, AHU, segunda seção de Angola, pastas 5 A e 5 B. See also Thiago Sapede, "Le Roi et le Temps, le Kongo et le Monde. Une histoire globale des transformations politiques du Royaume du Kongo (1780–1860)," PhD Dissertation, École des Hautes Études en Sciences Sociales, Paris, 2020, p. 424.

8. Jelmer Vos, *Kongo in the Age of Empire, 1860–1913: The Breakdown of a Moral Order* (Madison: University of Wisconsin Press, 2015), p. 20. See also Jelmer Vos, "Kongo Cosmopolitans in the Nineteenth Century," in Koen Bostoen, and Inge Brinkman (eds.), *The Kongo Kingdom: The Origins, Dynamics and Cosmopolitan Culture of an African Polity* (NYC: Cambridge University Press, 2018), p. 248.

9. Thornton, p. 125. See also Vos, *Kongo in the Age of Empire*, p. 26; David Birmingham, *A Short History of Modern Angola* (NY: Oxford University Press, 2015), p. 36.

10. Cécile Fromont, "The Kongo Kingdom," in John parker (ed.), *Great Kingdoms of Africa* (Oakland: University of California Press, 2023), p. 165.

11. "Ofício do British Vice-Cônsul em Luanda" on April 30, 1846, Ministério dos Negócios Estrangeiros, cx. 967, maço 1.

12. "Relatório do Governador de Angola" on August 6, 1838, AHU, segunda seção de Angola, pasta 3.

13. "Instruções Reservadas" on November 4, 1838, AHA, cód. 259, fls. 214-222v.

14. "Notas do Visconde de Sá da Bandeira" in 1844, in *Annaes Maritimos e Coloniaes* (Lisboa: Imprensa Nacional, 1844), parte não oficial, número 5, quarta série, p. 209; "Ofício do Governador de Angola" on August 31, 1845, AHA, cód. 16, fls. 125v.–126.

15. Roger Anstey, *Britain and the Congo in the Nineteenth Century* (NY: Oxford University Press, 1962), p. 15; Maeve Ryan, *Humanitarian Governance and the British Anti-Slavery World System* (New Haven: Yale University Press, 2022), p. 31.

16. Mary Wills, *Envoys of Abolition: British Naval Officers and the Campaign against the Slave Trade in West Africa* (Liverpool: Liverpool University Press, 2019), p. 49.

17. The Royal Gazette, February 21, 1824, pp. 239-240.

18. "Ofício" on March 10, 1860, AHU, segunda seção de Angola, pasta 26.1.

19. Leslie Bethell, "Britain, Portugal and the Suppression of the Brazilian Slave Trade: The Origins of Lord Palmerston's Act of 1839," *The English Historical Review*, 80, 317, 1965, pp. 761-84; João Pedro Marques, *The Sounds of Silence: Nineteenth Century Portugal and the Abolition of the Slave Trade* (New York: Berghahn Books, 2006). For West Africa, see

Colin Newbury, *The Western Slave Coast and its Rulers* (London: Oxford University press, 1961), p. 39; Silke Strickrodt, *Afro-European Trade in the Atlantic World: The Western Slave Coast, c. 1550–c. 1885* (London: James Currey, 2015), pp. 197–198. For West Central Africa, see Anstey, *Britain and the Congo in the Nineteenth Century*, chapter II. See also Gabriel Paquette, "Anglo-Portuguese Relations in the Mid-Nineteenth Century: Informal Empire, Arbitration, and the Durability of an Asymmetrical Alliance," *The English Historical Review*, 135, 575, 2020, pp. 836–859.

20. "Relatório do Ministério do Ultramar" in 1840, in *Annaes Marítimos e Coloniaes* (Lisboa: Imprensa Nacional, 1841), p. 161.

21. "Oficio do Comandante das Forças Navais Britânicas" on January 28, 1840, AHA, cód. 259.

22. Anstey, *Britain and the Congo in the Nineteenth Century*, p. 11.

23. Report on the State of the Slave Trade on December 31, 1845, PRO, FO 84, 572, 1845, fls. 358–375. For the wider context of British naval operations, see Richard Huzzey, *Freedom Burning: Anti-Slavery and Empire in Victorian Britain* (NY: Cornell University, 2012), Chapter 3.

24. Report on the Slave Trade by Gabriel and Jackson on February 14, 1848, PRO, FO 84, 719, 1848, fls. 61–74; BOGGPA, n°127, 12 February 1848.

25. "Instruções para o Governador de Benguela" on February 27, 1844, AHA, cód. 261.

26. "Relação dos Navios de Guerra Portugueses nas Costas Oriental e Ocidental da África" on April 13, 1844, FO 84, 521, fl. 67; *Annaes Maritimos e Coloniaes* (Lisboa: Imprensa oficial, janeiro de 1845), 2, quinta série, parte official, p. 31; *Annaes maritimos e coloniaes*, parte official, julho de 1845, 5ª serie, n. 8, p. 142. See also João Pedro Marques, *A armada portuguesa no combate ao tráfico de escravos em Angola (1839–1865)*, *Anais de História do Além Mar*, 1, 2000, pp. 161–912; Jorge Manuel Moreira Silva, "A Marinha Portuguesa no combate ao tráfico de escravos (1837–1904)," PhD Dissertation, Universidade de Lisboa, 2023, pp. 219–227.

27. Report on the Slave Trade by Gabriel and Jackson on February 14, 1848, FO 84, 719, fls. 61–74.

28. Draft of letter by Palmerston on November 11, 1846, FO 84, 630, fls. 99–101. Palmerston largely channeled views first espoused by Matson, who had been a naval commander in Central Africa. See Henry James Matson, *Remarks on the Slave Trade and African Squadron* (London: James Ridgway, 1848), pp. 77–79.

29. "Portaria do Ministério da Marinha e Negócios do Ultramar" on May 22, 1847, AHA, cód. 262, fl. 59v.; "Ofício do Governador de Angola" on December 19, 1849, AHA, cód. 19, fls. 2v.–3.

30. Letter of Edward Hannah on November 27, 1849, FO 84, 764, fls. 187–189.

31. Letter of the king of Ambriz on December 8, 1849, FO 84, 800, fls. 160–161.

32. Dispatch by Brand on December 20, 1849, FO 84, 764, fls. 197–200. See also Anstey, *Britain and the Congo in the Nineteenth Century*, p. 16.

33. Huzzey, *Freedom Burning*, p. 56.

34. Andrew Pearson, "Waterwitch: A Warship, its Voyage and its Crew in the Era of Anti-Slavery," *Atlantic Studies*, 13, 1, 2016, pp. 99–124.

35. George Brooks, *Yankee Traders, Old Coasters & African Middlemen. A History of American Legitimate Trade with West Africa in the Nineteenth Century* (Boston: Boston University Press, 1970), p. 287.

36. Thomas to Dobbin on June 20, 1856, in *Executive Documents, printed by Order of the House of Representatives during the Second Session of the Thirty-Sixth Congress (1860–1861)* (Washington: Government Printing Office, 1861), p. 39.

37. "Ofício do Governador de Angola" on January 17, 1841, AHA, cód. 15, fls. 25–25v.; "Ofício do Governador de Angola" on January 18, 1841, AHA, cód. 15, fls. 34v.–35.

38. Lawrence Jennings, "France, Great Britain, and the Repression of the Slave Trade, 1841–1845," *French Historical Studies*, 10, 1, 1977, pp. 101–125.

39. Lawrence Jennings, "French Reaction to the 'Disguised British Slave Trade': France and British African Emigration Projects, 1840–1864," *Cahiers d'études Africaines*, 18, 69–70, 1978, pp. 203–204.

40. Maeve Ryan, "The Price of Legitimacy in Humanitarian Intervention: Britain, the Right of Search, and the Abolition of the West African Slave Trade, 1807–1867," in Brendan

Simms and D. J. B. Trim (eds.), *Humanitarian Intervention: A History* (NYC: Cambridge University Press, 2011), pp. 231–255. See also Raphaël Cheriau, *Imperial Powers and Humanitarian Interventions: The Zanzibar Sultanate, Britain, and France in the Indian Ocean, 1862–1905* (NYC: Routledge, 2020), pp. 78–79.

41. A. H. Foote, *The African Squadron* (Philadelphia: William Geddes Printer, 1855), p. 7.

42. Cheriau, *Imperial Powers and Humanitarian Interventions*, p. 80. For African contexts, see Samba Mampuya, *Survivance et répression de la traite négrière du Gabon au Congo de 1840 a 1880* (Paris: Les Editions la Bruyere, 1990), p. 28. See also Serge Daget, *La Répression de la Traite des Noirs au XIXè Siècle* (Paris: Éditions Karthala, 1997), p. 538; Paul Michael Kielstra, *The Politics of Slave Trade Suppression in Britain and France, 1814–1848: Diplomacy, Morality and Economics* (London and NY: Macmillan Press, 2000), Chapter 5.

43. BGGPA, 18, January 10, 1846; Report on the slave trade by Edmond Gabriel and George Jackson on February 18, 1847, FO 84, 671, 1847, fls. 99–11.

44. Edouard Bouët-Willaumez, *Campagne aux côtes occidentales d'Afrique* (Paris: P. Dupont, 1850), p. 23; Kielstra, *The Politics of Slave Trade Suppression in Britain and France, 1814–1848*, p. 255.

45. Report on the slave trade by Edmond Gabriel and George Jackson on February 18, 1847, FO 84, 671, 1847, fls. 99–11.

46. Bouët-Willaumez, *Campagne aux côtes occidentales d'Afrique*, p. 23. See also Hubert Deschamps, "Quinze ans de Gabon (les débuts de l'établissement français, 1839–1853)," *Revue Française d'Histoire d'Outre-Mer*, 50, 1963, p. 313.

47. Gustau Nerín, *Traficants d'ànimes: Els negrers espanyols a l'Àfrica* (Barcelona: Editorial Pòrtic, 2015), pp. 233–234. For further context on French anti-slave trade naval operations, see Daget, *La Répression de la Traite des Noirs au XIXè Siècle*.

48. Revue Maritime et Coloniale (Paris: Librairie de Challamel Ainé, 1863), tome neuviéme, pp. 44, 63. For context, Mampuya, *Survivance et répression de la traite négrière du Gabon au Congo de 1840 a 1880*, pp. 199–201.

49. Jeff Pardue, "Antislavery and Imperialism: The British Suppression of the Slave Trade and the Opening of Fernando Po, 1827–1829," *Itinerario*, 44, 1, 2020, p. 185.

50. Édouard Bouët-Willaumez, "Les Colonies Françaises en 1852," *Revue Des Deux Mondes*, 14, 5, 1852, p. 941.

51. Hyacinthe Hecquard, *Voyages sur la cote et dans l'interieur de l'Afrique Occidentale* (Paris: Imprimerie de Benaud, 1853), p. 13.

52. Xavier Daumalin, "La domination informelle des milieux économiques marseillais en Afrique (1815–1880): acteurs, enjeux, limites," *Outre-Mers*, vol. 410–411, 1, 2021, pp. 63–82. See also Jean-Claude Nardin, "La Reprise des Relations Franco-Dahoméennes au XIXe Siècle: la Mission d'Auguste Bouët à la Cour d'Abomey (1851)," *Cahiers d'Études Africaines*, 7, 25, 1967, pp. 59–126; Pierre Trichet, "Victor Régis, L'Armateur Marseillais qui voulait une Mission Catholique à Ouidah," *Histoire et Missions Chrétiennes*, 2, 18, 2011, pp. 149–181; Flory, *De l'Esclavage à la Liberté Forcée*, pp. 67–68, 139. For his participation in the palm oil trade in Lagos, see Kristin Mann, *Slavery and the Birth of an African City: Lagos, 1760–1900* (Bloomington: Indian University Press, 2007), p. 122.

53. Elisée Soumonni, "Trade and Politics in Dahomey, 1841–1892," PhD Dissertation, University of Ife, Nigeria, p. 85. For ties between slave dealers and the Régis Maison, see Newbury, *The Western Slave Coast, and Its Rulers*, p. 42; Strickrodt, *Afro-European Trade in the Atlantic World*, p. 205. For the relationship between French traders and slave dealers in general, see Lawrence Jennings, "French Policy towards Trading with African and Brazilian Slave Merchants, 1840–1853," *Journal of African History*, 17, 4, 1976, pp. 515–528.

54. "Ofício da Secretário de Estado da Marinha e Ultramar" on September 16, 1844, Ministério dos Negócios Estrangeiros, cx. 967, maço 1. See also Marquez do Lavradio, *A Abolição da Escravatura e a Ocupação do Ambriz* (Lisboa: Livraria Bertrand, 1934), pp. 100, 119, 146; "Notas do Visconde de Sá da Bandeira em 1844," in *Annaes Maritimos e Coloniaes* (Lisboa: Imprensa Nacional, 1844), Parte Não Oficial, Número 5, Quarta Séria, 208. See also Simão José da Luz Soriano, *Revelações da Minha Vida* (Lisboa: Typographia Universal, 1860), p. 557.

55. "Ofício de John Foote" on August 23, 1843, Ministério dos Negócios Estrangeiros, cx. 967, maço 1.

56. Louis Edouard Bouët-Willaumez, *Commerce et Traite des Noires aux Côtes Occidentales d'Afrique* (Paris: Imprimerie Nationale, 1848), p. 166.

57. "Ofício reservado do Governador de Angola" on May 4, 1847, Ministério dos Negócios Estrangeiros, cx. 967, maço 1.

58. "Despacho Consular" on June 17, 1855, Ministério dos Negócios Estrangeiros, cx. 967, maço 4.

59. Pardue, "Antislavery and Imperialism," pp. 183–195. See also Ibrahim Sundiata, *From Slaving to Neoslavery: The Bight of Biafra and Fernando Po in the Era of Abolition, 1827–1930* (Madison: University of Wisconsin Press, 1996).

60. Philip Havik, "A Commanding Commercial Position: The African Settlement of Bolama Island and Anglo-Portuguese Rivalry (1830–1870)," in Toby Green (ed.), *Brokers of Change: Atlantic Commerce and Cultures in Precolonial Western Africa* (New York: Oxford University Press, 2012), pp. 333–377.

61. Anjuli Webster, "Inter-Imperial Entanglement: The British Claim to Portuguese Delagoa Bay in the Nineteenth Century." *Journal of World History*, 35, 1, 2024, p. 33–52.

62. F. L. Barnard, *A Three Years' Cruise in the Mozambique Channel* (London: Schulze & Co, 1848), p. 267. For context, see Patrick Harries, "The Hobgoblins of the Middle Passage: The Cape and the Trans-Atlantic Slave Trade," in U. Schmieder, Michael Zeuske, and K. Fullberg-Stolberg (eds.), *The End of Slavery in Africa and the Americas: A Comparative Approach* (Munster: LitVerlag, 2011), p. 49.

63. Linell Chewins and Peter Delius, "The Northeastern Factor in South African History: Reevaluating the Volume of the Slave Trade Out of Delagoa Bay and its Impact on its Hinterland in the Early Nineteenth Century," *Journal of African History*, 61, 1, 2020, p. 108. For the illegal slave trade to the Mascarenes islands at the time, see Marina Carter and Hubert Gerbeau, "Covert Slaves and Coveted Coolies in the Early 19th Century Mascareignes," *Slavery & Abolition*, 9, 3, 1988, pp. 194–208; Richard Allen, "Licentious and Unbridled Proceedings: The Illegal Slave Trade to Mauritius and the Seychelles during the Early Nineteenth Century," *The Journal of African History*, 42, 1, 2001, pp. 91–116; Hubert Gerbau, "La traite illégale aux Mascareignes des années 1810 aux années 1840. Les cas de l'île Bourbon," in Vijaya Teelock et Thomas Vernet (eds.), *Traites, esclavage et transition vers l'engagisme. Perspectives nouvelles sur les Mascareignes et le sud-ouest de l'océan Indien, 1715–1848* (Réduit, University of Mauritius Press, 2015), pp. 46–57.

64. Richard Allen, *European Slave Trading in the Indian Ocean, 1500–1850* (Athens: Ohio University Press, 2014), p. 169.

65. Matthew Hopper, *Slaves of One Master: Globalization and Slavery in Arabia in the Age of Empire* (New Haven: Yale University Press, 2015), Chapter 5. See also Edward Alpers, *The Indian Ocean in World History* (Oxford: Oxford University Press, 2013), Chapter 5; Abdul Sheriff, *Slaves, Spices, & Ivory in Zanzibar: Integration of an East African Commercial Empire into the World Economy, 1770–1873* (London: James Currey, 1987), pp. 201–228.

66. Leigh Muffet, "The Cape of Good Hope Colony and the British World Turned Upside-down, 1806–1836," *The Journal of Imperial and Commonwealth History*, 50, 6, 2022, p. 1044.

67. Edward Alpers and Benigna Zimba, "British abolition in Southeast Africa: The first 50 years," *Quarterly Bulletin of the National Library of South Africa*, 63, 1–2, 2009, pp. 5–15.

68. Newbury, *The Western Slave Coast and Its Rulers*, pp. 46–47, 48. See also Olatunji Ojo, "Document 2: Letters Found in the House of Kosoko, King of Lagos (1851)," *African Economic History*, 40, 1, 2012, pp. 37–126.

69. Huzzey, *Freedom Burning*, p. 144.

70. Huzzey, *Freedom Burning*, pp. 145–147. See Preye Adekoya, "The Succession Dispute to the Throne of Lagos and the British Conquest and Occupation of Lagos," *African Research Review*, 10, 3, 2016, pp. 207–226; Ayodeji Olukoju, "Lagos in the 19th Century," *Oxford Research Encyclopedia*, 2019, p. 3. See also Robert Smith, *The Lagos Consulate, 1851–1861* (London: The Macmillan Press, 1978), Chapter 2; Martin Lynn, "Consul and Kings: British Policy, 'the Man on the Spot', and the Seizure of Lagos, 1851," *The Journal of Imperial and*

Commonwealth History, 10, 2, 1982, pp. 150–167; Kristin Mann, *Slavery and the Birth of an African City: Lagos, 1760-1900*" (Bloomington: Indiana University Press, 2007), pp. 84–116. For an overview, see Silke Strickrodt, *Afro-European Trade in the Atlantic World: The Western Slave Coast, c. 1550–c. 1885* (Rochester: James Currey, 2015).

71. BOGGPA, 46, June 13, 1846; Figueiredo, *Indice do Boletim Official da Provincia d'Angola*, p. 47.

72. "Despacho reservado" on May 2, 1855, Ministério dos Negócios Estrangeiros, cx. 967, maço 4.

73. BOPPA, 332, 1852.

74. BOPPA, 351, 1852.

75. "Ofício de John Foot" on August 23, 1843, Ministério dos Negócios Estrangeiros, cx. 967, maço 1 (1844).

76. Phyllis Martin, *The External Trade of the Loango Coast, 1576–1870* (NY: Oxford University Press, 1972), p. 140; Susan Broadhead, "Trade and Politics on the Congo Coast: 1770–1870," PhD Dissertation, Boston University, 1971, p. 150; Mampuya, *Survivance et répression de la traite négrière du Gabon*, 1990, p. 170.

77. István Rákóczi, *O planalto do Bié: diários de viagem de László Magyar (1848-57)* (Lisboa: Colibri, 2019), p. 35. See also Norm Schrag, "Mboma and the Lower Zaire: A Socio-economic Study of a Kongo Trading Community, c. 1785–1885" (PhD Dissertation, Indiana University, 1985), pp. 40–43, 58, 61. See also John Monteiro, *Angola and the River Congo* (New York: Macmillan and Co., 1876), p. 31.

78. Thornton, *A History of West Central Africa to 1850*, pp. 344. For further context, see Sapede, "Le Roi et le Temps, le Kongo et le Monde," p. 427.

79. "Carta dos Príncipes do Congo" on March 19, 1842, AHU, segunda seção de Angola, pastas 5 A e 5 B. See also Thornton, *A History of West Central Africa to 1850*, p. 343.

80. AHA, cód. 67, f. 36.

81. Bouët-Willaumez, *Commerce et Traite des Noires aux Côtes Occidentales d'Afrique*, p. 167.

82. Rákóczi, *O Planalto do Bié*, p. 48.

83. "Carta do Governador de Angola" on August 31 1845, AHU, pasta 8; Sarmento, *Os Sertões d'Africa*, p. 27; Rákóczi, *O Planalto do Bié*, p. 39.

84. Report on the State of the Slave Trade on December 31, 1845, FO 84, 572, fls. 358–375.

85. "Ofício da Secretaria de Estado dos Negócios da Marinha e do Ultramar" on January 13, 1844, Ministério dos Negócios Estrangeiros, cx. 967, maço 1; "Portaria da Secretaria de Estado da Marinha e Ultramar" on April 27, 1844, AHA, cód. 261, fls. 145–145v.

86. "Instruções para o Capitão do Exército Antonio Joaquim de Castro" on May 31, 1845, AHA, cód. 768.

87. "Tratado entre o Rei do Congo e a Rainha de Portugal" on June 26, 1845, AHU, segunda seção de Angola, pasta 8.

88. "Acordo do Rei do Congo" on June 26, 1845, in António Brásio, *Spiritana Monumenta Historica*, 1, Angola, vol. 1. See F. Bontinck, "Notes Complement Aires Sur Dom Nicolau Agua Rosada e Sardonia," *African Historical Studies*, 2, 1, 1969, p. 106; Sapede, "Le Roi et le Temps, le Kongo et le Monde," p. 434.

89. "Carta de Joaquim de Castro" on July 7, 1845, AHU, segunda seção de Angola, pasta 8. See also Thornton, *A History of West Central Africa to 1850*, pp. 343–344.

90. "Portaria do Ministério da Marinha e Negócios do Ultramar" on January 26, 1847, AHA, cód. 262, fls. 40v.–41v.

91. "Carta do Governador de Angola" on October 13, 1853, BOGGPA, 423, 1853. See also Françoise Latour da Veiga Pinto, *Le Portugal et le Congo au XIX siècle: étude d'histoire des relations internationales* (Paris: P.U.F., 1972), p. 53.

92. Dispatch by Jackson on May 18, 1855, FO 84, 906, fls. 147–149. For higher numbers of soldiers in the expedition, see Richard Burton, *Two Trips to Gorilla Land and the Cataracts of the Congo* (London: Sampson Low, Marston, Low, and Searle, 1876), vol. II, p. 45. See also João Pedro Marques, "A ocupação do Ambriz (1855): geografia e diplomacia de uma derrota

inglesa," *Africana Studia*, 9, 2006, pp. 145–158; Miguel Bandeira Jerónimo, *A Diplomacia do Império: Política e Religião na Partilha da África, 1820–1890* (Lisboa: Edições 70, 2012), p. 48.

93. "Ofício do Governador de Angola" on May 24, 1855, AHA, cód. 248, fls. 15–16.

94. "Portaria" on January 20, 1855, Ministério dos Negócios Estrangeiros, cx. 967, maço 4.

95. "Portaria" on November 21, 1855, AA, p. 93.

96. Report of Edmond Gabriel in 1850, PRO, FO 84/792, p. 142. For similar numbers six years later, see Report on the slave trade by Gabriel on February 11, 1857, FO 84, 1013, fls. 130–150. See also Anstey, *Britain and the Congo in the Nineteenth Century*, p. 23.

97. Edward Reynolds, *Trade and Economic Change on the Gold Coast, 1807–1874* (NY: Longman, 1974), pp. 132, 137.

98. Mann, *Slavery and the Birth of an African City*, p. 127.

99. "Ofício do Governador de Angola" on March 2, 1851, AHA, cód. 19, fls. 156v.–157.

100. "Memória sobre o Ambriz" in 1852, AHU, papéis de Sá da Bandeira, maço 827; "Ofício do Governador de Angola" on February 1, 1853, AHU, segunda seção de Angola, pasta 19 (1). For the flow of goods from Ambriz into Luanda, which forced Luandan authorities to seek to restrict the flow of people between the two places, see "Ofício do Secretário Geral do Governo de Angola" on November 12, 1854, AHA, cód. 112, fls. 132–132v.; "Ofício do Governador de Angola" on December 28, 1854, AHA, cód. 21, fls. 166v.–167.

101. St. Helena Herald, n. 133, vol. III, 1855.

102. "Carta do Governador de Angola" on May 17, 1855, AA, 2a série, vol. XII, 47–50, 1950, pp. 25–26; "Ofício de Rodovalho" on May 21, 1855, Ministério dos Negócios Estrangeiros, cx. 967, maço 5; "Ofício do Governador de Angola" on May 24, 1855, AHA, cód. 248, fls. 15–16; Dispatch by Gabriel on July 9, 1855, FO 84, 960, fls. 244–248.

103. "Carta do Governador de Angola" on May 17, 1855, AA, 2a série, vol. XII, 47–50, 1950, pp. 25–26; "Ofício de Rodovalho" on May 21, 1855, Ministério dos Negócios Estrangeiros, cx. 967, maço 5; "Ofício do Comandante do Ambriz" on June 29, 1855, AGM, cx. 473. See Lavradio, *A Abolição da Escravatura*, p. 142. See also Sapede, "Le Roi et le Temps, le Kongo et le Monde," pp. 457–458.

104. "Ofício do Comandante do Navio Britânico Scourge" on September 12, 1855, AHA, cx. 2841; "Ofício do Comandante do Navio Britânico Scourge" on September 14, 1855, AHA, cx. 2841.

105. "Tratado entre sua Majestade a Rainha da Inglaterra e os Chefes do Ambrizete" on September 17, 1855, AHA, cx. 2841.

106. "Ofício do Comandante do Navio Britânico Scourge" on September 14, 1855, AHA, cx. 2841; "Declaração" on October 29, 1855, Ministério dos Negócios Estrangeiros, cx. 967, maço 5; "Ofício de João Maximo do Rodovalho" on November 8, 1855, AHU, segunda seção de Angola, pasta 22.

107. "Portaria" on January 20, 1855, Ministério dos Negócios Estrangeiros, cx. 967, maço 4.

108. "Ofício do Secretário Geral do Governo de Angola" on December 29, 1854, AHA, cód. 179, fls. 92–93; "Ofício da Estação Naval" on January 18, 1855, AGM, cx. 473; "Despacho de Edmond Gabriel" on December 30 1854, Ministério dos Negócios Estrangeiros, cx. 967, maço 4. See also Francisco Travassos Valdez, *Six Years of a Traveller's Life in Western Africa* (London: Hurst and Blackett Publishers, 1861), vol. II, p. 139.

109. Lavradio, *A Abolição da Escravatura*, p. 266.

110. Lavradio, *A Abolição da Escravatura*, p. 141.

111. Note of the British legation in Lisbon on September 8, 1855, Ministério dos Negócios Estrangeiros, cx. 967, maço 4; "Despacho reservado" on January 27, 1856, Ministério dos Negócios Estrangeiros, cx. 967, maço 5; "Despacho reservado" on March 25, 1856, Ministério dos Negócios Estrangeiros, cx. 967, maço 5. See also Lavradio, *A Abolição da Escravatura*, pp. 145, 175–187. For background, see Jerónimo, *A Diplomacia do Império*, p. 50; Anstey, *Britain and the Congo in the Nineteenth Century*, pp. 50–54.

112. "Proposta de Convenção entre Portugal e Inglaterra" on February 16, 1856, Ministério dos Negócios Estrangeiros, cx. 967, maço 5; "Ofício do Secretário Geral de Governo" on March 14, 1857, AHA, cód. 181, fls. 167–167v.

113. Lavradio, *A Abolição da Escravatura*, p. 206.

114. Vos, *Kongo in the Age of Empire*, p. 26.

115. "Carta do Rei do Congo" on June 29, 1855, BOGGPA, 1855, 514; AGM, Serra do Pilar, cx. 473. See also Sapede, "Le Roi et le Temps, le Kongo et le Monde," p. 459.

116. BOGGPA, 1857, 605, 6.

117. "Ofício do Governador de Angola" on August 4, 1855, AHA, cód. 248, fls. 20–22.

118. "Ofício do Governador de Angola" on September 10, 1856, AHA, cód. 248, fls. 33v.–34v.

119. "Carta do Rei do Congo" on October 12 1855, BOGGPA, 539, 1856.

120. "Ofício do Governador de Angola" on January 25, 1856, BOGGPA, 539, 1856.

121. "Ofício do Governador de Angola" on September 10, 1856, AHA, cód. 248, fls. 33v.–34v.

122. "Ofício do Governador de Angola" on May 23, 1856, AHA, cód. 248, fls. 23v.–24.

123. "Ofício do Governador de Angola" on May 23, 1856, AHA, cód. 248, fls. 23v.–24.

124. "Ofício do Governador de Angola" on May 23, 1856, AHA, cód. 248, fls. 23v.–24.

125. "Ofício do Governador de Angola" on May 23, 1856, AHA, cód. 248, fls. 23v.–24.

126. Dispatch by Gabriel and Jackson on June 11, 1855, FO 84, 906, fls. 171–174. For further context of British operations, see Anstey, *Britain and the Congo in the Nineteenth Century*, p. 21.

127. Edmond Gabriel on April 15, 1859, *Accounts and Papers of the House of Commons*, Slave Trade, Session January 24–August 28, 1860, vol. LXX, p. 40. See also Report on the State of the Slave Trade on April 15, 1859, FO 84, 1075, fls. 94–116. See also Monteiro, *Angola and the River Congo*, p. 105. For context, see Françoise Latour da Veiga Pinto, *Le Portugal et le Congo au XIXe Siècle: Étude d'Histoire des Relations Internationales* (Paris: P.U.F., 1972), p. 53.

128. Dispatch by Gabriel and Jackson on December 1, 1856, FO 84, 985, fls. 464–466v.

129. Report on the slave trade by Gabriel on February 11, 1857, FO 83, 1013, fls. 130–150.

130. Report on the State of the Slave Trade by Gabriel on February 25, 1858, FO 84, 1043, fls. 121–150.

131. Report on the State of the Slave Trade by Gabriel on February 25, 1858, FO 84, 1043, fls. 121–150. See also Sarmento, *Os Sertões d'Africa*, p. 28.

132. Dispatch by Gabriel and Jackson on August 25, 1856, fls. 295–299; "Ofício do Governador de Angola" on August 12, 1856, AHU, segunda seção de Angola, pasta 22 A; "Ofício do Secretário Geral de Angola" on September 9, 1856, AHA, cód. 857, fls. 6–6v.; "Ofício do Governador de Angola" on July 26, 1856, AHA, cód. 248, fl. 29. See also Sarmento, *Os Sertões d'Africa*, p. 22.

133. "Ofício do Governador de Angola" on June 2, 1856, AHU, segunda seção de Angola, pasta 22 A.

134. "Ofício do Governador de Angola" on August 12, 1856, AHU, segunda seção de Angola, pasta 22 A; "Ofício do Secretário do Governo de Angola" on February 19, 1857, AHA, cód. 226, fl. 53.

135. "Diário do Rio de Janeiro" on April 9, 1859, 99, ano XXXIV, p. 2.

136. "Decreto do Visconde de Athouguia" on November 7, 1855, BOGGPA, 594, 2/3. See also "Relação das Participações de Descobertas de Jazidas Minerais nesta Província," BOGGPA, 615.

137. "Registo de Participação de Francisco António Flores" on May 4, 1855, AHA, cód. 1261, fl. 1–1v.; "Registro de Representação de Francisco Antonio Flores (representado por seu procurador August Garrido)" on March 6, 1856, AHA cód. 1261, fls. 1v–2; "Ofício do Secretário Geral de Governo de Angola" on October 3, 1856, AHA, cód. 181, fls. 101–101v.; "Despacho 1121" on August 1, 1856, AHA, cód. 2619, fl. 170v; "Registo de Participação de Francisco Antonio Flores" on August 5, 1856, AHA, cód. 1261, fls. 3v.–4. For further information on Flores multiple investments in mining in Angola, see Monteiro, *Angola and the River Congo*, pp. 201–202, 204, 213, 270–271, 275. See also Valentim Alexandre, *Origens do Colonialismo Português Moderno* (Lisboa: Sá da Costa Editora, 1979), p. 52; Frederico Antonio Ferreira, "Investimentos Privados de Brasileiros na África Portuguesa: o Caso da Western Africa Malachite Copper Mines Company," XI Congresso Brasileiro de História Econômica, 2015.

138. "Ofício do Governador de Angola" on June 2, 1856, AHU, segunda seção de Angola, pasta 22 A.

139. Sarmento, *Os Sertões d'Africa*, p. 40.

140. Adolph Bastian, *Ein Besuch in San Salvador, der Hauptstadt des Konigreichs Kongo* (Bremen: Druck und Verlag von H. Strack, 1859), p. 51.

141. "Ofício do Secretário de Governo" on December 2, 1856, AHA, cód. 857, fls. 33v.–34v.

142. Report on the slave trade by Gabriel on February 11, 1857, FO 83, 1013, fls. 130–150.

143. Dispatch by Gabriel on July 30, 1858, FO 84, 1043, fls. 359–366.

144. "Francisco Antonio Flores, Algumas Reflexões a Respeito da Província de Angola" on December 2, 1859, AHU, papéis de Sá da Bandeira, maço 827.

145. Dispatch by Gabriel on July 30, 1858, FO 84, 1043, fls. 359–366.

146. "Ofício do Secretário do Governo de Angola" on November 12, 1856, AHA, cód. 857, fls. 30v.–31v. See also "Decreto" on July 3, 1857, in *Annaes do Conselho Ultramarino*, parte official, serie I, fevereiro de 1854 a dezembro de 1858 (Lisboa: Imprensa Nacional, 1867), p. 434.

147. "Carta de José Tavares da Costa e Moura" on November 20, 1856, BOGGPA, 586, 1856, p. 3.

148. "Carta de José Tavares da Costa e Moura" on November 20, 1856, BOGGPA, 586, 1856, p. 3; BOGGPA, 1857, 605, 6.

149. Bastian, *Ein Besuch in San Salvador*, p. 119.

150. Rákóczi, *O Planalto do Bié*, p. 48.

151. Vos, *Kongo in the Age of Empire*, p. 23.

152. Bontinck, "Pedro V, Roi de Kongo," p. 7.

153. "Extrato de um Relatório do Chefe do Conselho de Pedro V, o Tenente Zacharias da Silva Cruz, sobre a sua viagem a S. Salvador do Congo," BOGGPA, March 5, 1859, 701, p. 1. See also Pinto, *Le Portugal et le Congo au XIXe Siècle*, p. 59.

154. Bastian, *Ein Besuch in San Salvador*, pp. 131–132.

155. Bastian, *Ein Besuch in San Salvador*, pp. 131, 215, 135.

156. BOGGPA, 711, 1859, p. 3. See also Pinto, *Le Portugal et le Congo au XIXe Siècle*, p. 58.

157. "Carta de Francisco de Salles Ferreira," undated, AHU, papéis de Sá da Bandeira, maço 827. See also Alfredo de Sarmento, *Os Sertões d'Africa*, p. 52.

158. BOGGPA, 701, 1859, 1.

159. John Thornton, "Kongo's Incorporation into Angola: A Perspective from Kongo," in Maria Emelia Madeira Santos (ed), *A África e a instalação do sistema colonial* (c. 1885–c. 1930) (Lisbon: Instituto de Investigacao Cientifica Tropical, 2000), p. 352.

160. Cheriau, *Imperial Powers and Humanitarian Interventions*, p. 82. See also Renault, *Libération d'Esclaves et Nouvelle Servitude*, pp. 46–47.

161. Daumalin, "La domination informelle des milieux économiques marseillais en Afrique," pp. 63–82.

162. Jelmer Vos, "Without the Slave Trade no Recruitment: From Slave Trading to 'Migrant Recruitment' in the Lower Congo, 1830–1890," in Benjamin Lawrance and Richard Roberts (eds.), *Trafficking in Slavery's Wake: Law and the Experience of Women and Children in Africa* (Athens: Ohio University Press, 2012), pp. 45–64; Céline Flory, *De l'Esclavage à la Liberté Forcée: Histoire des Travailleurs Africains Engagés dans la Caraïbe Française au XIXe Siècle* (Paris: Karthala, 2015); Céline Flory, "Affranchir sans libérer: la pratique du "rachat" de captifs africains dans l'espace colonial français (XIXe siècle)," in Dominique Rogers and Boris Lesueur (eds.), *Libres après les abolitions? Statuts et identités aux Amériques et en Afrique* (Paris: Karthala, 2019), pp. 57–69.

163. Report on the State of the Slave Trade on April 15, 1859, FO 84, 1075, fls. 94–116.

164. Lawless to Clarendon on February 28, 1858, *British and Foreign State Papers (1858–1859)* (London: William Ridgway, 1867), vol. XLIX, p. 1050.

165. Schrag, "Mboma and the Lower Zaire," p. 114.

166. Schrag, "Mboma and the Lower Zaire," pp. 105–106. For the Bight of Benin, where French warships would also sometimes support the Régis firm's operations, see Newbury, *The Western Slave Coast and its Rulers*, p. 62.

167. Schrag, "Mboma and the Lower Zaire," p. 106.

168. Dispatch by Gabriel on October 1, 1857, FO 83, 1013, fls. 397–407.

169. "Relatório do Governador do Ambriz" on November 28, 1858, AHU, segunda seção de Angola, pasta 24 (2). See also Pinto, *Le Portugal et le Congo au XIXe Siècle*, pp. 117–119.

170. Report on the State of the Slave Trade on April 15, 1859, FO 84, 1075, fls. 94–116.

171. Bosse to MMC, 37, 24/6/59, FM, SG, Afrique VI, Gabon-Congo I, Dossier 1. See Broadhead, "Trade and Politics on the Congo Coast," p. 173.

172. Régis ainé to MMC, Marseille 18/5/62, Afrique, VI, Gabon-Congo XV; "Souzy, La Côte Occidentale d'África," *Revue Maritime et Coloniale*, tome neuvième, 1863, p. 606.

173. Jean-Claude Nardin, "La Reprise de Relations Franco-Dahoméennes au XIXe Siècle: La Mission d'Auguste Bouët à La Cour d'Abomey (1851)," *Cahiers d'Études Africaines*, 7, 25, 1967, pp. 59–126; Gaëlle Beaujean, "Le cadeau dans les relations diplomatiques du royaume du Danhomè au XIXe siècle," *Politique Africaine*, 165, 1, 2022, p. 84.

174. Robin Law, *Ouidah: The Social History of a West African Slaving Port, 1727–1892* (Athens: Ohio University Press, 2004), p. 218.

175. Vos, *Kongo in the Age of Empire*, p. 26.

176. Bosse to MAC 23/8/60; "La Côte Occidentale d'África," *Revue Maritime et Coloniale*, tome neuvième, 1863, pp. 600, 601; A. Vallon, "La Côte Occidentale d'Afrique," in *Revue Maritime et Coloniale* (Paris: Librairie de Challamel Ainé, 1863), tome neuviéme, p. 394.

177. Bastian, "Ein Besuch in San Salvador," p. 143.

178. Monteiro, *Angola and the River Congo*, pp. 117, 119, 122. See also Bontinck, "Pedro V, Roi de Kongo," p. 7.

179. Pinto, *Le Portugal et le Congo au XIXe Siècle*, p. 61.

180. "Extrato de um Relatório do Chefe do Conselho de Pedro V, o Tenente Zacharias da Silva Cruz, sobre a sua viagem a S. Salvador do Congo," BOGGPA, December 25, 1858, 691, p. 2. See also Bastian, *Ein Besuch in San Salvador*, p. 143.

181. "Extrato de um Relatório do Chefe do Conselho de Pedro V, o Tenente Zacharias da Silva Cruz, sobre a sua viagem a S. Salvador do Congo," BOGGPA, December 25, 1858, 691, p. 2. See also Bastian, *Ein Besuch in San Salvador*, p. 143.

182. René Pélissier, *Les Guerres Grises: Resistance et Revoltes en Angola (1845–1941)* (Orgeval: René Pélissier, 1977), p. 103; Thornton, "Kongo's Incorporation into Angola," p. 353; Birmingham, *A Short History of Modern Angola*, p. 36; Sapede, "Le Roi et le Temps, le Kongo et le Monde," p. 470.

183. Bontinck, "Pedro V, Roi de Kongo," p. 9. Following deeply entrenched traditions, burials of Kongo kings could only happen with the blessing of a priest dispatched from Luanda. The burial coincided with the crowning of the new king. King Garcia V, elected in 1803, reopened relations with the Portuguese in part so Luanda would send a priest to Mbanza Kongo to crown him. See Thornton, *A History of West Central Africa to 1850*, p. 285. It would take thirteen years for Luanda to send a priest to crown the king. See Sapede, "Le Roi et le Temps, le Kongo et le Monde," p. 406.

184. "Ofício do Governador de Angola" on November 23, 1858, AHU, segunda seção de Angola, pasta 24 (2). See also John Thornton, "Master or Dupe? The Reign of Pedro V of Kongo," *Portuguese Studies Review*, 19, 1–2, pp. 115–132; Thornton, "Mbanza Kongo/São Salvador," p. 75.

185. "Ofício do Secretário Geral de Governo de Angola" on December 9, 1858, AHA, cód. 115, fls. 46–46v. See Monteiro, *Angola and the River Congo*, pp. 116, 117–118. See also Broadhead, "Trade and Politics on the Congo Coast," p. 215; Birmingham, *A Short History of Modern Angola*, p. 36; Vos, *Kongo in the Age of Empire*, pp. 27, 44.

186. BOGGPA, 728, 1859, p. 2; Bontinck, "Pedro V, Roi de Kongo," pp. 11–12; Thornton, "Kongo's Incorporation into Angola," p. 353; Vos, *Kongo in the Age of Empire*, pp. 22–24; J. Delcourt, *Au Congo Français: Monseigneur Carrie, 1842–1904* (Brazzaville: Maison Libermann, undated), p. 12.

187. Douglas Wheeler, "Nineteenth-Century African Protest in Angola: Prince Nicolau of Kongo (1830?–1860)," *African Historical Studies*, 1, 1, 1968, pp. 40–59; François Bontinck, "Notes Complémentaires sur de Nicolau Água Rosada e Sardonia," *African Historical Studies*,

2, 1, 1969, pp. 101–119; Frederico Antonio Ferreira, "O Imperador e o Príncipe: A Participação do Governo Imperial Brasileiro na Questão Dinástica no Reino do Congo (1857–1860)," MA Thesis, Universidade Rural do Rio de Janeiro, 2015, Chapter 3; Sapede, "Le Roi et le Temps, le Kongo et le Monde," Chapter 8.

188. *Relatório do Governador Geral da Província de Angola Sebastião Lopes de Carvalho e Menezes referido ao Ano de 1861* (Lisboa: Imprensa Nacional, 1867), p. 13.

189. "Ofício do Secretário Geral de Governo" on December 9, 1858, AHA, cód. 115, fls. 46–46v. See also *Archivo Universal: Revista Hebdomadaria*, September 26 1859, 10 ano, 2a serie, no 13, p. 206.

190. "Ofício do Governo de Angola" on October 31, 1860, AHU, segunda seção de Angola, pasta 27. See also Thornton, "Master or Dupe?," pp. 121–122.

191. *Relatório do Governador Geral da Província de Angola Sebastião Lopes de Carvalho e Menezes referido ao Ano de 1861*, p. 8. See also Pelissier, *História das Campanhas de Angola*, pp. 134–135.

Chapter 7: *Making Forced Labor (Locally and Globally)*

1. "Ofício do Secretário do Governo Geral de Angola" on May 16, 1857, Arquivo Histórico de Angola (AHA), cód. 225, fls. 246v.–247v.

2. Mariana Candido, "The Expansion of Slavery in Benguela During the Nineteenth Century," *International Review of Social History*, 65, 28, 2020, p. 4.

3. Miguel Bandeira Jerónimo, *The "Civilising Mission" of Portuguese Colonialism, 1870–1930* (NY: Palgrave Macmillan, 2015).

4. Maeve Ryan, *Humanitarian Governance and the British Anti-Slavery World System* (New Haven: Yale University Press, 2022), pp. 165–166; Richard Anderson, "Abolition's Adolescence: Apprenticeship as 'Liberation' in Sierra Leone, 1808–1848," *The English Historical Review*, 137, 586, 2022, pp. 763–793.

5. Gad Heuman, "Apprenticeship and Emancipation in the Caribbean: The Seeds of Citizenship," in Whitney Nell Stewart and John Garrison Marks (eds.), *Race and Nation in the Age of Emancipations* (Athens: University of Georgia Press, 2018), pp. 107–120; Kate Boehme, Peter Mitchell, and Alan Lester, "Reforming Everywhere and All at Once: Transitioning to Free Labor across the British Empire, 1837–1838," *Comparative Studies in Society and History*, 60, 3, 2018, pp. 688–718. For the early history of apprenticeship, see Henry Lovejoy and Richard Anderson, "Liberated Africans and Early International Courts of Humanitarian Effort," in Richard Anderson and Henry Lovejoy, *Liberated Africans and the Abolition of the Slave Trade, 1807–1896* (Rochester: University of Rochester Press, 2020), p. 4.

6. François Zuccarelli, "Le régime des engagés à temps au Sénégal (1817–1848)," in *Cahiers d'Études Africaines*, 2, 7, 1962, pp. 420–461; Kelly Brignac, "Free and Bound: Abolition and Forced Labor in the French Empire," PhD Dissertation, Harvard University, 2021; Kelly Brignac, "African Indentured Labor in Senegal and Ste. Marie, Madagascar, 1817–1830," *Slavery & Abolition*, 43, 4, 2022, pp. 779–797; Juliana Barreto Farias, "Um novo cativeiro? O fim do tráfico de escravizados e os engagés à temps no Senegal (1817–1848)," *Afro-Ásia*, 65, 2022, pp. 281–337.

7. Natália Umbelina, *Travail forcé dans l'archipel de São Tomé et Príncipe: les serviçaes* (Paris: L'Harmattan, 2019). Tracy Lopes, "Continuities between the Slave Trade, "Legitimate" Commerce, and the Serviçal Trade: a Look at Four Families in Angola in the Mid- to Late Nineteenth Century," *Canadian Journal of African Studies*, 58, 3, 2024, pp. 555–575.

8. For French contexts in the Atlantic and Indian Oceans, see Céline Flory, *De l'Esclavage à la Liberté Forcée: Histoire des Travailleurs Africains Engagés dans la Caraïbe Française au XIXe Siècle* (Paris: Karthala, 2015); Céline Flory, "Affranchir sans libérer: la pratique du 'rachat' de captifs africains dans l'espace colonial français (XIXe siècle)," in Dominique Rogers and Boris Lesueur (eds.), *Libres après les abolitions? Statuts et identités aux Amériques et en Afrique* (Paris: Karthala, 2019), pp. 57–69; Brignac, "Free and Bound," Chapter 1; Brignac, "African Indentured Labor in Senegal and Ste. Marie," pp. 779–797; For British contexts, see Stephan Karghoo and Sayendra Peerthum, "Un Peuple Malheureux mais Fier"; "Africains Libérés et Engagés à l'île Maurice, vers 1811–1839," in Vijaya Teelock and Thomas

Vernet (eds.); *Traites, Esclavage et Transition vers l'Engagisme: Perspectives Nouvelles sur les Mascareignes et le Sud-Ouest de l'Océan Indien* (Réduit: University of Mauritius Press, 2015), pp. 95–111; Ryan, *Humanitarian Governance and the British Anti-Slavery World System*, p. 6; Kate Boehme, Peter Mitchell, and Alan Lester, "Reforming Everywhere and All at Once: Transitioning to Free Labor across the British Empire, 1837–1838," *Comparative Studies in Society and History*, 60, 3, 2018, pp. 688–718.

9. Yesenia Barragan, *Freedom's Captives: Slavery and Gradual Emancipation on the Colombian Black Pacific* (NYC: Cambridge University Press, 2021).

10. Magdalena Candioti, "El tiempo de los libertos: conflictos y litigación en torno a la ley de vientre libre en el Río de la Plata (1813–1860)," *História*, 38, 2019; Magdalena Candioti, "Free Womb Law, Legal Asynchronies, and Migrations: Suing for an Enslaved Woman's Child in Nineteenth-Century Río de la Plata," *The Americas*, 77, 1, 2020, pp. 73–99; Magdalena Candioti, "Interamerican Dialogues and Experimentations in the Spanish South American Gradual Abolitionist Process (1810–1870)," *Oxford Research Encyclopedia of Latin American History*, 2022, pp. 1–23. See also Magdalena Candioti, *Una historia de la emancipación negra. Esclavitud y abolición en la Argentina* (Buenos Aires: Siglo veintiuno editores, 2021), pp. 26–31.

11. Ryan, *Humanitarian Governance and the British Anti-Slavery World System*, p. 16.

12. Catherine Hall and Sonya Rose, "Being at Home with the Empire," in Catherine Hall and Sonya Rose (eds.), *At Home with the Empire: Metropolitan Culture and the Imperial World* (NY: Cambridge University Press, 2006), p. 7.

13. Richard Anderson, "Liberated Africans," *Oxford Encyclopedia of African History*, 2021, p. 9.

14. Bronwen Everill, *Abolition and Empire in Sierra Leone and Liberia* (NY: Palgrave Macmillan, 2013), pp. 43, 48, 49, 52.

15. Ndubueze Mbah, "The Black Englishmen of Old Calabar: Freedom and Mobility in the Age of Abolition in West Africa," *Radical History Review*, 1 144, 2022, p. 45.

16. Allen Howard, "New Insights on Liberated Africans: The 1831 Freetown Census," in Richard Anderson and Henry Lovejoy (eds.), *Liberated Africans and the Abolition of the Slave Trade, 1807–1896* (Rochester: University of Rochester Press, 2020), p. 121.

17. Samuel Nyanchoga and Michelle Liebst, "Rethinking Liberated Africans as Abolitionists: Bombay Africans, Resistance, and Ritual Integration in Coastal Kenya, 1846–1900," *Esclavages & Post-esclavages* 10, 2024.

18. Beatriz Mamigonian, "The Rights of Liberated Africans in Nineteenth Century Brazil," in Stephan Conermann, Mariana Dias Paes, Roberto Hofmeister Pich, and Paulo Cruz Terra (eds.), *Current Trends in Slavery Studies in Brazil* (Berlin: De Gruyter, 2023), p. 79.

19. Lisa Ford and Naomi Parkinson, "Legislating Liberty: Liberated Africans and the Abolition Act, 1806–1824," *Slavery & Abolition*, 2021, pp. 827–846.

20. Anita Rupprecht, "'When he gets among his Countrymen, they tell him that he is free': Slave Trade Abolition, Indentured Africans and a Royal Commission," *Slavery & Abolition*, 33, 3, 2012, pp. 435–455.

21. S. A. Cavell, "Abolition, the West India Colonies and the Troubling Case of Vice-Admiral Sir Alexander Cochrane, 1807–1823," *The Mariner's Mirror*, 107, 1, 2021, pp. 23–39.

22. Anita Rupprecht, "'An Anomalous Population': Recaptive Narratives in Antigua and the British Colonial Archive, 1807–1828," in Sophie White and Trevor Burnard (eds.), *Hearing Enslaved Voices: African and Indian Slave Testimony in British and French America, 1700–1848* (New York: Routledge, 2020), pp. 204–222.

23. Céline Flory, "Les migrations de travail à destination de la Guyane et des Antilles françaises: Sociétés post-esclavagistes, macule servile et genre," in Myriam Cottias and Hebe Mattos (eds.), *Esclavage et subjectivités: dans l'Atlantique luso-brésilien et français (xviie-xxe siècles)* (Marseille: OpenEdition Press, 2016); Brignac, "Free and Bound,"; Brignac, "African Indentured Labor in Senegal and Ste. Marie, Madagascar," pp. 779–797; Farias, "Um novo cativeiro?," pp. 281–337.

24. Padraic Scanlan, "The Colonial Rebirth of British Anti-Slavery: The Liberated African Villages of Sierra Leone, 1815–1824," *The American Historical Review*, 121, 4, 2016, pp. 1085–1113. See also Padraic Scanlan, *Freedom's Debtors: British Antislavery in Sierra Leone in the Age of Revolution* (New Haven: Yale University Press, 2017). For further background on

Sierra Leone, see Philip Misevich, *Abolition and the Transformation of Atlantic Commerce in Southern Sierra Leone, 1790s to 1860s* (Trenton: Africa World Press, 2019); Richard Anderson, *Abolition in Sierra Leone: Re-building Lives and Identities in Nineteenth-Century West Africa* (NYC: Cambridge University Press, 2020); Emma Christopher, *Freedom in White and Black: A Lost Story of the Illegal Slave Trade and its Global Legacy* (Wisconsin: University of Wisconsin Press, 2019).

25. Ryan, *Humanitarian Governance and the British Anti-Slavery World System*, pp. 3, 27, 36, 39.

26. Emma Christopher, *"'Tis enough that we give them liberty'? Liberated Africans at Sierra Leone in the Early Era of Slave Trade Suppression,"* in Robert Burroughs and Richard Huzzey (eds.), *The Suppression of the Atlantic Slave Trade: British Policies, Practices and Representations of Naval Coercion* (Manchester: Manchester University Press, 2015), p. 59. See also Suzanne Schwarz, "The Impact of Liberated African 'Disposal' Policies in Early Nineteenth-Century Sierra," in Richard Anderson and Henry Lovejoy, *Liberated Africans and the Abolition of the Slave Trade, 1807-1896* (Rochester: University of Rochester Press, 2020), pp. 47-53.

27. Henry Lovejoy and Richard Anderson, "Liberated Africans and Early International Courts of Humanitarian Effort," p 9; Ryan, *Humanitarian Governance and the British Anti-Slavery World System*, pp. 104-107. See also Kyle Prochnow, "Perpetual Expatriation: Forced Migration and Liberated African Apprenticeship in the Gambia," in Richard Anderson and Henry Lovejoy (eds.), *Liberated Africans and the Abolition of the Slave Trade, 1807-1896* (Rochester: University of Rochester Press, 2020), pp. 347-367.

28. Ryan, *Humanitarian Governance and the British Anti-Slavery World System*, Chapter 6. See also Richard Anderson, "The Diaspora of Sierra Leone's Recaptive Africans: Enlistment, Forced Migration, and "Liberation" at Freetown, 1808-1863," *African Economic History*, 41, 2013, pp. 101-138; Christopher, *"'Tis enough that we give them liberty'?* pp. 60-63; Kyle Prochnow, "'Saving an Extraordinary Expense to the Nation': African Recruitment for the West India Regiment in the British Atlantic World," *Atlantic Studies*, 2020, pp. 3-11; Laura Adderley and Sharla Fett, "Slave Trade Refugees and Imperial Agendas: The Resettlement of 'Liberated Africans' into British West Indian Regiments and Liberian Militias, 1808-60," in Martin Lemberg-Pedersen, Sharla Fett, Lucy Mayblin, Nina Sahraoui, and Eva Magdalena Stambøl (eds.), *Postcoloniality and Forced Migration: Mobility, Control, Agency* (Bristol: Bristol University Press, 2022), pp. 28-45; Kyle Prochnow, "The West India Regiments: African Soldiers, War, and Empire in The British Atlantic Tropics," PhD Dissertation, York University, 2022, pp. 59-82.

29. Farias, "Um novo cativeiro?," p. 325.

30. Flory, *De l'Esclavage à la Liberté Forcée*. See also François Renault, *Libération d'Esclaves et Nouvelle Servitude: Les Rachats de Captifs Africains pour le Compte des Colonies Françaises après l'Abolition de l'Esclavage* (Abidjan: Nouvelles Éditions Africaines, 1976); Flory, "Affranchir sans libérer: la pratique du 'rachat' de captifs africains dans l'espace colonial français (XIXe siècle)," pp. 57-69. See also David Northrup, "Freedom and Indentured Labor in the French Caribbean, 1848-1900," in David Eltis (ed.), *Coerced and Free Migration: Global Perspectives* (Palo Alto: Stanford University Press, 2002), pp. 204-228.

31. Jelmer Vos, "'Without the Slave Trade no Recruitment': From Slave Trading to 'Migrant Recruitment' in the Lower Congo, 1830-1890," in Benjamin Lawrance and Richard Roberts (eds.), *Trafficking in Slavery's Wake: Law and the Experience of Women and Children in Africa* (Athens: Ohio University Press, 2012), pp. 45-64; Flory, *De l'Esclavage à la Liberté Forcée*; Céline Flory, "Affranchir sans libérer: la pratique du 'rachat' de captifs africains dans l'espace colonial français (XIXe siècle)," in Dominique Rogers and Boris Lesueur (eds.), *Libres après les abolitions? Statuts et identités aux Amériques et en Afrique* (Paris: Karthala, 2019), p. 57-69.

32. Brignac, "African Indentured Labor in Senegal and Ste. Marie, Madagascar," pp. 779-797. See also Zuccarelli, "Le Régime des Engagés à Temps au Sénégal (1817-1848)," pp. 420-461.

33. Sudel Fuma, *Histoire d'un Peuple: La Réunion (1848-1900)* (Saint Denis: Université de la Réunion, 1994), pp. 30-48. See also Alessandro Stanziani, *Sailors, Slaves, and Immigrants: Bondage in the Indian Ocean World, 1750-1914* (New York: Palgrave Macmillan,

2014), p. 101; Alessandro Stanziani, "Travail, droits et immigration. Une comparaison entre l'île Maurice et l'île de La Réunion, années 1840–1880," *Le Mouvement Social*, 4, 241, 2012, pp. 47–64. See also Alessandro Stanziani, "Local Bondage in Global Economies: Servants, Wage Earners, and Indentured Migrants in Nineteenth-Century France, Great Britain, and the Mascarene Islands," *Modern Asian Studies*, 47, 4, 2013, pp. 218–1251; Alessandro Stanziani, *Bondage. Labor and Rights in Eurasia from the Sixteenth to the Early Twentieth Centuries* (NYC: Berghahn Books, 2014), pp. 186–187.

34. Jehanne-Emmanuelle Monnier, *Esclaves de la canne à sucre: engagés et planteurs à Nossi-Bé, Madagascar 1850–1880* (Paris: France: L'Harmattan, 2006), p. 121.

35. Monnier, *Esclaves de la canne à sucre*, p. 169.

36. Edward Alpers, "'Le Caractère d'une Traite d'Esclaves Déguisée (the nature of a disguised slave trade)'? Labor Recruitment for La Réunion at Portuguese Mozambique, 1887–1889," *Ufahamu: A Journal of African Studies*, 40, 1, 2018, p. 13. See also Virginie Chaillou-Atrous, "La reprise de l'immigration africaine à La Réunion à la fin du XIXème siècle: de la traite déguisée à l'engagement de travail libre," *French Colonial History*, 16, 2016, pp. 27–54.

37. Caree Banton, "Who Is Black in a Black Republic? Labor in the Remaking of Black Citizenship in Liberia," in Whitney Nell Stewart, John Garrison Marks and Julie Saville (eds.), *Race and Nation in the Age of Emancipations* (Athens: University of Georgia Press, 2018), p. 134. See Lisa Lindsay, *Atlantic Bonds: A Nineteenth-Century Odyssey from America to Africa* (Chapel Hill: University of North Carolina Press, 2017), pp. 97–98.

38. Beatriz Mamigonian, *Africanos Livres: A Abolição do Tráfico de Escravos no Brasil* (São Paulo: Companhia das Letras, 2017). See also Walter Hawthorne, "'Being Now, as It Were, One Family:' Shipmate Bonding on the Slave Vessel Emilia, in Rio De Janeiro and throughout the Atlantic World," *Luso-Brazilian Review*, 45, 1, 2008, p. 65; Jake Richards, "Anti-Slave-Trade Law, 'Liberated Africans' and the State in the South Atlantic World, c.1839–1852," *Past & Present*, 241, 1, 2018, p. 197.

39. Inés Roldán de Montaud, "En los Borrosos Confines de la Libertad: El Caso de los Negros Emancipados en Cuba," *Revista de Indias*, 251, LXXI, pp. 135. See also Inés Roldán de Montaud, *Origen, Evolución y Supresión del Grupo de Negros "Emancipados" en Cuba (1817–1870)* (Madrid: Consejo Superior de Investigaciones Científicas, 1982); Evelyn Jennings, "The Path to Sweet Success: Free and Unfree Labor in the Building of Roads and Rails in Havana, Cuba, 1790–1835," *International Review of Social History*, 2019, p. 16.

40. Matthew Hopper, *Slaves of One Master: Globalization and Slavery in Arabia in the Age of Empire* (New Haven: Yale University Press, 2015), p. 175. See also Lindsay Doulton, "The Flag that sets us Free: Antislavery, Africans, and the Royal Navy in the Western Indian Ocean," in Robert Harms, Bernard Freamon, and David Blight (eds.), *Indian Ocean Slavery in the Age of Abolition* (New Haven: Yale University Press, 2013), pp. 105–111.

41. Marina Carter, Sayendra Peerthum, and V. Govinden, *The Last Slaves: Liberated Africans in 19th Century Mauritius* (Port Louis: Center for Research on Indian Ocean Societies, 2003); Karghoo and Peerthum, "Un Peuple Malheureux mais Fier," pp. 95–111.

42. Hopper, "Liberated Africans in the Indian Ocean," p. 275. See also Doulton, "The Royal Navy's Anti-Slavery Campaign," pp. 222–231; Vijaya Teelock, *Bitter Sugar: Sugar and Slavery in 19th Century Mauritius* (Moka: Mahatma Gandhi Institute, 1998), p. 270; Gwyn Campbell, *Africa and the Indian Ocean World from Early Times to Circa 1900* (Cambridge: Cambridge University Press, 2019), p. 278; Raphaël Cheriau, *Imperial Powers and Humanitarian Interventions: The Zanzibar Sultanate, Britain, and France in the Indian Ocean, 1862–1905* (NYC: Routledge, 2020), p. 87.

43. Hopper, *Slaves of One Master*, p. 176.

44. "Ofício do Major Ajudante de Ordens J. C. S. Montez" on April 30, 1839, AHA, cód. 1081. For context, see José Curto, "Producing 'Liberated' Africans in the Mid-Nineteenth Century Angola," in Richard Anderson and Henry Lovejoy (eds.), *Liberated Africans and the Abolition of the Slave Trade, 1807–1896* (Rochester; University of Rochester Press, 2020), pp. 239–256.

45. "Termo do Capitão do Batalhão de Infantaria de Linha Agostinho Gonçalves dos Santos" on October 8, 1839, AHA, cód. 2563, fl. 178.

46. Sá da Bandeira, *O Tráfico da Escravatura e o Bill de Lord Palmerston* (Lisboa: Typ. De José Baptista Morando, 1840), p. 63.

47. Ryan, *Humanitarian Governance and the British Anti-Slavery World System*, pp. 161–162.

48. Dispatch by Brand on May 16, 1845, FO 84, 569, fls. 404–404v. For general context, see "Apprenticeship and the Negotiation of Freedom: The Recaptive Africans of the Anglo-Portuguese Mixed Commission in Luanda (1844–1870)," *Africana Studia*, 14, 2010, pp. 264–265; Samuël Coghe, "The Problem of Freedom in a Mid Nineteenth-Century Atlantic Slave Society: The Recaptive Africans of thee Anglo-Portuguese Mixed Commission in Luanda (1844–1870)," *Slavery & Abolition*, 33, 3, 2012, pp. 489–490; Ryan, *Humanitarian Governance and the British Anti-Slavery World System*, p. 22.

49. Commissioners to Palmerston on October 30, 1846, *Minutes of Evidence taken before the Duke de Broglie* (London: T. R. Harrison, 1847), p. 173. See also Luis Martínez-Fernández, "The Havana Anglo-Spanish Mixed Commission for the Suppression of the Slave Trade and Cuba's Emancipados," *Slavery & Abolition*, 16, 2, 1995, pp. 207, 209; Henry Lovejoy, "The Registers of Liberated Africans of the Havana Slave Trade Commission: Implementation and Policy, 1824–1841," *Slavery & Abolition*, 37, 1, 2016, p. 4. See also Anderson, "Liberated Africans," p. 11; Lovejoy and Anderson, "Liberated Africans and Early International Courts of Humanitarian Effort," p. 10.

50. Martínez-Fernández, "The Havana Anglo-Spanish Mixed Commission for the Suppression of the Slave Trade and Cuba's Emancipados," p. 209; Jennifer Nelson, "Liberated Africans in the Atlantic World: The Courts of Mixed Commission in Havana and Rio de Janeiro, 1819–1871" (PhD Dissertation, The University of Leeds, 2015), pp. 100–103; Jennifer Nelson, "Slavery, Race, and Conspiracy: The HMS Romney in Nineteenth-Century Cuba," *Atlantic Studies*, 14, 2, 2017, pp. 174–195. See also Ryan, Humanitarian Governance and the British Anti-Slavery World System, p. 139. For the early history of recaptives in the Caribbean, see Juan Luis Bachero Bachero, "La lucha contra la trata de esclavos en el Caribe: Los Tribunales del Vicealmirantazgo británicos, 1807–1825," *Hispanic American Historical Review*, 103, 4, 2023, pp. 589–616.

51. Alain Yacou, *Essor des Plantations et Subversion Antiesclavagiste à Cuba* (1791–1845) (Paris: Karthala, 2010), pp. 426–427.

52. Mr. Fox to Viscount Palmerston on October 15, 1834, in *Correspondence with the British Commissioners at Sierra Leone, Havana, Rio de Janeiro, and Surinam relating to the Slave Trade* (London: William Clowes and Sons, 1835), p. 35. See Ryan, *Humanitarian Governance and the British Anti-Slavery World System*, pp. 133–136.

53. Jennifer Nelson, "Apprentices of Freedom: Atlantic Histories of the *Africanos Livres* in Mid-Nineteenth Century Rio de Janeiro," *Itinerario*, 39, 2015, pp. 359, 360; Martine Jean, "Recaptive Africans, Slaves, and Convict Labor in the Construction of Rio de Janeiro's Casa de Correção: Atlantic Labor Regimes and Confinement in Brazil's Port City," *International Review of Social History*, 2019, p. 27.

54. Pedro Brandão de Sousa Culmant Ramos, "Homens de confiança: Moral, Antiescravismo e o Abolicionismo Inglês na Supressão do Tráfico Brasileiro de Escravos (1836–1846)," MA Thesis, UFRJ, 2016, Chapter 2.

55. Beatriz Mamigonian, "In the Name of Freedom: Slave Trade Abolition, the Law and the Brazilian Branch of the African Emigration Scheme (Brazil-British West Indies, 1830s–1850s)," *Slavery & Abolition*, 30, 1, 2009, pp. 41–66; Mamigonian, *Africanos Livres*, pp. 182–189, 201. See also Henrique Antonio Ré, "A abolição da escravidão não significa o estabelecimento da liberdade: os abolicionistas britânicos e os africanos libertados do tráfico, 1840–1854," *Clio*, 39, 2022, p. 482; Henrique Antonio Ré, "H. M. R. S. Crescent: Navio hospital e presiganga Britânica no porto do Rio de Janeiro, 1840–1854," *Revista de História*, 182, 2023, pp. 2–26.

56. Beatriz Mamigonian, "Conflicts over the Meanings of Freedom: The Recaptive Africans' Struggle for Emancipation in Brazil (1840s–1860s)," in Rosemary Brana-Shute and Randy J. Sparks (eds.), *Paths to Freedom: Manumission in the Atlantic World* (Columbia: University of South Carolina Press, 2009), pp. 239–240.

57. Mamigonian, *Africanos Livres*, pp. 360–399. See Alain Youssef, "Questão Christie em Perspectiva Global: Pressão Britânica, Guerra Civil Norte-Americana e o Início da Crise da Escravidão Brasileira (1860–1864)," *Revista de História*, 177, 2018, pp. 1–26; Alain Youssef, "O Império do Brasil na Segunda Era da Abolição," PhD Dissertation, USP, 2019, pp. 45–65; Isadora Mota, "On the Verge of War: Black Insurgency, the 'Christie Affair', and British Antislavery in Brazil," *Slavery & Abolition*, 43, 1, 2021, pp. 120–139 See also Ryan, *Humanitarian Governance and the British Anti-Slavery World System*, pp. 147–151.

58. Francisco Travassos Valdez, *Six Years of a Traveller's Life in Western Africa* (London: Hurst & Blackett, 1861), vol. II, pp. 114. For the wider context, see Ryan, *Humanitarian Governance and the British Anti-Slavery World System*, pp. 160–161.

59. Coghe, "The Problem of Freedom in a Mid Nineteenth-Century Atlantic Slave Society," p. 480.

60. Coghe, "The Problem of Freedom in a Mid Nineteenth-Century Atlantic Slave Society," p. 480.

61. "Mapa dos Escravos Apresados" on February 18, 1845, AHU, segunda seção de Angola, pasta 8.

62. "Bando" on March 26, 1845, AHA, cód. 522, fls. 215–216.

63. "Ofício do Alferes Ajudante de Ordens J. B. de Sampaio" on November 20, 1846, AHA, cód. 1082, fl. 17v.

64. Dispatch by Edmond Gabriel and George Jackson on February 6, 1847, FO 84, 671, fls. 56–58.

65. "Instruções para o Alferes do Batalhão de Linha de Luanda" on June 21, 1848, AHA, cód. 1178, fls. 26–26v.

66. "Portaria do Governador de Angola" on September 5, 1844, *Annaes Maritimos e Coloniaes*, 10, segunda série, p. 347. See "Ordem e Instrução ao Comandante da Corveta Relâmpago" on January 21, 1847, AHA, cód. 1178, fls. 1v.–2v.; "Ordens do Governo Geral da Província de Angola" on May 31, 1848, AHU, Miscelânea 766, maço 1. See also Simão José da Luz Soriano, *Revelações da Minha Vida* (Lisboa: Typographia Universal, 1860), p. 561.

67. S. A. Cavell, "Abolition, the West India Colonies and the Troubling Case of Vice-Admiral Sir Alexander Cochrane, 1807–1823," *The Mariner's Mirror*, 107, 1, 2021, pp. 26, 29.

68. Anita Rupprecht, "'When he gets among his Countrymen, they tell him that he is free': Slave Trade Abolition, Indentured Africans and a Royal Commission," *Slavery & Abolition*, 33, 3, 2012, pp. 435–455; Anita Rupprecht, "'He says that if he is not taught a trade, he will run away': Recaptured Africans, Desertion, and Mobility in the British Caribbean, 1808–1828," in Marcus Rediker, Titas Chakraborty, and Matthias van Rossum (eds.), *A Global History of Runaways: Workers, Mobility, and Capitalism, 1600–1850* (Berkeley: University of California Press, 2019), pp. 178–199; Rupprecht, "An Anomalous Population," pp. 204–223.

69. Kirsten McKenzie, *Imperial Underworld: An Escaped Convict and the Transformation of the British Colonial Order* (New York: Cambridge University Press, 2016), p. 119.

70. Hopper, *Slaves of One Master*, p. 177.

71. Ryan, *Humanitarian Governance and the British Anti-Slavery World System*, p. 5.

72. The Sessional Papers Printed by the Order of the House of Lords (vol. IX, 1844). See also Anderson, "Liberated Africans," p. 11.

73. Johnson Asiegbu, *Slavery and the Politics of Liberation, 1787–1861: A Study of Recaptive African Emigration and British Anti-Slavery Policy* (London: Longman, 1969), p. 190; Pearson, *Distant Freedom*, pp. 212–213. For the transfer of libertos to Cape Town, see Patrick Harries, "Middle Passages of the Southwest Indian Ocean: A Century of Forced Immigration from Africa to the Cape of Good Hope," *The Journal of African History*, 55, 2014, p. 186.

74. Lawrence Jennings, "French Reaction to the 'Disguised British Slave Trade': France and British African Emigration Projects, 1840–1864," *Cahiers d'études Africaines*, 18, 69–70, 1978, pp. 206–207.

75. Jelmer Vos, "'Without the Slave Trade no Recruitment': From Slave Trading to 'Migrant Recruitment' in the Lower Congo, 1830–1890," in Benjamin Lawrance and Richard Roberts (eds.), *Trafficking in Slavery's Wake: Law and the Experience of Women and Children in Africa* (Athens: Ohio University Press, 2012), pp. 45–64; Flory, *De l'Esclavage à la Liberté Forcée*.

76. Fuma, *Histoire d'un Peuple: La Réunion*, pp. 30–48.

77. Cheriau, *Imperial Powers and Humanitarian Interventions*, p. 82. See also Renault, *Libération d'Esclaves et Nouvelle Servitude*, pp. 46–47.

78. Jennings, "French Reaction to the 'Disguised British Slave Trade,'" pp. 206–207.

79. Francisco Travassos Valdez, *Six Years of a Traveller's Life in Western Africa* (London: Hurst and Blackett Publishers, 1861), vol. II, p. 48. See also William Gervase Clarence-Smith, *The Third Portuguese Empire, 1825–1875: A Study in Economic Imperialism* (Manchester: Manchester University Press, 1985), p. 39.

80. Coghe "Apprenticeship and the Negotiation of Freedom," p. 265.

81. "Ofício do Secretário de Governo Interino Antonio Manoel da Silva Heitor" on April 30, 1856, AHA, cód. 469. See also BOGGPA, September 6, 1856, 571, p. 1; *Boletim do Conselho Ultramarino* (Lisboa: Imprensa Nacional, 1869), vol. II, p. 307.

82. Maysa Espíndola Souza, "A Liberdade do Contrato: O Trabalho Africano na Legislação do Império Português, 1850–1910," MA Thesis, UFSC, 2017, pp. 53–54. See also Marta Macedo, "Coffee on the move: technology, labour and race in the making of a transatlantic plantation system," *Mobilities*, 16, 2, 2021, pp. 262–272.

83. *Boletim do Conselho Ultramarino* (Lisboa: Imprensa Nacional, 1869), vol. II, p. 677. See also "Decreto" on August 25, 1855, in *Annaes do Conselho Ultramarino*, parte official, serie I, fevereiro de 1854 a dezembro de 1858 (Lisboa: Imprensa Nacional, 1867), p. 187.

84. "Ofício do Governador de Angola" on July 22, 1856, Ministério dos Negócios Estrangeiros, cx. 985. See also Robert Nartey, "From Slave to Serviçal: Labor in the Plantation Economy of São Tomé and Príncipe, 1872–1932," PhD Dissertation, University of Illinois at Chicago, 1986, p. 70.

85. Sebastião Lopes de Calheiros e Menezes, *Relatório do Governo Geral da Província de Angola para o ano de 1861* (Lisboa: Imprensa Nacional, 1867), pp. 414–424. See BOGGPA, 518, 1855, 2–4. See also Souza, "A Liberdade do Contrato," pp. 58–61.

86. Macedo, "Coffee on the move," p. 266.

87. "Carta para o Marquês de Sá da Bandeira" on April 27, 1861, AHU, papéis de Sá da Bandeira, maço 827; "Carta para o Marquês de Sá da Bandeira" on July 8, 1861, AHU, papéis de Sá da Bandeira, maço 827. See also Bernardino Freire de Figueiredo Abreu e Castro, "Breve Notícia do Estado da Cultura nas Nossas Províncias Ultramarinas" on June 25, 1861, in *O Archivo Rural: Jornal de Agricultura, Artes e Sciencias Correlativas* (Lisboa: Typ. da Sociedade Typographica Franco-Portugueza, 1862), vol. IV, p. 325; Menezes, *Relatório do Governo Geral da Província de Angola para o ano de 1861*, p. 230.

88. *Annaes do Conselho Ultramarino*, parte não oficial, (Lisboa: Imprensa Nacional, 1868), p. 4. For the wider context, see César Rafael Jurante, "Os contratados de Angola para São Tomé e Príncipe: O impacto do contrato na colónia de Angola (1876–1887)," MA Thesis, ISCTE, Instituto Universitário de Lisboa, 2021, p. 37. See also Augusto Nascimento, "A crise braçal de 1875 em São Tomé," *Revista Crítica de Ciências Sociais*, 34, 1992, pp. 317–329.

89. Lopes, "Continuities between the Slave Trade, "Legitimate" Commerce, and the Serviçal Trade," pp. 555–575.

90. Gabriel and Huntley on October 10, 1861, in *Correspondence with the British Commissioners at Sierra Leone, Havana, the Cape of Good Hope, and Loanda from January 1 to December 31, 1861* (London: Harrison and Sons, 1862), p. 64; Annual report on the slave trade on September 30, 1866, *Accounts and Papers*, Slave Trade, 5 February–21 August 1867, vol. LXXIII, p. 63.

91. Pablo Eyzaguirre, "Small Farmers and Estates in São Tomé, West Africa," PhD Dissertation, Yale University, 1986, pp. 167, 188.

92. Letter from Uredenburg on August 17, 1865, fls. 158–161, FO 84, 1235. See also Menezes *Relatório do Governo Geral da Província de Angola para o ano de 1861*, pp. 242–243; "Carta do Governador de Angola" on March 29, 1862, AHU, Angola, pasta 30. For background, see Catherine Higgs, *Chocolate Islands: Cocoa, Slavery, and Colonial Africa* (Athens: Ohio University Press, 2012), Chapter 2; Augusto do Nascimento, "Escravatura, Trabalho Forçado e Contrato em S. Tomé e Príncipe nos Sécs. XIX e XX: Sujeição e Ética Laboral," *Africana Studia*, 7, 2004, pp. 183–217; Maciel Santos, "Trabalho Forçado na Época Colonial: Um Padrão a partir do Caso Português," *Hendu*, 4, 1, 2014, pp. 9–21; Mariana Candido, "Des

passeports pour la liberté? Libres, affranchis et esclaves dans les déplacements de population à destination de São Tomé. Les conceptions raciales dans l'Atlantique Sud (XIX siècle)," in Dominique Rogers and Boris Lesueur (eds.), *Libres après les abolitions? Status et identités aux Amériques et en Afrique* (Paris: Karthala editions, 2019), pp 72–92.

93. Menezes, *Relatório do Governo Geral da Província de Angola para o ano de 1861*, p. 331; "Extrato de Carta do Comodoro Horseby" on November 7, 1866, Ministério dos Negócios Estrangeiros, cx. 985.

94. British Legation in Lisbon on July 13, 1866, Ministério dos Negócios Estrangeiros, cx. 985.

95. Her majesty's acting commissary judge to Lord Stanley on September 30, 1868, in *Accounts and Papers*, Slave Trade, 10 December 1868–11 August 1869, 1868–1869, vol. LVI. For context, see Evelyn Hu-DeHart, "Chinese Coolie Labor in Cuba in the Nineteenth Century: Free Labor of Neoslavery," *Contributions in Black Studies*, 12, 1994, pp. 38–54; Evelyn Hu-DeHart, "La Trata Amarilla: The 'Yellow Trade' and the Middle Passage, 1847–1884," in Emma Christopher, Cassandra Pybus, and Markus Rediker (eds.), *Many Middle Passages: Forced Migration and the Making of the Modern World* (Berkeley and Los Angeles: University of California Press, 2007), pp. 66–184; Evelyn Hu-DeHart, "Chinese Contract Labor in the Wake of the Abolition of Slavery in the Americas: A New Form of Slavery or Transition to Free Labor in the Case of Cuba?," *Amerasia Journal*, 45, 1, 2019, pp. 6–26; Imilcy Balboa Navarro, "Las recontratas de Coolies. A medio camino entre la esclavitud y la libertad formal (Cuba, década de 1860)," *Tzintzun*, 74, 2021, pp. 127–160.

96. Paulo Cesar Gonçalves, "Piratas, anamitas e traficâncias: um estudo sobre o engajamento de trabalhadores na Macau oitocentista," *Revista Mundos do Trabalho*, 15, 2023, pp. 1–22. For the broader context beyond Macau, see Mònica Ginés Blasi, "Exploiting Chinese Labour Emigration in Treaty Ports: The Role of Spanish Consulates in the "Coolie Trade," *International Review of Social History*, 66, 2020, pp. 1–24; Mònica Ginés Blasi, "The International Trafficking of Chinese Children and its Conflicting Legalities in Mid-nineteenth Century Treaty-Port China," *Slavery & Abolition*, 44, 1, pp. 157–180.

97. Eric Guerassimoff, "Travail Colonial, Coolies et Diplomatie: Réclamations Chinoises autour du Contrat d'Engagement à Cuba au XIXe Siècle," in Eric Guerassimoff and Issiaka Mandé (eds.), *Le Travail Colonial* (Paris: Riveneuve Éditions, 2015), pp. 417–463. For the broader context of Chinese migrations, see Stanziani, *Sailors, Slaves, and Immigrants*, p. 92; Alessandro Stanziani, "Slavery and Post-Slavery in the Indian Ocean World," *Oxford Research Encyclopedia of African History*, 2020, pp. 13–14.

98. Menezes, *Relatório do Governo Geral da Província de Angola para o ano de 1861*, pp. 278, 289, 293.

99. Menezes, *Relatório do Governo Geral da Província de Angola para o ano de 1861*, pp. 85, 264,

100. Report on the State of the Slave Trade on April 15, 1859, FO 84, 1075, fls. 94–116.

101. "Decreto de 14 de dezembro de 1854," in *A Abolição do Tráfico e da Escravatura em Angola: Documentos* (Luanda: Ministério da Cultura, 1997), pp. 35–38. See A. de Oliveira Pires, *Algumas Reflexões sobre a Questão do Trabalho nas Possessões Portuguezas d'Africa* (Lisboa: Typographia Progresso, 1874), p. 31.

102. Daniel Domingues da Silva and Edward Alpers, "Abolition and the Registration of Slaves and Libertos in Portuguese Mozambique, 1856–76," *Journal of African History*, 62, 3, 2021, pp. 377–393.

103. Draft of Circular by Palmerston on December 1847, FO 84, 675, fls. 121–134.

104. Report by Edmund Gabriel in 1850, PRO, FO 84/792, p. 142. See also João Pedro Marques, *Sá da Bandeira e o Fim da Escravidão: Vitória da Moral, Desforra do Interesse* (Lisboa: Imprensa de Ciências Sociais, 2008), p. 49; Jerónimo, *The "Civilising Mission" of Portuguese Colonialism*, p. 24.

105. *Representação dos Principaes Moradores do Districto de Benguella* (Lisboa: Typographia, 1855), pp. 20–21.

106. Valdez, *Six Years of a Traveller's Life in Western Africa*, p. 116.

107. "Ata da Sessão da Junta Protetora dos Escravos e Libertos" on July 27, 1856, 1856, AHA, Angola, pasta 22-A, fl. 20v.

108. Frederico Welwitsch, "Cultura do Algodão em Angola" on August 20, 1861, *Jornal da Sociedade Agricola do Porto*, 10, 1861, p. 292.

109. "Ofício do Secretário Geral do Governo de Angola" on May 3, 1855, AHA, cód. 179, fls. 201v.–202.

110. Letter of the Luanda City Council on September 7, 1855, in *British and Foreign State Papers, 1855–1856* (London: William Ridgway, 1865), p. 936. For reactions to the 1854 decree in Mozambique, see Silva and Alpers, "Abolition and the Registration of Slaves and Libertos in Portuguese Mozambique," p. 5. For Benguela, see Esteban Salas, "Making Portuguese Colonial Governance: Slavery, Forced Labor, and Racial Ideology in the Interior from Benguela, 1760–1860," PhD Dissertation, University of Notre Dame, 2021, p. 108.

111. Letter of the Luanda City Council on September 7, 1855, in *British and Foreign State Papers, 1855–1856* (London: William Ridgway, 1865), p. 939. See also Dispatch by Gabriel on November 12, 1855, FO 84, 960, fls. 355–357; "Ofício do Governador de Angola" on September 22, 1855, AHU, segunda seção de Angola, pasta 22 A.

112. Letter of the Luanda City Council on September 7, 1855, in *British and Foreign State Papers, 1855–1856* (London: William Ridgway, 1865), p. 939. See also Dispatch by Gabriel on November 12, 1855, FO 84, 960, fls. 355–357; "Ofício do Governador de Angola" on September 22, 1855, AHU, segunda seção de Angola, pasta 22 A.

113. BOGGPA, 554, 1856, 3.

114. "Ofício do Governador da Fortaleza de São Pedro" in 1857, BML, cód. 66, fl. 55–56.

115. Camillia Cowling, *Conceiving Freedom: Women of Color, Gender, and the Abolition of Slavery in Havana and Rio de Janeiro* (Chapel Hill: UNC Press, 2013), p. 52.

116. BOGGPA, 5, 1868, 47.

117. Valdez, *Six Years of a Traveller's Life in Western Africa*, vol. II, p. 115.

118. BOGGPA, 5, 1868, 47. See also Tracy Lopes, "Punishing Crime: Jails and Confinement in Luanda, Angola, from 1836 to 1899," PhD Dissertation, York University, 2022, p. 85.

119. "Registro de Carta de Liberdade" on October 6, 1856, AHA, cód. 5613, fls. 6v–7; "Registro de Carta de Liberdade" on April 16, 1856, AHA, cód. 5613, fls. 5–5v.

120. "Mapa dos Números de Escravos" on June 4, 1865 (AHU, papéis da Sá da Bandeira, maço 824, AHU).

121. Lopes, "Punishing Crime," p. 86. See also Vanessa Oliveira, "Slave Labor and the Vulnerability of Enslaved Women in Mid-Nineteenth Century Luanda," in Jose Curto (ed.), *New Perspectives on Angola: From Slaving Colony to Nation State* (Peterborough: Baywolf Press/ Éditions Baywolf, 2021), pp. 160–161.

122. "Ata da Sessão da Junta Protetora dos Escravos e Libertos" on July 27, 1856, AHU, Angola, pasta 22-A, fl. 21.

123. BOGGPA, 1863, 1, 5.

124. "Ofício do Secretário Geral da Província de Angola" on June 30, 1847, AHA, cód. 325; "Ofício do Secretário Geral da Província de Angola" on July 1, 1847, AHA, cód. 325, fls. 171v.–172.

125. "Ofício do Secretário Geral da Província de Angola" on December 24, 1846, AHA, cód. 325, fl. 92v.

126. "Ofício do Juiz Ordinário" in November 1855, AHA, cód. 2843, fl. 11v.

127. "Ofício do Governador de Angola" on April 16, 1857, AHA, cód. 68, fls. 25–27.

128. *Relatório do Governador Geral da Província de Angola Sebastião Lopes de Carvalho e Menezes referido ao Ano de 1861* (Lisboa: Imprensa Nacional, 1867), pp. 82–83.

129. Menezes, *Relatório do Governo Geral da Província de Angola para o ano de 1861*, p. 67.

130. "Consulta do Conselho Ultramarino" on 5 de julho de 1856, Annaes do Conselho Ultramarino, parte official, série I, fevereiro de 1854 a dezembro de 1858, Lisboa, Imprensa Nacional, 1867, p. 372. For Cape Verde, see Daryle Williams, "Cape Verde at the End of Atlantic Slavery," *Slavery and Abolition*, 36, 1, p. 173.

131. "Ofício do Secretário do Governo" on September 20, 1856, AHA, cód. 857, fls. 13–13v.

132. *Arquivos de Angola*, 2a série, vol. XII, 47/50, 1955, p. 157.

133. BOGGPA, 653, 1858, 1.

134. BOGGPA, 653, 1858, 1. See also Cristina Nogueira da Silva, *Constitucionalismo e Império: A Cidadania no Ultramar Português* (Lisboa: Almedina, 2009), pp. 277–281.

135. "Relação dos Libertos registrados na Província d'Angola" entre 1854 e 1859, AHU, Angola, pasta 26–1; "Nota do número de libertos que têm sido registrados na Província de Angola depois do decreto de 14 de dezembro de 1854 até 31 de dezembro de 1863," AHU, Angola, pasta 34.

136. "Annaes do Município de Mossamedes (anos de 1838–1849)" on December 31, 1856, *Annaes do Conselho Ultramarino*, parte não official, fevereiro de 1854 a dezembro de 1858 (Lisboa: Imprensa Nacional, 1867), p. 490; "Segunda Memória lançada no Livro dos Annaes do Município de Mossamedes" in 1857, in *Annaes do Conselho Ultramarino*, parte não official, fevereiro de 1854 a dezembro de 1858 (Lisboa: Imprensa Nacional, 1867), p. 497; "Mapa da População de Mossamedes no Fim do Ano de 1857," *Anais do Conselho Ultramarino*, parte não oficial, série 1, agosto de 1858, p. 497.

137. "Carta do Governador de Mossamedes" on January 16, 1864, AHU, papéis de Sá da Bandeira, maço 827. See also José Curto and Arshad Desai, "The Early Demography of Moçamedes, 1839–1869: a Preliminary Analysis," *Historiæ*, 10, 2, 2019, pp. 11–32.

138. John Monteiro, *Angola and the River Congo* (New York: Macmillan and Co., 1876), p. 42.

139. Vredenburg to the Earl of Clarendon on June 12, 1869, *British and Foreign State Papers, 1869–1870*, vol. LX (London: William Ridgway, 1876), pp. 612–614. See also Monteiro, *Angola and the River Congo*, p. 189.

140. Marquez de Sá da Bandeira, *A Emancipação dos Libertos* (Lisboa: Imprensa Nacional, 1874).

141. Sá da Bandeira, *A Emancipação dos Libertos*, p. 13.

142. Projeto de Decreto em 25 de fevereiro de 1869, in *Jornal de Jurisprudencia* (Coimbra: Imprensa da Universidade, 1868), vol. 4, p. 689. See also *Diário do Governo* on February 27, 1869.

143. Leão, *Considerações sobre o Transporte de Pretos entre as Colonias Portuguezas d'África*, pp. 25–27. See also Miguel Bandeira Jerónimo, "The 'Civilisation Guild': Race and Labour in the Third Portuguese Empire, c. 1870–1930," in Francisco Bethencourt and Adrian Pearce (ed), *Racism and Ethnic Relations in the Portuguese-Speaking World* (New York: Oxford UP, 2012), pp. 173–199.

144. "Ofício do Governador do Golungo" on November 27, 1864, AHU, maço 824. See also João Pedro Marques, "O Retorno do Escravismo em Meados do Século XIX," *Análise Social*, XLI, 180, 2006, p. 687.

145. Report on the slave trade by Gabriel on February 25, 1860, FO 84, 1104, fls. 234–26ov. For British contexts in the Caribbean and the Indian Ocean, see Catherine Hall, "Reconfiguring Race: The Stories the Slave-Owners told," in Catherine Hall et al. (eds.), *Legacies of British Slave-Ownership: Colonial Slavery and the Formation of Victorian Britain* (NYC: Cambridge University Press, 2014), pp. 163–202; Doulton, "The Royal Navy's Anti-Slavery Campaign," p. 232.

146. Ulrike Lindner, "Indentured Labour in Sub-Saharan Africa 1870–1918: Circulation of Concepts between Imperial Powers," in Sabine Damir-Geilsdorf, Ulrike Lindner, Gesine Müller, Oliver Tappe, and Michael Zeuske (eds.), *Bonded Labour: Global and Comparative Perspectives* (Bielefeld: Transcript Verlag, 2016), pp. 59–83.

147. Felix Meyer, *A Questão do Trabalho Livre em Angola e o Estado Presente desta Província* (Lisboa: Typographia Progresso, 1874), p. 7.

148. Meyer, *A Questão do Trabalho Livre em Angola*, pp. 12–14.

149. Maria da Conceição Neto, "De Escravos a 'Serviçais', de 'Serviçais' a 'Contratados': Omissões, perceções e equívocos na história do trabalho africano na Angola colonial," *Cadernos de Estudos Africanos*, 33, 2017, pp. 107–129. See also Michel Cahen, "Seis teses sobre o trabalho forçado no império português continental em África," *África*, 35, 2015, pp. 129–155. For an overview, see Zachary Kagan Guthrie, "Forced Labor in Portuguese Africa," *Oxford Research Encyclopedia of African History*, 2022.

Page numbers in *italics* indicate figures.

A NOTE ON THE TYPE

THIS BOOK has been composed in Miller, a Scotch Roman typeface designed by Matthew Carter and first released by Font Bureau in 1997. It resembles Monticello, the typeface developed for The Papers of Thomas Jefferson in the 1940s by C. H. Griffith and P. J. Conkwright and reinterpreted in digital form by Carter in 2003.

Pleasant Jefferson ("P. J.") Conkwright (1905–1986) was Typographer at Princeton University Press from 1939 to 1970. He was an acclaimed book designer and AIGA Medalist.

The ornament used throughout this book was designed by Pierre Simon Fournier (1712–1768) and was a favorite of Conkwright's, used in his design of the *Princeton University Library Chronicle*.